If you do not understand
White Supremacy (Racism) –
what it is, and how it works –
everything else that you understand,
will only confuse you.

©Neely Fuller, Jr. (1971)

Introduction

Like a crawling infant attempting to walk, all errors that are made by any person who seriously attempts to produce justice, are errors that can only be revealed through the process of the attempt.

The <u>will</u> to produce justice is the first thing that must happen before justice can be produced.

The <u>will</u> to produce justice is, itself, the beginning of the end, of error.

Therefore, the <u>initial</u> purpose of this work is to help people to produce the <u>will</u> to produce justice.

Preface

Words can be thought of as "tools." Words can be used as "tools" for expressing thoughts through speech and/or writing, printing, etc., in order to produce some desired result. Words have been used to cause people to do many things that were either constructive or non-constructive. Words have been used to cause people to be violent, calm, bored, lazy, happy, sad, confused, and/or smart.

Words have been used to cause people to believe things to be true, when logic and evidence showed those things as <u>not</u> being true. Words have been used to cause people to say that they did things that they <u>did not do,</u> and to cause people to believe that something happened that <u>did not happen</u>. Words have been used to cause people to be the <u>non</u>-quality of people that no people should ever be. Words have been used to cause people to think, speak, and act to establish, maintain, expand, and refine The System of White Supremacy (Racism).

There are now, and there likely will be in the future, a great many words that, when used, will <u>not</u> motivate people to do the constructive things that should be done. The "mechanics" of the logic of choosing some words, and not others, should always be judged by the manner in which <u>truth</u> (that which is) is revealed. Truth should always be revealed in a manner that best promotes the production of justice and correctness (balance between <u>all</u> people, creatures, things, etc.).

There is reason to believe that it is the <u>duty</u> of every person in the known universe to study, and to think, speak and act, to do all that he or she can to find and/or produce words and/or the definitions of words, that can be used in a manner that will best help solve all problems, in the <u>most efficient</u> and the <u>most constructive</u> manner.

The words presented in this work are only a limited number of compensatory ways that a limited number of words can be used. Some of the words presented herein may have definitions that may or may not seem to <u>contradict</u> the definitions that have been used previously. Many Compensatory Definitions may or may not differ from definitions that are currently being used.

All words and all definitions, however, should be used at a time, place, and manner that do the most in producing the so-called language of "peace." There is reason to believe that "peace" can

i

be produced by using words in such a manner that people are motivated to use truth (that which is), in such a manner that justice and correctness is the result. There is reason to believe that truth, <u>plus</u> justice, <u>plus</u> correctness, equals "peace."

The evidence so far shows that no words, or combinations of words, have yet been invented and used, in a manner that has resulted in the establishment of "peace." Again, that is what words should do – motivate people to produce "peace" in all areas of activity: Economics, Education, Entertainment, Labor, Law, Politics, Religion, Sex, (including the <u>end</u> of) War/Counter-War in <u>all</u> of its forms.

The Importance of Correct Context

When using words, *context* is extremely important; one should ask, "What is the context in which the word is being used"? During the existence of The System of White Supremacy (Racism), many people have been taught and/or guided into promoting confusion and non-correct conflict by repeating or altering some of the words of a Non-White person in a manner that did not best reveal the truth of the *intended effect* of those words. Therefore, according to Compensatory Counter-Racist Logic, and in order to reveal truth in a manner that best promotes the production of Justice and correctness, the context in which anything said or done should be given correct consideration.

Introductory Remarks About
This Compensatory Counter-Racist Word-Guide

What It Is, and How To Use It

---

1. According to Compensatory Logic, there is reason to believe that the people of the known universe (as of now) are interacting with each other in a manner that is non-just and non-correct. Therefore, according to Compensatory Logic, there is reason to believe that each person now existing in the known universe has the "Assignment" of producing the interactions between people that are just and correct.

2. A major part of the problems that exist in the interactions of people, one to the other, can be revealed by studying the ways that people use words, think about words, and act and react to the ways that words are used.

3. Subjugated people are often taught and/or "enticed" to use words that they (themselves) cannot define or explain through the use of logic. This is done (by the subjugators) for the purpose of deceiving and confusing their Victims in a manner that results in their Victims often not being sure of what some words mean whenever those words are used to "say" whatever they "say." This results in many subjugated people thinking things that they should not think, and saying things that they do not intend to say. Many times, what is said "means less" to the person who says it, than it means to the person to whom it is said. At other times, the same words may mean something completely different to the person speaking, from what is heard (understood) by the person listening. Where there is confusion in the meaning of words, there is a great possibility of much deception, unnecessary malice, mistaken judgment, mistaken action, non-correct intent, and/or the general mistreatment of people.

4. Because they are often used with non-correct and/or confusing definitions, many words do not do what words should do. Some words, because of the ways that they have been used, should not be used at all. Some words and their definitions may appear to be contradictory to similar words.

iii

5. "Languages" are produced from combinations of "words" and/or "word-sounds." All languages change. The words in all languages are "tools." The "word-tools" in all languages should always be designed to serve the best and most constructive behavior of all of the people who use those words, and/or who are exposed to the effect(s) of those words. The use of <u>any</u> word should always produce the <u>most constructive</u> effect(s) on the thoughts, speech, and actions of all persons, and of all creatures anywhere and everywhere, at all times.

    In a known universe dominated by the behavior of persons who are the smartest and most powerful, all words should be used in a manner that best helps to result in the revelation of truth (that which is). The revealed truth should be used in a manner that causes all people to think, speak, and act in a manner that best helps to produce universal justice, correctness, and "peace" (between and among all people, all creatures and all things). According to Compensatory Logic, any comment that is made should always be the best possible comment that can be made.

6. This Compensatory Word-Guide pertains to word-terms that are, basically, associated with what is known as the "English" language. Word-terms that may or may not be associated with other languages may appear in this work. Consideration should be given to the possibility of confusion that may result from changes in the ways that some people understand how words are used. During the existence of The System of White Supremacy (Racism), many words have been invented, and/or used by the White Supremacists (Racistman and Racistwoman), to do deliberate non-just harm to the Non-White people of the known universe.

7. According to Compensatory Logic, no word or combination of words in any language should ever be used in a manner that either directly or indirectly helps to produce a result that is <u>non</u>-just, <u>non</u>-correct and/or <u>non</u>-constructive. All words, in every language, should always <u>best help</u> to reveal truth and/or to use truth (that which is) in such a manner as to result in the establishment of justice, correctness, and "peace" between and among all people, all creatures and all things in the known universe. All words, in every language, should be designed to cause people to think, speak, and act in the most constructive manner, at all times, in all places,

iv

and for the most constructive reasons. No language has, as yet, produced this result. Therefore, every effort should be made to make all language and the words of every language, serve as <u>tools</u> designed to motivate people to function, always and forever, in a manner that produces the most constructive result. All of these efforts, regardless of form, should always start with the <u>correct intent</u>.

8.   According to Compensatory Logic, there is reason to believe that the "best language" for any people to teach, learn, and use, is language that does the most to produce the following two results:

- <u>guaranteeing</u> that <u>no</u> person is <u>mistreated</u>; and
- <u>guaranteeing</u> that the person who <u>needs</u> help the most, <u>gets</u> the most [constructive] help.

To do this, there is reason to believe that it is correct for all persons to do their best to practice using constructive logic. This would include the practice of thinking about the cause(s) and the effect(s) of everything that is said, and everything that is done. This would include the practice of thinking about the most constructive use of every word - <u>before</u> the word is used. This would include the practice of making every situation a "school" - a "school" for learning ideas, and for using words to express those ideas in a manner that produces the most constructive result.

9.   The words and word-terms presented in this Compensatory Word-Guide are intended to [also] have the effect of causing people to think of <u>other</u> words, and/or of <u>newer</u> word combinations that, when used, will be of more constructive value than the words and their definitions, as presented. All comments that appear in connection with the word-terms should be used for guidance in improving a person's thought(s), speech, and/or action(s).

10. This work is, fundamentally, a Compensatory <u>Counter-Racist</u> Word-Guide. The "word-tools" presented in this Compensatory Counter-Racist Word-Guide are <u>specifically intended</u> to assist the user in thinking, speaking, and/or acting in a manner that best helps the process of replacing The System of White Supremacy (Racism) with The System of Justice (balance between people). According to Compensatory Logic, and based on evidence shown thus far,

there is reason to believe that Justice should replace Racism, and it should do so in all areas of activity – Economics, Education, Entertainment, Labor, Law, Politics, Religion, Sex, and War/Counter-War.

The System of White Supremacy (Racism) is specifically designed to result in the mistreatment of the Non-White people of the known universe. The material benefits produced by this System are very great. However, the cost in regards to the "Throw-away People" that it produces has proven that such a System never should have come into existence. The <u>words</u> that have been used to coordinate the workings of this System have greatly assisted in causing destruction between, among, and against the Non-White people of the known universe.

This skillful use of words by the White Supremacists (Racistman and Racistwoman, collectively) has resulted in great and ongoing deception, confusion, and non-correct animosity between, among, and against all of their Victims (Non-White people).

During the existence of White Supremacy (Racism), many words are used, many "topics" are talked about, and many facts and "events" are "required" to be remembered, that serve no constructive purpose. Many of these words are basically designed for and intended to be used in a manner that best helps to <u>confuse</u> and <u>retard</u> the Non-White people of the known universe. Many words are <u>intended</u> to be used to best help maintain, expand, and/or refine the practice of White Supremacy (Racism) as the major form of non-justice (non-balance) between people. In the process of teaching Non-White people, White Supremacists (Racists) make sure that they teach much that is of little constructive value, and much of what they teach that <u>is</u> of constructive value, is taught in a manner that is often unnecessarily complicated and confusing.

11.   The words that are in books, etc., are intended to cause some, most, or all people to think, speak, and/or act in some manner that is either <u>constructive</u> or <u>non-constructive</u>.

The words that are presented in this book, with their compensatory definitions, explanations, questions, etc., are designed with the intention of helping the Victims of White Supremacy (the Non-White people of the known universe) to select and use some words, in a manner that may be of greater value in the use of truth, in order to best help produce justice, correctness, and "peace."

12. The essential function of this Word-Guide, initially, is to assist in producing Compensatory Counter-Racist Clarity as it pertains to the use of words in regards to Compensatory Counter-Racist thought, speech, and action. The words that are used, in any and every language (including all "signs," "symbols," "pictures," and "insignias") should be carefully examined by those who use them. Every part of every form of communication should be studied, and all parts of every form of communication should promote thought and speech that best helps to inspire action that will swiftly and efficiently result in replacing The System of White Supremacy (Racism) with The System of Justice (balance between people). This should be the result of what happens in the use of any and all languages – past, present and future, and/or for as long as White Supremacy (Racism) or other forms of non-justice exist. It is important to study "new" words, or "new" definitions of words to find if they do, or do not, appear to be for the purpose of producing effects that are harmful to the production of justice (balance between people).

13. No word should be used for the purpose of "showing-off" the ability of a person to "show-off" his or her ability to "show-off" by using a word. The use of every word (written or spoken) should always produce a <u>constructive result</u>.

14. It is correct to study the many ways that all words are used by those persons who are suspected of practicing White Supremacy (Racism). Many words in what is called the "English" language (as in other languages) are carefully designed to be used in such a manner as to glorify "Whiteness," as it is associated with The System of White Supremacy (Racism). During the existence of The System of White Supremacy (Racism), nearly all things associated with "darkness" (and/or "dark" people) are regarded as "non-correct", "foreboding," and/or most worthy of ridicule. Words such as "light," "bright," "enlightened," "fair," etc., are taught to be used in association with that which is favored. Words such as "dark," "dim," "dim-witted," "dirt," "dirty,"

"dust," "dull," "grime," tarnished," etc., are taught to be used in association with that which is <u>not</u>-favored.

15. Words and their definitions should be studied carefully by all who are affected by their use. All words, when used, have a constructive effect or a <u>non</u>-constructive effect. The System of White Supremacy (Racism) functions in a manner that causes many Non-White persons to choose <u>not</u> to study and <u>not</u> to learn how important words are in preventing the production of justice (balance between people). The White Supremacists (Racistman and Racistwoman) have proven that they do not approve of the use of any words in a manner that seem to have the effect of helping to replace The System of White Supremacy (Racism) with The System of Justice (balance between people).

16. During the existence of The System of White Supremacy (Racism) and, according to Compensatory Counter-Racist Logic, it is correct to study carefully, and, where necessary, define and "re-define" all of the words that are being used, and all of the words that are likely to be used, that directly or indirectly control the thought, speech, and action(s) of both White people and Non-White people, in everything that pertains to Race, Racism, and Counter-Racism.

17. According to Compensatory Counter-Racist Logic, there is reason to believe that if the Victims of White Supremacy (Non-White people), by their own will and skill, control the ways that they use (or not use) words, it will have the effect of countering the ways that the White Supremacists (Racists) use words to help themselves maintain, expand, and refine The System of White Supremacy (Racism).

Summary Remarks to the User
of this
Compensatory Counter-Racist Codified
Word-Guide

White Supremacists (Racistman and Racistwoman, collectively) are greatly skilled in using all words in such a manner as to cause the thoughts of all people to make them <u>act</u> in a way that is either directly or indirectly supportive of The System of White Supremacy (Racism). Therefore, it is logical to study words, and to study how words are used in all situations. It is correct to always use words to reveal truth (that which is), and do so in a manner that best helps to produce justice and correctness (balance between people, creatures, things, "spirits," etc.). To accomplish this, it may be necessary to change the "thought-images" that the use of some words produce. To do this, it is necessary to change the definitions of many words.

It is not necessary to wait for others to change the ways that words are used. Words are "tools." "Tools" should be designed to do the best and most constructive job that <u>needs</u> doing. Words, and the ways that they are used, should be changed by whoever becomes aware that a change is needed in order to produce the <u>most constructive result</u>.

It is correct to listen carefully to what others are saying. It is correct to listen carefully to the words that are being used. It is correct to not be "ashamed" to ask for simpler explanations for everything that is not easily and quickly understood. It is correct to not hesitate to <u>thank</u> those who give information that is of constructive value.

For sure, it is correct to, at all times, practice using <u>all</u> words in a manner that best helps to produce thought, speech, and action that is effective in best helping to replace The System of White Supremacy (Racism) with The System of Justice (balance between people). It is correct for <u>each individual person</u> to do this at <u>all</u> times, in <u>all</u> of his or her interactions with others, in <u>all</u> areas of activity, including Economics, Education, Entertainment, Labor, Law, Politics, Religion, Sex and War/Counter-War.

It is correct to ask all others (White and Non-White) to do the same.

ix

A Basic Product of the System of White Supremacy (Racism).
Use this term as an "official title" for yourself, when introducing yourself, and/or when presenting your "credentials" to people for the basic purpose of speaking or acting in regards to matters of Race, Racism, and/or Counter-Racism. Other terms that can be used for the same purpose, are "A Victim of White Supremacy," "A Servant to White Supremacy," "A Prisoner of White Supremacy," etc.

> **Note:** During the existence of White Supremacy (Racism), the aforementioned "titles" of identification are among the best, correct, most accurate and truthful statements for self-identification that a Non-White person can make when speaking and/or acting about matters that pertain to Race, Racism, and/or Counter-Racism.

Able-bodied. Use this term with caution. When others use it, ask for a detailed explanation that you can easily understand.

> **Questions:** How "able" is which body? "Able" to do what? In order to satisfy who? Within The System of White Supremacy (Racism), is a "body" of a Non-White person "able" to do the same things as a "body" of a White person? If so, why? If not, why not? Within The System of White Supremacy (Racism), do the White Supremacists (Racists) do anything or say anything that hinders Non-White people in the "ability" to do some things that need doing? Within The System of White Supremacy (Racism), are Non-White people "able" to do the same things that White people do, in all areas of activity, including Economics, Education, Entertainment, Labor, Law, Politics, Religion, Sex, and War/ Counter-War? Does an "able body" also include an "able" mind? An "able" brain?

Acceptable White Losses/White Sacrifices. Use these terms to apply to those White persons who are willing (according to what they think is necessary), to "allow" themselves or other White persons to be deprived, maimed, or killed in order to establish, maintain, expand, and/or refine the practice of White Supremacy (Racism).

Acting White/Acting Black. Do not use these terms. Use, instead, the terms, "acting constructively" and/or "acting non-constructively." When others use these terms, ask for a detailed explanation of each term, so that you can easily understand. Also, ask for a detailed explanation of what acts are constructive, and what acts are non-constructive. Ask for a detailed description of which acts are most likely to help produce justice, and which acts are most likely not to help to do so.

> **Note:** According to Compensatory Counter-Racist Logic, all acts, by all people, at all times, should be acts that directly or indirectly help to end White Supremacy (Racism), help to produce justice (balance between people), and/or help to produce correctness (balance between people, creatures, things, etc.).

Acting with the Approval of Those in Power. <u>Use this expression</u> to apply to any person who is, for whatever reason, thinking, speaking, and/or acting in such a manner as to support, and/or tolerate, the practice of White Supremacy (Racism).

> **Note:** During the existence of White Supremacy (Racism), it is the White Supremacists (Racists) who are "in power" over the Non-White people of the known universe.

Acutely Ghetto-Impaired or "AGI" (Racial). <u>Use this term</u> to apply to the speech and/or action(s) of a Non-White person whose behavior indicates that he or she is extremely dangerous to him or herself and/or others (White or Non-White), as the direct or indirect result of the effects of The System of White Supremacy (Racism).

Administrative/Administrator. <u>Use these terms with caution</u>. When others use them, ask for a detailed explanation that you can easily understand.

> **Reason:** During the existence of The System of White Supremacy (Racism), the use of the terms "administrative," "administrator" and "administration" can be very confusing – particularly in regards to the interaction between White people and Non-White people.

> **Questions:** Who, exactly, are the true "administrators" during the existence of The System of White Supremacy (Racism)? Is it true that during the existence of White Supremacy (Racism), it is Racistman and Racistwoman (White Supremacists, collectively), who "administer" and/or "control" all major activity in regards to the Non-White people of the known universe? If not, how does The System of White Supremacy (Racism) continue to exist?

Adult. <u>Avoid using this word</u>. Use instead, the term "older people" and/or "younger people." When others use this term, ask them to explain, in exact detail, what an "adult" is, and what an "adult" is not. Ask them to explain, in exact detail, what an "adult" does and/or does not do in each and every area of activity, including Economics, Education, Entertainment, Labor, Law, Politics, Religion, Sex, and War/Counter-War.

> **Questions:** What is the purpose of a so-called "adult"? What is the purpose of a so-called "non-adult"? Who is "qualified" to say who is an "adult" and who is not? During the existence of White Supremacy (Racism), is an "adult person" who is Non-White, "equal" to or the same as an "adult person" who is White? During the existence of White Supremacy (Racism), how does a Non-White person function as an "adult person" if he or she is "required" to, or forced to speak and/or act according to the dictates of the White Supremacists (Racists)? How can a Non-White person function as an "adult person" (and not an "adulterated person") if he or she is subject to White Supremacy (Racism) in Economics, Education, Entertainment, Labor, Law, Politics, Religion, Sex, and War/ Counter-War?

Adultery. Avoid using this word. When others use it, ask for a detailed explanation that you can easily understand.

> **Questions:** Is it an act of "adultery" if, during the existence of White Supremacy (Racism), a White person willfully and deliberately engages in sexual intercourse with a Non-White person? Is The System of White Supremacy (Racism), itself "adulterous"? Is every White person who participates in The System of White Supremacy (Racism) an "adulterer" or an "adulteress"? Is every Non-White person a Victim of the sexual, political, economic, and religious "adultery" practiced among and against Non-White people by Racistman and Racistwoman (White Supremacists, collectively)?

> **Notes:** According to Compensatory Counter-Racist Logic, The System of White Supremacy (Racism) forces Non-White people to function as "children." According to Compensatory Counter-Racist Logic, a person who is forced to function as a "child" is an "adulterated person". According to Compensatory Counter-Racist Logic, a "child" cannot commit "adultery."

Advisor/Advocate. Use these words with caution. When others use them, ask for a detailed explanation that you can easily understand.

Questions: When a White Supremacist (Racist) gives "advice" to a Victim of White Supremacy (Non-White person), is the White Supremacist (Racist) acting as an "advisor," or as a "dictator"? Is "advocating" the practice of White Supremacy (Racism) the same as helping to promote the continuation of White Supremacy (Racism)?

Affectionkin/Aff[e]sexkin/Soul-Mate [Counter-Racist] – Use these terms to apply to Non-White males with females who are not close "blood kin" to each other, but who choose to confide in each other and to generally interact with each other with great and sincere affection and caring exactly like sister with brother - "blood kin" at it's very best, except that they may also engage in affectionate sexual intercourse, and/or "sexual play," with each other, and, also, not disapprove of each other's acts of sexual intercourse and/or "sexual play" with others [Non-White persons] when such acts are affectionate, caring, and directly or indirectly supportive of thought, speech, and/or action designed to help replace The System of White Supremacy (Racism) with The System of Justice (balance between people).

> **Notes:** Non-White persons who function as "affectionkin" and/or as "aff[e]sexkin," tell each other everything about each other without gossiping about others and, in the process of doing so, seek to be the ultimate "soul-mates," as characterized by affection, caring, truthfulness, honesty, knowledge, understanding and trust. When persons choose to be "affectionkin" and/or "aff[e]sexkin," it is correct for them to identify themselves as "affectionkin" and/or as "aff[e]sexkin," and to identify themselves as persons who are seeking to become ultimate "soul-mates" (to each other).

Affirmative Action. Avoid using this term. Instead, use the terms "Compensatory Constructive Action," and/or "Compensatory Counter-Racist Action." When others use this term, ask them to explain in detail, exactly what they mean. During the existence of The System of White Supremacy (Racism), the greatest and most powerful of all "affirmative action" programs is The System of White Supremacy (Racism).

> **Questions:** What, exactly, is an "action" that is "affirmative" and/or that is "affirmed"? What "action"? "Affirmed," according to whom? How? In order to accomplish what? Are not all "actions," "affirmative"? How can any "action" be an "action" if it is not "affirmed"? What kind of "action" is a "non-affirmative" action?

Suggestion: In all matters pertaining to the ending of White Supremacy (Racism) and replacing it with Justice (balance between people), it is best and correct to use the terms "compensatory-constructive action" and/or "Compensatory Counter-Racist action," in place of the term "affirmative action."

Affirmative Action (Racial). Use this term with caution. When talking about "affirmative action" in regards to Race, Racism, and/or Counter-Racism, use the term to mean effective action to end White Supremacy (Racism), or effective action to maintain White Supremacy (Racism). When others use this term, ask them to explain if they are in favor of "affirmative action" to end White Supremacy (Racism), or in favor of "affirmative action" to maintain White Supremacy (Racism).

> **Notes:** All actions are "affirmative." Any action that is not "affirmative," is not and cannot be an "action." During the existence of The System of White Supremacy (Racism), there exists only one proven form of racial "affirmative action." The correct title of that form of "affirmative action" is "The System of White Supremacy (Racism)."

African-American. Avoid using this term. When others use the term, ask for a detailed explanation that you can easily understand.

> **Notes:** According to Compensatory Counter-Racist Logic, the correct definition of an "African," "American," and/or "Asian" is any person that has succeeded in producing "peace" in the known universe using truth, justice, and correctness. No such person, creature, or thing has yet done so. Therefore, no such person, creature, or thing that can be correctly called "African," "American," or "Asian" now exists in the known universe.

African Diseases. Do not use this term. When others use it, ask for a detailed explanation of what they mean by saying that a "disease" is "African."

> **Note:** According to Compensatory Counter-Racist Logic, the word "African" means a person who does not mistreat anyone, does not allow anyone to be mistreated, and who also guarantees that the person who needs help the most, gets the most help.

African Dream/American Dream/Asian Dream. Use these terms to apply to the combined thought, speech, and action that is designed to, and intended to, result in the use of truth (that which is) in such a manner as to produce justice (balance between people), and correctness (balance between people, creatures, things, etc.), in all areas of activity/existence, including Economics, Education, Entertainment, Labor, Law, Politics, Religion, Sex, and War/Counter-War.

> **Notes:** According to Compensatory Logic, all "dreams" that are correct ("Correct Dreams") are designed to produce the same result(s) between and among people - the use of truth to produce justice, correctness and "peace." "Peace" is the logical result of the revelation of truth used in such a manner as to result in justice and correctness. According to Compensatory Logic, it is important to know and to understand that, in the absence of justice (balance between people), "Africans," "Americans," and "Asians" do not, and cannot exist.

Africanized Killer Bees. Do not use this term. When others use the term, ask for a detailed explanation that you can easily understand.

> **Reason:** No creature in the known universe other than a person, can be an "African," and/or can be "Africanized." An "African," and/or an "Africanized person," is a person who guarantees that no person is mistreated, and guarantees that the person who needs help the most, gets the most help. An "African" is also a person, who, at all times uses truth (that which is) in such a manner as to produce and maintain justice (balance between people) and correctness (balance between people, creatures, things, etc.). According to Compensatory Logic, it is best and correct to define and regard an "African" as the aforementioned. Things and creatures, other than people, cannot be "African," nor can they be "Africanized." Only people can be "African," and/or "Africanized."

> **Notes:** During the existence of The System of White Supremacy (Racism), people, creatures, and things that have been associated with the word "African," have been made sometimes to be associated with all that is dangerous, destructive, and/or "non-progressive." Therefore, according to Compensatory Counter-Racist Logic, any and all words that people use to motivate people, should be used in such a manner as to best cause people to think, speak, and/or act to find truth, and to use truth in such a manner as to produce justice and

correctness in all areas of activity, including Economics, Education, Entertainment, Labor, Law, Politics, Religion, Sex, and War/Counter-War.

The words and their meanings that should exist do not now exist in a form, and/or in combinations, that cause people to think, speak, and act in a just and correct manner. Words such as "Africa," "Africanized," "America," "Asia," etc., should be used in a manner that describes people as they <u>should</u> be. Since the people of the known universe are not now as they should be, it is, therefore, incorrect to describe any people as African," "Africanized," "American," "Americanized," "Asian," or "Asianized." According to Compensatory Logic, such persons are yet to be produced.

Afrikaner. <u>Avoid using this word</u>. When others use it, ask them to explain in a way that you can easily understand, exactly what an "Afrikaner" is, exactly what an "Afrikaner" is not, and exactly what is the ultimate objective [purpose] of an "Afrikaner."

Afrocentric/Americentric/Asiacentric. <u>Use these terms</u> (either individually or collectively), to apply only to an existing situation that includes all of the people in the known universe, and only when their thoughts, speech, and actions have resulted in (1) guaranteeing that no person is mistreated; and (2) guaranteeing that the person who needs help the most, receives the most help (at all times).

> **Note:** During the existence of White Supremacy (Racism) and according to Compensatory Counter-Racist Logic, a condition that is "Afrocentric," "Americentric" and/or "Asiacentric" does not, and cannot, exist.

Age of Consent. <u>Avoid using this term.</u> When others use it, ask for a detailed explanation that you can easily understand.

> **Questions:** What is the "age of consent" for Non-White persons while they are subject to The Law of White Supremacy (Racism)? Is there ever a correct time for a Victim of White Supremacy (Non-White person) to "consent" to have sexual intercourse with a White Supremacist (Racist)? Is it correct for a Racist (White Supremacist) or a Suspected Racist (Suspected White Supremacist) to dictate what the "age of consent" is, or is not, in regards to a Victim of Racism (a Victim of White Supremacy/Non-White person)?

Note: During the existence of White Supremacy (Racism), the term "age of consent" usually means what the White Supremacists (Racists) say that it means (in regards to Non-White people).

Aggression/Aggressor. Use these terms with caution. When others use them, ask for a detailed explanation that you can easily understand.

> **Note:** During the existence of White Supremacy (Racism), and according to Compensatory Counter-Racist Logic, all White persons who participate in the practice of White Supremacy (Racism) are the Masters of Aggression against the Non-White people of the known universe.

Albino. Avoid using this word. When others use it, ask for a detailed explanation that you can easily understand.

> **Reason:** The word "albino" is a confusing term that may or may not mean the same thing to different people, or may or may not mean something different to the same person at a different time.

> **Questions:** What, exactly, is an "albino"? What, exactly, is not an albino"? Is an "albino" a White person? Is a White person an "albino? Can a Non-White person be an "albino"? Can a Non-White person be a White person by being an "albino"? Can an "albino" be a member of the White Race (White Supremacists, collectively)? Who is correctly qualified to say who is and who is not an "albino," and who is correctly qualified to say what being an "albino" means or does not mean?

Alien/Alienated. Use these terms with caution. When others use them, ask for a detailed explanation that you can easily understand.

> **Questions:** Is a White Supremacist (Racist) "alienated" from the Victims of White Supremacy (the Non-White people of the known universe)? If so, "alienated" how? If so, "alienated" in which areas of activity? Do the White Supremacists (Racists) help cause the Non-White people of the known universe to be "alienated" from each other? Are the White Supremacists (Racists) deliberately "alienated" from the intention to produce justice (balance between people)?

All. <u>Use this word with caution</u>. Study the many ways that others use the word "all." When in doubt about using the word "all," practice using the expression "the most effective number."

> **Reason:** Sometimes people use the word "all" when, in truth, they should have said "some," or "many," or "most."

All-American. <u>Do not use this term</u>. When others use this term, ask for a detailed explanation that you can easily understand.

> **Notes:** According to Compensatory Logic, "Americans," "Africans," and "Asians," do not and cannot exist unless they, at all times, practice justice (balance between people) in all areas of activity (Economics, Education, Entertainment, Labor, Law, Politics, Religion, Sex, and War/Counter-War). Since justice (balance between people) does not now exist any place in the known universe, no "Americans" exist, no "Africans" exist, and no "Asians" exist. "Americans," "Africans," and "Asians" are people who guarantee that no person is mistreated and who guarantee that the person who needs help the most, gets the most [constructive] help. This is justice (balance between people). As of now, no such situation exists. As of now, no such people exist. Justice, and the people who practice it, are yet to be produced.

All Deliberate Speed. <u>Use this term with caution</u>. When others use it, ask for a detailed explanation that you can easily understand. When you choose to use this term, be prepared to explain, in detail, exactly what you mean, and what you do not mean. Also, be wary of the ways in which this term is used regarding matters of Race, Racism, and/or Counter-Racism. Study the ways in which the term is used as a means of promoting confusion and frustration in regards to efforts to produce justice (balance between people) through the process of ending Racism (White Supremacy). Study the ways that the term is used in regards to the process of replacing White Supremacy with Justice in every area of activity, including Economics, Education, Entertainment, Labor, Law, Politics, Religion, Sex, and War/Counter-War.

> **Questions:** In racial matters, what is meant by the term "all deliberate speed"? Who is best "qualified" to decide? How "deliberate" is "deliberate"? When and how is "speed" to be regarded as "speed"? Based on what? By whom?

All the Facts. Use this term with caution. When others use it, ask for a detailed explanation that you can easily understand. Ask questions.

> **Questions:** What, exactly, is "all of the facts"? How many "facts" are needed to reveal "truth"? Can "facts" be arranged in such a manner as to promote falsehood? Is a "fact" a "limited truth"? If truth is "that which is," how much of "that which is" must be revealed in order to reveal enough of "that which is not"? Is it a "fact" and a "truth" that during the existence of White Supremacy (Racism), every Non-White person in the known universe is a direct or indirect Victim of White Supremacy? Is every "fact" in the known universe "connected to" every other "fact" in the known universe? If so, does that indicate that "all the facts" in one situation, is at the same time, a part of "all the facts" in all situations?

Allies. Use this word with caution. Study the ways that others use the word "ally" or "allies."

> **Questions:** If a person is a so-called "ally," is that person an "ally" in all matters? Is it correct to think that a person is an "ally" in every area of activity? If a person is not an "ally" in all areas of activity, does that mean that he or she is an "enemy" in some areas of activity? Can a person be an "ally" in some things, and an "alien" in others? Are Victims of White Supremacy (Non-White people) "allied" with the White Supremacists (Racists) in some things, and "alienated" from the White Supremacists in others? Is it possible for a prisoner to be an "ally" of the prison master?
>
> What, exactly, is an "ally"? What, exactly, is not an "ally"? Are two persons "allies" if they "cooperate" with each other in any one or more areas of activity? If so, which area(s) of activity: Economics? Education? Entertainment? Labor? Law? Politics? Religion? Sex? War/Counter-War? What exactly is "cooperation?" Exactly how much "cooperation" with a person makes that person an "ally"? Does "cooperation" apply to words or deeds of "support" that is indirect, as well as direct? Are all of the White people who participate in any part of The System of White Supremacy (Racism) "allies" of each other? Are they "allies" in the maintenance of non-justice? Are they "allies" in the Universal Racist Conspiracy against the Non-White people of the known universe?

Alone. Use this word with caution. When, exactly, is a person "alone"? How "alone" is "alone"? "Alone" by "distance"? How much "distance"? By thought? What "kind" of thought? Can a person be "alone" in a crowd of other persons? If so, how? Why?

America. Use this word with caution. Use it to mean a person who does not mistreat anyone, who does not allow anyone to be mistreated and who, at all times, guarantees that the person who needs help the most, gets the most help in regards to every area of activity/existence, including Economics, Education, Entertainment, Labor, Law, Politics, Religion, Sex, and War/Counter-War.

Always, as long as White Supremacy (Racism) exits, do not regard any person as being in "America," and/or as being an "American." As long as non-justice (no balance between people) exists, do not regard any person as being "America," and/or as being "American." When others use the terms "America" or "American," ask them to explain, in a way that you can easily understand, exactly what they mean, and what they do not mean.

> **Notes:** The words "America," "American," etc., mean different things to different people. To some people, "America" is a place. To some people "America" is one or more persons. To some people "America" is a concept, and/or a combination of ideas. To some people "America" is a house, or a "flag," or a mountain. To some people "America" is a combination of most or all of these.
>
> According to Compensatory Counter-Racist Logic, "America" is, and, if correct, must and should be, any person in the known universe who does not mistreat anyone, does not allow anyone to be mistreated, and who guarantees that the person who needs help the most, gets the most help. According to Compensatory Logic, no person in the known universe is at this time correctly qualified to be identified as "America," and/or as being "American". The following are some Compensatory uses of the words "America" and/or or "American":
>
> America is an idea.
>
> America is a concept.
>
> America is a goal that is yet to be produced.
>
> America is not a place.
>
> America is not a current practice.
>
> America does not exist.

America is a product that is yet to be produced.

An "American" is always a person.

An "American" is not a rock, bird, a fish, a cloud, or piece of cloth.

An "American" is not a person who tells lies.

An "American" is not a Racist, and a Racist is not an "American".

An "American" does not mistreat, misuse or abuse any person, creature, or thing.

An "American" does not tolerate injustice.

An "American" does not seek, nor accept "praise".

An "American" does not brag, gossip, rape, rob, steal, or practice discourtesy.

An "American" kills only when necessary to maintain justice, correctness, and peace.

An "American" thinks, speaks, and acts as if he or she believes that a "force" exists that is greater than themselves and greater than all other people and creatures in the known universe.

Americans guarantee that the person who needs help the most, gets the most constructive help.

Americans are people who practice "Americanism," "Africanism," and "Asianism".

People who practice "Americanism" are yet to be produced. It is correct for all people in the known universe to do all they can to become "Americans" ("Africans," "Asians"). It is better for a person to say that he or she intends to be an "American," rather than to confuse themselves or others by pretending to be an "American".

Many people often have difficulty explaining exactly what an "American" is and what an "American is not. The term "American" is often used carelessly. To *appear* to be an "American" is not the same as *being* an "American". Being called an "American," or calling someone else an "American" is easy. Being an "American" is extremely difficult.

American Culture/American Flag/Americanism. Do not use these terms to apply to and/or to describe any person, place, or thing that now exists in the known universe. Use these terms only for describing the names or titles for thoughts, ideas, or intentions of producing a situation where no person is mistreated, and where the person who needs help the most, at all times, gets the most help.

> **Note:** As long as White Supremacy (Racism) exists, and as long as non-justice (non-balance between people) exists, "America," "Americans," and/or "Americanism" cannot exist.

American Dream (The). Use this term to mean, "Replace White Supremacy (Racism) with Justice" (balance between people). Use it to mean a condition in which The System of White Supremacy (Racism) has been replaced with The System of Justice (balance between people). Use it to mean the condition in which no person is mistreated in any area of activity, and in which the person who needs help the most, gets the most help in every area of activity. When others use the terms "The American Dream," "The African Dream," "The Asian Dream," "The European Dream," etc., ask for a detailed explanation of each term, and ask that each term be explained in a manner that you can easily understand.

> **Notes:** During the existence of White Supremacy (Racism) and, according to Compensatory Counter-Racist Logic, the terms "The American Dream," "The African Dream," and "The Asian Dream" all have the same meaning. The term "The European Dream" is a term that should be used only to ask a person who says that he or she is a "European," to define what "The European Dream" is, and what "The European Dream" is not. All definitions of all terms used should be explained, in detail, in regards to all areas of activity, including Economics, Education, Entertainment, Labor, Law, Politics, Religion, Sex, and War/Counter-War.

Anti-American. Avoid using this term. When others use it, ask for a detailed explanation that you can easily understand.

> **Reason:** According to Compensatory Logic, an "American" is a person who guarantees that no person is mistreated, and who guarantees that the person who needs help the most, gets the most help in all places, at all times and in all areas of activity.

13

Questions: Do "Americans" exist? Does a person who can be correctly called an "American" exist? If so, where? If so, how? If "Americans" do not exist, is it correct to say that they do not exist because people who are "anti-American" have prevented them from existing? If Americans do not exist, does that mean that all the people of the known universe are directly or indirectly "anti-American"? Is trying to be an "American" the same as <u>being</u> an "American"? Is it correct to say that an "American" is as an "American" does? If a person does not do what an "American" does, is that person "anti-American"? How can a person, place, creature, or thing be "anti-American" if an "American" does not exist?

Anti-Black and/or Pro-Niggerized Entertainment. <u>Use these terms</u> to apply to anything said or done for "fun," for "glory" and/or for "profit" that has the effect of producing or promoting thought, speech, or action that results in direct or indirect non-just and/or non-correct harm to Non-White people during the existence of White Supremacy (Racism).

Notes: During the existence of White Supremacy (Racism), most of what is said or done that involves or pertains to Non-White people in the area of entertainment, has the effect of producing or promoting thought, speech, and/or action between, among, or against Non-White people that is of no constructive value in the production of justice and/or correctness.

Suggestion: When talking about any "entertainment" in a manner that directly or indirectly involves Race, Racism, and/or Counter-Racism, say, and often repeat:

"During the existence of White Supremacy (Racism), most forms of "entertainment" is directly or indirectly designed to be supportive to The System of White Supremacy (Racism), and therefore, is likely to have an effect on the thoughts, speech, and actions of Non-White people that is non-constructive."

Anti-Capitalist. <u>Avoid using this term</u>. When others use this term, ask them to explain, in detail, exactly what they mean, and what they do not mean.

Questions: What, exactly, is a "Capitalist"? What, exactly, is an "anti-Capitalist"? Are all creatures, including people, "Capitalists"? If a person attempts to acquire something and succeeds in doing so, is he or she a "Capitalist"? Is White Supremacy (Racism) the most powerful system of "Capitalism" produced by the people of the known universe? Is a person who is opposed to White Supremacy (Racism), a so-called "anti-Capitalist"?

Anti-Communist. Use this term with caution. When others use it, ask for a detailed explanation that you can easily understand.

> **Questions:** What, exactly, is a "Communist"? What, exactly, is an "anti-Communist"? What is it that both a "Communist" and "anti-Communist" do in regards to each and every area of activity, including Economics, Education, Entertainment, Labor, Law, Politics, Religion, Sex, and War/Counter-War? What, exactly, do "Communists" and "anti-Communists" do that no one else does? What persons are best qualified to judge what an "anti-Communist" is or is not? If White Supremacy (Racism) is the most powerful form of "communism" in the known universe, is it possible that a White Supremacist (Racist) can, at the same time, be an "anti-Communist"?

Anti-Racist Expert. Use this term to apply only to that person, creature, spirit, etc., that has ended the existence of White Supremacy (Racism), and replaced it with The System of Justice (balance between people).

Anti-Semite/Anti-Semitic. Do not use these terms. When others use them, ask for a detailed explanation that you can easily understand.

> **Questions:** What, exactly, is a "Semite"? What, exactly, is an "anti-Semite"? What, exactly, does a "Semite" do that no one else does, in regards to each area of activity? What, exactly, is the ultimate objective of a "Semite"? What, exactly, is the ultimate objective of an "anti-Semite"? What are the "correct duties" of a "non-Semite" in regards to "Semitics" and "anti-Semitics"?

> **Note:** According to Compensatory Logic, it is correct to believe that the best person to answer the aforementioned questions is a person who is a "Semite".

Anti-Sexual Behavior/Anti-Sexual Intercourse/Anti-Sexual Play (counter-sexual behavior, counter-sexual intercourse, counter-sexual play). Use these terms to mean the same as any attempt by male persons to try (with each other), to copy, simulate, and/or "approximate," male with female sexual intercourse or "sexual play." Also, use these terms to mean the same as any attempt by female persons to try (with each other), to copy, simulate, and/or "approximate," female with male sexual intercourse or "sexual play." Use these terms in place of, and/or to mean the same as, "homosexual" behavior and/or "lesbian" behavior.

> **Reason:** The word "sex" applies to male and female, or male <u>with</u> female. It is not possible for a female person to have sexual intercourse with a female person, nor is it possible for a male person to have sexual intercourse with a male person. Male persons can only pretend that they are engaging in sexual intercourse and/or sexual "play" with [against] each other. Female persons can only pretend that they are engaging in sexual intercourse and/or sexual "play" with [against] each other.

Anti-Social. <u>Do not use this term</u>. When others use it, ask for a detailed explanation that you can easily understand.

> **Questions:** What, exactly, is "social"? What, exactly, is "anti-social"? What, exactly, is "non-social"? How "social" should a person be in order not to be "anti-social"? Is a White person "anti-social" if he or she does not try to spend all of his or her time and energy trying to end The System of White Supremacy (Racism)? Is a Non-White person "anti-social" if he or she does not try to spend all of his or her time and energy trying to produce a relationship with White people that does the most to produce justice (balance between people) in all areas of activity, including Economics, Education, Entertainment, Labor, Law, Politics, Religion, Sex, and War/Counter-War?

Anti-Terrorist. <u>Use this term with caution</u>. ·When others use this term, ask them to explain, in detail, exactly what they mean, and to do so in a manner that you can easily understand.

> **Questions:** What, exactly, is an "anti-terrorist"? What, exactly, is a "terrorist? What, exactly, is not a "terrorist"? Is a White person who practices White Supremacy (Racism), a "terrorist"? Is any person who speaks and acts to [try to] end White Supremacy (Racism), an "anti-terrorist"? Is a Non-White person who is subject to The System of White Supremacy (Racism), a Victim of "terrorism"?

Apartheid. <u>Do not use this word</u> except to explain it as having the same meaning as the term "White Supremacy (Racism)." Use the words "White Supremacy (Racism)" in place of the word "apartheid."

> **Reason:** According to Compensatory Counter-Racist Logic, the word "apartheid" is a refined and confusing term that is designed or intended to be used, to mean the same as the term "White Supremacy (Racism)," but without directly appearing to do so.

Apparent. <u>Use this word</u> to describe any circumstance that you have no doubt about.

Appropriate. <u>Use this word with caution</u>. Be wary of the way the word is used by others. Who decides what is "appropriate," and when, and for what reason?

Arab/Arabic. <u>Use these words with caution</u>. When others use them, ask for a detailed explanation that you can easily understand.

Aristocrat/Aristocratic. <u>Use these words with caution</u>. When others use them, ask for a detailed explanation that you can easily understand. What makes a person, place, creature, or thing an "aristocrat"? Can any person be an "aristocrat"? Can any "thing" be correctly called "aristocratic"? Why? According to whom? In order to accomplish what?

Aristocratic-Refined Racism (refined White Supremacy). <u>Use this term</u> to apply to those forms (styles) of White Supremacy (Racism) that are so sophisticated that, when practiced, they have the effect of being "soothing" and/or appearing to be non-harmful to its Victims (Non-White persons). This "nice-mannered" style of practicing White Supremacy (Racism), as employed by some Racistmen and Racistwomen, is so refined that its destructive causes or effects are usually completely "hidden" from most of its Victims (Non-White persons).

> **Note:** White Supremacy (Racism), as practiced in this supremely refined manner, could also be described as "Painless Poison Racism," and/or "Racism (White Supremacy) with a smile".

Army. <u>Use this word with caution</u>. When others use it, ask for a detailed explanation that you can easily understand. What, exactly, is an "army"? What, exactly, is not an "army"? Do the people who practice White Supremacy (Racism) function as an "army"?

Arrest. <u>Use this word with caution</u>. When others use it, ask for a detailed explanation that you can easily understand.

> **Questions:** What, exactly, is an "arrest"? When, exactly, is a person "arrested"? Is a person who is subject to The System of White Supremacy (Racism) "arrested"? Is The System of White Supremacy (Racism) a "prison system"? Is a Victim of White Supremacy (Non-White person) "confined" and/or "restricted"? Does The System of White Supremacy (Racism) require that, based on color, a Non-White person be confined, restricted, and/or "arrested" in regards to what he or she can do in matters of Economics, Education, Entertainment, Labor, Law, Politics, Religion, Sex, and War/Counter-War?

Art. <u>Use this word with caution</u>. When others use it, ask for a detailed explanation that you can easily understand. What, exactly, is "art"? What, exactly, is not "art"? Study the ways in which the word "art" is used.

Aryan/Aryan Blood. <u>Avoid using these terms</u>. When others use them, ask for a detailed explanation that you can easily understand.

> **Questions:** What, exactly, is "Aryan" and/or "Aryan blood"? When a person says that he or she is "Aryan," what should that person do in each area of activity? What is the correct relationship between a person who is an "Aryan," and a person who is a "non-Aryan"? What does an "Aryan" do that "non-Aryans" do not do, and for what purpose?

Asia/Asian/Asiatic. <u>Use these terms</u> to identify or describe those persons in the known universe who do not mistreat people, do not allow people to be mistreated, and who guarantee, at all times, in all areas of activity, that the person who needs help the most, gets the most help.

> **Reason:** When others use these terms, ask them to explain, in detail, exactly what they mean, and exactly what they do not mean. Ask them to explain the purpose for a person wanting to be an "Asia," "Asian," or "Asiatic" person, and ask them to explain the purpose in a manner that you can easily understand. Ask them to explain what an "Asiatic" person does that "non-Asiatic" persons do not do in matters of Economics, Education, Entertainment, Labor, Law, Politics, Religion, Sex, and War/Counter-War.

Asian Flu (Asian Influenza). <u>Avoid using this term</u>. When others use it, ask for a detailed explanation that you can easily understand. What, exactly, is the "Asian flu"? Does the "Asian flu" only affect "Asians"? What, exactly, is an "Asian"? Is the "Asian flu" a Racist (White Supremacist) name for a disease that is produced or spread by Non-White people?

Assassin/Assassination. <u>Use these words with caution</u>. When others use them, ask for a detailed explanation that you can easily understand. If assassinating a person means to kill that person, why not say that to assassinate a person means to kill that person?

Assignment, An. <u>Use this term</u> to apply to those things that White Supremacists (Racistman and Racistwoman, collectively), "require," or force Non-White persons to do that directly or indirectly helps to maintain, expand, and/or refine the practice of White Supremacy (Racism).

The term "An Assignment" is different from the term "The Assignment," and should be used as such. The term "An Assignment" should be used to apply to whatever it is that a Non-White person is "required" or forced to say or do that does not help him or her to accomplish "The Assignment."

> **Notes:** During the existence of White Supremacy (Racism), and according to Compensatory Counter-Racist Logic, "The Assignment" for all Non-White people is to speak and act to replace The System of White Supremacy (Racism) with The System of Justice (balance between people) in all areas of activity, including Economics, Education, Entertainment, Labor, Law, Politics, Religion, Sex, and War/Counter-War.

Assignment, The. <u>Use this term</u>. Use it to apply to: (1) those things that are said or done that best help to replace The System of White Supremacy (Racism) with the System of Justice (balance between people); and (2) those things that are said or done that best help to produce "peace" (the use of truth in such a manner as to result in the establishment of justice and correctness). Practice asking people questions like, "Have you done any work on 'The Assignment' today"?

<u>Use the term</u> "The [Compensatory] Assignment" to apply to the specific "assigned duty" that each Non-White person has to do all that he or she can to speak and act effectively to replace The System of White Supremacy (Racism) with The System of Justice (balance between people). This term can also be used to apply to all acts that help to produce correctness (balance between people, creatures,

things, etc), and should be used frequently as a constant reminder to all people of what Non-White people should, logically, be doing as their "basic reason for being" (in the known universe during the existence of White Supremacy/Racism).

Attack. Use this word with caution. Study the many ways that others use this word. Are there times when a so-called "attack" is, in truth, a "counter-attack"? During the existence of White Supremacy (Racism), is an "attack" on White Supremacy (Racism), in truth, a "counter-attack" on White Supremacy (Racism)? (See, "Counter-Attack").

Attitude. Do not use this word. Instead, use the word "intent" or "intention."

> **Reason:** The word "attitude" is often used in a manner that promotes confusion. Instead of saying that a person "has an attitude," or "has a bad attitude," say that he or she "could have the incorrect intentions," or that he or she is "using an incorrect means of trying to produce justice" (balance between people).

Attraction Enhancer(s)/Repulsion Enhancer(s). Use these terms to apply to anything added to the body of a person (including face, hands, hair, etc.), that is, apparently, intended to produce attention from other persons for reasons that may or may not be favorable to that person, and/or for reasons that may or may not be of constructive value to any persons.

Authority/Authorized. Use these words with caution. When others use them, ask for a detailed explanation that you can easily understand.

> **Questions:** What, exactly, is an "authority"? How, exactly, does an "authority" become "authorized" to be an "authority"? What "authority" "authorizes" a person to be an "author"? What persons are "authorized" to speak or act to produce justice (balance between people)? What persons are "unauthorized" to speak or act with "authority" against The System of White Supremacy (Racism)? Why?

> **Example for use**: When asked to name the "authority" that "authorizes" you to speak or act against Racism (White Supremacy) say, "As a Victim of Racism, I am authorized to speak and to act with authority against Racism (White Supremacy), by being a Victim of Racism."

Average American. Do not use this term. When others use it, ask for a detailed explanation that you can easily understand.

> **Reason:** According to Compensatory Logic, "Americans" do not exist. They are yet to be produced. According to Compensatory Logic, an "American" is a person who does not mistreat anyone, does not allow anyone to be mistreated, and, who at all times, guarantees that the person who needs help the most, gets the most help.
>
> According to Compensatory Counter-Racist Logic, there is no way for an "American" and The System of White Supremacy (Racism) to exist at the same time, in the same universe. According to Compensatory Logic, there is not now, nor can there ever be, any person that can be correctly recognized as an "Average American." A person is either an "American," or he or she is not an "American." There is not, nor can there be, any person that can be correctly called "Average American," "Half-American," "Part-American," "Semi-American," etc.

B

Baby Boy/Baby Girl (Racial). Use these terms with caution. Use them (generally) to apply to all of the Non-White people of the known universe who are directly or indirectly subject to The System of White Supremacy (Racism).

> **Note:** According to Compensatory Counter-Racist Logic, and during the existence of White Supremacy (Racism), all of the Non-White people of the known universe are the illegitimate, abused, retarded, handicapped, dependent and subject children ("babies") of the White Supremacists (Racistmen and Racistwomen, collectively).

Background/Personal History. Use these terms with caution. When others use them, ask for a detailed explanation that you can easily understand.

> **Questions:** What, exactly, is a person's "background"? How far back does a person's "personal history" go? What does a person's "personal history" include? What does it not include? Exactly how many people, creatures, and things are involved in each person's "historical background"? Is it likely that any person "knows" him or herself? Is it likely that any person has a complete

knowledge of any person? What person is "all-knowing"?
How much knowledge of a person is "enough knowledge"?

Bad. Do not use this word. Instead, use the words "incorrect"
and/or "tragic."

> **Reason:** Within The System of White Supremacy
> (Racism), the words "bad" and "good" have often been
> used to describe many things or conditions in a manner
> that is too confusing to too many people. Therefore, until
> the people of the known universe know and understand
> the truth (that which is) about what is "good" and what is
> "bad," it is best and correct not to use the words "good" or
> "bad" to describe any person, creature, thing, or total
> condition now in existence in the known universe.
> According to Compensatory Logic, it is best and correct to
> use the term "correct" instead of "good," and "incorrect"
> instead of "bad."

Bad Hair. Do not use this term. Either hair exists or it does not
exist. It is correct to say that hair does, or does not, exist. It is not
correct to say that hair is either "good," or "bad." Conflict and
confusion about what is "good hair" and what is "bad hair" should
not exist. As in all other matters, people or creatures should not be
mistreated because of the "appearance" or "type" of hair that is
associated with their bodies.

Balance Between People. Use this term to mean the same as the
word "justice" and/or use it to mean: (1) guaranteed absence of the
mistreatment of people, and (2) guaranteed condition of the person
who is in need of help the most, getting the most help.

Barbarian. Do not use this word. When others use it, ask for a
detailed explanation that you can easily understand.

> **Questions:** What, exactly, is a "barbarian"? What,
> exactly, is not a "barbarian"? Is a White Supremacist
> (Racist) a "barbarian"? Is a person who uses counter-
> violence to defend him or herself against the violence of a
> White Supremacist (Racist), a "barbarian"?

Basic Compensatory Constructive (Sexual) Arrangement. Use
this term to apply to any and all interaction(s) between a Non-White
male and a Non-White female that includes helping each other, in a
constructive and voluntary manner, by sharing time, energy, material
needs, information, and/or "companionship" that may or may not
include sexual intercourse and/or "sexual play".

Basic Compensatory Support Unit. Use these terms to mean the same as, and/or use them in place of, the term "family" in regards to Non-White people during the existence of White Supremacy (Racism).

> **Reason:**   Within The System of White Supremacy (Racism), Non-White people are not permitted to function as a "family," as "families," or as "nations". During the existence of White Supremacy (Racism), Non-White people are only permitted (by the White Supremacists) to function as "creature-people" who are allowed to interact with each other only in the manner of "prisoners" and as "prisoners," are only allowed to give assistance to each other according to the direct or indirect dictation of the White Supremacists (Racists).

Basic "Ten Stops" for Victims of Racism, The. Use these suggestions for helping self or others in promoting the production of Justice (balance between people):

(1)   Stop snitching (volunteering information about people for the purpose of gaining personal favors from Racists by deliberately causing non-just to others).

(2)   Stop name-calling.

(3)   Stop cursing.

(4)   Stop gossiping.

(5)   Stop being discourteous.

(6)   Stop stealing.

(7)   Stop robbing.

(8)   Stop fighting.

(9)   Stop killing, except under conditions of extreme emergency defense, and/or Maximum Emergency Compensatory Action against Racism.

(10)   Stop squabbling among yourselves and depending on Racists (White Supremacists) to settle the squabbles.

Beauty/Beautiful Person. Avoid using these words to describe any persons who exist in the known universe during any time that The System of White Supremacy (Racism) also exists. Instead of saying that a person is beautiful, say that the person is "attractive." When others say that a person is beautiful, ask them to explain, in detail, why that person is "beautiful," or is a "beauty."

Reason: During the existence of White Supremacy (Racism), the people of the known universe either practice or tolerate the practice of White Supremacy (Racism). According to Compensatory Counter-Racist Logic, a "beautiful person" does not practice, nor does he or she tolerate the practice of White Supremacy (Racism), or any other form of injustice (non-balance between people). Therefore, as long as White Supremacy (Racism) exists, and as long as injustice (non-balance between people) exists, there are no people in the known universe who can correctly be identified as "beautiful."

As long as the people of the known universe are not in balance with each other, it is best and correct to describe any persons who do things that "attract" you to them, as persons who are "attractive." It is important to know and to understand that people can "attract" other people for reasons that are correct, or for reasons that are incorrect.

Beauty Contest. <u>Do not use this term</u>. When others use it, ask for a detailed explanation that you can easily understand.

Questions: What, exactly, is "beauty"? What, exactly, is a "beautiful" person? What, exactly, is not a "beautiful" person? Who decides what or who, is "beautiful," and for what reason, and in order to accomplish what? If it is true that "beauty" exists, how can it be "contested"? Is injustice "ugly"? Can a person who practices injustice, and/or who tolerates injustice, be correctly regarded as "beautiful"? What person in the known universe is correctly qualified to decide who is "beautiful" and who is not? According to Compensatory Logic, it is incorrect to promote or participate in "beauty contests".

Beg/Begging. <u>Use these words</u> to apply to any and all requests for help by a person, or creature, unable to give adequate help to him, her, or itself or others, in order to produce a desired result, and/or accomplish a constructive goal. When others use the term "begging," ask for a detailed explanation that you can easily understand.

Notes: During the existence of White Supremacy (Racism), and according to Compensatory Counter-Racist Logic, any Non-White person who asks a White person for help in doing something of constructive value is not "begging". By asking for constructive help, the Non-White person is making a "Compensatory Investment Request". Anytime that one person gives help to another person for purposes of doing something of constructive value, the

24

something of constructive value, when done, was and is, an "investment" in humanity, justice, correctness, and "peace".

Being. Use this word to apply to any "body" that thinks, speaks, and/or acts. Study the ways that others use the words "being," "human being," "humane being," "non-humane being," etc.

Benign Neglect. Do not use this term. When others use the term, ask them to explain what they mean, and to do so in a manner that you can easily understand.

Best and Brightest (The). Do not use this term to describe any person. Instead, if it is necessary to describe a person as "smart," or "very smart," say that the person is "smart" or "very smart." Do not describe the person as "bright" to mean the same as "smart." When others use the word "bright" to mean "smart," ask them to explain, in detail, why they do so.

> **Questions:** Why use the word "bright" to mean "smart"? Does "bright," "light," and "white" mean the same as "smart"? Should it? If so, why?
>
> **Reason:** During the existence of White Supremacy (Racism), the term "best and brightest" is a term that, when used, has the direct or indirect effect of helping to promote the thought that "White," "bright" or extremely pale-skinned people are not only the "smartest" people, but that they are the "best" people in the known universe. The use of the term "best and brightest" implies that those persons who are regarded as the "worst and dullest," are "dark" or "Black" in color.
>
> During the existence of White Supremacy (Racism), the word "bright" is often associated with the word "white" and/or with the term "White people". The word "bright" is also often associated with the word "smart". The use of these words in this connective manner may easily cause a person to think, (directly or indirectly) that a "smart" person is a "bright" person who is [like] a "White" person, who is a "best" person at being "bright," "brilliant," "enlightened," etc.

Better. Use this word with caution. Study the many ways that others use the word.

Questions: What makes a person, place, creature, or thing "better"? "Better," as compared to what? When? How? In order to accomplish what? Is everything in the known universe "better" than everything else, for some purpose, at some time? Is the mountain "better" than the valley? Is the snow "better" than the rain? Is sky "better" than dirt? Is a "tall" person "better" than a "short" person? Is being smart "better" than being ignorant? Who is "smart"? Who is "ignorant"? When? Where? In regards to what? If a person is "smarter" than another person, is the "smarter" person "better"? If so, what is the correct way for the "smarter" person to interact with the "not-so-smart" person?

Bias. Do not use this word. The word is unnecessarily vague and non-specific. It is best and correct to use terms like "Racism," "sexism," "ageism," "mistreatment," etc. Words like "bias," "bigotry," "discrimination," "prejudice," etc., usually require too many words in attempting to explain what is meant and what is not meant.

Big Business. Use this term with caution. During the existence of White Supremacy (Racism), use it to mean the same as White Supremacy (Racism).

> **Reason:** During the existence of The System of White Supremacy (Racism), The System of White Supremacy (Racism) is the "biggest business" produced, maintained, and/or supported by the people of the known universe.

Big Government (Racial). Use this term to mean the same as, and/or to apply to White Supremacy (Racism).

Bi-Sexual and/or Transsexual. Do not use these terms.

Explanation:

(1)   A person is either male or female.

(2)   Any person who is neither male nor female is "non-sexual".

(3)   Any male person who attempts to be a female person, or any female person who attempts to be a male person, is engaged in anti-sexual and/or counter-sexual behavior.

(4)   Any person who attempts to be both male and female either alternatively or simultaneously is engaging in anti-sexual and/or counter-sexual behavior. Such persons function directly or indirectly in such a manner as to promote the destruction of sex (male-female) relationships.

Black. Use this word constructively. When using it to describe or identify people during the existence of White Supremacy (Racism), use it to apply to any color and/or "shade" of color – black, brown, red, tan, yellow, etc. Use it to apply to any "color" person, but do not use it to apply to persons "classified" as [the non-color] "white". Do not use the word "black" or the word "white," and/or words such as "brown," "yellow," "tan," "red," "purple," "rust," etc., in any manner that has the effect of belittling a person, or has the effect of promoting non-just or incorrect thought, speech, or action against any persons, creatures, things, etc. Always use the words "black," "brown," "tan," "red," "yellow," etc., in a manner that best reveals truth (that which is) for the purpose of producing justice (balance between people) and correctness (balance between people, creatures, things, etc.). Study the many ways that others use this word.

> **Note:** During the existence of White Supremacy (Racism), the White Supremacists (Racists) speak and act to use the words "black" and/or "dark" in such a manner as to cause people to think, speak, and act as if "black," "blackness," "darkness," etc., is "evil" or incorrect - especially in regards to color or "shades" of color, as it pertains to people (and sometimes creatures, or things).

Black Achievement/Black Progress. Use these terms and similar terms to apply to speech and/or action by Non-White persons that result in the following: (1) the end of White Supremacy (Racism); and/or (2) the establishment of Justice (balance between people).

Black Arts, The. Avoid using this term. If you choose to use this term, use it to mean some activity that is associated with replacing White Supremacy (Racism) with Justice (balance between people). When others use terms like "black art," "black comedy," "black drama," etc., ask for a detailed explanation that you can easily understand.

Black-Bag Jobs/Black-Balled. Do not use these terms. When others use these terms, ask for a detailed explanation that you can easily understand.

> **Reason:** During the existence of White Supremacy (Racism), it is correct to study all terms that include the words "black" or "dark" in order to reveal if the term is being used in a manner that directly or indirectly helps to promote thought, speech, and/or action in support of White Supremacy (Racism).

Black Book. Use this term to apply to any book that presents information that is directly or indirectly designed to help a person to think, speak, and/or act to replace The System of White Supremacy (Racism) with The System of Justice (balance between people).

Black Capitalism. Do not use this term. When others use it, ask for a detailed explanation that you can easily understand.

> **Questions:** What, exactly, is a "Capitalist"? Who is not a "Capitalist"? What is the exact difference between a person who is said to be a "Black Capitalist" and a person who is said to be a "White Capitalist"? What, exactly, is "capital"? What, exactly, is not "capital"? Is a White Supremacist (Racist) a "Capitalist"? Is a Non-White person the "capital" of the White Supremacists (Racists)? Can a Non-White person be a "Capitalist" and, at the same time, be subject to The System of White Supremacy (Racism)? If so, what, exactly, is the "capital" of a Non-White person who is subject to, and who is the "possession" of, those White persons who practice White Supremacy (Racism)? (See, "Capitalists").

Black Child. Use this term to apply [in your thinking] to any Black person who is directly or indirectly subject to White Supremacy (Racism) in any area of activity, including Economics, Education, Entertainment, Labor, Law, Politics, Religion, Sex, and War/Counter-War.

> **Notes:** During the existence of White Supremacy (Racism), the Non-White people of the known universe are directly or indirectly subject to, and dependent on, the White Supremacists (Racistmen and Racistwomen, collectively) of the known universe. Therefore, according to Compensatory Logic, the Non-White people of the known universe are immature, and are forced to function as the illegitimate children ("Race-Children"/"Race-Victims") of Racistmen and Racistwomen (White Supremacists, collectively).

Black Christian. Use this term with caution. When others use this term, ask for a detailed explanation that you can easily understand. What, exactly, is a "Black Christian"? Is it necessary to identify a "Christian," a "Hindu," a "Confucian," a "Muslim," a "Jew," or a "Pluralist" as "Black" or "White" or "Red," "Yellow" or "Brown"? If so, why?

Black Church/White Church. <u>Avoid using these terms</u>. Practice using the terms "church," or "churches." When others use these terms, ask them to explain, in detail, exactly what they mean. What, exactly, is "the Black church"? What, exactly, is "the White church"? "The Yellow church"? "The Red church"? Does a religion have a "color"? If so, what religion? If so, why? Is a "church" a person? If so, what person? If so, what color is that "church person"?

> **Questions:** Does a "Black church" practice a "Black religion"? If so, what, exactly, is the "religion" of a "Black church," and what is its ultimate goal? Does a "White church" practice a "White religion"? If so, what, exactly, is the "religion" of a "White church," and what is its ultimate goal?

Black Comedy. <u>Do not use this term</u>. When others use this term, ask for a detailed explanation that you can easily understand.

> **Reason:** The term "Black comedy" may be a term that, when used during the existence of White Supremacy (Racism), may have the effect of helping to promote thought, speech, and/or action in support of White Supremacy (Racism).

Black Community, The. <u>Do not use this term</u>. Instead, use "Black" or "Non-White" people, or "Victims of White Supremacy (Racism)".

> **Reason:** According to Compensatory Counter-Racist Logic and during the existence of White Supremacy (Racism), Non-White people do not, and cannot, function as a "community". A true "community" of persons does not function in subjugation to persons or groups of persons. During the existence of White Supremacy (Racism) and, according to Compensatory Counter-Racist Logic, only White people can function as a "community" - "The White Community" and/or "The Community of White Supremacists (Racists)".

Black Confine/Black Corral. <u>Use these terms</u> to apply to any place that the White Supremacists (Racists) directly or indirectly establish or choose to use to restrict Non-White people in regards to where Non-White people will or will not be "located".

Black Credentials. <u>Use this term</u> to apply to whatever a Black (Non-White) person thinks, says, or does in any area of activity during the existence of The System of White Supremacy (Racism) that proves that he or she is subject to, and is a Victim of, White Supremacy.

Black Crime. Do not use this term. When others use it, ask for a detailed explanation that you can easily understand. Does a "crime" have a "color"? What "color" is a "crime"? Is it a "crime" to be "Black"? If so, why?

Black Culture/White Culture. Use the term "Black Culture" to mean those things that the Black people of the known universe do as a reaction to the existence of The System of White Supremacy (Racism). Use the term "White Culture" to mean those things that the White people of the known universe do that directly or indirectly help to maintain, expand, and/or refine The System of White Supremacy (Racism).

> **Notes:** During the existence of "The White Culture" (White Supremacy), it is incorrect to describe any "culture" in the known universe as "African culture," "American culture" or "Asian culture," etc. According to Compensatory Counter-Racist Logic, it is not possible for the "African," the "American," or the "Asian" culture(s) to exist in the same universe, at the same time, with "The Culture of White Supremacy (Racism)".

> **Reason:** "The African Culture," "the American Culture," and "the Asian Culture," by definition, means the existence of justice (balance between people). "The Culture of White Supremacy (Racism)" by definition, means the existence of non-justice (non-balance between people) based on Race. According to Compensatory Logic, it is not possible for justice (balance between people), and non-justice (non-balance between people), to exist in the same universe, at the same time.

Black Day. Do not use this term. Instead, use the terms "it is [was] raining," "it is [was] sunny," "it is [was] snowing," "it is [was] cloudy," etc.

> **Note:** The terms "black day," "dark days," "gloomy days," etc., are sometimes used by White Supremacists (Racists) in a manner that helps promote thoughts that directly or indirectly support the practice of White Supremacy (Racism).

Black Death, The. Do not use this term. When others use the term, ask for a detailed explanation that you can easily understand.

> **Reason:** The term "The Black Death" is used directly or indirectly to promote thinking that helps support White

Supremacy (Racism). This is done by associating "death," "killer diseases," "darkness," "blackness," etc., with harm that comes from the existence of Black people.

Black English. Do not use this term. Instead, use the terms "correct English," "constructive English," "compensatory English," and/or "Counter-Racist English." Use these terms to apply to the use of English "words" in a manner that best helps to produce or promote thought, speech, and action that best helps to replace The System of White Supremacy (Racism) with The System of Justice (balance between people).

Black Family. Do not use this term. Instead, use the terms "Black group," "Black kin," "Black kin-group," "close kin," "kin-group," "kin-company," "companion-kin," etc.

> **Reason:** During the existence of White Supremacy (Racism), the White people of the known universe who participate in White Supremacy (Racism) are all members of the "White Family." The White Family and The System of White Supremacy (Racism) are one and the same. Being a White person and participating in The System of White Supremacy (Racism), is the same as being a member of the "White Family."
>
> During the existence of White Supremacy (Racism), a "Black family" does not, and cannot, exist. What does exist are "combinations" of Black people who interact with each other, in a manner that is weak and pitiful, while rendering direct or indirect service to Racistman and Racistwoman (the "White Family" or "White Supremacists," collectively).

Black Fascism. Use this term to mean the subjugation of all White people, by Black people, for the basic purpose of glorifying Black people. This is a non-existent form of fascism.

Black Flag/White Flag. Avoid using these terms. When others use them, ask for a detailed explanation that you can easily understand. What is a "Black flag" used for, and why? What is a "White flag" used for, and why? Why Black? Why White? Does the use of the terms "White flag" or "Black flag" somehow help to promote thought, speech, and/or action in support of White Supremacy (Racism)? Study the ways in which "White" is used in regards to "flags," and compare it with the way in which "Black" is used.

Black Future. <u>Do not use this term</u>. When talking about the "future," describe it either as "constructive" or "destructive," and/or either "correct" or "non-correct."

> **Reason:** There is reason to believe that White Supremacists (Racists) have promoted the use of the word "black" in a manner that causes people to think that everything "black" is evil or non-constructive, including those "things" that have no "color."

> **Questions:** What "color" is a "future"? What "color" is "the past"? What "color" is "the present"? Why, deliberately try to think of the past, the present, or the future as having a "color"?

Black Ghetto Thug. <u>Use this term</u> to apply to any Black (Non-White) person who says that he or she prefers to glorify, enjoy, and/or "profit" from being a "thug" by doing harm to other Black (Non-White) people. When others use the terms "thug," "thug-life," "ghetto thug," or "Black ghetto thug" ask for a detailed explanation that you can easily understand.

> **Notes:** According to Compensatory Logic, a person who chooses to be a "Black-ghetto thug" should, the moment that the choice is made, kill himself or herself. This is the best and correct thing that a "Black ghetto thug" can do for himself or herself and/or for others, including those that he or she "cares" about most, if such persons exist.

Black (happens to be). <u>Do not use this expression</u> to apply to a Black person. When a person uses the expression, "happens to be Black," it is correct to ask for a detailed explanation that can be easily understood.

> **Questions:** Is it correct to say or imply that a Black person is black because of a "happening"? An accident? A disease? Is a Black person black because of a "mistake"? Is a Black person Black because of deliberate, careful, and constructive intent? Is being Black an "excuse" for <u>not</u> being White?

> **Reason:** During the existence of White Supremacy (Racism), it is incorrect to say or imply that a person who is "Black" was not "created," but something that "happened." The term "happens to be Black" seems to be useful only as a form of indirect "apology" for a person

being "dark" or "black" in skin color appearance. It is incorrect to use this term in this manner. People do not "happen to be black," any more than some trees "happen to be green." There is reason to believe that "colors" do not "happen" anymore than the existence of anything else that "happens". "Color," like everything else in the known universe, is produced. There is reason to believe that "blackness" exists in the appearance of Black people because it is correct for "blackness" to exist in the appearance of Black people, and that the existence of that Black person is the result of a creative action that was deliberate and correct.

Black Hats/White Hats. Use these words with caution. Study the ways in which others use these terms.

> **Reason:** In the White Supremacist (Racist) Culture, the words "black hats" or "white hats" are sometimes used to promote the thought that "bad" people wear "black" hats, and that "good" people wear "white" hats. "Goodness" or "badness," in any person should not be associated with the color or non-color of a hat.

Black Heart/Black-Hearted. Do not use these terms. When others use them, ask for a detailed explanation that you can easily understand. Is a heart "Black"? Is a heart "White"? Are these terms used in a manner that indirectly support thinking in support of White Supremacy (Racism)?

Black (and) Hispanic. Do not use this term. When others use this term, ask for a detailed explanation that you can easily understand.

> **Questions:** Can a person be "Black" and, at the same time, be "Hispanic"? Can a person be "White" and, at the same time, be "Hispanic"? If so, why? If so, in order to accomplish what? Does a person need to be "classified" as "Black," "Brown," "Red," "Yellow," "Tan," or "White" in order to be "Hispanic"? If so, why? If so, in order to accomplish what?

> **Notes:** When a person says to you that he or she is "Hispanic" or "Latino," ask him or her if he or she is "White" or "Non-White." If he or she says that he or she is "White," ask him or her if he or she has ever participated in the practice of White Supremacy (Racism) in any one or more areas of activity. Some White persons who practice the religion of White Supremacy (Racism)

and/or The Culture of White Supremacy (Racism), sometimes pretend to be "Hispanics," "Latinos," "Christians," "Jews," "Confucians," "Conservatists," etc.

Black History. <u>Do not use this term</u>. Instead use the term "the past." When asked about your "history" say, "my history is everything that ever happened before the beginning of time, and since the beginning of time". When asked about how much history is "enough," say, "all, and only that which is necessary to best help to reveal truth, and to use truth in such a manner as to produce justice and correctness among all the people, creatures and things of the known universe." When others use the term "Black history," ask them to explain, in detail, what they mean.

Black Institution. <u>Do not use this term</u>. Instead, use the expression "Counter-Racist thought, speech, and action by Non-White persons."

> **Reason:** During the existence of The System of White Supremacy (Racism), "Black Institutions" do not, and cannot, exist. The "proof" that a "Black Institution" did exist, will come at the exact time that White Supremacy (Racism) ends.

Black Jew. <u>Do not use this term</u> unless asked to do so by a person who asks you to use the term as a title of identification for him or her. When a person uses the terms "Jew," "Black Jew," or "White Jew," ask for a detailed explanation that you can easily understand, but avoid using any of the terms yourself except to identify yourself.

> **Questions:** What, exactly, is a "Jew"? What, exactly, is not a "Jew"? Are "Jews" Black? Are "Jews" White? Do people who call themselves "Black Jews" or "White Jews" practice the same "religion"? Do they do the same things in all areas of activity – Economics, Education, Entertainment, Labor, Law, Politics, Sex, and War/Counter-War?

Black Leader(s). <u>Do not use this term</u>. Instead, use the term "Black spokesperson," and use it to mean a Black person who speaks about Race, Racism, Counter-Racism, justice, and/or non-justice.

> **Reason:** During the existence of White Supremacy (Racism), the only proven leaders of Black people are those White people who practice White Supremacy (Racism). During the existence of White Supremacy (Racism), it is the White Supremacists (Racists), who have

proven to have the most power and the most influence over what Black people do, and not do.

Black Lie. Do not use this term. When others use the term, ask for a detailed explanation that you can easily understand. Does a lie have a "color"? What "color" is a lie? If a lie has a "color," who decides that the "color" of that lie is black? Who has seen the "color" of a lie?

> **Note:** There is reason to believe that the term "black lie" is, or has been, used in a manner that has directly or indirectly helped to promote White Supremacist (Racist) thought, speech and/or action.

Black Lifestyle. Avoid using this term. When others use it, ask for a detailed explanation that you can easily understand. What is "life"? What is "style"? What makes a "lifestyle," Black? What is its purpose? Is its purpose constructive? If so, how? When? Where?

Blacklisted. Do not use this term. When others use it, ask for a detailed explanation that you can easily understand. What makes a so-called "Black list" black? Is it necessary to refer to a "list" as "Black"? If a "Black list" is derogatory, what is a "White list"? Why?

Black Magic. Do not use this term. When others use it, ask for a detailed explanation that you can easily understand. Does magic have a "color"? What color is it? Is the term "black magic" intended for use by White Supremacists (Racists) to associate the word "black" with that which is evil, incorrect, or undesirable? What is the purpose of saying that magic is "black"?

Blackmail. Do not use this term. When others use it, ask for a detailed explanation that you can easily understand. Regard the term "blackmail" as having the same lack of logic value as the terms "black lie," "black list," "black magic," etc.

Black Man/Black Woman. Do not use these terms. Instead, use the terms "Black Male" or "Black Female".

Explanation:

No Non-White person can be correctly called a "man" or a "woman," and, at the same time, be subject to White Supremacy (Racism) because no Non-White person can function as man, or as a woman and, at the same time, submit to, or cooperate with, White Supremacists (Racists), in any manner, directly or indirectly. That person, at the time, can only function as a male or female child, subject, and/or victim.

Black Mark. Avoid using this term. When others use it, ask for a detailed explanation that you can easily understand. Is the term used in a manner that directly or indirectly promotes derogatory thought, speech, and/or action against "blackness," or against Black people?

Black Middle-Class. Do not use these terms. Do not try to find or produce words that describe a "Black middle-class," or words that describe "Black middle-class values." As long as White Supremacy (Racism) exists, speak of the "classes" of people of the known universe as "the powerful class" and "the powerless class."

As long as White Supremacy (Racism) exists, think, speak, and act as if all Black (Non-White) people function as part of the "powerless class." This means that during the existence of White Supremacy (Racism), the Black or Non-White people of the known universe function with less power than the White people who practice White Supremacy (Racism). The Black and Non-White people function as Victims of the "powerful class." All of the White people of the known universe who participate in the practice of White Supremacy (Racism) are members of the "powerful class." There are no "classes" of Victims of White Supremacy. Victims of White Supremacy [Non-White people] are simply Victims of White Supremacy.

Black Monday (Tuesday, etc.) Do not use these terms. When others use them, ask for a detailed explanation that you can easily understand. What, exactly, makes a day "black"? Why is the word "black" often used to describe a situation in a manner that is derogatory, unhappy, destructive, unwanted, etc.?

Black Mood. Do not use this term. When others use it, ask for a detailed explanation that you can easily understand. How can a "mood" be "black," or "green," or "orange"? What "color" is a mood? How many moods are in "color"? Where is the "proof"?

Black Muslim/Black Christian/Black Pluralist. Avoid using these terms. The use of these terms may, unnecessarily, confuse the practice of a religion with the "color" of a person. According to Compensatory Counter-Racist Logic, it is correct to associate the practice of a "religion" with the "color" (or "non-color") of people only with those people who practice the religion of White Supremacy (Racism). During the existence of White Supremacy (Racism), the religion of White Supremacy (Racism) is the only "religion" that requires a person to be identified by a specific category of "color" or "non-color".

Black Nationalism. Avoid using this term. When others use it, ask for a detailed explanation that you can easily understand. What, exactly, is "Black nationalism," and what, exactly, is its purpose? How can "Black nationalism" exist within, and/or at the same time, that White Supremacy (White nationalism/Racism) exists?

> **Suggestion:** Instead of advocating' "Black nationalism," use the expression, "Replace White Supremacy (Racism) with Justice (balance between people)."

> **Reasons:** During the existence of White Supremacy (Racism), the only reason for any person to say anything about Black people, and/or about people being associated with a "Nation" is to help them to think, speak, and act in such a manner as to end White Supremacy (Racism) and replace it with Justice.

> The term "Black Nationalism" has often been thought to mean the same as the "glorification" of Black people because they are "Black". Some people have thought the terms to mean some form of deliberate expression of hostility toward White people because they are "White". Some people have thought that the term "Black Nationalism" means to promote thought, speech, and action that is designed to help Black people only, without any regard to what happens to White people.

> **Notes:** Since the use of this term in the aforementioned manner has sometimes promoted confusion and/or unintended animosity between White and Non-White people, or among Non-White people, themselves, it may be best and correct to use the term "Counter-Racism," "Counter-Racist Activity" and/or "Anti-White Supremacy Activity." The only logical and constructive reason for talking about or seeking to promote "Black nationalism," is for the purpose of replacing White Supremacy (Racism) with Justice (balance between people).

Black People's Contributions. Do not use this term.

> **Reason:** This is an insulting way of talking about any people, in regards to their "useful" activities in the known universe. All of the people in the known universe do

some things that are of constructive value, and do many things that are of destructive value.

Notes: No people in the known universe <u>have proven</u> to be the quality of people that they should be. To say that Black people have made "useful contributions" to the world, is to say that a Black Person is worth something of "value" only if he or she has done something that White people (or Black people) say is a "worthy contribution." This is not correct. All persons are "worthy persons" simply by being persons. All people, as persons, make "contributions." All people, as persons, "contribute" to the "world activity" that is sometimes constructive and sometimes destructive. No person, however, is the "quality" of person that a person should be.

Black Person. <u>Use this term</u> to apply to any person classified as, or who generally function as a "Black," "Brown," "Red," "Yellow," or "Non-White" person. Use it to mean a person whose physical structure is composed of elements that produces significant and/or pronounced skin color that is other than "White" in general appearance.

Black Power. <u>Use this term</u> to mean:

(1) Any word or deed or any combination of words or deeds that proves effective against White Supremacy (Racism) when employed by the Victims of White Supremacy (Non-White people).

(2) The sum total of all thought, speech, and action by Black (and/or Non-White) people that helps to reveal truth, promote justice, and/or promote correctness.

Black Pride. <u>Do not use this term</u>.

Reason: According to Compensatory Counter-Racist Logic, there is no need to use the terms that are intended to promote "pride" in "being Black." There is only a need to replace White Supremacy (Racism) with Justice (balance between people). Black people are Black people. Being a Black person does not require "pride" in being a Black person, nor does it require shame. "Black" is "Black." "Black" is a correct fact. "Black" is what it is. A person should not be any more "proud" being Black than he or she would be "proud" having ears, eyes, feet, or the ability to breathe.

Black and Proud (I am). <u>Do not use this term</u>. Instead, say, "It is my duty to do my best to speak and act to replace The System of White Supremacy (Racism) with The System of Justice (balance between people)."

> **Notes:** The expression "I am Black and proud" or "I am "White and proud" serves no constructive purpose. If a person is Black, there is no need to either be proud or ashamed. If a person is White, there is no need to either be proud or ashamed. If a person is "tall," or "short," or "happy," or "smart," there is no need to either be proud or ashamed. In a world dominated by non-justice (non-balance between people), what is needed is for each person to do his or her best to guarantee that no person is mistreated, and to guarantee that the person who needs the most help, gets the most (constructive) help.

Black Race. <u>Do not use this term</u>. Use the terms "Black people" and/or "Non-White people".

> **Reason:** In the known universe, a "Black Race" of people does not exist. In the known universe, there is only one group of people who function as a "Race". All of the "members" of that "Race" group are people who classify themselves as "White" people. The "Race group," itself, is called "The White Race." Not all White people function as "members" of "The White Race". Only those White persons who have the <u>ability to choose</u> to function as "members" of "The White Race," are members of "The White Race."
>
> All of the people who have chosen to function as "members" of "The White Race" are "Racists" (White Supremacists). These Race/ Racist people are dominant over, and are dedicated to, the mistreatment of all of the Non-White people of the known universe. This practice of dominance and mistreatment based on "race membership," is Racism. Therefore, "Race" is Racism, Racism is, functionally, White Supremacy, and White Supremacy is, functionally, Racism.
>
> The only functional "Race of People" in the known universe is the "White Race," and/or the "White Nation," the "Race Nation," "Racistman," and "Racistwoman." All of these "Race People" collectively, function as White Supremacists (Racists). During the existence of White Supremacy (Racism), Non-White people do not, and cannot, function as Racist people, or as the "Black Race."

Black School(s). <u>Do not use this term</u>. Use the word "school," or the terms "learning place," "teaching center," etc.

>**Reason:** Whenever and wherever a person is learning, that person is in "school." Whenever and wherever a person is not learning, that person is not in "school." It is incorrect to use the terms "Black school," or "White school" as it pertains to people. People "learn." People "teach." A "school" is any situation where any person is teaching or being taught, and learning. It is always important to know and to understand what is being taught and why.

>**Note:** During the existence of White Supremacy (Racism), those White persons who practice White Supremacy (Racism) try to teach and to learn only those things that will best help to maintain, expand, and/or refine The System of White Supremacy (Racism).

Black Sheep of the Family. <u>Do not use this term</u>. When others use it, ask for a detailed explanation that you can easily understand. What, exactly, does it mean for a person to be called the "Black sheep" of a family? Why "Black"? Is there something incorrect about being "Black"? Is there something incorrect about a sheep being "Black"? About a person being "Black"? If so, what? If so, according to whom, and for what reason?

>**Note:** This expression has often been used in a manner that has directly or indirectly helped to promote thought, speech, and action that are destructive to Black (Non-White) people. This expression helps to promote thought, speech, and action that glorify White Supremacy (Racism).

Black Supremacy/Black Supremacist. <u>Do not use these terms</u>.

>**Reason:** During the existence of White Supremacy (Racism), there is neither "Black Supremacy," nor are there any people who are "Black Supremacists." There is no way for "Black Supremacy" or "Black Supremacists" to exist at the same time in the same universe with White Supremacy and White Supremacists. During the existence of White Supremacy (Racism), these terms serve no useful or constructive purpose. The term "Black Supremacy" does not describe a situation that exists. It only describes a situation that <u>could</u> exist, if White

Supremacy (Racism) <u>did</u> <u>not</u> exist. "Black supremacy" is an idea; White Supremacy (Racism) is a fact.

> **Note:** According to Compensatory Counter-Racist Logic, it is correct to think, speak, and/or act to replace White Supremacy (Racism) with no form of "supremacy" other than justice and correctness.

Black Underclass. <u>Do not use this term</u>. Use the term, "Victims of White Supremacy." When others use this term, ask for a detailed explanation that you can easily understand.

> **Note:** As long as White Supremacy (Racism) exists, all Black (Non-White) people are a "class" that is "under" or subject to the White Supremacists (Racists) of the known universe.

Blacken (His/Her Name). <u>Do not use this expression</u>. The term promotes thinking that directly or indirectly helps to promote the maintenance of White Supremacy (Racism).

> **Questions:** How, exactly, does a name of a person acquire a "color"? Why "black"? What was the color of the person's name before it was "blackened"? What does the "blackened" (or tarnished) name mean, and why? According to whom? In order to accomplish what?

Black(ened) Reputation. <u>Do not use this term</u>. When others use it, ask for a detailed explanation that you can easily understand. Ask specific questions. What "color" is a "reputation" before it is made to be "black" or "blackened"? Is there any reason why a "reputation" would be associated with "color"? If so, why? If so, according to whom? If so, in order to accomplish what?

During the existence of The System of White Supremacy (Racism), there is reason to believe that the use of the terms "blackened reputation" or "black reputation" helps to promote thought, speech, and/or action in support of White Supremacy (Racism). Instead of using these terms, use the term "questionable reputation." According to Compensatory Logic, all "reputations" are questionable.

Blacks. <u>Do not use this word</u> to apply to Black people; instead, use the term "Black people".

> **Reason:** According to Compensatory Counter-Racist Logic, and as long as White Supremacy (Racism) exists, it is correct to use the term "Black people" to include any

and all people who are classified as, or who function as, Non-White people. This includes people who are "brown," "dark brown," "light brown," "beige," "tan," "yellow," "light yellow," "dark yellow," etc.

During the existence of White Supremacy (Racism), the word "blacks" has often been used to apply to Black (Non-White) people as a way of implying that Black people are not truly "people". The White Supremacists (Racistmen and Racistwomen, collectively), often use words and images in such a manner as to promote the belief that "Blacks" are not "people" but some form of grotesque "animal," "creature," "thing" and/or as a whole, a species of "monstrosities" that may or may not appear to resemble "people".

Note: During the existence of White Supremacy (Racism), Black people will, sometimes, make themselves look and act in a "grotesque" manner in order to please White people, by appearing to be "things," instead of people.

Blacks and Browns. Do not use this term. When others use it, ask for a detailed explanation that you can easily understand.

Questions: Is a Black person also "brown"? How "black" is "black"? How many people who are said to be "Black," also appear "brown"? How many people who are said to be "brown" are "classified' as "Black"? Is "brown" a "shade of Black"? Can a person who is said to be "Black," also have parts of his or her body that sometimes "appear" to be "brown," or "tan," or "dark yellow"? Who invented the term "Blacks and Browns," and what constructive purpose is the use of this term intended to serve?

Blacks and Jews. Do not use this term. When others use it, ask for a detailed explanation that you can easily understand.

Questions: What, exactly, is a "Black" person? What, exactly, is a "Jew"? Can a "Jew" be "Black"? Is "Black" a "religion"? Is "Jew" a "religion"? What are the basic characteristics of a person who is "Black"? What are the basic characteristics of a person who is a "Jew"? What, exactly, does a "Black" person do that nobody else does, in regards to Economics, Education, Entertainment, Labor, Law, Politics, Religion, Sex, and War/Counter-War? What, exactly, is a "Jew" required to do that nobody else is required to do, in regards to all areas of activity?

Notes: When a person introduces him or herself to you as a "Jew," ask, "What can I expect of you as a "Jew" in the way(s) that you will relate [interact] to me in all areas of activity, and in order to accomplish what"? Also, when a person says that he or she is a "Jew," ask him or her if he or she is "White" and ask, as a "White" person, if he or she participated in the practice of White Supremacy (Racism) at any time, in any area of activity. Instead of using the term "Blacks and Jews" use the term "Jews and non-Jews." Some White persons who practice the religion of White Supremacy (Racism), sometimes pretend to be "Jews," "Christians," "Muslims," "Atheists," etc.

Blacks and Puerto Ricans/Cubans/Pacific Islanders. Do not use these terms. Use the term "Black people," "White people," and "White Supremacists (Racists)." When others use the term "Blacks and Puerto Ricans" ask for a detailed explanation that you can easily understand.

Note: During the existence of White Supremacy (Racism), there are only three major categories of people in the known universe: (1) White people, (2) Non-White people ("Black," "Brown," "Red," "Yellow," etc.), and (3) White Supremacists (Racists).

Blame/Blameworthy. Use these words with caution. Study the ways that others use these words. Ask yourself and ask others many questions.

Questions: Is being "blameworthy" the same as being "responsible"? Who should be "blamed" for the continued existence of White Supremacy (Racism) - the people who practice White Supremacy (Racism), or the people who are the Victims of White Supremacy (Non-White people)? Both? Who should be "blamed" for the violence and counter-violence that result from the continued existence of White Supremacy (Racism)? Is it correct to "blame" a Non-White person for his or her incorrect behavior that is the result of being subject to White Supremacy (Racism) in one or more areas of people activity?

If Non-White people should be "blamed" for "allowing" themselves to be made subject to White Supremacy (Racism), is it correct to "blame" them for whatever they choose to do or say about ending White Supremacy (Racism)? If a person is taught exclusively and systematically to think, speak, and act in the manner of a monster or monstrosity, is it correct to "blame" that person? Should the "teacher" be "blamed"? Should the "student" be "blamed"? If so, how much? If so, what should be the result of the "blame"? How many people should be "blamed" for allowing White Supremacy (Racism) to exist? Some? Many? All? None?

Blemish (on his or her record). <u>Do not use this expression</u>. Instead, say "record of incorrect speech or action."

> **Reason:** There is no such thing as a "blemish" on a person's "record," "character" or "reputation." Can anyone "see" this "blemish"? If so, is it "red"? Is it "brown"? Is it "pink"? Is it round or square, or "shapeless"?

Blue-Collar Worker. <u>Avoid using this term</u>. When others use it, ask for a detailed explanation that you can easily understand.

> **Questions:** What, exactly, is the definition of a so-called "blue-collar worker"? What, exactly, does a "blue-collar" have to do with "work"? What, exactly, is "work"? Do "work classifications" help to promote a form of non-just "royalism"? Does such "work" and "blue-collar" classifications help to directly or indirectly promote the maintenance of White Supremacy (Racism)?

Born Again Christian. <u>Avoid using this term</u>. When others use it, ask for a detailed explanation that you can easily understand. What is the difference between a "born-again Christian" and a "Christian" who is not "born again"? Does the use of the term "born again Christian," help to <u>eliminate</u> confusion, or does it help to <u>promote</u> it?

Boss. <u>Use this word with caution</u>. When others use it, ask for a detailed explanation that you can easily understand. What, exactly, is a "boss"? Is it necessary for a "boss" to be in the form of a person? Is it better for a "boss" of people to be in the form of a "code," or in the form of a "set of laws" for thought, speech, and action? Why not call a "boss" by the title of "advisor," or "instructor," or "director"?

> **Reason:** The word "boss" has sometimes been associated with persons who practice "Racist-slavery" (White Supremacy).

44

Boundary. <u>Use this word with caution</u>. Study very carefully the ways that people use the words "boundary," "borders," "dividing lines," etc. Particularly, study the ways that some White persons use these words during the existence of The System of White Supremacy (Racism).

> **Reason:** During the existence of White Supremacy (Racism), those White persons who practice White Supremacy (Racism), "set" many "boundaries," etc., in such a manner as to best help to maintain, expand, and/or refine the practice of White Supremacy (Racism).

Boys. <u>Use this word</u>. In racial matters, generally, use it to "identify" all Non-White male persons, collectively, and/or without naming individual persons, who directly or indirectly exist in subjugation to the Racistman and Racistwoman (White Supremacists, collectively). Study the ways that the word is used, has been used, or can be used. Seek to use the word in a manner that accurately and truthfully defines what a "boy" is, and what a "boy" is not. In every way, seek to use the word in a manner that best reveals the true difference between what is a "man," and what is a "boy." (See, "Baby Boy").

> **Question:** According to the logic that is required in replacing White Supremacy (Racism) with Justice (balance between people), how can a Non-White person be a "man" and, at the same time, be subject to The System of White Supremacy (Racism)?

Brave. <u>Use this word with caution</u>. When others use it, ask for a detailed explanation that you can easily understand.

> **Note:** What is sometimes called "bravery" may, truthfully, be "extreme insanity." Many acts, however, require what may be called "bravery," regardless of their "insane" characteristics.

Bright. <u>Use this word with caution</u>. Do not use this word to mean the same as the word "smart." To do so, is to associate the word "smart" with the word "light," "right," or the non-color "white." It is incorrect to associate only "whiteness" with "smartness," in regards to people.

> **Note:** During the existence of The System of White Supremacy (Racism), terms like "bright future," and "bright student," etc., help to produce thoughts that help to support White Supremacy (Racism).

Brighter Day, A. <u>Do not use this term</u>. Instead, use the expression "a day of opportunity."

> **Reason:** The term "brighter day," when used during the existence of White Supremacy (Racism), sometimes causes some people to associate the word "bright" with the word "white." The term "bright" is often associated with "White" people being associated with making a day "bright" – which, in turn, is said to make a day "better" or "good." The use of the terms "bright" or "brighter" are also often used to indicate that things, places, or people who appear to be "dark," "gloomy," "dull," etc., are, somehow not "better," or "pleasing," or "correct."

> **Notes:** All "days" are a part of the same "day/night" condition. "Darkness" and "light" serve the purposes that they are designed to serve. White Supremacists (Racists) speak and act, and cause others to speak and act, as if "dark days," as well as "dark people," should be regarded as "evil," "incorrect" and/or "unpleasant".

Brown. <u>Use this word with caution</u>. During the existence of White Supremacy (Racism), use the word "brown" to mean a shade of "Black," or a shade of "Non-White" when associating the word with the "color," or the "racial-classification" of a person. When talking about the "color" of a person, do not use the word "Brown" unless you use it to mean a "shade" of "Black," or "Non-White." In other words, a "brown," "tan," "red," "beige," or "yellow" person is a "shade" of "Black" in "appearance," or in accords with Compensatory Counter-Racist Classification Logic.

Buck-Naked. <u>Do not use this term</u>. Instead, use the term "naked" or "completely naked".

> **Reason:** The term "buck-naked" has sometimes been used as a "slang" term by White Supremacists (Racists) for the purpose of "making fun" of "primitive" Non-White people whose bodies are not covered.

> **Note:** Non-White people, particularly Black males, have sometimes been called "Bucks" by those White persons who practice White Supremacy (Racism).

Business Clothes/Business Suit. <u>Use these terms with caution</u>. Study the ways in which others associate "doing business" with clothes or body covering. What effect does a particular "form" of body covering have on how people think, speak, and/or act toward each other? What should the effect be? Should a "naked" person be regarded as a person who is worthy of "doing business" in a constructive manner? If so, why? If not, why not?

C

Capital. Use this word with caution. When others use it, ask for a detailed explanation that you can easily understand. What, exactly, is "capital"? What, exactly, is not "capital"?

> **Note:** It can be said that anything that a person has "possession" of, or control of, may or may not be "capital." This includes "possession" of, or control of, him or herself.

Capitalist/Communist. Use these words with caution. When others use them, ask for a detailed explanation that you can easily understand.

> **Questions:** What, exactly, is a "capitalist"? What, exactly, is not a "capitalist"? Is a person a "capitalist" if he or she owns, possesses, or uses something that is of "value"? If so, what, when, where, and/or how much? Is a person a "communistic-capitalist" if he or she shares a "common interest" with another person who owns, possesses, or uses something that is of "socio-material value"? If a person "socializes" with a person who is a "capitalist," is that person a supporter of "capitalism" by "socializing" as if he or she has something of "value" in "common" with the person who is a "capitalist"? Does such "socializing" make both of people "socialistic supporters of communistic-capitalism"?
>
> What does "Communism" or "Capitalism" do to eliminate Racism (White Supremacy)? If "Communism" or "Capitalism" eliminates Racism, why is Racism still the dominant motivating force among the people of the known universe?
>
> **Notes:** "Capitalist," "capitalism," "socialism," "socialist," "socialize," "communist" and "communistic," are words that mean many different things to many different people.

Caucasian/Caucasoid. Use these words with caution. When others use these words, ask for a detailed explanation that you can easily understand.

Questions: What, exactly, is a "Caucasian"? What, exactly, is not a "Caucasian"? How many "characteristics" does a "Caucasian" have that a "non-Caucasian" does not have? What, exactly, does a "Caucasian" do that a "non-Caucasian" does not do in each area of activity, including Economics, Education, Entertainment, Labor, Law, Politics, Religion, Sex, and War/Counter-War?

Notes: According to Compensatory Counter-Racist Logic and during the existence of White Supremacy (Racism), there are only three basic "racially-associated" categories of people in the known universe: White people, Non-White people, and White Supremacists (Racists). The naming of any other "categories" are sometimes used by White Supremacists (Racists) for the purpose of producing confusion in the thinking of their Victims (Non-White people).

Center (right of/left of). <u>Do not use these terms</u> in ways that pertain to "political differences." When others use these terms, ask for a detailed explanation that you can easily understand.

Questions: What, exactly, is the "political center"? Does it mean the same as the term "dominant force"? If so, what is that "dominant force"? Is the "dominant political force" among the people of the known universe, The System of White Supremacy (Racism)? If so, what is the "left," or the "right," of that "center" that is the "dominant force" that functions as The System of White Supremacy (Racism)?

Note: When talking about the interactions between the people of the known universe, the terms "center," "left-of-center," and/or "right-of-center," are confusing.

Character. <u>Use this word with caution</u>. When others use this word, ask for a detailed explanation that you can easily understand. What, exactly, is "character"? What, exactly, is not "character"? Which persons are best qualified to decide what is, and what is not, "character"?

Character (blot on his or her). <u>Do not use this expression</u>. Instead, say "record of his or her non-correct speech or action."

Reason: To say that a person has a "blot" on his or her "character" or "reputation" is to (directly or indirectly)

48

promote thought, speech, and/or action in support of White Supremacy (Racism).

Questions: What does a "blot" on a "character" look like? How, exactly, does a "reputation" receive something called a "blot"? Is a "blot" or "spot" often associated with something dark, destructive and/or out of place? Is the "color" of a "blot" on a person's "character" the same as the "color" of a Non-White person? Why is a "blot" that is not seen, called a "blot"?

Character (good). Do not use this term. When others use it, ask for a detailed explanation that you can easily understand. What, exactly, is "character"? What, exactly, is "good character"? What, exactly, is a "good person"? Can a person who is not a "good" person, be of "good" character? If so, how? By doing what? Which persons are best qualified to decide what persons possess "good character," and what persons do not? Can a person be a White Supremacist (Racist) and, at the same time, possess "good character"?

Character (having). Use this term with caution. When others use it, ask for a detailed explanation that you can easily understand. What, exactly, is "character"? What, exactly, is not "character"? Which persons are "qualified" to decide which persons "have character" and which persons do not? Use this term to mean to have the correct intentions, at all times in all areas of activity, including Economics, Education, Entertainment, Labor, Law, Politics, Religion, Sex, and War/Counter-War.

Notes: To "have character" does not, necessarily, include "being smart," and/or knowing what to do or how to do it. "Having character" does mean having the intention of: (1) guaranteeing that no person is mistreated, and having the intention of (2) guaranteeing that the person who needs help the most, gets the most help.

Character (shady). Do not use this term. When others use it, ask for a detailed explanation that you can easily understand. What, exactly, makes a "character" "shady"? Why "shady"? "Shady," as compared to what? For what reason?

Note: During the existence of White Supremacy (Racism), the term "shady character" is sometimes used to (directly or indirectly) promote the thought that "dark" people are "evil," "dangerous," and/or generally more "treacherous" than White people.

Character (stained). <u>Do not use this term</u>. Use, instead, "incorrect speech and/or action," "incorrect intent," "incorrect characteristics," etc.

> **Questions:** How can a person have a "stained character"? How can a person see the "color" of "something" [a stain] in a person's "character"?

> **Reason:** White Supremacists (Racists) often use words in a manner that promotes thinking that is derogatory in regards to persons, creatures, or things that are "dark" and/or "black" in appearance. The word "stain" is often associated with a condition of darkness. It is also often associated with something that is detrimental, annoying, and/or undesirable.

Character (swarthy). <u>Do not use this term</u>. When others use terms like "swarthy character," "shady character," etc., ask for a detailed explanation that you can easily understand. Ask questions.

> **Questions:** What, exactly, is "character"? What, exactly, is the correct "color" of "character"? Instead of using the term "swarthy character" to apply to any person, use the expression, "I do not know what I should know about him or her."

> **Note:** During the existence of White Supremacy (Racism), the term "swarthy character" has been used to imply that a person, who is "dark" in appearance, is dangerous, repulsive, "tricky," and/or "mysteriously incorrect" <u>because</u> he or she is "dark" in appearance.

Child/Children. <u>Use these words with caution</u>. When others use these words, ask for a detailed explanation that you can easily understand.

> **Reason:** According to Compensatory Counter-Racist Logic, all Non-White persons are "children" as long as they are subject to The System of White Supremacy (Racism).

> **Questions:** What, exactly, is a "child"? Are Non-White people "children" if they are forced to think, speak, and act as "children" because of The System of White Supremacy (Racism)? When, exactly, is a person "grown" (completed his or her growth)? Is being "grown" a matter of comparing each person with another person? If so, by

measuring what speech or action, with what speech or action? During the existence of White Supremacy (Racism), is every Victim of White Supremacy (Non-White person), an "illegitimate, abused, child-subject" of every White Supremacist (Racist)?

Notes: As long as White Supremacy (Racism) exists, it is incorrect for any Non-White person to make remarks like, "When I was a child..." He or she should, instead say, "When I was a younger person..."

Children Having Children. Use this term. Use it mostly to apply to all Non-White persons who produce offspring while subject to White Supremacy (Racism).

Notes: According to Compensatory Counter-Racist Logic, and as long as White Supremacy (Racism) exists, all of the Non-White people of the known universe either directly or indirectly function as the retarded, handicapped, weak and illegitimate "children" of the White Supremacists (Racistmen and Racistwomen, collectively). The White Supremacists (Racists) dominate and function as the "supreme illegitimate parents" of the Non-White people in every area of activity – Economics, Education, Entertainment, Labor, Law, Politics, Religion, Sex, and War/Counter-War.

Chinks (Racial). Do not use this word to identify or make remarks to or about any person who is called "Chinese," or "Asian." It is incorrect to call any person by any name or any title except the name or title that the person asks to be called.

Chosen People, The. Avoid using this term. When others use it, ask for a detailed explanation that you can easily understand.

Questions: Are not all people "chosen"? What people are "chosen" and for what purpose? Which people have been "chosen" to produce justice (balance between people) and/or to produce "peace" among all people, all creatures, and all things in the known universe? Where is the "proof"? Who has been "chosen" to decide what is "proof" and what is not "proof," of who has or has not been "chosen"? Why? When? How?

Note: Justice has not been produced; peace has not been produced.

Church. Use this word with caution. When others use it, ask for a detailed explanation that you can easily understand.

> **Questions:** What, exactly, makes a "church," a "church"? Is a "church" a "building"? Is a "church" a person? Can one person be a "church"? If so, what are the things that a person must do if he or she intends to be a "church"? Is it correct for one "church" to be different from another? If so, different in what ways? Can a "church" be the same "church," and be a different "church," at the same time? If a person is a "church," what does that person do that a person who is not a "church," do?

Churchism. Use this term to apply to the practice of worshipping or praising the rituals, images, ceremonies, songs, buildings, symbols, popularity, etc., of a church, temple, etc., without practicing the religion for which the idea of church, temple, etc., is intended.

Church and State (separation of). Avoid using this term. When others use the term, ask for a detailed explanation that you can easily understand. What, exactly, is a "church"? What, exactly, is a "state"? Is a "church" a person? Is a "state" a person? Can a person be a "church," and a "state" at the same time? If so, how can that person be a "state" that is "separate" from a "church," and at the same time, be a person that can be correctly called an "individual" (un-divided) person?

Church Work. Avoid using this term. When others use it, ask them to explain, in detail, exactly what they mean when they say that they are doing "church work."

Citizen. Use this word with caution. When others use it, ask for a detailed explanation that you can easily understand.

> **Questions:** What exactly, is a "citizen"? What, exactly, is a "non-citizen"? Is it possible for a "non-citizen" to receive better treatment than a "citizen"? If so, how? Why? Is it possible for one person to be treated as more "citizen" than another? If so, how? Why? What, exactly, is a "second-class citizen," and how can a person be a "second-class citizen," and, at the same time, be "worthy" of being called a "citizen"? Is a "second-class citizen," in truth, a "non-citizen"? Can a "creature" (animal, etc.) be treated as a "citizen" without having the "title" of "citizen"? If a Non-White person is subject to The System of White Supremacy (Racism), is that person a "citizen" of anything, or a "citizen" of nothing?

Citizen's Council. <u>Use this term with caution</u>. When others use the term, ask for a detailed explanation that you can easily understand. What, exactly, is a "citizen's council" and what, exactly, is its ultimate purpose?

Civic Duty. <u>Use this term with caution</u>. When others use it, ask for a detailed explanation that you can easily understand. What, exactly, is a "civic duty"? Are some "civic duties" more important than others? If so, which ones? Is it a "civic duty" to speak and act to replace The System of White Supremacy (Racism) with The System of Justice (balance between people)?

Civil/Civilized. <u>Use these terms with caution</u>. When others use these terms, ask for a detailed explanation that you can easily understand.

> **Questions:** What, exactly, is "civil" or "civilized"? What, exactly, is a "civil," or a "civilized" person? Where are they? What does a "civil" or "civilized" person do in each area of activity - Economics, Education, Entertainment, Labor, Law, Politics, Religion, Sex, and War/Counter-War? What, exactly, is "uncivil"? What, exactly, is "uncivilized"? What, exactly, is an "uncivil" or "uncivilized" person? Are all people "uncivil," and/or "uncivilized"?
>
> **Note:** According to Compensatory Counter-Racist Logic, it is not possible for "civilization" to exist and White Supremacy (Racism) to exist among the people of the known universe <u>at the same time</u>. (<u>See</u>, also, "Uncivil" and "Uncivilized").

Civil Law. <u>Use this term with caution</u>. When others use it, ask for a detailed explanation that you can easily understand. What, exactly, is the difference between a "law" that is "civil" ("civilized") and a "law" that is "not civil" ("uncivilized")?

Civil Rights. <u>Do not use this term</u>. Instead, use the term "correct duties." When others use this term, ask for a detailed explanation that you can easily understand. What, exactly is a "right" that is not "civil"? If a "right" is not "civil," how can it be a "right"?

> **Notes:** The term "correct duties" means thought, speech, and action using truth (that which is), to produce justice (balance between people), and correctness (balance between people, creatures, things, etc.). This includes thought, speech, and action that is designed to replace

The System of White Supremacy with The System of Justice. The term "correct duties" can also mean "Counter-Racist duties" (duties to replace White Supremacy with Justice).

Civil Servant/Civil Service. <u>Avoid using these terms</u>. When others use these terms, ask for a detailed explanation that you can easily understand. What, exactly, is "civil service"? What, exactly, is a "non-civil" servant? Is it possible for a person who is a White Supremacist (Racist) to practice "civilized service"? In a known universe in which non-justice and non-correctness dominates the behavior of the Non-White people, are there any people who are truly practicing "service" that is "civil" or "civilized?

Civil War. <u>Do not use this term</u>. Instead, use terms like "war," "counter-War," "non-war" and/or "the war." When others use the term "civil war," ask them to explain, in detail, how a "war" can be a "war" and, at the same time, be "civil" ("civilized").

> **Questions:** Do people kill or maim each other in a "civil war"? What is "civil," or "civilized" about killing or maiming people, that is different from "non-civil" or "non-civilized" killing or maiming people?

> **Notes:** According to Compensatory Logic, "war" is any conflict between, among, or against any persons, creatures, things, and/or "spirits." "Counter-War" is speech and/or action that is designed to cause "war" to result in "non-war" (non-conflict). "The War" is a term that, during the existence of White Supremacy (Racism), means any conflict between White people and Non-White people that is the direct or indirect result of the existence of White Supremacy (Racism).

Classical Music. <u>Use this word</u> to apply to any and all "sounds" that produce a constructive effect on the ways that the greater number of people, creatures, and/or things, think, speak, and/or act for the greatest period of time. When others use this term, ask for a detailed explanation that you can easily understand.

> **Notes:** According to Compensatory Logic, there is reason to believe that the difference between "music" and "noise" is that "music" is any sounds that helps a person to think, speak, and/or act in a manner that produces a <u>constructive</u> result; whereas "noise" is any sounds that helps a person to think, speak and/or act in a manner that produces a <u>non-constructive</u> result.

Classified Information. Use this term with caution. When others use this term, ask for a detailed explanation that you can easily understand. If you decide that some information that you have should be put into a "class" that you think is correct, simply say to yourself and/or to others, that the information is, in fact, "classified information."

Closest Person/Closest Mate. Use these terms to apply to that person of opposite/complimentary sex with whom you have direct and intimate contact, and with whom both you and the person know everything about one another that each of you regard as "worth" knowing, and with no conflicts resulting from any of your interactions with each other in regards to all areas of activity.

Code White. Use this term to apply to the intent and the actions of White Supremacists (Racistmen and Racistwomen, collectively) that directly or indirectly result in the establishment, maintenance, expansion, and refinement of The System of White Supremacy (Racism) in any one or more areas of activity. Also, use the terms "Code White" and/or "The White Code" to apply to any situation wherein the existence of White Supremacy (Racism) is the dominant motivating factor by people, in regards to the activities of the people of the known universe.

Code Work. Use this word to apply to the process of making a detailed plan for thinking, speaking, and acting to produce the best possible result for which the plan was made.

> **Note:** During the existence of White Supremacy (Racism), every person in the known universe should be producing a "Counter-Racist Code" (plan) for thinking, speaking, and acting to replace The System of White Supremacy (Racism) with The System of Justice (balance between people) in every area of activity (Economics, Education, Entertainment, Labor, Law, Politics, Religion, Sex, and War/Counter-War).

Codify. Use this word to apply to any and all thought, speech, and action that is designed and intended to produce a specific result that consistently and efficiently satisfies those who seek to produce the result. Use it to apply to a way of getting things done, the same way, each time it's done.

Colonialism/Colony. Avoid using these terms. When others use them, ask for a detailed explanation that you can easily understand. Also, do not associate "colonialism" with Racism, or White

Supremacy. Call "Racism" White Supremacy, and call "White Supremacy" Racism.

> **Questions:** What, exactly, is a "colony"? What, exactly, is not a "colony"? Is a "colony" a person? Is a "colony" a Victim? Is a "colony" a place? Are all of the people of the known universe who are subject to White Supremacy (Racism), a "colonized" people – a "Race colony"?

Color/Colored (Racial). Use these words with caution. When others use the term, ask for a detailed explanation that you can easily understand. Do not say that any person is "colored." The term "Black" and/or "Non-White" should be used to describe all of the people of the known universe who are "classified" as "Non-White," and/or who are treated/mistreated as "Non-White," by people who are "classified" as "White" and/or people who function as White Supremacists (Racists). Why not use the term "Non-White" to describe and/or identify all Non-White people during the existence of White Supremacy (Racism)?

> **Notes:** According to Compensatory Counter-Racist Logic, it is best and correct to minimize confusion by using only those terms of description and identification that best serves the purpose of helping people to effectively think, speak, and act to correctly replace The System of White Supremacy (Racism), with The System of Justice (balance between people). This purpose is best served by using the term "Non-White" instead of the term "colored," as a means of describing/identifying all of the people of the known universe who are not White.

Color Blind/Color-Blind Society (Racial). Do not use these terms. When others use these terms, ask for a detailed explanation that you can easily understand. Perhaps "color" should exist; perhaps "Racism" and "Race" should not. Ask questions. Discuss. Study. Conclude.

> **Questions:** Why be "blind" to "color" if "color" does, in fact, exist? If a person, place, creature, or thing has "color," is it correct for that "color" to be seen? If not, why not? Is it correct to pretend that a person who has "color" is "color-less"? If so, why? If so, "less" of what "color"? If so, "color-less," in order to accomplish what, that would be of constructive value? What is incorrect about recognizing the existence of "color"? Should "color" exist? If "color" in people should exist, what should the existence of "color" in people, mean? Should "height" exist? Should "weight" exist? Should "sex" exist? Is

56

there a difference between "color" and "Racism"? What is the difference? According to whom?

Colored Blood/Black Blood/Indian Blood/White Blood, etc. <u>Do not use these terms</u> as a means of identifying the "racial" categories of any person, and/or as a means of identifying the "geographical origin" of any person or creature. When others use these terms, ask for a detailed explanation that you can easily understand.

> **Questions:** What, exactly, is the "colored blood" of a "Black person"? What "color" is the blood of a "colored person"? Does a Black person have "black" blood? Does a White person have white blood? Does a "brown" person have "purple" blood? Does talk about "colored people" having "black blood" or "Asian blood" serve a constructive purpose? Does the use of such terms best help to produce justice (balance between people), or does it help to maintain The System of White Supremacy (Racism)?

Colorful Language. <u>Do not use this term</u>. When others use it, ask for a detailed explanation that you can easily understand. Ask questions. What, exactly, makes "colorful language" so-called "colorful," and/or "full of color"? Why "color"? What "color"? Why is language that is considered "offensive," "obscene," "trashy," or "vulgar" sometimes given the title of "colorful language"?

Colorism. <u>Avoid using this word</u>. When others use it to apply to people in matters of Race, Racism, and/or Counter-Racism, ask for a detailed explanation that you can easily understand.

Colorless (Racial). <u>Avoid using this word</u>. When speaking or writing about "White" people, do not describe them as "color-less" unless they ask you to do so. When others use the word "colorless" in matters of Race, Racism, and/or Counter-Racism, ask questions.

> **Questions:** Is "White" a "color"? If "White" is a "color," does that mean that people who are "White" are, in fact, "colored people" with a "White-colored" appearance? Does being "White" mean being "colored," but having less "color" than someone or something that has more "color"? Is a "colorless" person a "Black," and/or "Non-White" person? How "full" is a "color" that is "full"? Is a "Black" person a "full color" person? Is a "White" person a "less color" person? Can a person be "color-less" and be "White" at the same time? Can a person be "White" and "Non-White" at the same time? Can a person be "Black"

and "White" at the same time? How "white" is "white"?
How "colorless" is "less color"?

Combatants/Non-Combatants.   Use these terms with caution.
When others use these terms, ask for a detailed explanation that you
can easily understand.

> **Questions:**   What, exactly, is a "combatant"?   What,
> exactly, is a "non-combatant"? If a "civilian" supports a
> "soldier," is that "civilian" the same as a "soldier" who
> supports another "soldier"? What, exactly, is a "fight"?
> What, exactly, is a "war"? Is all "fighting" a "war"? Is all
> "war" the same as "fighting"? Is a "soldier" the same as a
> "civilian" if he or she is not a "combatant" in a "war"?
> During a "war," are all people "combatants"? If a person
> resists being mistreated through deceit or through
> violence, is that person a "combatant soldier"? Are the
> White people who have chosen to participate in The
> System of White Supremacy (Racism), "combatants" for
> The System of White Supremacy (Racism)?

Combat Zone. Use this term with caution. When others use it, ask
for a detailed explanation that you can easily understand. When you
use this term, use it to mean any situation where people, creatures,
or other forces act toward one another in any manner that results in
willful, deliberate, and/or harmful behavior.

> **Note:**   During the existence of The System of White
> Supremacy (Racism), all Non-White people exist in the
> (Racial) "combat zone."

Common. Use this word with caution. When others use it, ask for a
detailed explanation that you can easily understand. What, exactly,
is "common" and what is not? To what degree is "something in
common," truly "something in common"?   When?   Where?
"Common" to whom? As compared to what? When, exactly, is
something the "same as" something "else"? Can something be "in
common" with "something else" and, at the same time, be different
from that "something else"? If so, how "different"? If so, how much
different from being in "common"? How "common" is "common"?

> **Notes:**   During the existence of White Supremacy
> (Racism), the White people who have chosen to practice
> White Supremacy (Racism) have produced the most
> powerful force of people "in common" among the people of
> the known universe. That most powerful people force is
> The System of White Supremacy (Racism).

Common Basic Objective.   <u>Use this term</u> to apply to any combination of willful thought, speech, and action by a person that dominates all other combinations of willful thought, speech, and action.   Racism is the Common Basic Objective of Racists (White Supremacists).

Common Sense. <u>Avoid using this term</u>. When others use this term, ask for a detailed explanation that you can easily understand. Instead of using this term, use the term "correct thinking" and/or "correct thought".

> **Reason:**   "Thoughts" and/or "motivations" are either <u>correct</u> or <u>incorrect</u>. A "correct thought" is a thought that best helps to produce speech and/or action that result in justice (balance between people) and correctness (balance between people, creatures, things, etc.) and/or peace (the result of truth being revealed and used in such a manner as to help produce justice and correctness).

> **Questions:** How "common" is "common sense"?   What exactly is "common sense" in matters of all the areas of activity?

Commonwealth.   <u>Use this word with caution</u>.   When others use it, ask for a detailed explanation that you can easily understand.

> **Questions:**   What, exactly, is "wealth" in "common"? What does this term mean if it does not mean a form of "communism," and/or "community-ism"?   Is a "commonwealth," people who have one or more things "in common"? If so, what things "in common"? How many things? Most things? A few things? Everything? How are "things in common" correctly measured?   Are there things, habits, thoughts, etc., in a "commonwealth" that are not "in common"? Is a "member" of a "commonwealth" also a "member" of a "commune"? Is a "member" of a "commonwealth," a "communist"? What, exactly, is the difference between a "commonwealth" and a "commune," "community," "democracy," and a "republic"?

Commune. <u>Avoid using this word</u>. When others use it, ask for a detailed explanation that you can easily understand.   Avoid describing any situation as a "commune," and/or as a "community" (of people) unless you are referring to the "commune" or "community" of those White persons who participate in the practice of White Supremacy (Racism).

Questions: What, exactly, is a "commune"? What, exactly, is a "non-commune"? What, exactly, is a "community"? What, exactly, is a "non-community"? Are all people a part of a "commune" or "community"? Are all people, either directly or indirectly a part of the same "commune," or "community"? If so, in what ways? If so, in which areas of activity? Where? When? How? Why? If not, where, when, how and why not? If two or more persons do something "with" each other, is that a form of "commune," or "community"? If so, why? If not, why not?

If Black people exist in subjugation to a System of White Supremacy (Racism) in all areas of activity, how can those Black people, at the same time, function as a "Black commune," or as a "Black community"? Is it possible for people to be a "community" of "color" and, at the same time, be subject to a "community" of people of "non-color"? If all people have "something in common," do they belong to the same "commune"? If all people are "members" of the same "commune," how can their situation be correctly called a "commune"?

Are such people a "nation"? Is a "nation" a "commune" or a "community"? If a "nation" is a "commune" or a "community," does that mean that every person in the known universe who directly or indirectly "communes" with another person, is, in truth, a "member" of the same "nation" as that other person? Is it possible for a person to be an "equal member" of a "commune," a "community," or a "nation," and, at the same time, be subject to the "commune," "community," or "nation" that he or she is an "equal member" of? If so, how can a person be "subject to" something or someone and, at the same time, be "equal to" that same something or someone? How can one "commune" or "community" be subject to another "commune" or "community" and, at the same time, be "worthy" of being called a "commune" or a "community"?

Notes: During the existence of The System of White Supremacy (Racism), there is no "Black community." There are only White people, White Supremacists (Racists) and Victims of White Supremacy (Non-White people). During the existence of White Supremacy (Racism), the Non-White people of the known universe can be correctly identified either collectively or individually, as "Victims," and/or "Victim Units" – not as any "commune" or "community."

60

Communicate. Use this word with caution. When others use it, ask for a detailed explanation that you can easily understand.

> **Questions:**   When do people "communicate"?   Is it possible for people to talk to each other and, at the same time, not "communicate" with each other? Do Non-White people and White people [truly] "communicate" with each other within The System of White Supremacy (Racism)? Do the White Supremacists (Racists) of the known universe "communicate" with each other about how to continue to maintain, expand, and/or refine The System of White Supremacy (Racism)?   If not, how does The System of White Supremacy (Racism) continue to exist? If so, what methods do they use to "communicate" the ways that they practice White Supremacy (Racism) in Economics,   Education,   Entertainment,   Labor,   Law, Politics, Religion, Sex, and War/Counter-War? Do Non-White people "communicate" with each other, or do they "talk at" each other?   If the Non-White people of the known universe "communicate" with each other, why are they subject to The System of White Supremacy (Racism)?

Communist/Communism. Avoid using these terms. When others use these terms, ask for a detailed explanation that you can easily understand. Do not say that a person is a "communist" unless that person asks you to do so. Do not say that a "condition," "situation," or "system" is "communist" or "communistic" unless you can specifically identify what makes them "communist" or "communistic" in each area of activity.   Compare what you say about a "communistic" condition, situation, or system with conditions, situations, or systems that are said to be "non-communistic" or "non-communist."

Be very specific when you explain the differences between a "communist" or "communistic" condition, etc., and a condition that is "capitalist," "democratic," "dictatorial," "fascist," "free," "republican," "royalist," "socialist," "terroristic," "totalitarian," "utopian" or "White Supremacist (Racist)."

"Communism," in general, is a word that is or can be used in so many ways that, when used alone, cannot be defined in any "special" way because it can be defined in many "special" ways.   As a description of a "socio-material system," the word can be used to describe anything that any person says or does that is, or seems to be, "in common" with what another person is saying or doing. The most "common" form of "communism" and the most dominant form among the people of the known universe is "Racial Communism" (White Supremacy).

"Communism" can be said to mean: (1) the sum total of all social and material functions of the Racist Community; (2) White Capitalism, collectively; (3) the sum total of all "White Capitalism"; (4) "Universal Racism" (White Supremacy); and (5) the basic "common" interest of the "Master Commune" (White Supremacist, collectively).

Community. Avoid using this word. When others use it, ask for a detailed explanation that you can easily understand.

> **Questions:** What, exactly, is a "community"? What, exactly, is not a "community"? Where, exactly, is a "community"? Is there conflict in a "community"? If there is conflict in a "community," how much conflict can exist in a "community" and, at the same time, be "correctly qualified" to be called a "community"? If a "community" is "overpowered" by another [hostile] "community," is the "over-powered community" still a "community"? Can a subjugated people be a "community"? How can people who are subject to a "hostile community," function as a "community"? If they are "subjects," how can they, at the same time, be worthy of being correctly called a "community"? If Non-White people are subject to a "White community" (organized White Supremacists, collectively), how can those Non-White people be a "community" and, at the same time, be a people who are subject to the dictates of Racists (White Supremacists)?

Community Standards. Avoid using this term. When others use this term, ask for a detailed explanation that you can easily understand.

> **Questions:** What, exactly, is a "community"? What, exactly, is a "community standard"? How many of what people, when, where, and how, produce or support, which "standard" of what "community"? Which persons are "correctly qualified" to decide what is and what is not a "community standard"? Based on what? Is White Supremacy (Racism) a "community standard"? Is being a Victim of White Supremacy (Non-White person) a "community standard"? What is the basic purpose of a "community standard" that is dominated by The System of White Supremacy (Racism)? What is the "community standard" of White Supremacy (Racism) in regards to Economics, Education, Entertainment, Labor, Law, Politics, Religion, Sex, and War/Counter-War?

Community Ties. Avoid using this term. When others use it, ask for a detailed explanation that you can easily understand.

> **Notes:** During the existence of White Supremacy (Racism), and according to Compensatory Counter-Racist Logic, the only "community" of people in the known universe, is the "community" of White Supremacists (Racists). Other terms that apply to White Supremacy are "The System of White Supremacy," "The White Community," "The White Nation," "Racistman and Racistwoman," "The White Race/Racists," etc.

Comparable Worth/Non-Comparable Worth. Use these terms with caution. When others use these terms, ask for a detailed explanation that you can easily understand. Study and discuss the word "comparable," and the word "worth" whenever and wherever they are used. Ask yourself and others why the words are used the way they are used, when they are used, and by whom.

> **Questions:** Is anything "worth" anything when compared with something other than itself? What causes something or someone to have "worth"? Is a bird "worth" more than a bee? Is an ant "worth" more than a flower? Are rocks "worth" more than water? What is a Non-White person "worth"? What is a baby "worth"? Is a person, place, creature or thing "worth" something by simply existing? "Worth" something to who? When? Where? "Worth" what, for what? What determines "worth"? Who decides what "worth" is? Who decides what is of "worth" and what is "worthless"? Is it whomever has the most power to decide? What is something "worth" that is not compared with something else? What is a work of art "worth"? What, exactly, does a baby do that makes it "worth" something? Something like what? Why? What person is qualified to say that a baby is "worth" nothing because it "does" nothing? Is it correct to say that a baby does all that it needs to do simply by being a baby? What "work" is "worth" doing? What part of the same "job" is "worth" more than another part of the same "job"?

Compensate/Compensation/Compensatory. Use these terms and always use them with definitions that best promote the production of justice (balance between people), the production of correctness (balance between people, creatures, things, etc.), and/or the promotion of the elimination of White Supremacy (Racism). When others use these terms, ask for a detailed explanation that you can easily understand. Be particularly wary of the ways that others may or may not use these terms. Study, in detail, the ways that these terms are used in each area of activity.

> **Notes:** According to Compensatory Counter-Racist Logic, to "compensate" means to "make up" for what is "missing." What is "missing" during the existence of White Supremacy (Racism), is the practice of Justice (balance between people) by the people of the known universe. Because White Supremacy (Racism), itself, is the most powerful form of injustice among the people of the known universe, there is no way to start to "compensate" for the absence of Justice without first ending White Supremacy (Racism) in all areas of activity.

Compensatory Communications Associate. Use this term to apply to any person with whom you (or others) talk to, receive information from, give information to, or engage in activity with, for the purpose of helping to produce justice and/or for the purpose of helping to end Racism (White Supremacy) according to a compensatory and/or "codified" method of thinking, speaking, and/or acting.

Compensatory Concept/Compensatory Logic. Use these terms to apply to thought that is intended to result in speech and action that compensates (takes the place of) that which does not exist, by bringing it into existence.

> **Example**: If Justice (balance between people) does not exist, a person may compensate for its non-existence by thinking of a way to produce a system of speaking and/or acting that results in Justice being made to exist. The only way to compensate for the non-existence of Justice is through thoughts (concepts) that produce acts that guarantee that no person is mistreated, and guarantee that the person who needs help the most, gets the most constructive help.

> **Notes:** The way to find out if the concept was "logical" (in producing the intended result) is when the intended result is produced. Until then, the "concept" and the "logical process" for producing the intended result is none other than "thoughts about intentions".

Compensatory Counter-Racist Contact [Waltz]. Use this term to apply to the practice of Non-White persons making voluntary contact with persons only for the purpose of doing or saying things in a manner that best helps to promote the replacement of The System of White Supremacy (Racism) with The System of Justice (balance between people).

The main characteristics of all of these voluntary contacts are specifically designed to minimize conflict by consisting of no activity that is not of constructive value. These contacts should be infrequent and only as necessary. Each occasion of contact should be brief. All talk that is trivial, unnecessary, and/or non-constructive, must be avoided. This is the meaning of the "waltz." It means persons "making contact" with each other, and "breaking contact" with each other in a manner that is similar to a "dance" of constructive [rhythm-like] harmony.

These constructive Counter-Racist Contacts apply to each and every area of activity, including Economics, Education, Entertainment, Labor, Law, Politics, Religion, Sex, and War/Counter-War. They apply to all situations, at all times, as long as The System of White Supremacy (Racism) has not been replaced with The System of Justice (balance between people).

> **Notes:** The Compensatory Counter-Racist Contact [Waltz], when practiced correctly, is guaranteed to best help to minimize conflict, minimize confusion, minimize frustration, and greatly improve the production of The Quality Relationship(s) between all persons, White and Non-White.

Compensatory Counter-Racist Copulation. Use this term to apply to all acts of mutual sexual intercourse, and/or "sexual play" (between Non-White persons) that help to promote thought, speech, and/or action that is directly or indirectly effective in opposing The System of White Supremacy (Racism).

> **Notes:** According to Compensatory Counter-Racist Logic, it is, at all times, correct to speak and/or act in support of any and all acts of Compensatory Counter-Racist Copulation. It is incorrect to regard any act(s) of sexual intercourse, and/or "sexual play," as being more "decent," more "patriotic," and/or correctly "superior" to any act(s) of Compensatory Counter-Racist Copulation.

Compensatory Counter-Racist Family. Use this term to apply to any one or more persons while thinking, speaking and/or acting effectively in any manner that best helps to replace The System of

White Supremacy (Racism) with The System of Justice (balance between people).

Compensatory Counter-Racist Networking. Use this term to apply to any and all exchanges of views, ideas, concepts, etc., in conversations between individual Victims of White Supremacy [Non-White persons], one to another, on an "as-needed" basis for the purpose of solving problems that are directly or indirectly associated with the goal of replacing The System of White Supremacy (Racism) with The System of Justice (balance between people), guaranteeing that no person is mistreated and guaranteeing that the person who needs help the most, gets the most help.

Compensatory Counter-Racist Suggestion. Use this term to apply to any combination of words that a person uses with the intention of best helping to result in ending The System of White Supremacy (Racism).

Compensatory-Functional Definition. Use this term to mean:

(1)   The "meaning" of a word or term expressed in a manner that is more useful in helping to reveal truth, and/or in helping to promote justice or correctness.

(2)   The "use" of a word or term in a manner that is more effective in helping to eliminate falsehood, non-justice, and/or incorrectness.

(3)   The "use" of a word or term in such a manner that it helps to eliminate confusion in the thought, speech, and/or action of people who are unjustly subject to other people.

Compensatory-Functional Identification. Use this term to mean:

(1)   The "meaning" of a word or term expressed in a manner that is more useful in helping to reveal truth, and/or in helping to promote justice or correctness.

(2)   A name, title, number, etc., that a person uses to identify him or herself, that he or she considers to be an accurate description of what he or she is, and/or does, all, or most of the time.

Compensatory-Functional Supreme Value. Use this term to apply to the absence of falsehood, non-justice, and incorrectness.

Compensatory Investment Request. Use these terms to apply to any and all activities that are based on a Non-White person asking a White person to help him or her to acquire something of needed constructive value. When accused of "begging" White people to help you to do something that is of constructive value, it is correct to say that you are asking for and/or seeking "compensatory capital," "compensatory capital investment," "compensatory investment support" and/or "compensatory social investment," etc.

Compensatory Law. Use this term to apply to the Law of the Universe that eliminates imbalances.

Compensatory Marriage/Counter-Racist Marriage. Use these terms to describe the "marital arrangements" that a Non-White male and Non-White female have with each other while they are subject to The System of White Supremacy (Racism).

> **Reason:** According to Compensatory Counter-Racist Logic, The System of White Supremacy (Racism) functions in such a manner as to prevent Non-White males and Non-White females from having major control over their actions and reactions in every area of activity, including Economics, Education, Entertainment, Labor, Law, Politics, Religion, Sex, and War/Counter-War. Therefore, according to Compensatory Counter-Racist Logic, The System of White Supremacy (Racism) functions in such a manner as to prevent Non-White males and Non-White females from functioning as "married people."

Compensatory Nuance-Niche. Use this term to apply to a "situation" or condition existing during the existence of The System of White Supremacy (Racism) that, for whatever reason, known or unknown, allows a Non-White person to gain something of constructive value, in a constructive manner, apparently "in spite of," and/or because of, a minor, calculated, non-calculated, temporary, and/or careless so-called "flaw" in The System of White Supremacy (Racism).

Compensatory Self-Support Requests [Racial]. Use this term to apply to the act of any Non-White person asking White persons [only] for whatever constructive help is needed during the existence of White Supremacy (Racism). This constructive help is requested by individual Non-White persons, as needed, whenever, and wherever necessary in regards to any and all areas of activity (Economics, Education, Entertainment, Labor, Law, Politics, Religion, Sex, and War/Counter-War).

Note: It is correct to regard all "Compensatory Self-Support Requests" as a logical activity for Non-White persons who seek to avoid robbing, stealing, etc., as a reaction to deprivation caused or promoted by the White Supremacists (Racistman and Racistwoman, collectively). (See, also, "Compensatory Investment Request"].

Compensatory Universal Prayer. Use this term to apply to the act of inhaling air and mentally counting from one to ten before exhaling, while (at the same time) thinking about "The Supreme Source" of the power that allows a body to inhale and exhale the air that supports the functions of the body repeatedly, and without any "conscious" effort.

>**Notes:** While utilizing this Compensatory Universal Prayer, a person can think of the number ten as a reminder that "The Source of All-Power" is the sum-total of "everything" that is "nothing," and "everything" that is "everything" (the sum total of the known plus the unknown).

Compensatory Variables. Use this term to apply to those things that happen that are unexpected, and that are also of constructive value to you or others, especially when there were many reasons to believe that nothing constructive could, or would, happen. Use it to mean those "unknown" factors that are "at work" that suddenly, and without notice or warning, result in a condition not being what it was thought to be, planned to be, or predicted to be.

>**Notes:** "Compensatory Variables" are factors or events that sometimes happen in favor of a person when he or she is trying to do his or her best to speak and/or act in support of the production of justice under conditions of seemingly hopeless confusion, and/or when everything and everyone seems to be working against him or her. "Compensatory Variables" are factors or events that come into existence in ways that seemingly have no immediate explanation, and are sometimes referred to as "fate," "luck," "destiny," or "Acts of God".

Complain/Complaint. Use these terms with caution. When talking about something that happens that pertains to Race, Racism, and/or Counter-Racism, practice saying that you are making a "report" instead of saying that you are making a "complaint." Say that you are "reporting," not "complaining." Say that you are "reporting" an unjust act and/or an incorrect condition, rather than "complaining" about the act or condition.

Reason: When a person is said to be "complaining," that person is often thought of as a person who is "griping" or "whining" and is, therefore, not "worthy" of being "seriously regarded." A "complaint" is often regarded as speech and/or action that is not "justified," and/or not worthy of serious consideration.

Note: It is correct to be wary of the intentions of people who often claim that you are "complaining," "griping" or "whining" when, in truth, you are reporting an unjust or incorrect condition or when you are reporting a suggestion for correction.

Comrade. Avoid using this word. When others use it, ask for a detailed explanation that you can easily understand. Avoid saying that you are the "friend," or the "comrade" of any person, creature, place, or thing. During the existence of White Supremacy (Racism) and/or other forms of non-justice and/or incorrectness, practice saying that you are directly or indirectly "associated with," and/or "subject to" people, creatures, places, and things of the known and unknown universe.

Instead of saying that a person is a "friend" or a "comrade" of yours, practice saying that he or she is an "associate". When doing or saying something that a Suspected Racist (Suspected White Supremacist) requires you to do or say, or forces you to do or say, identify yourself as an "accomplice" of that Suspected Racist (Suspected White Supremacist).

Note: During the existence of The System of White Supremacy (Racism), all of the Non-White people of the known universe are the direct or indirect "accomplices" of those White persons who practice the crime of White Supremacy (Racism).

Concentration Camp. Use this term with caution. When others use it, ask for a detailed explanation that you can easily understand. Study all of the ways in which the term "concentration camp" can be correctly and constructively used, and use the term correctly and constructively.

Note: During the existence of The System of White Supremacy (Racism), all of the Non-White people of the known universe are "inmates" of the Concentration Camp (System) of White Supremacy (Racism).

Conditions (could be worse). <u>Do not use this term</u>. Instead use the expression, "Conditions could be better. I will do my best to make them as they should be."

Confidential. <u>Use this word with caution</u>. When others use the word, ask for a detailed explanation that you can easily understand. Use it mostly to apply to any form of constructive communication between Victims (Non-White persons) of White Supremacy.

> **Notes:** It is incorrect to think, speak, or act as if the word "confidential," means the same as the word "secret". During the existence of White Supremacy (Racism), it is best and correct for Non-White persons to think, speak, and act as if it is not possible or necessary to "keep secrets" from The White Supremacists (Racists).

Confiscation. <u>Use this word with caution</u>. When others use it, ask for a detailed explanation that you can easily understand. What, exactly, is "confiscation"? What, exactly, is not "confiscation"? Is The System of White Supremacy (Racism) the greatest, most powerful and most non-just system of "confiscation" ever produced by people within the known universe?

Conflict of Interest. <u>Use this term with caution</u>. When others use it, ask for a detailed explanation that you can easily understand. Is the existence of White Supremacy (Racism) in "conflict" with the "interest" of those persons who are trying to replace White Supremacy (Racism) with Justice (balance between people)?

Conquest. <u>Use this word with caution</u>. When others use it, ask for a detailed explanation that you can easily understand. Use the word "conquest" to mostly describe anything done by White persons that directly or indirectly help to establish, maintain, expand, and/or refine The System of White Supremacy (Racism) in any area of activity (Economics, Education, Entertainment, Labor, Law, Politics, Religion, Sex, and War/Counter-War).

Conservative [General]. <u>Use this term</u> to apply to one who speaks and/or acts to save and/or protect any person, place, thing, etc. When others use this term, ask for a detailed explanation that you can easily understand.

Conservative [Racial]. <u>Use this term</u> to apply to a White person who speaks and/or acts to maintain White Supremacy (Racism) by any effective means directly or indirectly. Always ask questions when the word "conservative" is used.

Constitution, The. Use this term to mean any and all words that are used in "association with" each other in such a manner that best help to replace White Supremacy (Racism) with Justice (balance between people). This includes those words that pertain to any area of activity. Think, speak, and act as if any words that have the effect of helping to produce Justice (balance between people), as being words that are a part of "The Constitution," and/or a part of the "Constitutional process." Always say that you are in favor of using the "Constitutional process" for replacing White Supremacy with Justice. Always say that "The Constitution" should always be used in a manner that best promotes the production of Justice (balance between people).

Constructive. Use this word in a manner that describes or identifies thought, speech, or action that best helps to promote the production of justice (balance between people), or correctness (balance between people, creatures, things, etc.). Also, use the word "constructive" to mean thought, speech, or action that helps to replace White Supremacy (Racism) with Justice. Study the ways that others use this word. Ask questions. "Constructive" for whom? "Constructive" how? "Constructive," in order to accomplish what? Everything said and everything done is either constructive or non-constructive.

Constructive Engagement. Use this term to mean any interaction between people, creatures, things, etc., that produces thought, speech, and action that results in the use of truth (that which is) in a manner that produces justice (balance between people), and in a manner that produces correctness (balance between people, creatures, things, etc.).

Contact. Use this word with caution. When others use it, ask for a detailed explanation that you can easily understand.

> **Questions:** What, exactly, is "contact"? What, exactly, is "non-contact"? When people talk to each other, are they in "contact" with each other? Does "contact" mean to touch a person's body? Is there, in truth, a way to maintain "eye contact" without "touching" the eye that is "contacted"? Is "looking" at a person the same as "making contact" with that person? Are White people and Non-White people in "contact" with each other? How often do White people and Non-White people make "body contact" with each other, by touching each other's bodies, and for what reasons? Has the "body contact" proven to be of constructive value? When? Where? Why? How?
>
> Has "body contact" between White people and Non-White people for purposes of sexual intercourse and/or "sexual

play," proven to be of constructive value? If so, when?
Where? How? Has such "contact" helped to end The
System of White Supremacy (Racism), or has such
"contact" helped to make The System of White Supremacy
(Racism) stronger? What form(s) of "contact" between
White people and Non-White people are best for helping
to produce Justice (balance between people) in each area
of activity – Economics, Education, Entertainment, Labor,
Law, Politics, Religion, Sex, and War/Counter-War?

Containment. Use this word with caution. When others use it, ask
for a detailed explanation that you can easily understand. Keep in
mind that, during the existence of White Supremacy (Racism), all of
the Non-White people of the known universe are being "contained" by
the White Supremacists (Racists) of the known universe. During the
existence of White Supremacy (Racism), the Non-White people are
also being "restrained," "restricted," "repressed," "confined,"
"subjugated," "victimized," etc. The System of White Supremacy
(Racism) is specifically designed to "contain," "restrict," and victimize
all of the Non-White people in all areas of activity.

Contra(s). Avoid using this term. When others use the term, ask for
a detailed explanation that you can easily understand. Ask
questions. "Contra" what?   "Contra" to what? "Contra" why?
"Contrary"? "Contradiction"?

Contract. Use this word with caution. When others use it, ask for a
detailed explanation that you can easily understand. Ask questions.

> **Questions:** During the existence of White Supremacy
> (Racism), do White people and Non-White people have a
> "contract" with each other? If so, is that "contract,"
> correct? What kind of "contract" do White people and
> Non-White people have with each other in each area of
> activity? Should White people and Non-White people
> have the exact same "contract" with each other that
> White people have with other White people? If so, why?
> If not, why not? What, exactly, is the "contract" that
> White people have with each other? Is it the "White
> Supremacy (Racism) contract"? If it is not, what kind of
> "contract" is it?
>
> Why does it appear that the White people of the known
> universe have a "contract" with each other that is more
> powerful than the "contract" that they have with Non-
> White people, and why does it appear that the contract is
> more helpful to White people? Is it correct for the Non-
> White people of the known universe to produce a

"Counter-Racist Contract" (Counter-Racist Code of behavior) that is specifically designed to replace White Supremacy (Racism) with Justice (balance between people)?

Notes: Because of the existence of White Supremacy (Racism), all of the Non-White people of the known universe function according to a socio-material "contract" with the White Supremacists (Racists) of the known universe. This "Race contract" guarantees that White people and Non-White people interact with each other and with themselves, in such a manner that The System of White Supremacy (Racism) is maintained, expanded, and/or refined, in all places, at all times, in all areas of activity, including Economics, Education, Entertainment, Labor, Law, Politics, Religion, Sex, and War/Counter-War. It is correct that The System of White Supremacy (Racism) be replaced with a System that guarantees that no person is mistreated, and that guarantees that the person who needs help the most, gets the most help.

Cooperation. Use this word with caution. When others use it, ask for a detailed explanation that you can easily understand. Be particularly wary of the ways that the word is used by White persons whom you suspect may be White Supremacists (Racists).

Questions: What, exactly, is "cooperation"? Do people "cooperate" with each other in many ways that they do not name as "cooperation"? Do prisoners "cooperate" with the prison-masters, at least to the extent that they (the prisoners) are prisoners? Is one person "cooperating" with another person if he or she is buying, selling or trading something that is directly or indirectly associated with that other person? If two people "share" something "with" each other, are they "cooperating" with each other? If one person gives something to, or receives something from another person, are those persons "cooperating" with each other?

If a person is subjugated by another person, does that mean that he or she is also "cooperating with" the person to whom he or she is [being] subjugated? If a person does anything that a White Supremacist (Racist) asks, demands, or wants that person to do, does that person "cooperate with" that White Supremacist (Racist)? Is it correct to say that "cooperation" is, for all practical purposes, the same as "collaboration"? During the existence of White Supremacy (Racism), do all Non-White people "cooperate" and/or "collaborate" with the White Supremacists (Racists) of the known universe – either directly or indirectly in all areas of activity?

Correct Intentions. <u>Use this term</u> to apply to the proven acts of guaranteeing that no person is mistreated, guaranteeing that the person needing help the most, gets the most [constructive] help, and guaranteeing that creatures and things are employed in a manner that is non-abusive, non-wasteful, and is productive of the most constructive result.

> **Note:** Any person who has not shown by his or her actions that he or she has guaranteed the aforementioned constructive actions cannot be truthfully said to have the "correct intentions." This is according to Compensatory Logic.

Correctness. <u>Use this word</u> to mean thought, speech, and/or action that result in a balance between people, creatures, things, etc., in all areas of activity-existence. Use the term "correctness" to mean that every person, creature, and thing interacts in a manner that is totally constructive, and in a manner that produces and maintains "peace" within the known universe. Study the many ways that others use the words "correct" and/or "correctness." Ask questions and seek answers given by others in regards to what, when, where, how and why something is "correct," or "not correct." What is the ultimate purpose of an act, or a condition, that is "correct"?

> **Notes:** Do not use the word "correct" to mean the same as the word "right." The word "correct" should be used, basically, to mean balance between people, creatures, things, etc. The word "right" should be used to mean the completed result of everything that has finally and totally been put into balance between and among all of the people, creatures, and things in the known universe.
>
> "Correctness" is a part of the process that helps to produce what is "right". "Righteousness," and/or what is "right," cannot be accomplished without Justice (balance between people) and correctness (balance between people, creatures, things, etc.), being produced and maintained, every place in the known universe. It is, therefore, best to say that something is "correct," rather than to say something is "right."

According to Compensatory Logic, the people of the known universe do not know enough, nor do they understand enough, to say what is or is not, "right." According to Compensatory Logic, the people of the known universe can seek to become "righteous" through the process of practicing justice and correctness. In addition, when speaking of "correct" thought, speech, or action in regards to the use of the word "respect," it is incorrect to ever ask someone to "give you [some] respect" and/or "show [some] respect." Instead, it is best and correct to use expressions like, "May I ask you to regard this matter correctly"? "Respect" comes from oneself ("self-respect"). "Correct action," correct consideration, etc., comes from any person, creature, thing, etc.

Correct Speech. Use this term to apply to those things spoken during the existence of White Supremacy (Racism) in a manner that proves to be effective in best helping to replace White Supremacy (Racism) with Justice (balance between people).

Counter-Attack. Use this term with caution. When others use it, ask for a detailed explanation that you can easily understand. Do not confuse an "attack" with a "counter-attack." For example, during the existence of White Supremacy (Racism), it is the White Supremacists (Racists) who are, at all times, "attacking" the Victims of White Supremacy (Non-White people). The White Supremacists (Racists), through The System of White Supremacy (Racism), are always "on the attack" against Non-White people in all areas of activity (Economics, Education, Entertainment, Labor, Law, Politics, Religion, Sex, and War/Counter-War).

The people (White and Non-White) who are effectively thinking, speaking and/or acting to replace White Supremacy (Racism) with Justice (balance between people), are "on the counter-attack" against The System of White Supremacy (Racism).

> **Note:** During the existence of White Supremacy (Racism), all Non-White persons are always the Victims of a Racist attack by those White persons who participate in the practice of White Supremacy (Racism).

Counter-Racism. Use this term. During the existence of White Supremacy (Racism), use it exclusively to mean any thought, speech, and/or action that is effective in ending White Supremacy (Racism), and/or to mean any thought, speech and/or action that is effective in replacing White Supremacy (Racism) with Justice (balance between people).

Notes: During the existence of White Supremacy (Racism), it is correct to think, speak, and/or act as if the only form of [functional] Racism that exists in the known universe is White Supremacy. During the existence of White Supremacy (Racism) and according to Compensatory Counter-Racist Logic, it is best and correct to think, speak, and act as if White Supremacy is Racism, and Racism is White Supremacy.

Counter-Racist. Use this term to apply to:

(1)   A person who may or may not be a Victim of Racism, and who speaks and/or acts to eliminate Racism (White Supremacy).

(2)   A person who speaks and/or acts in a manner that helps to produce justice and correctness.

Counter-Racist Intellisex.   Use this term to apply to any acts of sexual intercourse and/or "sexual play" that is specifically intended to produce the revelation of information in a manner that results in thought, speech, and/or action that is effective in helping to replace The System of White Supremacy (Racism) with The System of Justice (balance between people).

Counter-Racist Labor Union. Use this term to apply to any two or more persons [while they are] speaking and/or acting effectively (laboring/working) to replace The System of White Supremacy (Racism) with The System of Justice (balance between people) in any and/or all areas of activity (Economics, Education, Entertainment, Labor, Law, Politics, Religion, Sex, and War/ Counter-War.

> **Note:** "Labor" is any "work" (use of time and energy) that is designed or intended to accomplish a goal.

Counter-Racist Logic (Counter-Racist Science).   Use these terms to apply to thought, speech, and/or action that are designed to result in replacing The System of White Supremacy (Racism) with The System of Justice (balance between people), which means guaranteeing that no person is mistreated, and guaranteeing that the person who needs help the most, gets the most help.   Prefer to use these terms instead of the terms "Black History," "Black Studies," (etc.).

> **Notes:** There is reason to believe that "logic" came with the creation of all that has been created.   The use of Logic has revealed that, for every "cause," there is an "effect," and for every "effect" there is a "cause".   The use of Logic has revealed that, for every

"beginning," there is an "end," which produces another "beginning". The use of Counter-Racist Logic and/or Counter-Racist Science will reveal that Racism, in the form of White Supremacy, was produced by people for the purpose of dominating and mistreating the Non-White people of the known universe for the basic purpose of providing so-called "benefits" for the White people of the known universe.

The System of White Supremacy (Racism) was produced by people, through a logical process that was designed to result in the establishment, maintenance, expansion, and refinement of the System of White Supremacy. The System of White Supremacy (Racism) has successfully operated in all Nine Areas of (People) Activity. Therefore, it is logical to believe that the System of Justice (balance between people) can be produced by people, through a logical process that is designed to replace The System of White Supremacy (Racism).

Counter-Racist and Production of Justice Studies. Use this term to apply to the "basic title" to describe, announce, teach, study and/or learn about anything that pertains to Race, Racism, Counter-Racism and/or the production of Justice (balance between people).

Counter-Racist System. Use this term to apply to the sum total of all words and all deeds that help to eliminate Racism (White Supremacy) and/or help to establish justice and correctness.

Counter-Terrorism. Use this term to apply to effective speech and/or action against those White persons who participate in the practice of White Supremacy (Racism). Also, use it to mean any effective speech or action against those persons who say or do those things that directly or indirectly help to produce or promote great and unjust fear among the people of the known universe. When others use this term, ask for a detailed explanation that you can easily understand. Particularly, pay attention to the many ways that some people use the words "terrorism," or "terrorist."

> **Questions:** What, exactly, is "terrorism"? What, exactly, is a "terrorist"? Does a "terrorist" cause someone to be "terrified"? What, exactly, is "counter-terrorism"? Are the White Supremacists (Racists) the most powerful producers of great fear among the Non-White people of the known universe? Is The System of White Supremacy (Racism), the most feared of all socio-material Systems among the Non-White people of the known universe? Is

77

speech and action to stop the "terrorism" caused by the existence of White Supremacy (Racism), the most constructive form of "counter-terrorism" that can be practiced by the people of the known universe?

Counter-Violence. <u>Use this term</u> to mean any effective speech and/or any effective action against, and/or to stop persons, creatures, or forces that are "violent." When others use the terms "violent," "counter-violent," and/or "non-violent," ask for a detailed explanation that you can easily understand.

Counter-War. <u>Use this term</u> to apply to:

(1)   Speech and/or action to stop a person, animal, etc., from doing unjust and/or incorrect harm.

(2)   The sum total of all words and all deeds that helps to eliminate Racism (White Supremacy), and helps to replace Racism (White Supremacy) with Justice (balance between people).

Country. <u>Use this word with caution</u>. When others use it, ask for a detailed explanation that you can easily understand. During the existence of White Supremacy (Racism), do not use the word "country" or the word "nation," to mean any "group" of people, other than the combined interactions between those White persons of the known universe who practice White Supremacy (Racism).

> **Questions:** How can a "country" be a "country" if it is subject to a "country"? What makes a "country," a "country"? Is it possible that one or more persons can be called a "country" but, in truth, not be a "country"? Is any "collection" of people a "country"? What, exactly, is a "collection" of people? How, exactly, do people of the same "country" interact with each other at all times, in all places, in all areas of activity, including Economics, Education, Entertainment, Labor, Law, Politics, Religion, Sex, and War/ Counter-War? Is a person in a "country," or is a "country" in a person? Can one person be a "country"? Can two persons be a "country"? When is a "country" not a "country"? If a "country" does not function as a "country," how can it be correctly called a "country"?

> **Notes:** During the existence of The System of White Supremacy (Racism), the only "country" and/or "nation" that exists in the known universe is The System of White Supremacy (Racism) - which is "The Race Nation," "The

Racist Nation," "The White Nation," and/or "The One Nation." Therefore, as long as White Supremacy (Racism) exists, it is incorrect to describe any "place" in the known universe as a "country," or a "nation," or a "state".

As long as White Supremacy (Racism) exists, it is best and correct to describe "places" as being "areas of the world," and/or "areas of the known universe," such as "the northeastern part of the world," "the area of the planet called Brazil," "the area of the planet called China," etc. Use terms like "Asia," or "Africa," or "America" to mean the same as the concept of Justice.

Country (my/our/this). <u>Do not use these terms</u> as long as White Supremacy (Racism) exists. If you are "classified" as a "Non-White" person, do not use the words "my country" "this country" or "our country." Instead say "my country to be," or "our country to be."

> **Reason:** During the existence of White Supremacy (Racism), the only people in the known universe who "have" a "country" are those White persons who practice White Supremacy (Racism). The "country" that they "have," is themselves. They, themselves, are a "country." They are not only a "country" (nation) they are the only "country" (nation) of people in the known universe. During the existence of White Supremacy (Racism), all other "countries" or "nations" are an illusion. They do not exist.
>
> As long as White Supremacy (Racism) exists, no Non-White person can function as a "country" [nation]. They may or may not appear to function as a "country" or "nation." During the existence of White Supremacy (Racism), people may or may not be called by the "titles" of a "country." Some may or may not be called "minor people," "minority people," "ethnic people," and/or by other names or titles.
>
> Regardless of what Non-White people are called, and regardless of what Non-White people call themselves, no people in the known universe function as a "country" or "nation" except those White people who practice White Supremacy (Racism). The Non-White people of the known universe function as Victims of the System ("country"/"nation") of White Supremacy (Racism). All of the Non-White people of the known universe function as subjects to the White Supremacist nation.

Coward/Cowardice.   Avoid using these terms.   When others use them, ask for a detailed explanation that you can easily understand. What, exactly, is a "coward"?   What, exactly, is not "cowardice"?   Is any person who fears another person, a "coward"?   Is the fear of doing what should be done to replace White Supremacy (Racism) with Justice (balance between people), a form of "cowardice"?   Can it correctly be said that all people at some time, in some place, function in a "cowardly" manner?   If so, does this mean that all people should be correctly regarded as "cowards"?

> **Note:**   There is reason to believe that calling a person a "coward" is incorrect, and serves no constructive purpose.

Cream of the Crop.   Do not use this term.

> **Reason:**   During the existence of White Supremacy (Racism), the term "cream of the crop" may directly or indirectly cause some people to think, speak, and/or act as if that which is "white" ("cream-like") in appearance, is "better" or "best," particularly when the "cream-like" appearance is applied to a person.   When this happens, such thought, speech, and/or action helps to promote ideas and practices that help to support White Supremacy (Racism).

Create.   Use this word to apply only to those acts by who is usually called "God," "Allah," "Jehovah," "All-Power," "the Great Spirit," "the Creator," etc.   Do not say that any person in the known universe "creates."   Instead, say that the people of the known universe do things like, "arrange," "discover," "dislocate," "produce," "re-arrange," "relocate," "repair," etc.

> **Notes:**   People do not "create"; people only "reproduce," "arrange," and/or "rearrange" that which has been created.   The Creator "creates."   People and all other creatures only "arrange" that which have already been "created."   Since the creation of the known universe, the greatest, most powerful <u>political</u> and sophisticated "arrangement" that has ever been produced by people is The System of White Supremacy (Racism).

Creation versus Evolution.   Avoid using this term.   When others use it, ask for a detailed explanation that you can easily understand. Is that which "evolves" in the "process of being created"?   Is that which is "being created," the result of an "evolving process" that was "created" for the purpose of "evolving"?   Is something "created" from nothing? Does nothing "evolve" into something? If so, was the "nothing" created so that it could "evolve" into "something"?

> **Note:** It has been said that in order for something to "evolve," it had to be "created," and in order for something to be "created," it had to "evolve." [**Examples**: "time," "space" "nothingness," etc.]

Creator, The. Use this phrase to apply to that force called "God," "the Great Spirit(s)," "the Master of All," "the Best Knower," "All-Power," etc. Do not object to others using whatever names or titles for the "Creator" that they choose to use.

Credit to your (his, her, our) Race. Do not use these terms to apply to any Non-White person. Instead, say "Using truth in such a manner as to best produce justice and correctness between and among all people, creatures, and things."

Creed. Use this word with caution. When others use it, ask for a detailed explanation that you can easily understand. Be aware of any contradictions and/or any confusion-making remarks that may be produced when the word is used.

Crime/Criminal. Use these words with caution. When others use these words, ask for a detailed explanation that you can easily understand.

> **Questions:** What, exactly, is a "crime"? What, exactly, is a "criminal"? Is a "crime," a "law" that has been "violated"? Is a "criminal," a person, creature, etc., that has "violated" a "law"? Does not every creature in the known universe "violate" some "law," some place at some time? Is not every person in the known universe, some "form" of "criminal"? Is the mistreatment and/or the misuse of any person, creature or thing, a "crime"? If not, why not? Is The System of White Supremacy (Racism), a "criminal" system? Are all of the White people who participate in The System of White Supremacy (Racism), "criminals"? Are all of the Non-White people who are subject to The System of White Supremacy (Racism), "criminals"?

Crime (does not pay). Do not use this term. When others use it, ask for a detailed explanation that you can easily understand. Expect most attempts at an explanation to be confusing.

Crime of Crimes. Use this term to apply to the System of Racism (White Supremacy). There is no combination of speech, and/or action among the people of the known universe, that is greater than the crime of Racism (White Supremacy) in promoting falsehood, non-justice, and incorrectness.

Crime Victim. Use this term with caution. When others use it, ask for a detailed explanation that you can easily understand.

> **Questions:** What, exactly, is a "crime"? What, exactly, is a "Victim of a "crime"? Is White Supremacy (Racism) a "crime"? Is a Victim of White Supremacy (Non-White person) a "Crime Victim" in all areas of activity, including Economics, Education, Entertainment, Labor, Law, Politics, Religion, Sex, and War/Counter-War? If so, why and how? If not, why not?

> **Note:** During the existence of White Supremacy (Racism), and according to Compensatory Counter-Racist Logic, White Supremacy (Racism) is the "crime of crimes" and all of the Non-White people in the known universe are "Crime Victims."

Criminal Law. Avoid using this term. When others use it, ask for a detailed explanation that you can easily understand.

> **Questions:** What, exactly, is a "crime"? What, exactly, is a "law"? Is every violation of a "law," a "crime"? Is every "crime" a violation of a "law"? Is the existence of White Supremacy (Racism), a violation of "law"? Is the existence of White Supremacy (Racism) a "crime"? If a White person practices White Supremacy (Racism), is he or she guilty of violating "criminal law"?

Crusade. Avoid using this word. When others use it, ask for a detailed explanation that you can easily understand. What, exactly, is a "crusade"? What, exactly, is not a "crusade"?

Cult. Do not use this word. When others use it, ask for a detailed explanation that you can easily understand. What, exactly, is a "cult"? What, exactly, is not a "cult"? Can any activity correctly be called a "cult"? Is every person in the known universe a "member" of a "cult"? Is The System of White Supremacy (Racism) a "cult"? Is it correct for a "cult" to exist? If so, for what purpose? If not, why not?

Culturally-Deprived. Avoid using this term. When others use it, ask for a detailed explanation that you can easily understand.

Questions: What, exactly, is "culture"? What, exactly, is not "culture"? Is there such a thing as a "correct culture"? If so, what is it? If so, where is it? If so, who or what is being "deprived" of it? If a person is "culturally-deprived," what does that person do in each area of activity (Economics, Education, Entertainment, Labor, Law, Politics, Religion, Sex, and War/Counter-War)? What does a person do if he or she is not "culturally-deprived"?

Culture. Use this word to mean, "That, which is done". When others use this word, ask for a detailed explanation that you can easily understand.

> **Note:** Whatever a person does, is the "culture" of that person, at the time he or she is doing whatever it is that he or she is doing.

Culture (Correct). Use this term to mean the type of "culture" that is yet to be produced among the people, creatures, and things of the known universe. Use it to mean "culture" that comes into existence through the use of truth in such a manner as to produce Justice (balance between people) and correctness (balance between people, creatures, things, etc.) in all thought, all speech and all action, as it pertains to all areas of activity. Use this term to mean the correct way to interact with and relate to every person, creature, and thing in all areas of activity. Do not use the term "Correct Culture" to mean "Black Culture," "White Culture" "Ethnic Culture," or any other "culture" known to exist.

Culture (The White). Use this term to apply to the direct or indirect subjugation of Non-White people by White Supremacists (Racists), in one or more areas of activity: Economics, Education, Entertainment, Labor, Law, Politics, Religion, Sex, and War/Counter-War. (See, "Culture").

Cultured. Avoid using this word. When others use it, ask for a detailed explanation that you can easily understand. (See, "Culture").

Custom. Use this word to mean anything that is done more than once, for the same reason. Study the ways that others use the word. When others use the word, ask for a detailed explanation that you can easily understand.

Customer. Use this word with caution. When others use it, ask for a detailed explanation that you can easily understand. What, exactly, is a "customer"? What, exactly, is not a "customer"? Can a person be a "customer" indirectly? Is every person in the known universe a "customer"?

Cycle Racism (Closed-Circle Racism). <u>Use this term</u> to apply to Racism (White Supremacy) that is practiced in such a manner that only those who are practicing it can prove its existence and/or its seriousness.

D

Dance. <u>Use this word</u> to mean any self-movement of the body of a person or creature that is designed to, or intended to accomplish a purpose that is either constructive, or destructive.

> **Notes:** During the existence of White Supremacy (Racism), Racistman and Racistwoman (White Supremacists, collectively), are the greatest, most powerful, most skillful and most impressive "dancers" in the known universe. They are the proven "masters of dance" when compared to the Non-White people of the known universe.

Dangerous. <u>Use this word with caution</u>. When others use this word, ask for a detailed explanation that you can easily understand.

> **Example**: Is it correct for speech and action that is designed to produce justice (balance between people) to be "dangerous" to the continuation of The System of White Supremacy (Racism)?

Dark. <u>Use this word with extreme caution</u>. When others use the words, "dark," "darkened," "darkness," etc., study very carefully the ways that such words are used. Study the ways that the words may often be used in a derogatory, non-constructive, and/or incorrect manner. Study the many ways that the words are used in a manner that directly or indirectly help to promote thought, speech, and/or action that is supportive of The System of White Supremacy (Racism). Ask questions about the "peculiar" ways that the word "dark" is sometimes used.

Dark Ages. <u>Do not use this term</u>. When others use it, ask for a detailed explanation that you can easily understand. What, exactly, is "age" that is "dark"? How can "age" be "dark"? Why and how did someone decide to start using terms like, "The age of enlightenment"?

> **Notes:** During the existence of The System of White Supremacy (Racism), the use of the word "dark" is often

intended to cause people to think, speak, and/or act as if "dark" means the same as "tragic," "evil," "dangerous," "destructive," etc., particularly when "dark" or "darkness" is associated with the physical appearance of people.

Dark Chapter. <u>Do not use this term</u>. When others use it, ask for a detailed explanation that you can easily understand. (<u>See</u>, also, "Dark," "Dark Ages").

Dark Clouds. <u>Use this term with caution</u>. Study the ways that others may choose to use the term.

> **Notes:** During the existence of White Supremacy (Racism), Racistman and Racistwoman (White Supremacists, collectively) sometimes use these words in such a manner as to associate "dark clouds" with evil, or with incorrectness, while using the words "light clouds," "white clouds" and "bright clouds" with so-called "prettiness," "goodness" or "correctness". Racistman and Racistwoman sometimes do this in a manner to promote the thought that "dark" people, like "dark clouds" are also evil, ugly, and/or incorrect. They also use expressions like "his future looks dark and cloudy," and "every dark cloud has a silver lining," and "keep the dark clouds away," specifically to promote the thought that "dark" people are a source of evil and/or dreadful events. The term "dark cloud" should apply to clouds that appear to be "dark" – not to "moods," "situations," etc.

Dark Deeds. <u>Do not use this term</u>. When others use it, ask for a detailed explanation that you can easily understand. Does the use of this term in some way help to promote thought, speech, and/or action that are directly or indirectly supportive of White Supremacy (Racism)? What, exactly, is a "dark deed"? Why call a "deed" (something that is done) "dark"? What, exactly, is a "light deed"? What is a "gray" deed? What is a "white" deed?

Dark Horse. <u>Do not use this term</u> except to describe a creature (animal) that is usually described as a horse that is "dark" in appearance. <u>Do not use the term</u> "dark horse" to describe a person. When others use this term to describe a person, ask them to explain why that person is or should be described as such.

Dark Journey. <u>Do not use this term</u>. When others use the term, ask for a detailed explanation that you can easily understand. If a "journey" is "movement," what "color" is "movement?" Study the ways that the word "dark," "darkest," and "darkness" are sometimes used.

Dark (keep in the). Avoid using this term. Never use it to mean "keeping a person from knowing," or "keeping a person from understanding". Do not use the term to mean that "darkness" and "ignorance" is somehow, one and the same. This is the way that some White Supremacists (Racists) use the term. They do this as an indirect means of associating ignorance and confusion with "dark" people. It is not correct to use the term "keep in the dark" in this manner. It is best and correct to say, "Keep (a person) from knowing," or "keep (a person) from understanding".

Dark Mood. Do not use this term. When others use it, ask for a detailed explanation that you can easily understand.

> **Questions:** How can a "mood" be "dark"? What, exactly, is a "mood"? Does a "mood" have "color"? How many "colors" can a "mood" have? What, exactly, is a "mood" that is "dark"? What, exactly, is a "light mood," or a "white mood"? Is there a way to know the difference between a "dark" or "black" mood, and a "light" or "white" mood? How? Why? According to whom? Why speak of "moods" in such terms?

> **Note:** It is important to know and understand that White Supremacists (Racistman and Racistwoman, collectively), usually speak of "darkness" in such a manner as to directly or indirectly promote fear, contempt, hostility, and hatred of "dark," "Black," and/or Non-White people.

Dark Realities. Use this term with caution. When others use it, ask for a detailed explanation that you can easily understand. What, exactly, is a "reality" that is "dark," and why would a person describe a "reality" as being "dark"? Why not say that a "reality" is a "reality"? Is there such a thing as a "light reality"? Do such terms serve any constructive purpose? If so, how? If so, as applied to what? When? Where? In order to accomplish what?

> **Note:** White people who have chosen to participate in The System of White Supremacy (Racism) usually associate the use of the words "dark," "darkest," and/or "darkness" with places, things and people regarded as worthless, dangerous, and/or "undesirable."

Dark Side. Use this term with caution. When others use it, ask for a detailed explanation that you can easily understand. Do not, however, use the term "dark side" to describe any person's "personality," and/or a person's "character." Do not say things like, "I have seen the 'dark side' of her character, and I do not like it."

> **Notes:** It is correct to describe the "dark side" of the moon as being the "dark side" of the moon. The "dark side" of the moon does exist. There is no reason to believe that a "character" or "personality" does have, or can have, a "dark side." To apply such a description to the "character" or "personality" of a person is to (directly or indirectly) promote thinking that supports and/or glorifies White Supremacy (Racism).

Darkest Hour. <u>Do not use this term</u>. When others use it, ask them why, and how they can say that an "hour" (a measure of time) is "dark"? Study, and ask questions about the ways that the words "dark," "darkest," "darkness," etc., are sometimes used. Are such words used in a manner that directly or indirectly supports thought, speech, and/or action against "dark" (Non-White) people?

Darkest Moment(s). <u>Do not use this term</u>. When others say something like "dark moment," "darkest hour" or "dark times," ask them why they choose to speak of a measure of time, as being "dark." Ask them to explain the way that they judge the "color" of "time."

> **Note:** White Supremacists (Racists) usually promote the belief that "darkness" should usually be associated with that which is "evil," unpleasant, non-constructive, etc., particularly if such "darkness" is associated with the physical appearance of Non-White people.

Darkness (forces of). <u>Do not use this term</u>. When others use this term, ask for a detailed explanation that you can easily understand.

> **Questions**: What, exactly, are the "forces of darkness"? Are Non-White people the "forces of darkness"? Is there anything incorrect about a "force of darkness"? If so, what would it be, and why? Why use such term as "forces of darkness"?

> **Note:** White Supremacists (Racists), usually make a major effort to use the words "dark," "darkest," "darkness," etc., in such a manner as to directly or indirectly produce thought, speech, and/or action that is harmful to "dark" and/or Non-White people.

Darkness (heart of). <u>Do not use this term</u>. When others use it, ask for a detailed explanation that you can easily understand. Study the many ways that the words "dark," "darker" and/or "darkness" are used.

Darky. <u>Do not use this word</u>.

> **Reason:** The word "darky" has usually been used for no better purpose than to make fun of, or to show the intent to "devalue" the physical appearance and the general "worth" of a person who appears to be, is said to be, and/or is "classified" as Non-White within The System of White Supremacy (Racism).

Death. <u>Use this word</u> to apply to: (1) The presence of life and/or (2) Non-justice and incorrectness. (<u>See</u>, also, "Life," "Living," and "Non-Existence").

Decent. <u>Use this word</u>. When describing people, do not use the words "good" or "righteous." Use, instead, the word "decent," but only use it to describe a person during an occasion when that person is speaking and/or acting effectively to replace White Supremacy (Racism) with Justice (balance between people). When others use the word "decent" to describe a person, ask for a detailed explanation that you can easily understand.

> **Notes:** During the existence of White Supremacy (Racism), and according to Compensatory Counter-Racist Logic, no person in the known universe has proven to be qualified for the title of "decent person." Because no person has acquired the will and the ability to do what is necessary to replace White Supremacy (Racism) with Justice (balance between people), no person is correctly qualified to be called "decent."
>
> During the existence of White Supremacy (Racism), the people of the known universe, so far, proven themselves "indecent" in all of their activities including Economics, Education, Entertainment, Labor, Law, Politics, Religion, Sex, and War/Counter-War.

Deed. <u>Use this word</u> to mean, "The absence of time".

Deliberate Speed. <u>Avoid using this term</u>. When others use it, ask for a detailed explanation that you can easily understand.

Questions: What, exactly, is "deliberate speed"? What, exactly, is "speed" that is not "deliberate"? How can the difference between "deliberate speed" and "non-deliberate speed" be measured? What persons are qualified to judge? Is it correct for every person in the known universe to use "all deliberate speed" to speak and act to replace White Supremacy (Racism) with Justice (balance between people)?

Democracy. Avoid using this word. When others use it, ask for a detailed explanation that you can easily understand.

Questions: What, exactly, is a "democracy"? Where, exactly, does a "democracy" exist? Does a "democracy" produce justice (balance between people)? Is The System of White Supremacy (Racism), a "democracy"? Is any existing "democratic system" more powerful than The System of White Supremacy (Racism)? Is it possible for a "democracy" to be "capitalist," "communist," "fascist," and/or "socialist" at the same time? Can a government be "democratic" and "royalist" at the same time? Can a person be subject to The System of White Supremacy (Racism) and, at the same time, be a "member" of a "democracy"?

Democrat. Avoid using this word. When others use it, ask for a detailed explanation that you can easily understand. Avoid calling yourself a "Democrat." During the existence of White Supremacy (Racism), avoid calling yourself by any "political" or "governmental" name or title other than "Victim of Racism," and/or "Victim of White Supremacy."

Note: As long as White Supremacy (Racism) is the dominant motivating "political-governmental" force among the people of the known universe, terms like "democrat," "republican," "aristocrat," "communist," "capitalist," "socialist," "conservative," "liberal," etc., all have meanings that are often, or always, confusing.

De-Niggerization. Use this term to apply to:

(1) The process of finding truth, and using truth in a manner that promotes the elimination of White Supremacy (Racism).

(2) Speech and/or action that promotes the elimination of Racism (White Supremacy) and the establishment of justice and correctness.

Depression. <u>Avoid using this word</u>. Instead, use the words "injustice," "non-justice," "incorrectness," "non-correctness" and/or "imbalanced condition." When others use this word, ask for a detailed explanation that you can easily understand.

> **Questions:** What, exactly, is "depression"? Can a person be "depressed" because he or she is "oppressed"? Is a "condition of depression" any situation that is non-just, non-correct, and/or "non-peaceful"? Is a "depressed condition" simply the absence of "peace"? Is a condition of "peace" simply the combination of truth being used in such a manner as to have produced justice (balance between people), and correctness (balance between people, creatures, things, etc.)? Is The System of White Supremacy (Racism) also "the greatest depression"?

Destructive. <u>Use this word</u> to mean any thought, speech, and action that does not (directly or indirectly) help to produce justice (balance between people), correctness (balance between people, creatures, etc.), and/or peace. Also, use this word to generally apply to the existence of The System of White Supremacy (Racism). Study the ways that others use the word "destructive" and the word "constructive." Practice asking for detailed explanations of all uses of the words "constructive," or "destructive" that helps to contribute to confused thought, speech, or action.

Detention. <u>Use this word with caution</u>. Study the many ways that this word can be used. When others use the words "detention," and/or "detained," ask for a detailed explanation that you can easily understand. What, exactly, happens when a person is being "detained"? Is being "detained," the same as being "arrested"? Is "detention" a form of "arrest"? Is "detention" a form of "restriction"?

> **Note:** During the existence of White Supremacy (Racism), and according to Compensatory Counter-Racist Logic, all of the Non-White people of the known universe are being "detained" (restricted) by the White Supremacists (Racists).

Devastated People, The. <u>Use this term</u> to apply to all Non-White persons (particularly <u>Black</u> males) during the existence of White Supremacy (Racism).

Develop/Development. <u>Use these words with caution</u>. When talking about producing something and/or when talking about anything associated with production, use the word "produce," instead of the word "develop." Use the word "production" instead of the word "development."

> **Reasons:** During the existence of White Supremacy (Racism), the words "develop," and "development" are too often used to mean the same as "white," "bright," "light," "right," "progressive," advanced," etc., and are used in such a manner as to be directly or indirectly associated with the thought(s), speech, and action(s) of the White people of the known universe.
>
> During the existence of White Supremacy (Racism), the word "undeveloped" is too often used to mean the same as "dark," "black," "dull," "non-progressive," "non-constructive," "negative," "negated," etc., and is used in such a manner as to be directly or indirectly associated with the thought, speech, and action of Non-White people.

Diaspora. Do not use this word to apply to any situation involving Non-White people as Victims of White Supremacy (Racism). When others use the word, ask them to give a detailed explanation that you can easily understand.

Dictate/Dictator. Use these words with caution. Mostly use the words, "master dictators," or "master dictatorship" to describe the people of the known universe who, collectively, practice White Supremacy (Racism). Do not, however, call any specific person, a "dictator." Instead, use expressions like, "The dictatorship is the cause of the problems we are having" or "he (or she) is acting like a dictator, instead of like a correct and helpful supervisor." When others use the terms "dictator," "dictatorship," "dictate," "dictatorial," etc., ask for a detailed explanation that you can easily understand. What, exactly, is a "dictator"? What, exactly, is a "dictatorship"? How can an individual, judge that he or she is, or is not, being "dictated" to? Is it possible for a person to be "free" and, at the same time, be "dictated" to?

> **Note:** During the existence of White Supremacy (Racism), it is correct to think, speak, and act as if White Supremacy (Racism) is the greatest "dictatorship" produced by people among the people of the known universe.

Dingy. Do not use this word. Instead use the word "dark."

Reason: The word "dingy" has often been associated with the word "dinge." The word "dinge" has been used by White Supremacists (Racists) as a "slang" word to make derogatory "fun" of the dark appearance of Non-White people. The word "dinge," when used by some White Supremacists (Racists) and applied to a person, usually means that the person whose skin is very dark, is not only dark in appearance, but also that the person is "filthy" or "unworthy," because he or she is "dark."

Note: White Supremacists (Racists) have sometimes described a Non-White person as "a dinge" or, "the dinge."

Direct Order. Avoid using this term. When others use it, ask for a detailed explanation that you can easily understand. What, exactly, is a "direct order"? What, exactly, is an "indirect order"? Is an "indirect order" intended to have the same "power" or importance as a "direct order"? If so, why and how? If not, why not? What is the intended result?

Dirt/Dirty. Avoid using these terms unless you are using them to apply to actual "dirt" – as on the surface of the earth. Do not use expressions like, "dirty book," or "dirty look," or "dirty talk," etc. Do not say that someone gave you a "dirty deal".

Reason: The words "dirt" or "dirty" have been used by the White Supremacists (Racists) to often mean the same as "dark and evil," "dark and filthy," or "dark and unworthy." White Supremacists (Racists) have often used the words "dirt" or "dirty" in such a manner as to associate "dirt," "dirty," "dark," "filth" and "evil" with "Black," "Brown," "Red," "Yellow," or any Non-White people. Thus, according to many White Supremacists (Racists), the words "dirty," "dark" and "evil," all mean the same – particularly when applied to Non-White people.

Notes: It is important to study the ways that people use the words "dirt," or "dirty". When someone uses terms like "dirty words," "dirty talk," etc., ask him or her if he or she means, "incorrect words" or "incorrect talk." Ask him or her why he or she uses the word "dirty" in that manner.

Dirt-Cheap. Do not use this term. Do not use terms like "dirty book," "dirty look," "dirty name," "dirty talk," "dirty woman," "dirty words," etc. When others use the term "dirt-cheap," ask for a detailed explanation that you can easily understand. Is dirt, "cheap"? How important is "dirt"? If dirt is a source that supports nourishment, is it correct to say that "dirt" is "cheap"?

> **Note:** During the existence of White Supremacy (Racism), dirt is thought of as being "dark," and by being "dark," (like Non-White people), both "dirt," and Non-White people are generally thought of as "worthless".

Disaster, The. Use this term specifically to apply to the "quality" of, and/or absence of "quality" in, the interactions between the White people and the Non-White people of the known universe, during the existence of The System of White Supremacy (Racism). Use this term to apply to the tacky, trashy, and/or terroristic "arrangement" that White people and Non-White people have with each other in every area of activity, including Economics, Education, Entertainment, Labor, Law, Politics, Religion, Sex, and War/Counter-War.

> **Note:** Another term that can be used that means the same as "The Disaster," is "The Tragic Arrangement."

Discriminate/Discrimination. Use these words with caution. Do not use these words to mean the same as, or in place of Racism and/or White Supremacy. When speaking or writing about White Supremacy, call it "White Supremacy," or call it "Racism," or call it both. During the existence of White Supremacy (Racism), use the term "White Supremacy (Racism)" instead of the less specific terms "discrimination," and/or "racial discrimination." When others use the term "racial discrimination," ask them if they mean, "White Supremacy (Racism)".

> **Notes:** The term "racial discrimination" can easily be used to mean something other than White Supremacy (Racism). Therefore, during the existence of White Supremacy (Racism), it is best and correct to use the term "White Supremacy (Racism)," and not the term "racial discrimination." The word "discrimination," itself, simply means, "to choose". The term White Supremacy (Racism) means much more than "choosing" - it means practicing the crime of dominating, subjugating, depriving, exploiting, and generally mistreating Non-White people on the basis of White people being White, and Non-White people being Non-White.

Disease. Use this word with caution. Be careful about what you say is a "disease," or what you say is not a "disease." Give attention to what others call a "disease." Think about the word "disease" and the different ways that it is used, or can be used. Think about the ways that the word is not used.

> **Questions:** What, exactly, is a "disease"? What, exactly, is not a "disease"? Is "insanity" a "disease"? If so, what, exactly, is "insanity"? Does White Supremacy (Racism), cause its Victims (Non-White people) to be afflicted with the "disease" of "insanity"?

Dislocate/Dislocated/Dislocation. Use these words. Particularly, use these words to describe a situation or condition wherein you, or others, are directly or indirectly unjustly and incorrectly forced to move from one place to another. Do not confuse the word "dislocate" with the word "relocate."

> **Example**: During the existence of The System of White Supremacy (Racism), the White people of the known universe, generally speaking, have the "privilege" of relocating either among or away from Non-White people. During the existence of White Supremacy (Racism), the Non-White people of the known universe are dislocated whenever the White Supremacists (Racists) decide to cause them to be dislocated.

> **Notes:** "Dislocation" is not the exact same as "relocation." "Dislocation" is "relocation" caused by an unjust or incorrect force. A person who is "dislocated" should receive dislocation compensation from those who caused him or her to be dislocated.

Disorder/Disorderly Conduct. Use these terms with caution. When others use them, ask for a detailed explanation that you can easily understand. What, exactly, is a "disorderly" situation? "Disorderly" as compared with what? Is a condition of White Supremacy (Racism) "disorderly" when compared with the condition of justice (balance between people)?

> **Note:** During the existence of White Supremacy (Racism), Racistman and Racistwoman (White Supremacists, collectively), produce conditions that make it easy for them to accuse and punish Non-White persons in regards to activities that are "disorderly."

Disrespect/Disrespectful. Avoid using these words. Instead, use the words, "discourteous" or "discourtesy".

Notes: According to Compensatory Logic, all "respect" of, and for, a person, is "self-respect," and all "self-respect" is produced entirely by and for the person who "has" it. The only way for a person to be "disrespectful" is to tell him or herself things that are true, while knowing that those things <u>are</u> <u>not</u> true. This produces the absence of "respect," which is the same as "disrespect". "Respect" means refusing to lie to oneself [self-respect], and being willing to inform all others of that refusal to lie to oneself.

Divorce. <u>Use this word with caution</u>. When others use this word, give attention to the limited manner in which the word is used, most of the time. Study the word "marriage," and study the word "divorce." Use these words with great caution and precision.

Questions: What, exactly, is a "divorce"? Is it possible for persons to be "divorced" from each other each time that one expresses animosity or disinterest toward the other? Are people "divorced" from each other during periods when they kiss, embrace, and/or engage in sexual intercourse or "sexual play" with persons other than each other? Are two people "divorced" if one person refuses to engage in sexual intercourse with the other? When, exactly, are people "married"? What do people do (or not do) from one minute to the next that "proves" that they are "married" at a particular moment? Can people be "married in one way, and "divorced" in another way, at the same time? Could it be that people are "divorced" most of the time that they say they are "married"?

During the existence of White Supremacy (Racism) does the power of the White Supremacists (Racists), prevent Non-White people from being truly "married" to any person, White or Non-White? Is it possible for a racially subjugated people to be "married"? Are such people "qualified" for "marriage"? Are such people actually "divorced" from themselves, from each other, and from those who subjugate them? How can people be "married," and be subject to the dictatorship of a hostile and unjust people, at the same time?

Doctor. <u>Use this word with caution</u>. Study the many ways this word is used by others. Ask for explanations. What, exactly, is a "doctor"? Does a "doctor" solve problems? Is the word "doctor" used too often to describe what a person is, or does?

Note: According to Compensatory Logic, it is a self-required act of courtesy to always call a person by the title of "doctor" if he or she asks to be called "doctor".

Domestic/Domesticated. Avoid using these words. Study the many ways these words are used by others. Ask questions.

> **Questions:** What, exactly, is a "domestic" person? What, exactly, is the function of a person who has been "domesticated"? Why call a person a "domestic servant"? Is not every person a "servant" – either for correctness or for incorrectness? What is the reason for calling a person a "domestic servant"? What is meant by the expression, "foreign and domestic"? If a Non-White person has been "domesticated" by the White Supremacists (Racistman and Racistwoman), is that person also a "foreign-subject" to the White Supremacists? Are the Victims of White Supremacy (Non-White persons) the "domestic and foreign servants" of, by, to, and for, the White Supremacists (Racistmen and Racistwomen, individually and collectively)?

Domestic Enemies. Do not use this term. Use, instead, the term, "The Enemy," and use it to mean those White persons [broadly] who have chosen to participate in the practice of White Supremacy (Racism) in any one or more of the Nine Major Areas of (People) Activity (Economics, Education, Entertainment, Labor, Law, Politics, Religion, Sex, and War/Counter-War). When others use the term, "The Enemy," ask for a detailed explanation that you can easily understand.

> **Questions:** Is "the enemy" the "greatest enemy" – greater than all other "enemies"? What is the best and correct way to choose "the enemy" of justice (balance) among the people of the known universe? Since justice (balance between people) does not exist among the people of the known universe, is it correct to say that all of the people of the known universe are "the enemy"? If correct, whose "enemy"? "The enemy" to themselves?
>
> Are the smartest people in the known universe "the greatest enemy" to the production of justice (balance between people)? Are the White Supremacists (Racists) of the known universe also the smartest people in the known universe and, therefore, "the greatest enemy" to the production of justice (balance between people)? Is there any logical and correct reason that the White

Supremacists (Racists) should not be called, collectively, by the title "The Enemy" [of justice]?

Domestic Violence. <u>Do not use this term</u>. Instead of the term, "domestic violence," use the word, "violence".

> **Reason:** "Domestic violence" and/or violence that is "domesticated," does not exist. "Violence" is <u>violence</u>; <u>indirect</u> violence is <u>violence</u>; <u>counter</u>-violence is <u>counter-violence</u> (violence used to counteract violence that is being used); and <u>anti</u>-violence is <u>anti-violence</u> (speech and/or action that is used to <u>stop</u> all forms of violence).
>
> <u>Non</u>-violence is <u>non-violence</u> (the <u>complete absence</u> of violence). The only form of "violence" that is <u>ever</u> correct is <u>counter</u>-violence, that helps to produce <u>anti</u>-violence, that results in <u>non</u>-violence.
>
> **Note:** <u>Counter</u>-violence is an act of correct and justified counter-force that is great enough to disrupt and/or contribute to the halting of any act of incorrect or <u>non</u>-justified force.

Domino Theory (the). <u>Do not use this term</u>.

> **Reason:** "Dominos" is a so-called "game" that has often consisted of objects that are black and white in appearance, with the white part of the objects used for the purpose of giving the objects their "value." During the existence of White Supremacy (Racism), and according to Compensatory Counter-Racist Logic, there is substantial reason to believe that the "game" of "dominos," and/or any use to which "domino objects" are put, is directly or indirectly intended to support the idea and practice of White Supremacy (Racism).

Doom and Gloom. <u>Do not use this term</u>. Instead of saying that a situation is one of "doom and gloom," say that the situation is "incorrect."

> **Reason:** The term "doom and gloom" is used in a manner that associates destruction with darkness. Darkness is not, within itself, destructive. Darkness is a correct part of the known universe. Darkness, like light, serves a correct purpose when presented, used, or regarded correctly. White Supremacists (Racists) prefer to associate "darkness," not only with "dark" people [Non-White

people], but also, with doom and danger, and with any situation that is regarded as destructive, depressing, ugly, unworthy, threatening, etc.

Dress for Success. <u>Use this term with caution</u>. Use it to mean placing something on the body of a person in such a manner that the something has the effect of best helping to replace White Supremacy (Racism) with Justice (balance between people). When others use this term, ask for a detailed explanation that you can easily understand.

> **Question:** During the existence of White Supremacy (Racism) how can a Non-White person "dress" in such a manner as to result in "success" in the replacement of White Supremacy (Racism) with Justice (balance between people)?

Drug Abuse. <u>Avoid using this term</u>. Instead, use the expression, "incorrect use of chemicals."

> **Note:** As long as White Supremacy (Racism) exits, it is the White Supremacists (Racists), who are to blame for most of the incorrect use of chemicals among the people of the known universe.

Duty. <u>Use this word with caution</u>. When others use it, ask for a detailed explanation that you can easily understand. When talking about "duty," always say that it is the basic "duty" of every person in the known universe to do all that he or she can to produce justice (balance between people), and to produce correctness (balance between people, creatures, things, etc.). During the existence of White Supremacy (Racism), it is also the basic duty of every person in the known universe to do all that he or she can to replace The System of White Supremacy (Racism), with The System of Justice (balance between people).

E

East/Eastern. <u>Use these words with caution</u>. When others use them, ask for a detailed explanation that you can easily understand. Use words like "East," "West," "North," "South" etc., with great caution. Do not use words like "eastern culture," "western culture," "far east," "middle east," "near east," "near west," etc.

> **Questions:** What, exactly, is "east"? Who determines what is and what is not, "east"? What, exactly, is the truth about what is "east" and what is "west"? Is "east," a

direction? Is "east," a place? Can "east" be any place? Is there truly any such thing as "eastern culture"? Is there any such thing as "eastern food"? If "east" is a direction, is "food" a direction? Is "food" a direction-culture? If so, which "direction"? High? Low? Up? Out? If a person eats a grape, is that person or that grape a "part" of "eastern culture," or is he, she or it, a "part" of "western culture"?

How "far" is the "Far East?" "Far East" from what? "Far East" from whom? According to whom? Is it the White Supremacists (Racists) who decide what is and what is not "East," and the purpose "East" serves?

Who decides what is an "East Indian" or what is a "West Indian," and for what ultimate purpose? Does an "East Indian" become a "North Indian" when he or she goes "North"? If so, "North" of what? If so, "North" of whom? What, exactly, is an "East European" when he or she travels to the "West" of wherever he or she was? Can people be correctly identified by or "classified" by direction and/or distance?

Eat Crow. Do not use this term in association with the "slang" use that has sometimes been used as an attempt to "apologize" for having made an error.

> **Reason:** A crow is a bird that is black in color. During the existence of White Supremacy (Racism), the White Supremacists (Racistman and Racistwoman, collectively) have often associated the blackness of a crow with things that are evil, dangerous, useless, unworthy, etc. White Supremacists (Racists) have sometimes said things like, "if I'm wrong, I'll eat crow." It is best for persons to say, "If I am incorrect, I will apologize and try to compensate."

Eclectic–Pluralism. Use this term to mean:

(1)   A compensatory-functional "religion" based on principles derived from two or more "systems" of religion.

(2)   A compensatory-functional "religion" based on principles derived from two or more social and material "systems" or concepts.

(3)   The concept and practice of making many principles into one, and/or one principle into many.

(4)　A compensatory-functional or transitional "religion," which includes methods of speech, and/or action that can be used by Victims of Racism (Non-White people), as a compensatory-functional means of helping to counteract the effects of such victimization, in any one or more areas of activity.

(5)　A "religion" that can be used to help a Victim of Racism (Non-White person) to find the "best" religion.

(6)　A "temporary" religion for Victims of Racism (Non-White people) that can be used, either in whole or in part, to counteract those parts of other "religions" that may, directly or indirectly, function in support of Racism (White Supremacy).

Eclectic Pluralist.　Use this term to mean any Victim of Racism (Non-White person) who practices one or more "parts" of Eclectic-Pluralism, and who identifies him or herself as a person who thinks, speaks, and acts in support of the concept of Eclectic-Pluralism.

Eclipse/Eclipsed.　Use these words with caution.

>　**Reason:**　During the existence of White Supremacy (Racism), the words "eclipse" or "eclipsed" have sometimes been used by White Supremacists (Racists) to apply to the appearance and/or the speech or action of dark (Non-White) people. The White Supremacists (Racists) have used the words "eclipse" or "eclipsed" to mean "darkness" in the form of "dark" people, who "get in the way" of White people and hinder White people in making "progress."

Economical.　Use this word to apply to speech and/or action that result in justice and correctness. When others use this word, ask for a detailed explanation that you can easily understand.

Economics.　Use this word with caution. When others use this word, ask for a detailed explanation that you can easily understand. According to Compensatory Logic, "economics" applies to anything pertaining to the use of time and energy (when, where, how, and what for).

Use this word to apply to the process of speaking, and/or acting in a manner that truth is revealed and used in a manner that produces justice and correctness at all times, in all places, in all areas of activity. Use this word to apply also to any use of time and energy - particularly time and energy that produces a constructive result.

During the existence of White Supremacy (Racism), it is best and correct to speak of "economics" as the correct use of time and energy to replace White Supremacy (Racism) with Justice (balance between people).

> **Questions:** What, exactly, is "economics"? What, exactly, is not "economics"? Is the correct use of time and energy the best and only form of "economical" activity in existence?

Education/Educated Person. Use these terms with caution. When others use these terms, ask for a detailed explanation that you can easily understand. When you choose to use the word "education," or the term "educated person," use them to mean the following:

> "Education" means the process of learning all things, about all things, or the process of learning all things about one thing.

> "Educated person" means a person who has learned all things about all things, or a person who has learned all things about one thing.

> **Notes:** Since all things are interrelated, to learn all things about one thing is to learn all things about all things. It is incorrect to be ashamed of not being "educated." It is also incorrect to be arrogant toward others or brag because of something that you have learned. Knowledge does not make one person "better" than another. Knowledge only helps a person to be smarter, and/or smart, about some things, some of the time. Becoming "educated" is only the *process* of learning what one does not know. There is reason to believe that no person in the known universe is "educated," and/or has an "education." It is correct to say that there exists no such person as an "educated person."

> It is important to know and understand that, as long as The System of White Supremacy (Racism) is the dominant motivating force in the interactions between the people of the known universe, those White people who practice White Supremacy (Racism) will resist allowing Non-White people to "learn enough" to replace White Supremacy (Racism) with Justice (balance between people).

> In seeking to learn, it is correct for every Non-White person to help produce "The Quality Relationship" with

White persons by asking White persons to teach all Non-White people everything that White people know that is of constructive value. Every person in the known universe should be taught everything that is of constructive value. Such teachings should include everything that needs to be known in every area of activity, including Economics, Education (processes), Entertainment, Labor, Law, Politics, Religion, Sex, and War/Counter-War.

Educational Excellence. Use this term. During the existence of White Supremacy (Racism) use this term to apply to all things learned that are useful in producing the result of replacing White Supremacy (Racism) with Justice (balance between people). When others use this term, ask for a detailed explanation that you can easily understand.

> **Reason:** According to Compensatory Logic, "education" is a process - a process that never ends until *all* things are known and understood. During the existence of White Supremacy (Racism), those things that are learned that do not directly or indirectly contribute to the result of replacing White Supremacy (Racism) with Justice (balance between people) should not be regarded as "educational excellence," and/or as "excellence in education." Things learned that do not help to replace White Supremacy (Racism) with Justice (balance between people) are, in effect, things learned that directly or indirectly support White Supremacy (Racism).

Effective Majority (The). Use this term to apply to:

(1)   A term referring to the power of the total number of those persons classified as White, and who practice White Supremacy (Racism) in the known universe;

(2)   Those White persons, collectively, who directly or indirectly dominate the Non-White people of the known universe through the practice of Racism; and

(3)   White Supremacists (collectively).

> **Explanation**: The term "Effective Majority" refers to the White people of the known universe, but only those who practice Racism (White Supremacy). The term does not refer to all White people, nor does it necessarily refer to the numerical majority of White people who may be situated at a particular place, at a particular time. Those

White persons who practice White Supremacy exercise more power over people than any other people in the known universe. They do this in spite of all efforts made by other White persons and Non-White persons to stop the practice of White Supremacy.

Even though White Supremacy (Racism) may or may not have been established, maintained, expanded, and/or refined by <u>all</u> White people, or even by <u>most</u> White people, it has always been maintained by those White persons who had the will and the ability to effectively make White Supremacy the major force. This makes them the "Effective Majority," the majority that is most effective in the exercise of power. If this were not true, there would not have been or could not have been anything in the known universe that could be correctly called White Supremacy. Therefore, those White people who do not practice Racism (White Supremacy), as well as those Non-White people who do not want to be Victims of Racism, are not the Effective Majority. They are the "Ineffective Majority," the "Powerless Majority," and/or the "majority" with "minority" power.

Eggshell White. <u>Do not use this term</u>. When others use the terms "eggshell white," "off-white," "pure white," "white-on-white," "near white," etc., ask for a detailed explanation that you can easily understand. Ask for a functional definition of the word "White" as it applies to people.

> **Questions:** What, exactly, is "white"? What, exactly, is not "white"? Is there such a thing as a "shade" of "white"? If so, is a "shade" of "white" a "color"? If so, how can someone or something be "White," and have "color," and/or a "shade of color," at the same time? Is the "color" of an eggshell "white"? How can anything, including an eggshell, be "white," and "non-white," at the same time? Can a "White" person be a "natural tan," and also be "White"?

Eight Ball. <u>Use this word with caution</u>. When others use it, ask for a detailed explanation that you can easily understand. Study the many ways that games, sports, and other forms of so-called "entertainment," or "recreation," are used by White Supremacists (Racists) to produce or promote thought, speech, and/or action that is supportive of The System of White Supremacy (Racism).

> **Questions:** What, exactly, is a so-called "eight ball"? In games such as pool, is the eight ball black for reasons

having to do with the promotion of thinking in support of White Supremacy (Racism)? In games such as pool, why is the "master of balls" (sometimes called the "cue ball" – the ball from which all other balls "take their cue"), a white ball?

Notes: During the existence of White Supremacy (Racism), the White Supremacists (Racists) of the known universe do everything that they can to cause all people, at all times to think, speak, and act in support of The System of White Supremacy (Racism) in all areas of (people) activity, including Economics, Education, Entertainment, Labor, Law, Politics, Religion, Sex, and War/ Counter-War.

Eight-Balling (Racial). Use this term to apply to:

(1)   A term used in a ball game called "pool".

(2)   In racial terms, to mean that a White person is directly or indirectly the cause of a Non-White person doing any kind of unjust harm to another Non-White person. The purpose for this tactic is to hide the fact that the harm done was caused by the White person who was the "master" of the situation, and not the Non-White person who acted as a mere ignorant, arrogant, and/or fearful tool and servant.

(3)   The practice of White Supremacists (Racists) using their power in such a manner as to force, bribe, and/or terrify some Non-White person into acts of harm to another Non-White person.

Embarrass/Embarrassment. Use these words to apply to, and/or to describe all of the interactions ("The Arrangement") between the White people and the Non-White people of the known universe, during the existence of White Supremacy (Racism).

Use the term "The Embarrassment" to describe the general interactions between White people and Non-White people during the existence of White Supremacy (Racism). Identify White Supremacy (Racism) itself, as "The Great Embarrassment," and/or as "The Tragic Arrangement". Say things like, "there is no way for justice to exist as long as 'The Great Embarrassment' exists," and "The Great Embarrassment" (White Supremacy), should be replaced by "The Quality Relationship" (Justice).

When talking about what is said to be an "embarrassing" situation say, "Nothing is more embarrassing than the existence of White Supremacy (Racism)."

Emergency. Use this word with caution. Study the many ways that others choose to use this word. Particularly, study the ways that White Supremacists (Racists) and/or Suspected White Supremacists (Suspected Racists), choose to use the word.

> **Questions:** What, exactly, is an "emergency"? What, exactly, is not an "emergency"? What person is qualified to judge what is and what is not an "emergency"? What, exactly, is a "state of emergency"? Is the existence of White Supremacy (Racism), a condition that can be correctly called a "state of emergency," and/or an "emergency condition"?

Eminent Domain. Avoid using this term. When others use it, ask for a detailed explanation that you can easily understand. Study the ways that White Supremacists (Racists) may choose to use the term for purposes of stealing from Non-White people. Is The System of White Supremacy (Racism) a form of "Eminent Domain"?

Employed/Employment. Use these words with caution. Use the word "employed" to mean whatever it is that a person or a creature does. Think, speak, and act as if every person, every creature, and every thing in the known and unknown universe is, at all times, "employed" – either constructively, or destructively.

> **Reason:** "Employed," means doing something. Every person, creature, and thing in the known and unknown universe, does something.

> **Examples**: During the existence of White Supremacy (Racism), all of the Non-White people of the known universe are directly or indirectly "employed" as Victims of, and servants to, The System of White Supremacy (Racism). Racistman and Racistwoman (White Supremacists, collectively), are the "employed"/ "employee"/"employers" who dominate and control (directly or indirectly) the manner in which their Victims (Non-White people) are "employed".

> During the existence of White Supremacy (Racism), Racistman and Racistwoman dominate and control the "employment" of the Non-White people of the known universe in every area of activity, including Economics, Education, Entertainment, Labor, Law, Politics, Religion, Sex, and War/Counter-War.

Enemy. Use this word. During the existence of White Supremacy (Racism), use the word "enemy," and/or the term, "the enemy" to mean those White persons who have chosen not to do all that they can to replace White Supremacy (Racism) with Justice (balance between people). When others use the word "enemy," and/or the term "the enemy," ask for a detailed explanation that you can easily understand. When White persons use the word "enemy," and/or the term "the enemy," ask if they mean "the enemy" of justice (balance between people).

During the existence of White Supremacy (Racism), use the term "the enemy" to apply only to those White persons who practice White Supremacy (Racism), and/or who refuse to oppose White Supremacy (Racism). During the existence of White Supremacy (Racism) do not use the word "enemy," and/or the term "the enemy" to apply to any person who is not a White Supremacist (Racist). If a person who is not a White Supremacist (Racist) does harm to you, and/or attempts to do harm to you, do not say that the person is an "enemy" and/or is "the enemy." Say that he or she is an "opponent."

> **Notes:** According to Compensatory Counter-Racist Logic and during the existence of White Supremacy (Racism), it is correct to blame the White Supremacists (Racists) for any and all harm that comes to those who are subject to the White Supremacists (Racists). During the existence of White Supremacy (Racism), all of the Non-White people of the known universe are directly or indirectly subject to the White Supremacists (Racists).

Enemies (Foreign and Domestic). Avoid using this term. When others use this term, ask for a detailed explanation that you can easily understand.

> **Questions:** What, exactly, is a so-called "domesticated enemy"? How can a person or a creature be "domestic" or "domesticated" and, at the same time, be an "enemy"? Are not all "enemies" foreign? How can an "enemy" to a person be anything other than "foreign" to that person? How can persons who are "enemies" be anything other than "foreign" to each other?

Enlightened. Do not use this word to mean the same as the word "smart". Instead, use the word "learned" or the term, "very smart."

> **Reason:** During the existence of The System of White Supremacy (Racism), those White persons who have chosen to participate in the practice of White Supremacy

(Racism) have chosen to use words in a manner that best helps to support that practice. One of those words is "enlightened."

White Supremacists (Racistman and Racistwoman) use the words "enlighten" and/or "enlightened" in association with the terms "smart," "very smart," "learned," "intelligent," etc. They also use these same words to mean "light" or "lightened," while directly or indirectly associating the words "light," or "lightened" with the word "white." They do this so that people will think that the words "enlightened," "enlighten," "light," bright, brilliant, and "white" are associated with the word "smart." Thus, being a White person is made to mean the same as being an "enlightened" and/or [a] smart person.

Notes: According to Compensatory Counter-Racist Logic, it is incorrect to use words that help promote thinking in support of "White" (meaning smart) and "Black" (meaning ignorant). For example, during the existence of White Supremacy (Racism), the expression "being in the dark" has often been used to mean the same as "not knowing," or, "not being smart."

White Supremacists (Racists), in their production of "Racist Language" have used words such as "enlightened" in association with the words "smart," and "wise," and also in association with the words "white," "bright," and "right." They do this to promote the thought that White Supremacy (Racism) is, and should be, "preferable" to anything that may be supportive of "darkness" – particularly "dark," "Black," and/or "Non-White" ("non-enlightened") people.

Entertainment. Use this word with caution. When others use it, ask for a detailed explanation that you can easily understand.

Questions: What, exactly, is "entertainment"? What, exactly, is not "entertainment"? Can politics (people relations) be a form of "entertainment"? Can Religion"? Education? Sex? War? Is White Supremacy (Racism) a form of "entertainment" for those who have chosen to practice it? Should any constructive work be regarded as the very best form of "entertainment"? During the existence of White Supremacy (Racism), should correct "entertainment" be only those things that people do that are intended to help replace White Supremacy (Racism) with Justice (balance between people)?

Note: During the existence of White Supremacy (Racism), those White persons who have chosen to participate in the practice of White Supremacy (Racism), do nothing for "entertainment" that is not intended to help maintain, expand, and/or refine The System of White Supremacy (Racism).

Entitled. Use this word with caution. When others use the words "entitle," "entitled," and "entitlement," ask for a detailed explanation that you can easily understand.

Questions: Who is "entitled" to what? When? Where? Why? Is every person in the known universe "entitled" to do what he or she can to replace White Supremacy (Racism) with Justice (balance between people)? Is every person in the known universe "entitled" to do his or her duty? Is it logical that every person is "entitled" to do his or her duty to replace White Supremacy (Racism) with Justice (balance between people), in every area of activity, including Economics, Education, Entertainment, Labor, Law, Politics, Religion, Sex, and War/Counter-War? During the existence of White Supremacy (Racism) is there any greater "entitlement"?

Note: When talking about people and what they are all "entitled" to, say, "A person is basically entitled to produce justice and correctness, and to work to guarantee that others do the same".

Environmental Error Factor(s). Use this term to mean anything that is the cause of, and/or that helps to be the cause of, something happening that should not happen. Also, use this term to apply to anything that exists in a situation that helps to prevent something being done that should be done.

Notes: "Environmental Error Factors," in many situations, are caused or promoted by persons, either intentionally, or unintentionally, and either directly or indirectly. Sometimes a "situation" can be produced that is very constructive for a specific time, place, and purpose. Sometimes when the time, place or purpose changes without all, most, or some of the factors in that situation also changing, the result may be the establishment of one or more "Environmental Error Factors." For example, it is important to be aware of what is said to be an "improvement" in a situation when a study may show that the "improvement" may also cause a change in the overall situation, and that the change produces harm in the form of one or more "Environmental Error Factors."

An "Environmental Error Factor" may be a door located in a place where a door should not be, or may be a machine that does not function correctly. It may be a tree or a wall that may hinder a view of something that should be seen. It may be a force or an object that hinders movement. It may be a thing that is likely to fall (or rise) and do harm. "Environmental Error Factors" may be a few things that are difficult to see, or many things that are "looked" at, but are not "seen" or understood. It can also be said, correctly, that among the people of the known universe, the most powerful "Environmental Error Factor" produced by people within the known universe, is The System of White Supremacy (Racism).

E. Pluribus Unum. Use this term with caution. When others use it, ask for a detailed explanation that you can easily understand.

Questions: What, exactly, is meant by the expression "many becoming one"? "Many" becoming "one," what? For what purpose? What is the proof that "many" have become "one"? Should every person think, speak, and act as "one person"? Is it correct for every person to think, speak, and act in such a manner as to replace White Supremacy (Racism) with Justice (balance between people)? If not, why not?

Equal (Racial). Use this word with caution. When others use it, ask for a detailed explanation that you can easily understand. Ask questions. Should all people be "equal" to one another? If so, how? If so, "equal" in what manner – according to what? "Equal" height? "Equal" weight? Does being "equal," mean that every person must, at all times, eat the same food, in the same amount?

Notes: When talking about people, and thinking about the word and concept of "equality," it may be best to use the word "justice," rather than the terms "equal," "equality," or "equal opportunity." According to Compensatory Logic, the word "justice" means no person is mistreated, and the person who needs help the most, gets the most help. It is important to know and to understand that justice (balance between people) and White Supremacy (Racism) cannot exist, in the same universe, at the same time.

Equal Opportunity. Use this term with caution. When others use this term, ask for a detailed explanation that you can easily understand.

> **Questions:** What, exactly, is an "equal opportunity"? "Equal opportunity" to do what? How? Where? When? How much of what is necessary to give a person a so-called "equal opportunity"? "Equal opportunity" as compared with whom? In order to have "equal opportunity," is it necessary to have this "equality of opportunity" in all areas of activity (Economics, Education, Entertainment, Labor, Law, Politics, Religion, Sex, War, and Counter-War)? If not, why not?

> **Notes:** When talking about "equal opportunity," it is best to use the term "production of justice." "Production of justice" and/or "producing justice" means to think, speak, and act in such a manner as to result in no person being mistreated, and result in the person who needs help the most, getting the most help.

Equality (Racial). Avoid using this word. Instead, use the word "justice" (balance between people), and/or guaranteeing that no person is mistreated and guaranteeing that the person who needs help the most, gets the most help. When others use the word "equality," and/or the term "equal justice," ask for a detailed explanation that you can easily understand.

Espionage/Counter-Espionage. Use these terms with caution. When others talk of "espionage," "counter-espionage," "spying," "counter-spying," etc., ask for a detailed explanation of all of these terms in a manner that you can easily understand.

> **Questions:** Is an act of "espionage" for the purpose of "secretly" gaining information about something or someone, in order to best do harm to someone? Is "counter-espionage" for gaining information that another has, in order to protect against any harm that may come as the result of the use of the information gained?

> Is the entire system of White Supremacy (Racism), a direct and indirect "system of espionage," specifically designed to do harm to Non-White people for the socio-material benefit of White people? Is it "counter-espionage" for a Non-White person to seek to learn about any information that White Supremacists (Racists) may have about anything? Is it correct for a Victim of White

Supremacy (Non-White person) to know everything that the White Supremacists (Racists) know?

Ethical. Avoid using this word. Instead, use the word "correct." When others use this word, ask them to explain, in detail, exactly what they mean, and do not mean. Ask them to explain in a manner that you can easily understand why something is "ethical" or "unethical."

> **Notes:** According to Compensatory Counter-Racist Logic, everything that "happens" in the known universe is either correct or incorrect. Correctness means balance between people, creatures, things, etc., that exists within the known (and unknown) universe. During the existence of White Supremacy (Racism), "correctness" does not exist, and the use of the word "ethical" is confusing.

Ethnic/Ethnic Group. Do not use these terms. When others use these terms, ask for a detailed explanation that you can easily understand. Ask questions.

> **Questions:** What, exactly, is ethnic"? What, exactly, is an "ethnic group"? What, exactly, is the difference between an "ethnic group" and a "nation," "tribe," "gang," "club" or "association"? What makes a "group," "ethnic"? Is an "ethnic group" "ethnic" all of the time? What, exactly, makes a "group," a "group"? When? Where? How? Why? Is every person in the known universe a "member" of an "ethnic group"? Is every person who has ever taken a drink of water from a stream, a member of an "ethnic group"? Do "tall" people go swimming? If a person who is "tall" goes swimming, does that mean that the person is a "member" of an "ethnic group" of "tall swimmers"?

> When one person kills another person, is it possible that both persons can be "members" of the same "ethnic group"? How can both persons be "members" of the same "ethnic group" when one person is a "killer" and the other is the person "killed"? Is it "communistic" to be a "member" of an "ethnic group"? Is it "fascist"? Is it "sexist," or "Racist"? Are persons who exist in the same universe also "members" of the same "ethnic group"? If so, how "universal" is a "universal person"? If so, how "ethnical" is that person? Based on how much of what? Why?

European Continent. Do not use this term. Use the words "European" or the "Europeans" to describe a person, only if asked to do so by that person, who describe themselves as such. When others use the term "European Continent," ask for a detailed explanation that you can easily understand. Ask questions.

> **Questions:** What, exactly, makes the "European continent" the "European continent"? According to whom? Why? For what ultimate purpose? What, exactly, is "European"? What, exactly, is "Europe"? Is a person who is called a "European," a "White" person? If so, why? When, exactly, if ever, is a "European" not a "European"? When, exactly, if ever, is a "White" person, not a "White" person?

Evidence. Use this word with caution. When others use it, ask for a detailed explanation that you can easily understand.

> **Questions:** What, exactly, is "evidence"? What, exactly, is "evident"? Is "evidence" something that "evolved," and then became known and understood? If so, "evolved" how? If so, became known and understood by whom? How much of what may be called "evidence" is, in truth "evident"? Is it possible that "evidence" is not "evidence," but only "appears" to be "evidence"? Does enough "evidence" exist to prove that White Supremacy (Racism) is a major criminal system? Does enough "evidence" exist to prove that the White people who participate in The System of White Supremacy (Racism) are the "Master Criminals" of the known universe?

> **Note:** During the existence of White Supremacy (Racism), the people who are best qualified to say that they have "evidence" that they are, and have been, victimized by the existence of White Supremacy (Racism), are the Non-White people of the known universe.

Evil Empire/Evil Religion. Use these terms to apply to The System of White Supremacy (Racism).

Evil Shadow/Shadow of Evil/Evil Darkness, etc. Do not use these terms. When others use them, ask for a detailed explanation that you can easily understand.

> **Reason:** "Shadows" are "black" and "dark" in appearance. Within The System of White Supremacy (Racism), the word "shadow" and the concept of a "shadow," is often

associated with the idea of something or someone, being evil, incorrect, harmful, threatening, malicious and/or destructive.

Existence. Use this word to mean, "function".

Exotic. Use this word with caution. When others say that a person is "exotic" or if they say that something that the person is doing is "exotic," ask for a detailed explanation that you can easily understand.

> **Reason:** Male White Supremacists (Racists) sometimes use the word "exotic" to apply to Non-White females whom they (the White Supremacists) regard as "primitive-sexy," "simple-minded sexy," or "seductively treacherous".

Expert. Use this word to apply to: (1) One who never makes a mistake; (2) one who knows all things about all things; or (3) one who knows all things about one thing.

> **Note:** During the existence of White Supremacy (Racism), the only "experts" on White Supremacy (Racism) and how it is practiced, are the White Supremacists (Racists), themselves.

Explorer(s). Use this word with caution. When others use it, ask for a detailed explanation that you can easily understand. Ask questions.

> **Questions:** What, exactly, is an "explorer"? Who is it that "explores"? Who is it that does not "explore"? Does a newborn baby "explore"? If a person asks a question, is that person an "explorer"? Are all people "explorers"? Do White Supremacists (Racists) "explore" for the purposes of helping to maintain, expand, and/or refine The System of White Supremacy (Racism)? Do the Victims of White Supremacy (Non-White people) "explore" by seeking ways of avoiding the harm that White Supremacy (Racism) produces?

Extremist. Avoid using this word to apply to any person, place, or thing. When others use the word to apply to a person, ask for a detailed explanation that you can easily understand. Does the use of the word explain "enough"? Does it mean "extremely"? Extremely what? Extremely correct? Extremely non-correct? "Extreme" as compared to what? When, exactly, is a person an "extremist"? When, exactly, is a person not an "extremist"?

Notes: White Supremacists (Racists) have sometimes used the word "extremist" to apply to Non-White persons who do not agree with the existence of, and/or who express opposition to, The System of White Supremacy (Racism).

F

Fact. Use this word with caution. When others use it, ask for a detailed explanation that you can easily understand.

> **Questions:** What, exactly, is a "fact"? Can "facts" be used to prove "truth"? What, exactly, is "truth"? Can "facts" be used to prove or to produce falsehood? How many "facts" are necessary in order to reveal "truth"? Enough "facts"? All the "facts"? What, exactly, are "enough facts"? "Enough" of what kind of "facts"? What kind of "facts" does it take to make "enough facts"? Is it possible to present too many "facts"? Are some "facts" more important than others? In matters of Race, Racism, and Counter-Racism, which persons are correctly qualified to decide which "facts" are the most important and why?

Faded into Obscurity. Do not use this term. Instead, use the word "forgotten."

> **Reason:** The term "faded into obscurity" may be used or have a meaning that directly or indirectly helps to promote Racist (White Supremacist) thought, speech, and action.

> **Questions:** Does "fade" mean to become "light" or "white"? Does "obscurity" mean to become "white," "lost in darkness" and, therefore, of no value?

Failure. Use this word with caution. Think, speak, and act as if there is no "failure" in what a person is trying to do until he or she stops trying to do it, and never tries again.

Fair. Do not use this word in any way that is directly or indirectly associated with the word "justice" (balance between people), or is directly or indirectly associated with being correct, or "right" or "righteous." Study the many ways that others choose to use the word "fair."

Reason: During the existence of White Supremacy (Racism), "fair" means, "White." Since "fair" is usually associated with the words "White" or "Whiteness," it does not mean, and should not be used to mean, "just" and/or "justice" (balance between people).

During the existence of White Supremacy (Racism), Racistman and Racistwoman (White Supremacists, collectively), often use the words "fair," "White," "just" and/or "justice," to mean one and the same thing. They use the word "fair" in a manner that is likely to cause many persons to believe that, in order for a person to practice justice (balance between people), the person must be or should be "fair" and/or "White."

It is incorrect to use the word "fair" in any manner that is likely to directly or indirectly help to promote the idea that justice or correctness is, or should be, associated with a person being "White" in appearance, or according to a "classification" by Racistman and Racistwoman (White Supremacists, collectively).

Study the following words and word-terms, and think about how they are sometimes used to help support White Supremacy (Racism) by associating the word "fair" with words such as "balanced," "beautiful," "blessed," "favored," "gentle," "good," "goodness," "intelligent," "just," "pretty," "wholesome," etc.:

"fair employment"	"fair play"
"fairest"	"fair price"
"fair game"	"fair princess"
"fair-haired boy"	"fair sex, the"
"fair lady (or "lady-fair")"	"fair-trade"
"fair market"	"fair treatment"
"fair-minded"	"fair weather"

Do not use any of the aforementioned terms. Do not use any terms that are similar in meaning to any of the aforementioned terms. Remember, the word "fair" means "White." Whenever you can, use the word "correct" in place of the word "fair." ("Correct employment," "correct lady," "correct market," "correct-minded," "correct play"). Another word that can be used in place of the word "fair" is the word "constructive." ("Constructive employment," "constructive trade," "constructive treatment", etc.

Fair (be). <u>Do not use this term</u>. Instead, use the terms "produce justice," "produce balance between people," and/or the words, "guarantee that no person is mistreated, and guarantee that the person who needs help the most, gets the most help."

> **Reason:** During the existence of White Supremacy (Racism), the word "fair" and the word "justice" have been used in such a manner as to cause people to think, speak, and act as if "being fair," "being just," and "being White," are one and the same. The use of the word "fair" in this manner, only helps to promote the thought that the existence of The System of White Supremacy (Racism) is not only correct, but that the White people who practice White Supremacy (Racism) are a "just people," because they are "White" ["fair"].

Fair Trial. <u>Do not use this term</u>. Use, instead, the term "Production of Justice Process."

> **Reason:** During the existence of White Supremacy (Racism), the word "White" is often associated with the word "fair," which is often made to mean the same as "just," and/or "justice." It is <u>incorrect</u> to say or imply, that the words "White," "fair," and "justice" mean or should mean, the same thing.

> To equate "whiteness" with "fairness," and then to equate "fairness" with Justice (balance between people) is to help promote the belief that a White person, and/or a system of domination based on a person being "White" and/or "fair," is the best and correct way to produce justice. The word "justice" should <u>not</u> be in any way used in association with the word "fair" and the ways that the words "fair" and "White" are used within The System of White Supremacy (Racism).

> It is best and correct for the word "justice" to always be used in association with speech, and/or action that is designed to or intended to <u>guarantee that no person is mistreated</u> and <u>guarantee that the person who needs help the most, gets the most help</u>. During the existence of White Supremacy (Racism), it is best and correct <u>not </u>to use terms like "fair play," "fair employment," "fair trial," "fair fight," "fair appraisal," etc. During the existence of White Supremacy (Racism), it is best and correct to (instead) use terms like "correct play," "correct employment," "correct trial," "correct fight," "correct appraisal," etc.

Fairy Godmother. <u>Do not use this term</u>.

> **Reason:** The use of the term "Fairy Godmother" is, in effect, supportive of White Supremacy (Racism). "Fairy" is most often associated with the word "fair" and the word "White". The word "fair" is often said to mean the same as the word "just" — as in "justice." In practice, the use of the term "Fairy Godmother" usually helps produce the thought that White ("fair") Mother who is just ("fair") like "God" – according to the White Supremacists (Racists).

Faith-Based Initiative. <u>Use this term with caution</u>. Use it to apply to all efforts made to produce justice and correctness in all areas of activity-existence, including Economics, Education, Entertainment, Labor, Law, Politics, Religion, Sex, and War/Counter-War. This also includes efforts made to promote the belief that the people of the known universe were produced for the purpose of finding the difference between what is just, and what is not just, what is correct and what is not correct, and what is "wrong" and what is "right." This also includes using all learning to guarantee that no person is mistreated, that the person needing the most help, gets the most help, and to guarantee that all creatures, and all of the materials of the known universe be preserved and "employed" in a constructive manner. When others use the term "faith-based initiative," ask them to explain, in detail, exactly what they mean, and what they do not mean.

Falsehood. <u>Use this word</u> to mean, "That, which is not true".

Familiar Mystery (The Most). <u>Use this term</u> to apply to the White persons of the known universe who participate in the practice of White Supremacy (Racism).

> **Reason:** A Non-White person (Victim of White Supremacy) may spend his or her entire existence in subjugation to, and in the presence of, a White person who is a White Supremacist (Racist) and never understand how that White person helps to make White Supremacy (Racism) "work".
>
> The entire System of White Supremacy (Racism) functions through the everyday actions of many White persons who seem to be "ordinary" in all that they say and do but, in effect, the many "small" things that they do (and not do) is the power that maintains The System of White Supremacy (Racism). Like the universe, White Supremacy

(Racism) can make its Victims (Non-White people) aware of its existence without making them understand how it "works."

One may feel heat or cold, but one may not understand exactly what it is, how it works, or what will be its ultimate effects. Many White people who practice White Supremacy (Racism) do so in a manner that is similar to the making of heat and cold. A Victim of White Supremacy (Non-White person) may "feel" the power of the White Supremacists (Racists) without understanding what is happening, or why.

During the existence of White Supremacy (Racism), a Non-White person can be "very close" to a White person who is a White Supremacist (Racist) without knowing and understanding the many ways that the person practices White Supremacy (Racism). The Non-White person may do many things "with" that White person, including working, playing, studying, laughing, crying, traveling, having sexual intercourse, etc., and still not understand how that White person practices White Supremacy (Racism) while doing these things. To many Victims of White Supremacy (Racism), the White Supremacists (Racists), both individually and collectively, are "the most familiar mystery".

Note: In the workings of White Supremacy (Racism) many "look," but few "see". "See" what? "See" what they're looking at.

Family. Use this word with caution. Use it, generally, to mean any two or more persons who, at all times, willfully and deliberately give as much constructive help to each other as often as they can in all areas of activity. When others use the word "family," ask for a detailed explanation that you can easily understand (if their use of the word "family" is somehow confusing to you).

During the existence of White Supremacy (Racism), practice thinking, speaking, and acting as if a "family," and/or your use of the term "family life," is a correct condition that you are (or should be) trying to produce through the process of ending White Supremacy (Racism), and replacing it with Justice (balance between people).

Reason: During the existence of The System of White Supremacy (Racism), the White Supremacists (Racistman and Racistwoman, collectively), do not allow Non-White people to function as "family," as "members" of a "family" and/or as an "extended family." As long as White Supremacy (Racism) exists, there can only be one family of people in the known universe. That family is the family of White Supremacists (Racists), or more specifically, "The White Family," and/or "The Racist Family".

In a social-material system dominated by White Supremacists (Racists), no family, no nation, and no tribe exists other than the family, nation, and/or tribe of White Supremacists (Racists). All other families, nations, and/or tribes are none other than individual persons who may or may not seem to be functioning as independent units of two or more persons. The truth is they are only individual persons. Persons who are Non-White are all subject to the Family of White Supremacists.

White persons are not subject to the Family of White Supremacists. Such White persons are either, themselves, White Supremacists, or they are individual persons who, at all times, function against the White Supremacists.

The only other categories of White people are those who function neither for White Supremacy, nor against it. These White people are considered to be, and function as, infantile or senile persons. It is not possible for any White person to be subject to White Supremacy. Each White person must function (as long as White Supremacy exists), as a White Supremacist, an anti-White Supremacist, a senile person, or an infantile person. As long as White Supremacy exists, the word family always means, in function, the "White Family", and/or the "Family of White Supremacists (White Supremacists, collectively)".

Note: Senile and infantile persons are persons who, because of physical or mental limitations, are generally incapable of doing harm to others.

Family Reunion. Do not use this term to apply to any Non-White persons who are directly or indirectly subject to The System of White Supremacy (Racism). Instead, use the terms "kin-assembly," "kin-contact," "kin-visit(s)," and/or "compensatory kin-visits."

> **Reason:** During the existence of White Supremacy (Racism), and according to Compensatory Counter-

Racist Logic, the White Supremacists (Racistmen and Racistwomen, collectively) do not allow the Non-White people of the known universe to function as so-called "families." The White Supremacists (Racists) force all Non-White persons to function only as direct or indirect so-called "Subject-units," "Victim-units," "Work-units," etc., in service to The System of White Supremacy (Racism).

Family Values. Do not use this term. When others use it, ask for a detailed explanation that you can easily understand.

> **Questions:** What, exactly, is a "family"? What, exactly, are "family values" during the existence of White Supremacy (Racism)? How can a Non-White person practice "family values" while, at the same time, serve and be subjugated by the System of White Supremacy (Racism)? While subject to White Supremacy (Racism), how can a Non-White person practice any "family values" that is not dominated by White Supremacists (Racistmen and Racistwomen, collectively) in all areas of activity?

Fanatic. Avoid using this word. When others use it, ask for a detailed explanation that you can easily understand. Ask questions.

> **Questions:** What, exactly, is a "fanatic"? Who, exactly, is a "fanatic"? When? About what? Is every person in the known universe a "fanatic" about something at some time? Is a White Supremacist (Racist) a "fanatic"? Is a person who is seriously opposed to White Supremacy (Racism), a "fanatic"? Is a person a "fanatic" if he or she is serious about producing justice (balance between people)?

Fascism/Fascist. Do not use these terms except to apply to White Supremacy (Racism), as it is usually practiced in its most direct, most obvious, and most violent form.

Father. Use this word with caution. During the existence of White Supremacy (Racism), use the title "father" to describe Non-White persons only because you must do so to avoid conflict in regards to "name-calling," and/or the promotion of discourtesy.

> **Reason:** As long as Non-White people are subject to Racistman and Racistwoman (White Supremacists, collectively), no Non-White person is allowed to function

as a "father," or "parent," to anybody or anything. Racistman and Racistwoman (White Supremacists, collectively) do not allow Non-White people to function as men. They force Non-White males to function as "boys". As people who function as dependent/subject "boys," Non-White males are only allowed to function as "play fathers." As long as White Supremacy (Racism) exists, Non-White persons are "allowed" to pretend that they are "fathers".

As long as White Supremacy (Racism) exists, all of the Non-White people of the known universe are subject to, and are the Victims of, Racistman and Racistwoman (White Supremacists, collectively). Under White Supremacy (Racism), the Non-White people of the known universe are subject to, and are the victims of, the powerful and abusive "Great White Father" and "Great White Mother" (White Supremacist males and females, collectively). The Great White Father and the Great White Mother function as "Race Father" and "Race Mother" (father and mother of Racism/White Supremacy). They dictate to Non-White people what to do, and not do, and they enforce what they dictate.

Some suggestions pertaining to the use of the words "father," "mother," "son," "daughter," etc., as applied to Non-White persons during the existence of White Supremacy (Racism) are as follows:

"father-less"	"sister-less"
"mother-less"	"brother-less"
"uncle-less"	"son-less"
"husband-less"	"niece-less"
"wife-less"	"daughter-less"

The use of the word "less" at the end of the words "father," "mother," etc., means that if a person is Non-White, and subject to White Supremacy (Racism), that person is functioning as less of a father, less of a mother, etc., than he or she should be, and is functioning as more of a Victim of Racefather and Racemother (White Supremacists, collectively). During the existence of White Supremacy (Racism), Racefather and Racemother (White Supremacists, collectively), practice master control over all Non-White people in all areas of activity, including Economics, Education, Entertainment, Labor, Law, Politics, Religion, Sex, and War/Counter-War.

Some examples of the use of words like "father-less," "mother-less," etc., for Counter-Racist purposes, are as follows:

1. "My father-less name is Ricardo Chinn."
2. "My mother-less resides at 1010 Hope Street."
3. "My cousin-less, Mary Jones, is in need of help."
4. "His son-less, is house-less."

Fatherless/Motherless. Use these words. Practice using them to apply to Non-White people (in general) during the existence of White Supremacy (Racism). When others use the words "fatherless" or "motherless," etc., ask for a detailed explanation that you can easily understand.

> **Questions:** How, exactly, can a person be "fatherless" or "motherless"? Does this mean that the "father" is less of a "father" than a "father"? Does this mean that the "mother" is less of a "mother" than a "mother"? What, exactly, are the "qualifications" for being a "father" or a "mother"? How many different types of "fathers" and "mothers" exist in the known universe?

> **Note:** During the existence of White Supremacy (Racism) those White persons of the known universe who have chosen to practice White Supremacy (Racism), by doing so, function as the "Race Fathers," and the "Race Mothers," of the Non-White people of the known universe.

Fear. Use this word to apply to the absence of knowledge and/or understanding of how to compensate for the lack of knowledge and/or understanding.

Fired. Use this word with caution - or not at all when talking about being removed from a "job".

> **Reason:** All of the people of the known universe are, at all times, "employed." They are, at all times, either "employed" in something that is constructive or "employed" in something that is non-constructive. When people are "fired" from one form of "employment," they are, in truth, transferred to another form of "employment."

> **Note:** Everything that exists is, at all times "employed" – including rocks, water, leaves, and newborn babies.

First Americans/Native Americans. Do not use these terms except to apply to persons who have guaranteed that no person is being mistreated, and who have guaranteed that the person who needs help the most, gets the most help in all Nine Areas of (People) Activity, including Economics, Education, Entertainment, Labor, Law, Politics, Religion, Sex, and War/Counter-War.

> **Reasons:** As long as White Supremacy (Racism) is the dominant socio-material force among the people of the known universe, there is not, nor can there be, any person, creature, or thing that can be correctly called "American." An "American" is, by correct definition, a person who guarantees that no person is mistreated, and guarantees that the person who needs help the most, gets the most help. An "American" is a person who does not mistreat anyone, nor does he or she allow anyone to be mistreated, at any time, in any place, in any area of activity.

An "American" does not practice Racism (White Supremacy). An "American" is not a Victim of, nor is he or she subject to, Racism (White Supremacy). An "American" is what an "American" does, and does not do. An "American" is not a person who seeks to do justice, but who actually does justice – at all times, in all places, in all areas of activity. There is no correct evidence that proves that an "American" exists. Therefore, the people of the known universe should be called what they are, based on the way that they function in regards to their interactions with each other. During the existence of White Supremacy (Racism) the people of the known universe interact with each other as:

1. White people, as White Supremacists (Racists).

2. White people, not as White Supremacists (not Racists).

3. Non-White people, as Victims of White Supremacy (Racism).

First World/Second World/Third World. Avoid using these terms. When others use these terms, ask for a detailed explanation that you can easily understand. What, exactly, is the "First World," "Second World," and "Third World"? What do these terms mean during the existence of The System of White Supremacy (Racism)?

Flag, Compensatory. Use this term to mean any activity that has a constructive result.

Notes: According to Compensatory Logic, any person, creature, or thing that engages in any activity that produces a constructive result is, at that exact time, a "compensatory flag." According to Compensatory Logic, and, when it is of constructive value to do so, it is correct to use a question mark ("?") as a so-called "Compensatory Universal Flag". A question mark ("?") may be used to indicate all of the things in the universe that are not known and understood that should be known and understood, by all who don't know and understand.

Follow. Use this word with caution. When others use the words "follow" or "follower," ask for a detailed explanation that you can easily understand.   Study the many different ways in which the words "follow" or "follower" is used. Ask many questions.

Questions: What does it mean to "follow" someone? Is agreeing with an idea that another person has, the same as "following" that person? If so, "following," how? If so, "following," where? Can a person "follow" a person in one "thing" and at the same time, not "follow" that person in another "thing"?

Follow the Logic. Use this term to apply to a suggestion to someone to think of ways to think, speak and/or act to get something done (problem-solving) in the best way that it could ever be done by any person, creature or force in existence - past or present.

Force. Use this word with caution. Study the many ways that others use the word "force." Ask questions.

Questions: What, exactly, is "force"? Is there such a thing as "direct force" and "indirect force"? What, exactly, is "hidden force"? Does it exist? How does it work if it does exist? Can one person truly "force" another person to do something, or does that other person "choose" to do that something? Is a person always "forced" to react to a "greater force"? Is White Supremacy (Racism) a "force"? If so, is it the strongest socio-material "force" that governs the interactions of the people of the known universe? Is education a "force"? Is sexual intercourse and "sexual play" a "force"? Is religion a "force"? If so, which religion is the greatest "religious force" among the people of the known universe? What, exactly, is the difference between a person being "forced" to do something, and that person "choosing" to do something?   Do people "choose" to submit to "force" or are they "forced" to submit to "force"? When? What "force"? How? Why?

Forces of Darkness/Forces of Light. Avoid using these terms and, whenever possible, do not use these terms at all. When others use them, ask for a detailed explanation that you can easily understand. Ask questions.

> **Questions:** Why do some people say that people are the "forces of darkness" and/or the "forces of light"? What people? How? Are "dark people" a "force of darkness" and, if so, what does that mean? Are White people a "force of light" and, if so, what does that mean? Is "darkness" a force that is correct or a force that is incorrect? Is "light" a force that is correct or a force that is incorrect? Instead of using the terms "forces of darkness," or "forces of light" as it pertains to the actions of people, use the terms "correct force," or "incorrect force."
>
> **Note:** White Supremacists (Racists) have often used the words "darkness" and/or "dark" to apply to people, places, creatures, and things in such a manner as to associate them with that which is dangerous, evil, unjust, and/or incorrect.

Foreign/Foreign-looking/Foreign-sounding. Use these terms with caution. When others use them, ask for a detailed explanation that you can easily understand. Also, study the ways that people may use the word "alien." During the existence of White Supremacy (Racism), practice using the word "foreigner(s)" or the word "alien" to apply mostly to those White persons, collectively, who participate in the practice of White Supremacy (Racism). Ask questions.

> **Questions:** Is The System of White Supremacy (Racism) "foreign" to The System of Justice (balance between people)? Does a White Supremacist (Racist) regard any person who is not White as "foreign" or as an "alien"? Are all people, at some time, "foreign-looking," or "foreign-sounding," or "foreign-acting" to each other?

Foreigner and/or Alien (Racial). Use these terms to mean:

(1) To a Racist - anyone who is a Victim of Racism is a "foreigner and/or alien" to a Racist.

(2) To a Victim of Racism (White Supremacy) - anyone who is a Racist or who practices White Supremacy.

(3) To a White Supremacist (Racist) - anyone who is classified as Non-White.

Fornication. Use this word to apply to any act of sexual intercourse and/or "sexual play" between persons who are deceitful, hypocritical, and/or otherwise untrustworthy in their relationship with each other.

Founding Fathers, The. Avoid using this term.

> **Reason:** It is best to simply say what an individual person did or did not do in regards to something that was done or said that is useful to remember. It is not necessary, and may be confusing to call that person by the title of, "Founding Father."

> **Questions:** What, exactly, is a "Founding Father"? Does the term mean "father" of the "foundation"? Who, or what is the "foundation" of anything? Who, or what, is the "foundation" of the known universe? Would that "foundation force" be the "founding father"? Does "founding" or "foundation" mean the "beginning"? Where or when, exactly, did anything "begin"? Who or what is the "foundation" of anything that had a "beginning"? How many "differing forces" and/or how many different people take part in the "start," or the making of the "foundation"? Where, exactly, is the "beginning" of the "beginning," and by what, or whom?

Fraud. Use this word to mean, "To do unjust or incorrect harm through the use of deceit." When others use the word "fraud," ask for a detailed explanation that you can easily understand.

> **Notes:** The most useful weapon employed by Racistman and Racistwoman (White Supremacists, collectively), is deception. Racists (White Supremacists) often use the "violence" of deceit to confuse and subjugate their Victims (Non-White people). "Fraud" (deceit), when used by a White Supremacist (Racist) against a Victim of Racism (Non-White person), is a form of indirect violence. It is correct to regard it as such.

Free/Freedom Fighter/Free Enterprise/Free Speech, etc. Avoid using any of these terms and any similar terms. When others use these or similar terms, ask for a detailed explanation that you can easily understand. Ask questions.

> **Questions:** What, exactly, is "free"? Who, exactly, is "free"? In the known universe, is any thing, any person, or any creature "free"? "Free" how? "Free" to do what?

Is a White Supremacist (Racist) "free" to make Non-White people subject to White Supremacy (Racism)? Is a Non-White person "free" not to be subject to White Supremacy (Racism)? Is a person who is subject to injustice (imbalance between people) "free"? Is a person "free" if he or she does not know and understand those things that he or she needs to know and understand?

Friend. Use this word with caution. Use the word "associate" to apply to any person (White or Non-White) with whom you interact with, in any manner, in any area of activity (Economics, Education, Entertainment, Labor, Law, Politics, Religion, Sex, and War/Counter-War). When others use this word, ask for a detailed explanation that you can easily understand. Ask questions.

> **Questions:** What, exactly, is a "friend"? What, exactly, are the qualifications for "friendship"? Is there any way to prove "friendship," other than by producing justice and correctness between and among all people, all creatures, and all things? During the existence of White Supremacy (Racism), how can a White person, "qualify" for "friendship" with a Non-White person without speaking and acting effectively to replace White Supremacy (Racism) with Justice (balance between people)? Can a White Supremacist (Racist) be a "friend" to any person who is not a White Supremacist (Racist), and/or to any person who is not White?

Functional. Use this word to mean, "Effective existence". (See "Existence").

Fuzzy Idea/Fuzzy Plan/Fuzzy Thinking. Do not use these terms. Instead, use the terms "incorrect idea," "confusing idea," "incorrect plan," or "confused thinking," etc.

> **Reason:** The word "fuzzy" has often been used by Racists (White Supremacists) to describe the hair of many of the Non-White people of the known universe, and to "make fun" of it. It could be that the White Supremacists (Racists) use the word "fuzzy" not only to apply to the appearance of the hair of Non-White people, but also to associate the word "fuzzy" with what they judge as the inability of Non-White people to "think clearly." Because of the ways that the White Supremacists (Racists) choose to use the word "fuzzy," it is non-constructive and incorrect to use this word to describe or apply to weak, unclear, confusing, and/or non-constructive ideas, plans, thoughts, etc.

G

Gal. <u>Do not use this word</u>. Instead, use the words "female," "girl," "lady" and/or "woman." Use the words "females," "women" and/or "ladies" to apply to female persons. Practice using the word "lady" to apply to a female person, regardless of her age, and/or her "classification," "status," etc.

> **Reason:** As long as White Supremacy (Racism) exists, both White females and Non-White females can be correctly called "ladies." However, during the existence of White Supremacy (Racism), Racistman and Racistwoman (White Supremacists, collectively), do not allow Non-White females to function as women. Racistman and Racistwoman (White Supremacists, collectively), require that only White females can function as women. During the existence of White Supremacy (Racism), Non-White females are forced to serve as victimized girls – not women. The word "gal" is sometimes regarded as "derogatory". For that reason, it should not be used.

> **Note:** During the existence of White Supremacy (Racism), Non-White people are not allowed to function as men and women – only as "boys" and "girls" who are subject to White men and women.

Gamble. <u>Use this word with caution</u>. When others use the word "gamble," ask for a detailed explanation that you can easily understand. Ask questions.

> **Questions:** Are you a person who has "gambled"? Which persons in the known universe have never taken a "chance" on the "unknown"? Who has not done something without being certain of what the result would be?

> **Notes:** An "investment" is not the same as a "gamble." An "investment" is based on a plan that is based on a logical study of known action and reaction, and based on a study of known cause and effect.

Game. <u>Use this word with caution</u>. When others use it, ask for a detailed explanation that you can easily understand. Ask questions. What, exactly, is a "game"? What, exactly, is not a "game"? Is there such a thing as "the game of love"? Is there such a thing as "the game of war"? What, exactly, is the difference between a so-called "game" and a "business"?

Gang/Gangster. Use these terms with caution. When others use these terms, ask for a detailed explanation that you can easily understand.

> **Questions:** What, exactly, is a "gang"? What, exactly, is the purpose of a "gang" that is different from the purpose of two or more people who interact with each other in a manner different from what is regarded as "gangsterism"? What, exactly, is the difference between a "gang" and a "nation"? Is a "gang member" a "gangster"? Is a member of a "Race" a "gangster"? If the purpose of a "Race" is to practice "Racism," is a person who is a "Race-member" a "gangster"? If White Supremacy is Racism, and Racism is a form of "gangsterism," is White Supremacy, therefore, the most powerful, and the most destructive form of "gangsterism" in the known universe?

> **Note:** When talking about "gangs" or "gangsters," instead of using the terms "Black gangs," "Latino gangs," "Asian gangs," etc., to apply to Non-White people "uniting" to mistreat each other, simply say, "numerous Non-White people uniting to mistreat each other in support of White Supremacy (Racism)."

Gay. Use this word with caution. When others use this word, ask for a detailed explanation that you can easily understand. Ask detailed questions.

> **Questions:** What, exactly, is "gay"? Is "being gay" the same as "being happy"? Is "being gay" the opposite of "being sad"? Why do some people who are "homosexual" seem to prefer being called "gay," rather than "anti-sexual" or "counter-sexual"? Why "gay"? Is the word "gay" used to mean anything? To mean everything? To mean nothing? Does the use of the word "gay" prove that any word can be "made" to mean anything that the user decides that it should mean?

Genocide. Use this word with caution. When others use it, ask for a detailed explanation that you can easily understand.

> **Questions:** What, exactly, is "genocide"? What, exactly, is not "genocide"? If "genocide" means to put great numbers of people to death, what is meant by a "great number"? How many people? All? Most? Is it necessary for all of the "deaths by genocide" to occur at the same place, at the same time? If so, what is meant by the

"same place"? What is meant by the "same time"? One day? Two days? Eighteen months? Forty years?

Do White Supremacists (Racists) intend to kill all of the Non-White people of the known universe, or do they only intend to kill "enough" Non-White people to make it easier to dominate the remainder? What, exactly, is "cultural genocide"? Is "culture" whatever a person is doing at the time that he or she is doing it? If so, is it "genocide" to "kill" a person's "culture" by forcing that person to stop doing whatever it is that he or she is doing? To commit "cultural genocide," is it necessary to "kill" the "culture" by killing the person who practices the "culture"?

Notes: During the existence of White Supremacy (Racism), the word "genocide" has often been used in a manner that produces confusion. When applied to the actions taken by White Supremacists (Racists) against their Victims (Non-White people), it is apparent that the White Supremacists (Racists) have not been willing to kill them all. It is also apparent that they have also chosen to kill great numbers of them and/or have them kill each other, and to continue this killing, apparently, endlessly. It is also apparent that, in order for the White Supremacists (Racists) to continue to kill Non-White people endlessly, there must be Non-White people available for killing.

According to Compensatory Logic, a White Supremacist (Racist) cannot continue to be a White Supremacist (Racist) unless he or she has Non-White people to dominate, use, abuse, and/or kill. Most of the White people who participate in the practice of White Supremacy (Racism) have shown that they do not desire to enact so-called "total dead body genocide" against their Victims (Non-White people).

They apparently prefer killing in large numbers. They enjoy bragging on themselves for being able to kill unlimited numbers of Non-White people for "fun," "glory" and "profit". They also enjoy bragging on themselves for being so-called "humane" enough to "allow" many Non-White people to continue to exist. The ultimate goal of the most sophisticated White Supremacist (Racist) is eternal White Supremacy for the sake of eternal White Supremacy (Racism).

Gentleman. <u>Use this word</u> to apply to any male person while he is doing or saying something that appears to be "pleasing," "harmless," "non-offending" or "non-violent," according to the judgment of at least one other person. When others use the word "gentleman," ask for a detailed explanation that you can easily understand.

Gentlemate. <u>Use this term</u> instead of the terms "boyfriend" or "husband" when referring to an "intimate" male [sexual] companion during the existence of White Supremacy (Racism).

Getting Ahead. <u>Avoid using this term</u>. When others speak of someone "getting ahead" of someone else, ask for a detailed explanation that you can easily understand. Ask questions.

> **Questions:** What, exactly, is "getting ahead"? "Getting ahead" of what? "Getting ahead" of whom? How? For what reason? What person in the known universe is "ahead" of what other person? In the absence of justice (balance between people), are any of the people of the known universe "ahead" of any other people in regards to the production of justice? In the absence of justice (balance between people), what people can truthfully claim to be "ahead" of any other people?

> **Notes:** During the existence of White Supremacy (Racism) and according to Compensatory Counter-Racist Logic, the basic and correct use of the term "getting ahead" means to think, speak, and act in such a manner as to result in replacing White Supremacy (Racism) with Justice (balance between people) in all areas of activity, including Economics, Education, Entertainment, Labor, Law, Politics, Religion, Sex, and War/Counter-War.

Getting the Kinks Out. <u>Do not use this term</u>. When others use terms like "getting the kinks out" or "kinky behavior" or "kinky sex," ask for a detailed explanation that you can easily understand.

> **Reason:** During the existence of White Supremacy (Racism), the word "kinky" has been used to apply to the hair of Non-White people, and has often been made to be something to ridicule and to make jokes about. The White Supremacists (Racists) have also promoted the use of the words "kink" or "kinky," to mean something unpleasant, "out of order," offensive, not "normal," or something that should not exist.

Ghetto (Racial). Use this word to apply to any Non-White person who is directly or indirectly restricted and/or dominated by White Supremacists (Racists) at any time in any place, in any area of activity.

Explanation:

In racial matters, ghetto is not a "place". Ghetto is any Non-White person who is subject to White Supremacy (Racism). In any socio-material condition dominated by White Supremacy, all Non-White people are unjustly restricted and/or dominated (ghettoized) on the basis of color, at all times, in all places, in all areas of activity.

Ghetto Glorification. Use this term to apply to any behavior by one or more Non-White person that helps to produce, promote, and/or praise, speech or action that is primitive, savage, silly, stupid, and/or in other ways destructive, that directly or indirectly support White Supremacy (Racism).

Examples: Non-White persons speaking and/or acting in support of one or more of the following:

- Being discourteous.

- Fighting (for purposes other than self-defense, necessary defense of others, and/or necessary defense of major constructive possessions/ property).

- Killing (for purposes other than self-defense, necessary defense of others, necessary defense of major constructive possessions/ property, and/or the enactment of Maximum Emergency Compensatory Action).

- "Name-calling".

- Promoting the destructive use of sound (producing "noise").

- Robbing and stealing.

- Showing contempt for Non-White females.

- "Showing-off" the ability to belittle Non-White people, based on what they have or have not acquired because of what the White Supremacists (Racists) have allowed them to acquire.

- "Showing-off" the ability to belittle Non-White people because Non-White people are not White people.

- Planning "newer styles" of doing harm to Non-White people.

- Singing songs, and/or using "slang" terms that glorify Non-White people doing harm to other Non-White people.

Ghettoized (Racial). <u>Use this word</u> to apply to the condition of a Non-White person who is directly or indirectly restricted, dominated, and/or subject to the power of White Supremacists (Racists) in any one or more areas of activity.

Ghetto Smart (Racial). <u>Use this term</u> to apply to: (1) the ability of a Non-White person to say and/or do things that may impress other Non-White persons, but is of little or no value in the production of justice or correctness; and/or (2) the ability of a Victim of Racism (Non-White person) to say or do many unjust, incorrect, silly, and/or stupid things, with great style or efficiency.

Gifted. <u>Use this word</u> to apply to every person, creature, or thing in the known universe. Study the ways that others use the word "gifted".

> **Reason:** According to Compensatory Logic, every person, creature, or thing in the known universe created by "The Creator" (All-Power) is a "gift" from The Creator. As a result of "receiving" the "gifts" of his or her mind, body and spirit from The Source of Creation, it is logical to think that these "gifts" were given to each person for the purpose of doing "The Assignment" of "problem-solving" and doing so in a manner that is the most constructive.

Gifted Student. <u>Use this term with caution.</u> When others use it, ask for a detailed explanation that you can easily understand. Are all students "gifted"? Are all persons "gifted"? Are all creatures "gifted"? Is existence, itself, a "gift"?

Girl. <u>Use this word with caution.</u> Instead, practice using the word "lady."

> **Reason:** White Supremacists (Racists) sometimes call Non-White females "girls" or "gals" with the intent of being insulting. Therefore, it is best and correct to use

the word "female" or the word "lady" to apply to all Non-White female persons. As long as White Supremacy (Racism) exists, all White female persons should be called "females," "ladies," and/or "women." Non-White female persons should not be called "women."

As long as White Supremacy (Racism) exists, it is not possible for Non-White females to function as "women." They are only allowed to function as "females" and/or as "ladies." A female who is a woman who functions as a partnership with a man and since a man, by definition, cannot be subject to racism, no female person, White or Non-White, can function as a true partnership with a Non-White male. This means that, as long as White Supremacy (Racism) exists, no Non-White female person is allowed to function in partnership with any person, White or Non-White, but only as a subject female, and/or subject "lady," in service to those White men and White women who practice the partnership of White Supremacy (Racism). During the existence of White Supremacy (Racism), Black males and Black females are only allowed to have a weak "arrangement" with each other – not a true "partnership."

Notes: During the existence of White Supremacy (Racism), all Non-White persons function as male and female "boys," "girls," "ladies" and/or "gentlemen" (gentle males), etc., but not as men, and not as women. During the existence of White Supremacy (Racism), only White males function as men, and only White females function as women.

Gloomy. Do not use this word. The words "gloom" and/or "gloomy" are often used to mean, not only "dark," but also unpleasant and/or possibly dangerous.

Notes: During the existence of White Supremacy (Racism), the words "dark," "darkened," "darkness," or "darky," have not only been used to apply to the physical appearance of "dark" (Non-White) people, but also to their behavior.

During the existence of White Supremacy (Racism) the word "dark" is made to be associated with word-expressions like "doom and gloom," "gloomy day," "gloomy mood," "gloomy forecast," "dark and gloomy," etc. Instead of the word "gloomy," use the term "non-constructive," but only if the situation you are describing is truly of non-constructive value.

God. Use this word according to the "requirements" of your chosen "religion," and/or according to your chosen socio-material beliefs. When others use the word "God," ask for a detailed explanation that you can easily understand. Do not argue with people about the meaning or non-meaning of the word "God." Some terms other than the term "God" that you may or may not choose to use, are "Allah," "All-Power," "Jehovah," "The Creator," "The Great Spirit," "The Supreme Master," "The Known, plus the Unknown," etc.

God and Country. Do not use this term. When others use terms like "God and country," "God's country," etc., ask for a detailed explanation that you can easily understand. Ask questions.

> **Questions:** Is a person's "God" and a person's "country," one and the same? Should a person's "God" and a person's "country," be one and the same? What is the reason for calling a place by the title, "God's country"? What "place" is not "God's country"? What is meant by "God"? What is meant by "country"? What "land" is not "God's land"? Where is it? What air? What water? What universe?

God-Fearing. Avoid using this term. Instead, practice using the term "God-serving." Also, do not confuse the word "God" with the many ways that people sometimes use the word "Lord."

> **Reason:** Many White persons who regard themselves as "royalty" and who regard themselves as being "without fault," often call themselves by the title of "Lord." Also, according to Compensatory Logic, it is probably better for a person to do what he or she thinks should be done, not because he or she has "fear of God," but because he or she desires to do what God "wants done".

Good. Avoid using this word, particularly when talking about the behavior of any of the people of the known universe. Avoid describing any situation that involves people as being a "good" situation. Practice using the word "good" as a "greeting," such as wishing a person "good morning," or "good evening," or "good day," etc. When describing the behavior of people, practice describing that behavior as being either "correct" or "incorrect" – not as "good," or "bad." Study the many ways that others choose to use the words "good" and "bad."

Reason: There is reason to believe that in a world that is dominated by the non-just and/or incorrect acts of people and other creatures, "goodness" does not exist. There is reason to believe that "goodness" can only exist when there is no injustice and no incorrectness (no imbalance between people, creatures, and things). Other words that can be used instead of the word "good" are words such as "pleasing," "pleasant," "fine," "nice," etc.

Suggestions:

1. Describe some White people as "nice."
2. Describe some Non-White people as "nice."
3. Describe no people as "good."

Questions: What, exactly, is a "good person"? Does a "good" person do anything that is non-just or non-correct? Do "good people" allow a situation to exist that is non-just or non-correct? Do "good" people think "good" thoughts, speak "good" words, and do "good" deeds, at all times, in all places, in all areas of activity? Do "good" people always tell the truth? Do "good" people use truth (that which is) in such a manner as to practice justice and correctness, at all times, in all areas of activity? How many "good people" now exist in the known universe, and what should be expected of them?

Good Black People/Good White People. Do not use these terms. When others use these terms, ask for a detailed explanation that you can easily understand. Ask questions.

Questions: What, exactly, is a "good" person – White or Non-White? What persons in the known universe are correctly qualified to say, truthfully, which persons are "good" and which persons are not "good"? Are White Supremacists (Racists) "good"? Are persons who allow themselves to be Victims of White Supremacists (Non-White persons) "good"? What, exactly, makes a person "good"? What, exactly, does a "good person" do in each area of activity?

Reason: In a known universe in which the people interact with each other unjustly and incorrectly, there is reason to believe that "good people" are yet to be produced. Therefore, until justice and correctness is established (in all areas of activity), it is best to describe people as "pleasant," "pleasing," "energetic," "nice," "productive," "attractive," "serious," etc., but not "good."

136

Notes: According to Compensatory Counter-Racist Logic, there is reason to believe that no person in the known and understood universe knows enough about "goodness" to describe any person, creature, etc., as being "good." There is reason to believe that only the Power that created people, creatures, etc., and placed them in the universe, can correctly judge what is "good," and what is not "good." Instead of using the term "good person," practice using terms like "nice person," "considerate person," "reasonable person," "helpful person," etc.

Good Education. <u>Do not use this term</u>. When others use this term, ask for a detailed explanation that you can easily understand. If a person has learned much, say that he or she has "learned much".

> **Reason:** There is reason to believe that no "educational process" has resulted in people being "good." Therefore, there is reason to believe that no "educational process" now in existence can correctly be called a "good education." Because of the dominance of White Supremacy (Racism) and other forms of non-justice (non-balance between people) among the people of the known universe, no person can "prove" that he or she has learned how to be "good." No person can, under such conditions, function as a "good person" or say that he or she is "educated."

> **Note:** According to Compensatory Logic, there is reason to believe that only people who are "good" can produce a "good education" - an "education" that results in people being the quality" of people that they <u>should be</u> as it pertains to every area of activity.

Good Faith. <u>Avoid using this term</u>. Instead, use the term "<u>correct intent</u>," and/or "correct intentions." Is "good faith" the <u>same</u> as "correct intent"? Study the ways that others use the term "good faith".

Good Hair. <u>Use this term with caution</u>. When others use this term, ask for a detailed explanation that you can easily understand. Ask questions.

> **Questions:** What, exactly, is "good hair"? What, exactly, is "no-good hair"? When, exactly does hair become "good" or "no-good" and why? What persons are qualified to judge? How, exactly, does "good hair" look? Is it "long"? Is it "short"? Is it "stiff"? Is it "limp"? Is it gray, or black,

or yellow, or white, or orange or pink? Is it "twisted"? If so, how "twisted"? Is it "spiraled"? If so, "spiraled" how? "Spiraled" how many times? Is it "straight" If so, "straight" how, or "straight" in how many "different directions"? Should so-called "good hair" be called "correct hair" or "healthy hair"?

Notes: During the existence of White Supremacy (Racism), people are taught that the "good hair," and/or that the "best hair" grows from the heads of White people. The existence of hair is either correct or non-correct. The existence of hair on people, creatures, etc., was produced and placed by "The Creator" of hair. Any argument against the existence of hair is an argument against "The Creator" of hair. Hair is <u>hair</u>. Hair was created to serve a correct purpose. Depending on conditions, there may be "too much" hair, or "not enough" hair to serve a constructive purpose. Hair should not be used as a reason to mistreat people – or to praise people.

Good Looking. <u>Do not use this term</u>. Use, instead the terms "nice looking," and/or "attractive" (when describing your reactions to the appearance of people).

Reason: As long as the people of the known universe do not practice justice (balance between people) and correctness (balance between people, creatures, things, etc.), at all times, in all areas of activity, it is incorrect to describe <u>any</u> person as "good," and/or as "good looking."

Good Speaker. <u>Do not use this term</u>. Instead, use the term, "constructive informer."

Reason: It is best and correct not to describe any person in the known universe as being "good." Among the people of the known universe, the examples of "goodness" are yet to be produced. Therefore, if a person reveals constructive information through the use of speech, it is best and correct to say that the person is a "constructive informer" – not a "speaker of goodness," and/or a "good speaker." It is also correct to use the terms "constructive speaker," "productive speaker," "truthful speaker," etc.

Good Time(s). <u>Do not use this term</u> to apply to any circumstances now in existence in the known universe. Instead use the terms "enjoyable time(s)," "pleasant time(s)," "nice time(s)," "thrilling time(s)," etc.

Reason: It is incorrect to describe a "time" as being "good" as long as non-justice and/or non-correctness exists any place in the known universe. During the existence of The System of White Supremacy (Racism), it is incorrect to say, or imply, that the thought, speech, and action of the people of the known universe has resulted in the establishment of "time" [deed(s)] that could correctly be described as "good."

Gook. <u>Do not use this word</u>. The word "gook" has often been used by White Supremacists (Racists) as a type of "name-calling" insult applied to Non-White people.

Notes: Other such words, usually intended to be insulting are "Chinaman," "chinks," "goonies," "japs," "rice niggers," "slopes," "yellow bastards," etc. It is correct to use the names and titles for each person that the person uses to name, describe, or identify him or herself.

Gossip. <u>Use this word</u> to apply to anything said about a person, with the intention of doing social or material harm to that person, without that person being immediately informed of what is being said, who is saying it, and why it is being said. This pertains particularly to things said about a person that are intended to criticize, belittle, and/or express contempt for that person.

Government. <u>Use this word</u> to apply to (1) one or more persons speaking and/or acting effectively to promote one or more objectives, in one or more areas of activity; and/or (2) a functional system of thought, speech, and action.

Government (Correct). <u>Use this term</u> to mean a system of thought, speech, and action by persons, animals, etc., that function in such a manner that has produced the revelation of truth and the practice of justice and correctness, at all times, in all areas of activity.

Government (Incorrect). <u>Use this term</u> to describe all of the "relationships" between all people, all creatures, all things, etc., during the existence of White Supremacy (Racism) and during the non-existence of justice, correctness, and peace between and among the people of the known universe. When others use the terms "incorrect government," "correct government" and/or "perfect government," ask for a detailed explanation that you can easily understand. Ask questions.

Questions: What, exactly, is "correct government"? What, exactly is "incorrect government"? What, exactly, is "perfect government"? Does a "correct government" exist? If so, where, and how does it function during the existence of The System of White Supremacy (Racism)? Can a "correct government" exist within and/or regardless of the existence of The System of White Supremacy (Racism)?

Use the term "Incorrect Government to apply to:

(1)   Thought, speech, and/or action by people that has not produced justice and correctness, in all places, in all areas of activity, including Economics, Education, Entertainment, Labor, Law, Politics, Religion, Sex, and War/Counter-War.

(2)   Any person, who dominates another person or persons by practicing falsehood, non-justice, and/or incorrectness in any one or more areas of activity.

(3)   White Supremacy (Racism).

Notes: According to Compensatory Counter-Racist Logic, "correct government" and The System of White Supremacy (Racism) do not, and cannot, exist in the same universe at the same time. Therefore, during the existence of White Supremacy (Racism) all so-called "government" by people is "incorrect" and/or "non-perfect" government. According to Compensatory Logic, "Correct Government" is yet to be produced by the people of the known universe.

Government Official. Use this term to apply to: (1) any person with maximum power over others in any one or more areas of activity; and (2) any person, while speaking, and/or acting effectively to promote one or more objectives in any one or more areas of activity.

Government (Racist). Use this term to apply to:

(1)   One or more persons classified as White, while speaking and/or acting effectively to promote White Supremacy (Racism).

(2)   The sum total of all thought, speech, and action by White persons who practice White Supremacy.

(3)   White Supremacists, collectively.

Government (Subversive). Use this term to apply to:

(1)   The sum total of all thought, speech, and action by a person that produces falsehood, non-justice, and incorrectness in any one or more areas of activity.

(2)   The sum total of all thought, speech, and action, by White persons who practice White Supremacy (Racism).

(3)   One or more persons speaking and/or acting effectively, to endanger the existence of any other person, while that person is speaking and/or acting to produce justice

(4)   One or more persons speaking and/or acting to prevent one or more persons from producing justice

(5)   White Supremacy (Racism).

Government (The). Use this term with caution. When others use it, ask for a detailed explanation that you can easily understand.

> **Reason:** During the existence of The System of White Supremacy (Racism), it is confusing to simply say "the government." As long as White Supremacy (Racism) is the dominant socio-material force among the people of the known universe, it is correct to avoid using the term "the government" unless the term is being used to mean "The Government of White Supremacy (Racism)."

> **Questions:** What, exactly is "the government"? What, exactly, is "a government"? How many people make a "government"? What, exactly, is "participation" in "government"? When? How? By whom? Does each and every individual person "participate" in a "government" every minute of every day?

> Does a "government" have "laws"? If so, and if an individual person is at anytime doing or saying something that "violates" one of the "laws" of a "government," can it truthfully be said that he or she is a "true participant" or a "true supporter" of that "government"? Is there really any such thing as "a government within a government"? If so, how can that be possible? Can a person be a White Supremacist (Racist), and at the same time, be a "supporter" or a "member" of any "government" other than the "government" of White Supremacy ("The White Nation" and/or "The Race Nation")? Is there any "government" any place in the known universe, established by people, which is more powerful than "The

Government of White Supremacy (Racism)"? If so, where is it? If so, what is the name of that "government"? If so, how does that "government" function?

Government (The Master). Use this term to apply to:

(1)   The sum total of all thought, speech, and action by those White persons who practice White Supremacy (Racism).

(2)   Government of, by, and for those persons who are Racists (White Supremacists).

(3)   White Supremacy and/or the only "functional" government among the people of the known universe.

Grandparent. Use this term with caution. When talking with others about "parents" and/or "parents" who are "great" or "grand" ("grandparents") ask questions. Ask questions and seek answers that you can easily understand. What, exactly, is a "parent"? What, exactly, is a "grandparent"? What, exactly, is a "Master Parent" and/or "Super-Parent"?

> **Notes:** During the existence of White Supremacy (Racism), it is best and correct to use the following terms to apply to those White people of the known universe who practice White Supremacy (Racism): "Master Parent(s)"/ "Master-Grandparent(s)"; and/or "Race Parent(s)"/"Race-Grandparent(s)".

Gray area. Do not use this term as a "slang" term that is said to mean the same as, "somewhere between black and white," or, "somewhere between this and that." If the term, "gray area" is used to express uncertainty, say, "I am not sure," rather than saying, "That's a gray area."

> **Reason:** During the existence of White Supremacy (Racism) it is best and correct not to talk about "color" in any manner that directly or indirectly may have the effect of promoting thought, speech, or action in support of White Supremacy (Racism).

Great. Use this word with caution. When others use this word, ask for a detailed explanation that you can easily understand. Ask questions. What, exactly, "makes" a person, creature, place, or thing, "great"? Is every person, creature, place, or thing, "great"? If so, "great" in what way – when, where, and according to whom? If not, why not? To minimize confusion, instead of the word "great," use "distinctive," "powerful," "prominent," "masterful," "unique," etc.

Great Spectator. Use this term to apply to Non-White people in general, including people sometimes referred to as Black, particularly people sometimes referred to as "Negro," or "Negroid" during the existence of White Supremacy (Racism).

> Explanation: The term "Great Spectator" generally means that Black people, and/or Negroes, are, basically, on-lookers. It means that Black people and/or Negroes generally do not do anything of great and/or significant value themselves by their own will but, for the most part, spend their time watching and waiting to see what White people will or will not do. The term also means that, under White Supremacy (Racism), no Non-White person does anything of significant value that is not started, supervised, and/or endorsed by White persons. The term means that under most conditions, Black people are best qualified to look and maybe to copy, but not to lead or start any activity, that is constructive.

Great White Father/Mother. Avoid using these terms. Instead choose to use terms such as "White Supremacists," "Racistman," "Racistwoman," "Racist(s)," "Master Parent(s)," "Race-Parent(s)," "Racist Parent(s)," etc.

> **Reason:** During the existence of White Supremacy (Racism), the use of the terms "Great White Father" and/or "Great White Mother," may or may not be regarded by some as terms that are less "business-like" when applied to serious thought, speech, or action intended to replace White Supremacy (Racism) with Justice (balance between people).

Greater Confinement. Use this term to mean:

(1)   "Jail," "Prison," etc.

(2)   Generally any "greater than usual" restriction of a Non-White person that is directly or indirectly caused and/or promoted by White Supremacists (Racists).

(3)   Any form of physical and/or mental confinement of Non-White persons "greater" than that which is usually imposed on them by the very existence of White Supremacy (Racism) itself.

Greatest Insult, The. Use this term to apply to all acts of sexual intercourse, "sexual play," or anti-sexual intercourse ("homosexual" or "lesbian" activity) between a White person and a Non-White person, during the existence of White Supremacy (Racism).

> **Reason:** During the existence of White Supremacy (Racism) and according to Compensatory Counter-Racist Logic, there is no greater insult to, no greater act of direct Racist aggression, and no greater act of physical and mental victimization, that a White person can commit against a Non-White person, than an act of sexual intercourse, "sexual play," and/or so-called "homo-sex" (anti-sex), whether mutual, or non-mutual.

> **Notes:** The only way that a White person can engage in sexual intercourse and/or "sexual play" with a Non-White person without the Non-White person being insulted and victimized in every way, is for The System of White Supremacy (Racism) to have ended before the acts of sexual intercourse and/or "sexual play" occur. During the existence of White Supremacy (Racism), such acts are an insult to the production of Justice (balance between people).

Greatest War in History, The. Use this term to apply to all acts of destruction caused by or promoted by those White persons who practice White Supremacy (Racism), against the Non-White people of the known universe.

Grotesque. Use this word to apply mostly to the so-called "Black life-style" ("Black culture") as it pertains to the substantial behavior of many Non-White people while subject to The System of White Supremacy (Racism). Use it to apply to the speech and action of those Non-White people who have had the most contact with the most destructive influences of The White Supremacists (Racists).

The "grotesque" behavior of Non-White people that results from, and/or is promoted by, The System of White Supremacy (Racism), can be described as pitiful, primitive, silly, stupid, confused, tacky, trashy, terroristic and/or generally non-constructive. Another major expression of "grotesque" behavior is the tendency of a person to be serious about things that are silly, and silly about things that are serious.

Grown/Grown-Up. Use these terms with caution. When others say that someone is "grown" or is a "grown-up" person, ask them to explain, exactly, what they mean. Ask them to explain how, when, and where, does any Non-White person qualify for the title of "grown person" while he or she is subject to The System of White Supremacy (Racism). Ask many questions, and seek answers that you can easily understand. It may be best and correct to say that a person is "growing".

Questions: Who is "grown-up"? What, truthfully, is a "grown person"? "Grown" as compared with what? "Grown" as compared to whom? How "grown up" is "grown up"? Can a person be "grown up" and, at the same time, be subject to other persons who treat that person like a subject-child? Can a person be "grown up," and, at the same time, be dominated by persons who function as malicious masters of that person in all areas of activity? How can any Non-White person be a "grown person" (Universal Man or Universal Woman) while, at the same time, being forced to function as a subject to, and a Victim of, White Supremacists (Racistman and Racistwoman)?

Notes: In a known universe in which White Supremacists (Racists) make the major decisions about what the Non-White people are "allowed" to do or not do, no person can truthfully be called "grown" or "grown up." All of the people in the known universe are either "growing" or "not growing" into the type of people that people should be. People should be "perfect." Any person who is not "perfect," is not "grown" and/or "grown-up." Since no person currently existing in the known universe has proven that he or she is "perfect," it is incorrect to describe any existing person as "grown" or "grown up."

Guidelines. <u>Use this word with caution</u>. When others use this word, ask for a detailed explanation that you can easily understand. Ask questions.

Questions: What, exactly, is a "guideline"? Is a "guideline" the same as a "law"? If not, why are people who are sometimes accused of not following "guidelines" often treated as if they have violated a "law"? When, exactly, is a "guideline" a "law"? When, exactly is a "law" a "guideline"? Who is qualified to judge?

Notes: It is correct to be wary of words like "guidelines," "policies," "rules," "regulations," etc. Such words can sometimes be used in a manner that is dangerously confusing. Such words are sometimes unexpectedly used as if they mean the same as "law(s)." A person may or may not be punished for not following a "guideline"; but if a "guideline" is used as a "law," a person may sometimes be punished for not following that "guideline" "rule," "regulation," general practice," etc. When confusion results, people are often mistreated. Many of the people who use such terms, use them to confuse and mistreat other people.

Guilt/Guilty. Use these words with caution. When others use the words "guilt," "guilty" or "not guilty," ask for a detailed explanation that you can easily understand. Ask questions.

> **Questions:** Which persons in the known universe are "guilty" or "not guilty" of tolerating injustice? Are Non-White people "guilty" of allowing themselves to be subject to the System of White Supremacy (Racism)? Which White people are "guilty" of practicing White Supremacy (Racism), and which White people are "not guilty"? Are some "more guilty" than others? If so, which ones? If so, what persons are correctly qualified to judge which White persons are "most guilty" of practicing White Supremacy (Racism), and which White persons are "less guilty," or "not guilty." In judging "guilt" or "non-guilt," what persons are correctly qualified to take the necessary action to stop the White people who are "guilty" of practicing White Supremacy (Racism) from practicing White Supremacy (Racism)?

Guttersex. Use this word to apply to any act of sexual intercourse and/or "sexual play" that persons engage in for mutual pleasure, while at the same time, having no reason to believe that such acts help to promote the replacement of The System of White Supremacy (Racism) with The System of Justice (balance between people). "Guttersex" generally may or may not also be described as: "Bawdy-sex," "Carnal-sex," "Debauched-sex," "Deception-sex," "Disgusting-sex," "Erotic-sex," Ghoulish-sex," "Illegal-sex," etc.

H

Habitat. Use this term to apply to any specific place where much time and energy is spent.

> **Example**: Under White Supremacy, no Non-White person has a "home" - he or she only has a "habitat". White Supremacists do not permit their subjects to have and/or to function as a "home". In any socio-material system

dominated by White Supremacists, "homes" for Non-White people do not exist. (See, "Home").

Half-White. Do not use this term. Do not use terms that are similar to this term. Do not use terms like "part-White," "dark-White," "off-White," "part-Indian," "part-Mexican," part-colored," "mulatto," etc. As long as White Supremacy (Racism) exists, practice limiting all "classifications" of people, in regards to color, to three - "White," "Non-White," and "White Supremacists (Racists)." Use the term "Non-White" to include any person(s) who are not "White" and not "classified" as "White."

> **Note:** During the existence of White Supremacy (Racism), the White Supremacists (Racists) produce or promote all "racial classifications" in a manner that best helps to maintain, expand, and/or refine the practice of White Supremacy (Racism).

Handicapped/Retarded. Use these terms with caution. When others use these terms or terms similar to these, ask for a detailed explanation that you can easily understand. Ask questions.

> **Questions:** What, exactly, is a "handicapped person"? What, exactly, is a "retarded person"? What, exactly, is a "defective" or "disabled" person? "Defective," how? "Retarded," how, and in regards to what? Is a White Supremacist (Racist) a "defective" person? Is a Victim of White Supremacy [Non-White person] a "handicapped" person? A mentally, physically, socially, and materially "retarded" and "handicapped" person? Can a person be "handicapped" and/or "retarded" in all areas of activity, all at the same time?

> **Notes:** During the existence of White Supremacy (Racism), it is correct to say that all Non-White persons are "handicapped" and "retarded" by Racistman and Racistwoman (White Supremacists, collectively). During the existence of White Supremacy (Racism), it is correct to say that the White Supremacists (Racists) willfully, deliberately and unjustly cause Non-White people to be "handicapped" and/or "retarded," in all areas of activity including Economics, Education, Entertainment, Labor, Law, Politics, Religion, Sex, and War/Counter-War.

Handsome. Use this word to apply to persons who uses his or her hands to do many things that are of major constructive value. Do not use the word "handsome" as a word to describe the way that a person looks in regards to his or her "appearance." When others use this word, ask for a detailed explanation that you can easily understand.

> **Note:** When talking about a person's "physical appearance," it is best and correct to use the word "pleasing" rather than words like "handsome," "beautiful," "lovely," etc.

Happy/Happiness. Use these words with caution. When others use these words, ask for a detailed explanation that you can easily understand. Ask questions.

> **Questions:** What, exactly, is "happiness"? Should a person be "happy" under conditions dominated by White Supremacy (Racism)? It is correct for all people to seek to be "happy" by thinking, speaking, and acting to replace White Supremacy (Racism) with Justice (balance between people)? Can "happiness" be guaranteed by people? Is it logical for a person to be "happy" at all times, in all circumstances? Does "happiness" happen only in moments? If "happiness" were "constant," would "happiness" <u>not</u> be "happiness," but functional "boredom"? Is it logical for a person to "pursue happiness," or is it logical for a person to think of "happiness" as something that "happens" when it "happens" – then stops – then "happens" again – then stops again?

Harass/Harassment. Use these words with caution. When others use words or word-terms like "harass," "harassment," "sexual harassment," "age harassment," etc., ask for a detailed explanation that you can easily understand.

> **Questions:** What, exactly, is "harassment"? When, exactly, is "harassment," not "harassment"? Is The System of White Supremacy (Racism) a system of the "harassment" of all of the Non-White people of the known universe?

> **Notes:** Study the many ways that people speak and act toward each other in all that they say and do. Study the things that could be called "harassment" (that many people do and say) in Economics, Education, Entertainment, Labor, Law, Politics, Religion, Sex, and War/Counter-War. Be wary of the ways that many who are opposed to justice (balance between people) choose to

use and define the word "harassment." It is very easy to accuse a person of "harassment" and, when considering the intention of those who are in a position to make the most powerful decisions, "harassment" can be very easy, or very difficult to prove.

Harmony. Use this word to apply to two or more bodies, "minds," things, etc. functioning in a continuous and constructive interaction with one another, and doing so in a manner that is pleasing to all involved.

Hate. Use this term to mean an aggressive submission to fear. Explanation: One "hates" what one fears.

Have/Having. Use these words to apply to any circumstance in which a person "has access" to a person, place or thing in a manner that results in physical or mental comfort (or discomfort), pleasure (or displeasure), and/or satisfaction (or dissatisfaction). Study the ways in which a person says that they "have" or do not "have" something.

> **Questions:** Can a person "have" something by only seeing it, feeling it, hearing it, tasting it, or smelling it – without the opinion of another person either "owning" or "possessing" what was seen, felt, heard, tasted or smelled? If a person is thinking about something (or someone) without (at the same time) seeing or touching that something (or someone), does that person "have" that something (or someone) only in his or her thoughts?

Haven't got a Chinaman's chance. Do not use this expression. The use of this expression may be regarded as a way of "poking fun" at the misfortune or the mistreatment of people who call themselves "Chinese." It is incorrect to "make fun" of the misfortune(s) or the mistreatment of any person or any creature.

Head of Household. Use this term with caution. When others use it, ask for a detailed explanation that you can easily understand. As long as White Supremacy (Racism) exists, never use the term "Black head of household." Instead, it is best and correct to use the term "Black spokesperson in the house."

> **Reason:** During the existence of White Supremacy (Racism), no Black (Non-White) person is the true "head" of any "household," nor are Non-White persons the "heads" of any other "organized" place, facility, etc.

During the existence of White Supremacy (Racism), Racistman and Racistwoman (White Supremacists, collectively), are the functional "heads" of Non-White people's "households."

Health/Healthy. Use these words with caution. When others use these words, ask for a detailed explanation that you can easily understand. Ask questions.

> **Questions:** Who can say, truthfully, what a "healthy person" is? In a known universe dominated by injustice and incorrectness, can it be truthfully said that any person is "healthy"? If so, "healthy," how? Mentally? Physically? Socially? Can a person be "healthy" without being "healthy" in all areas of his or her existence? Can a person be "healthy" and, at the same time, "behave" incorrectly? Can a person be "healthy" and, at the same time, practice Racism (White Supremacy)? Can a person be "healthy" and, at the same time, be a Victim of Racism (Victim of White Supremacy)?

Health Hazard. Use this term to apply to all situations that are unjust and/or incorrect in any area of activity-existence. This includes "health hazards" caused and/or promoted by the practice of White Supremacy (Racism) among the people of the known universe. When others use this term, ask for a detailed explanation that you can easily understand. Ask questions about what "health-hazards" exist in the areas of Economics, Education, Entertainment, Labor, Law, Politics, Religion, Sex, and War/Counter-War.

> **Questions:** Is the existence of White Supremacy (Racism), a "hazard" to the mental "health" of the people of the known universe? Is every Victim of White Supremacy [Non-White person] qualified to say that White Supremacy (Racism) has proven to be a "health hazard"? If not, why not?

Heathen. Do not use this word. When others use it, ask for a detailed explanation that you can easily understand. Ask questions.

> **Questions:** What, exactly, is a so-called "heathen"? Who, exactly, is a "heathen"? Who, exactly, is not a "heathen"? Who, exactly, is qualified to say, truthfully, who is, and who is not, a "heathen"? Is a White Supremacist (Racist) a "heathen"? Are Victims of White Supremacy (Non-White persons) "heathens"? Are people

who tolerate injustice (imbalance between people), "heathens"?

Note: It is correct to avoid "name-calling." There is reason to believe that it is incorrect to call any person a "heathen" unless that person says that he or she is, a "heathen."

He likes Black Females – She likes Black Males/He likes White Women – She likes White Men. Do not use these terms, or similar terms. When others use these terms and/or similar terms, ask for a detailed explanation that you can easily understand. As long as White Supremacy (Racism) exists, instead of saying that people "like" each other, say that they are, "attracted to each other" and/or that they, "find comfort with each other."

> **Reason:** According to Compensatory Counter-Racist Logic, it is correct to believe that when people "like" each other and/or when they "love" each other, justice (balance between people) is the result. Since justice (balance between people) does not exist between and among the people of the known universe, there is no proof that people "like" each other, or "love" each other, and/or that they "like" or "love" themselves. In a socio-material system dominated by White Supremacists (Racists), people are "attracted" to each other and/or feel "comfortable" with each other for purposes that have not resulted in justice (balance between people).

> **Notes:** During the existence of White Supremacy (Racism), White people and Black people, are often sexually "attracted" to each other, and always for the incorrect reasons. As long as White Supremacy (Racism) is the dominant motivating force among the people of the known universe, sexual intercourse and/or "sexual play" between White people and Non-White people only serves to make The System of White Supremacy (Racism) stronger.

Sexual intercourse and/or "sexual play" between White persons and Non-White persons during the existence of White Supremacy (Racism) is dominated and controlled by the White Supremacists (Racists) and, as such, helps to make Non-White people into sexual and political "simpletons and misfits" (extremely weak-minded and silly persons) in regards to their understanding of White Supremacy, and its effects.

151

Heritage. Use this word to apply to anything that has a direct or indirect effect on what happens to a person, creature or thing. When others use this word, ask for a detailed explanation that you can easily understand.

> **Questions:** What, exactly, is any person's "heritage"? What, exactly, is not that person's "heritage"? Is a person's "heritage" everything that has ever happened in that person's "past"? If so, how much of that person's "past"? Does a person's "past" include everything that has ever happened before that person became a "part" of the known universe? What about the "unknown" universe?

> **Notes:** When speaking of your "heritage" as a Non-White person, say, "My heritage is everything that has ever happened before the beginning of time, and since the beginning of time; and/or, "My heritage is The Assignment of replacing The System of White Supremacy (Racism) with the System of Justice (balance between people)".

Hero/Heroine. Use these words to apply to only those persons, spirits, creatures, things, etc., that have actually produced justice, correctness and peace between and among all people, spirits, creatures, things, etc., throughout the known universe. Do not use the words "hero" or "heroine" to apply to or to describe any person, spirit, creature, thing, etc., who is only trying to produce justice, correctness, and/or "peace."

> **Reason:** According to Compensatory Logic, and in a known universe in which "peace" does not exist, no person, spirit, creature, or thing has proven to be qualified for the title of "hero" or "heroine." In the absence of "peace," "heroes" and "heroines" do not exist.

High/Low. Avoid using these words in reference to people. Instead of "higher-up" in reference to people, say "strong people," or "powerful people." Instead of saying "low-down" in reference to people, say "weaker people" or "power-less people."

> **Notes:** During the existence of The System of White Supremacy (Racism), the most powerful people in the known universe are those people, collectively, who practice White Supremacy (Racism). The most powerless people in the known universe are those people, collectively, who are functionally "classified" as "Non-

White" (The Victims of The System of White Supremacy/ Racism).

High-Class Person. <u>Do not use this term</u>. When others use it, ask for a detailed explanation that you can easily understand. Ask, what exactly, is "high class"? What, exactly, is a "high-class" person? What, exactly, is "class"? What person is correctly qualified to say? Is any person correctly qualified to say? Is it correct not to say? What constructive purpose does the term "high class person" serve?

> **Notes:** During the existence of White Supremacy (Racism) and according to Compensatory Counter-Racist Logic, it is incorrect to use the terms "high-class," "middle-class," or "low class" to apply to any person(s). Instead, it is correct to use the terms "Powerful Class" (those who practice White Supremacy) and "Powerless Class" (those who do not or cannot practice White Supremacy, and/or those who are the Victims of White Supremacy).

High-Crime Area. <u>Do not use this term</u>. When others use the term, ask for a detailed explanation that you can easily understand.

> **Questions:** What, exactly, is a "crime"? What, exactly, is a "high-crime area"? What, exactly is the definition of an "area"? Who decides what an "area" is and what an "area" is not? What, exactly, makes an area, an "area"? How many factors make a "crime," a "high crime"? Is The System of White Supremacy (Racism) a "high crime"? If so, why? If not, why not? During the existence of White Supremacy (Racism), what crime against the people of the known universe is greater than the crime of White Supremacy (Racism)?

> **Suggestion:** Instead of using the term "high-crime area" (during the existence of White Supremacy), use "The Race-War Zone" and/or "The Race-Victim Zone" – which mean all places in the known universe wherein Non-White persons are directly or indirectly subject to The System of White Supremacy (Racism).

> **Notes:** The term "high-crime area" should not be used. This term is usually used in a manner that is "tricky," or very confusing. When used by White Supremacist (Racists), the term "high-crime area" is often used to apply to places where Non-White people are situated. It is important to know and understand that during the existence of White Supremacy (Racism), <u>all</u> people commit

"crimes" in some or all areas of activity, including Economics, Education, Entertainment, Labor, Law, Politics, Religion, Sex, and War/ Counter-War. It is important to know and understand that during the existence of White Supremacy (Racism), White Supremacy (Racism) itself, is, "The Crime of Crimes."

High Yellow. <u>Do not use this term</u>. When others use it, ask for a detailed explanation that you can easily understand. Is "yellow" a "color"? If so, how can a "color" be "high"? Can a "color" be "low"? If so, how?

> **Note:** During the existence of White Supremacy (Racism), the term "high yellow" is usually applied to the "shade" of color of persons, in such a manner as to support thought, speech, and action that supports White Supremacy (Racism).

Higher Education. <u>Do not use this term</u>. Instead, use the terms "education," "the education process," or "the learning process." Speak of the "education process" as the <u>process</u> of learning <u>all</u> things about <u>all</u> things, and/or the <u>process</u> of learning <u>all</u> things about <u>one</u> thing, and how all things relate to, react to and/or interact with, all things, people, creatures, etc., either directly or indirectly.

> **Questions:** What, exactly, is the purpose of a "higher education"? What exactly <u>is</u> a "higher education" that is different <u>in purpose</u>, from an "education" that is <u>not</u> "high"? Why would any person "divide" education into something that can be called "higher education" and "lower education"? Why would any person in the known universe invent a system of "higher education" and "lower education"? Are <u>all</u> of the people of the known universe "entitled" by the fact of their existence, to <u>know</u> <u>everything that they need to know</u> in order to produce, and/or maintain justice and correctness? Is the purpose of an "education" to produce comfort and prosperity for <u>all</u> persons? If not, why not?
>
> Is it the <u>duty</u> of the <u>smart</u> people of the known universe to teach and to give maximum constructive support to all of the people of the known universe who are not so "smart"? What, exactly, is an "education"? Should it be to teach <u>every</u> person <u>everything</u> that he or she "needs" to know? What persons are "correctly qualified" to say which <u>Non-White</u> persons should, or should not, be taught? During the existence of The System of White Supremacy (Racism), is it correct to teach <u>all</u> people what to do to

154

replace White Supremacy (Racism) with Justice (balance between people)?

Reason: "Education" is a <u>process</u>. There is no "high education" or "low education". There is no "complete education" now in existence among the people of the known universe. All learning is important. Everything that is learned is used for a purpose that is either correct or incorrect and/or either constructive or destructive. It is correct to regard all learning and all teaching as an ongoing and unlimited process – one that <u>never</u> stops as long as the ability to learn exists.

Higher-Ups/Upper Class. <u>Do not use these words</u> to apply to any person in the known universe. Instead, use the words "White Supremacists (Racists)," "Racistman and Racistwoman," "The Powerful People" and/or "The Powerful Class". These terms are all White Supremacists, collectively. (<u>See</u>, "High-Class Person").

Historian. <u>Use this term</u> to apply to persons who know about <u>something</u> that has happened, and who are able to inform others of that something. "Master Historians" are persons who know and understand <u>everything</u> that has happened and who are able to inform others of everything that has happened.

Holiday. <u>Use this word with caution</u>. When others use it, ask for a detailed explanation that you can easily understand. What, exactly, is a "holiday"? What, exactly, is the purpose of a "holiday"? Does "holiday" mean "holy day"? Does it mean a "day" that is "whole"? Are some days not "holy," or "whole"? Who is correctly qualified to say what is, and what is not, a "holiday"? Is any day of less "value" than any other day? If so, why? According to whom? (<u>See</u>, "Holy").

Holy. <u>Use this word with caution</u>. When others use it, ask for a detailed explanation that you can easily understand. What, exactly, does the word "holy" mean? Does the word "holy" mean the same thing to all people at all times in all places? How many things are "holy"? How many things are not "holy"? Are people "holy"? What people? When? If people are "holy," what, exactly, makes them so? "Holy" for what purpose? Is one person "holier" than another? If so, why? How? What is the test? Who is correctly qualified to judge?

Holy Land. <u>Avoid using this term</u>. When others use the term, ask for a detailed explanation that you can easily understand.

Questions: What "land" is "holy"? What "land" is not "holy"? What makes "land" "holy"? Is "land" "holy" at one time, and not at another? If some "land" is moved from "land" that is "holy," is the "land" that is moved, the same "holy" land? Is the air that passes over the "holy land," "holy air"? Is the water that is under "holy land," also "holy water"? If the water moves to another place, is the water still "holy water"? Is it correct to bury people in, or to grow food from, only that "land" which is "holy"? Who is correctly qualified to say what is, or what is not, "holy land"?

Holy Matrimony. Avoid using this term. When others use it, ask for a detailed explanation that you can easily understand. What, exactly, is "holy matrimony"? What, exactly, is not "holy matrimony"? What person is correctly qualified to judge that "matrimony" between persons is "holy," or not "holy"?

Holy War. Use this term to apply to: (1) The sum total of all thought, speech, and action against falsehood, non-justice, and incorrectness; and/or (2) The sum total of all thought, speech, and action to eliminate Racism (White Supremacy).

Home/Homeland. Use these words with caution. When others use them, ask for a detailed explanation that you can easily understand. What, exactly, is a "home"? What, exactly, is a "homeland"? What, exactly, makes a "home," a "home"? How much land is necessary to make "land" a "homeland"? What persons are correctly qualified to judge, and to decide, what will be the "home" and/or "homeland," for themselves, and/or others?

> **Notes:** During the existence of White Supremacy (Racism) and according to Compensatory Counter-Racist Logic, it is incorrect for any Non-White person to describe any situation that he or she is in, as "home," or "homeland." It is correct to describe such situations as "assigned-location," "housing," "Race-camp(s)," "Race-reserve," "residence," "Victim-camp" and/or "Victim-house".

> **Reason:** As long as a Non-White person is subject to White Supremacy (Racism) in any one or more areas of activity, he or she does not have a "home"; he or she can only have an "assigned house," "assigned semi-shelter," "assigned place of residence," etc. The house, semi-shelter, place of residence, etc., is "assigned" to that Non-White person by those who, directly or indirectly, have the power to decide who will or will not "reside," or be "housed," when, where, and under what conditions. Racistman and Racistwoman (White Supremacists, collectively) do not allow Non-White people to "reside,"

156

"camp," or place themselves in any situation that allows them the power to truthfully call that situation "home".

A house is not a "home." A so-called "country" is not a "home," nor is it a "homeland" to any Non-White person who is directly or indirectly subject to The System of White Supremacy (Racism). A house, no matter how "attractive," or "comfortable," can never be correctly called a "home" to a person who is required to think, speak, and act in subjugation to Racists (White Supremacists).

Notes: What a "home" is or is not may be argued by many, but, as long as White Supremacy (Racism) exits, it is incorrect for any Non-White person to regard a "home" as any "place," "condition," etc., that is directly or indirectly "assigned" to him or her by Racistman and/or Racistwoman (White Supremacists, collectively).

"Home" for a Non-White person can only be produced in the absence of White Supremacy (Racism). Therefore, as long as White Supremacy (Racism) exists, it is correct to avoid saying that any Non-White person has a "home," or a "homeland." Instead, it is correct to say that he or she has an "assigned location," "assigned space," "camp," "house," "location," "Race Camp," "Race Space," "Race Reserve," "reservation" and/or "residence".

Home-less. Use this word to apply to any Non-White person who is subject to the power of White Supremacists (Racists), either directly or indirectly, in any area of activity. Do not confuse the term "home-less" with the word "house-less." When others use the word "home-less," ask them if they mean "house-less." A person can be "homeless" without being "houseless".

> **Reason:** A person who has a "house," may not, necessarily, have a "home." During the existence of White Supremacy (Racism), many Non-White people may be "sheltered" by "houses," but none of them can truthfully say that they have a "home" (in the known universe). (See, "Home," "Homeland").

Home-Maker. Use this term with caution. Do not use it to apply to any Non-White person who is subject to the direct or indirect power of White Supremacists (Racists). When others use this term, ask for a detailed explanation that you can easily understand.

Reason: As long as White Supremacy (Racism) exists, no Non-White person is allowed to have a "home." At best, he or she is only allowed to have "shelter" in a "house," "hut," "apartment," "residence," "camp," etc. (See, "Home," "Homeland," "Home-less").

Home-Rule. Use this term with caution. When others use it, ask for a detailed explanation that you can easily understand.

Questions: What, exactly, is "home-rule"? What does the term mean – and to whom? What, exactly, is a "home"? Can a person have "home-rule," while at the same time be subject to the unjust power of others in any one or more of the major areas of activity (Economics, Education, Entertainment, Labor, Law, Politics, Religion, Sex, and War/Counter-War)?

Notes: According to Compensatory Counter-Racist Logic, no Non-White person can "rule" a "home," nor have a "home" to "rule," as long as he or she is directly or indirectly subject to White Supremacy (Racism). As long as White Supremacy (Racism) exists, all Non-White persons, with all of their material possessions, are "ruled" by Racistman and Racistwoman (White Supremacists, collectively).

Honorary White Person. Do not use this term. When others use it, ask for a detailed explanation that you can easily understand. Also ask them to explain what it does not mean.

Notes: According to Compensatory Counter-Racist Logic and during the existence of White Supremacy (Racism), there is no such person as an "honorary White person". In racial matters, there exist only three classifications of people in the known universe: White, Non-White, and White Supremacists (Racistman and Racistwoman).

The "Non-White" classification includes all "shades" of Black people ("Brown", "Tan", "Yellow", "Red"). The "White" classification includes all "White" people. The "White Supremacist (Racist)" classification includes all White people who are not only "White," but who also practice White Supremacy (Racism) - which is the mistreatment and the non-just subjugation of Non-White people (by White people) based on the "color" of people.

158

So-called "honorary White people" are, in truth, those Non-White people who are chosen by the White Supremacists (Racistmen and/or Racistwomen) to provide special services to The System of White Supremacy (Racism) in return for special material and/or "praise-worthy" benefits.

A slave does not stop being a slave because he or she sometimes rides the same horse as the Master.

Hostage. <u>Use this word</u>. During the existence of White Supremacy (Racism), use the word "hostage" mostly to apply to any Non-White person (Victim of White Supremacy).

> **Notes:** During the existence of White Supremacy (Racism) and according to Compensatory Counter-Racist Logic, all of the Non-White people of the known universe function as the direct or indirect "hostage" of those White persons who practice White Supremacy (Racism). It is correct to study all of the ways that Non-White people function as "hostages" in each area of activity, including Economics, Education, Entertainment, Labor, Law, Politics, Religion, Sex, and War/Counter-War.

House. <u>Use this word</u>. When using the word "house" or "housing" to apply to some form of body shelter for Non-White persons, do not use the words "house" or "housing" to mean the same as "home."

> **Reason:** During the existence of White Supremacy (Racism) and according to Compensatory Counter-Racist Logic, the Non-White people of the known universe are "allowed" to "occupy" houses, land, space, etc. White Supremacists (Racistman and Racistwoman) do not allow Non-White people to have a "home."

> **Note:** During the existence of White Supremacy (Racism), many Non-White persons may or may not occupy houses, but no Non-White person occupies a house that he or she can correctly call his or her "home." (<u>See</u>, "Home," and "Homeland").

House Arrest. <u>Use this term</u>. During the existence of White Supremacy (Racism) use it to apply to any "sheltered-restriction" of Non-White persons, by those White persons who practice White Supremacy (Racism). Also, study the ways that the word "arrest" is used.

Questions: When, exactly, is a person "under arrest"? Have all of the Non-White people of the known universe been placed "under arrest" by all of the White Supremacists (Racists)? What, exactly, is the difference between being "arrested," and being "restricted," "detained," "retained," "retarded," and/or "confined"? Is there such a thing as "house arrest"? Is there also such a thing as "neighborhood arrest"? "Section arrest"? "Area arrest"? What is the basic or functional difference between "arrest" and "restriction"? Is a person who is "restricted" to an area, also "arrested"? "Detained"? "Retained"?

Note: During the existence of White Supremacy (Racism), and according to Compensatory Counter-Racist Logic, all of the Non-White people of the known universe are directly or indirectly "arrested" by The System of White Supremacy (Racism) at all times, in all places, in all areas of activity.

House-Keeper. Use this term with caution. When others use this term, ask for a detailed explanation that you can easily understand. What, exactly, is a "house-keeper"? "House-husband"? "House-woman"? "House-person"? What, exactly, does a person do to "keep" a house? Is cleaning a house "keeping" a house? If so, why?

House-Wife. Do not use this term. When others use it, ask for a detailed explanation that you can easily understand. Ask questions. Is a "wife," the "wife" of a "house"?

> **Notes:** When talking about Non-White males and Non-White females who have pledged to have an "intimate personal," or "marital arrangement" with each other during the existence of White Supremacy (Racism), use the word "spouse" instead of "housewife," "househusband," "husband," "wife," etc.
>
> During the existence of White Supremacy (Racism), it is best and correct to also use the terms "C-Spouse" (Compensatory Spouse) and/or "V-Spouse" (Victim of White Supremacy Spouse) to apply to Non-White male and female persons who are "married" to each other. The term "V-Spouse" and/or "Victim Spouse" can also be used to correctly apply to any Non-White person who is "married" to a White person, during the existence of White Supremacy (Racism).

160

Human/Humane. Use these terms with caution. Do not use either of these terms to describe any person or any creature now in existence, any place in the known universe. When others use the terms "human," "human beings," "humane," and/or "humane beings" to apply to persons, ask for a detailed explanation that you can easily understand.

> **Notes:** In a known universe in which White Supremacy (Racism) and other forms of non-justice dominate what people do or not do, no person functions as a "human" and/or "humane" being. In a known universe in which the most powerful people (White Supremacists, collectively) do not allow justice to exist, "human" and/or "humane" people are yet to be produced.
>
> A "human," and/or "humane" being is a being that practices justice (balance between people) at all times, in all places, in all areas of activity, including Economics, Education, Entertainment, Labor, Law, Politics, Religion, Sex, and War/Counter-War.

Humanitarian. Use this word with caution. Study, carefully, the ways that others use this word and ask for a detailed explanation that you can easily understand. Does it mean practicing justice (balance between people)? If not, what does it mean? What should it mean?

Human Nature. Do not use this term. Instead, say what people do that is of constructive value, or that is of non-constructive (or destructive) value. Do not describe what any person does, or doesn't do as so-called "human nature," and/or as "natural humaneness." When others use this term, ask for a detailed explanation that you can easily understand. Ask questions.

> **Questions:** What, exactly, is so-called "human," or "humane" "nature"? When, exactly, is a person "human"? When, exactly, is a person "non-human," as directed by "non-nature"? What, exactly, is the so-called "nature" of a person who is "human" and/or "humane"?

Human Race. Do not use this term. A so-called "Human Race" is a non-existent "Race". When others use the term "Human Race," ask for a detailed explanation that you can easily understand.

> **Explanation**: According to Compensatory Counter-Racist Logic, there is no such thing as a "Human Race". The

words "human" and/or "humane" are directly contradictory to the word "Race". It is not possible for any "beings" to be "human" or "humane," and at the same time, be a "Race," and/or practice Racism. It is not possible for any person to be a "human" or "humane person", and at the same time, be a Racist or practice Racism. "Racism" is mistreatment of people, based on color.

A "human" or "humane" person is not a Racist, and a Racist is not a "human" or "humane" person. The objective of a human and/or humane person is not the same as the objective of a Racist, nor do they practice the same things for the same reasons. A person who is human and/or humane, knows and understands truth, and uses truth in such a manner as to produce justice, and correctness, at all times, in all places, in all areas of activity. A person who is a Racist practices falsehood, non-justice, and incorrectness, for the purpose of establishing, maintaining, expanding, and/or refining Racism (White Supremacy).

Human Rights. Avoid using this term. Instead, use the terms "justice," and/or "producing justice." Other expressions that can be used are, "using truth in such a manner as to produce justice and correctness," and/or, "guaranteeing that no person is mistreated, and guaranteeing that the person who needs help the most, gets the most help". When others use the term "human rights," ask them to explain, in detail, exactly what a "human right" is in regards to every area of activity.

> **Notes:** The term "human rights" is used to mean many different things to the people of the known universe. What is regarded as "human," or "humane" to one person, may or may not be regarded as meaning the same to another person.

I

Ignorant. Use this word with caution. According to Compensatory Logic, it is incorrect to call a person "ignorant." To call a person "ignorant" may be regarded as "name-calling," and may help to promote unnecessary or non-constructive conflict. Rather than say that a person is "ignorant," it is best and correct to say that the person apparently, "does not know" and/or, "does not understand." When others use this word, ask for a detailed explanation that you can easily understand. Be specific, but also be courteous in your discussions.

Questions: What, exactly, is an "ignorant person"? Are all people "ignorant" about something at some time? Is there any person in the known universe who "knows," and who understands everything that he or she should "know," and understand? What person knows and understands everything about economics, religion, and/or sex? What person or what creature, knows and understands everything about existence and non-existence? Is a person "ignorant" if he or she does not know everything about everything?

Notes: There is reason to believe that every person with a partially functioning brain knows and/or understands something about something. Therefore, it is incorrect to "praise" any person because of what he or she knows or understands. It is also incorrect to make "fun" of a person because he or she does not know or understand certain things at a particular time. All persons are "ignorant" about something that they should know. All persons are born "ignorant" and all persons will die "ignorant".

Every person knows something that some other person does not know. Some people learn some things slowly; others learn quickly. No person, however, is "better" than any other person because of what he or she knows. Sooner or later, each person can or will learn something of constructive value, and pass it on to others what he or she has learned.

The Law of Compensation operates in a manner that requires each person to learn from others, either directly or indirectly. This condition causes people to depend on one another, whether they want to or not. When people are forced by circumstances to depend on each other, they are less likely to kill or "disable" each other. In this regard, it is probably correct that no person knows "enough" about what he or she needs to know.

Too many people become arrogant toward others when they think they "know enough". It is incorrect for any person to be arrogant or aggressive towards others in order to "show-off" what he or she has learned for the purpose of mistreating others. Any person who uses what he or she has learned for purposes of mistreating

163

others, should be stopped by anyone who has the knowledge and understanding of how best to stop them. This is necessary in order to produce justice and correctness.

Illegal. Use this word with caution. Study the many ways that others use this word.

> **Reason:** During the existence of White Supremacy (Racism), many things that a Non-White person does, are regarded as "illegal" if what is done is directly, or indirectly, judged by the White Supremacists to be a "threat" to White Supremacy (Racism).

> **Note:** According to Compensatory Counter-Racist Logic, White Supremacy (Racism) is an "illegal," "illegitimate," incorrect, non-just, and subversive form of socio-material government.

Illegal Alien. Avoid using this term. Study the ways that others use the term. Ask questions.

> **Questions:** What, exactly, is an "alien"? What, exactly, is an "illegal alien"? What, exactly, is an "alien" that is "legal"? Are White Supremacists (Racists) "alien" to Non-White people? Are Non-White people, who are subject to White Supremacy (Racism), treated as if they are "illegal" and/or "alienated"? Are the White people who participate in the practice of White Supremacy (Racism) "illegally alienated" from promoting the production of justice (balance between people)?

Illegitimate. Use this word with caution. Study the ways that others use it.

> **Questions:** What is an "illegitimate child"? Is any child or any person "illegitimate"? During the existence of White Supremacy (Racism), are the Non-White people of the known universe the "illegitimate" children of the White Supremacists (Racists)? Is White Supremacy (Racism) an "illegitimate" form of government? Are the White Supremacists (Racistman and Racistwoman, collectively) "illegitimate" governors of the Non-White people of the known universe?

Note: According to Compensatory Logic, that which is "illegitimate," may be that which is "correct," and that which is "legitimate," may be that which is "incorrect."

I love America/I love Africa. Do not use these terms. When others use them, ask for a detailed explanation that you can easily understand. Ask questions.

> **Questions:** What do these terms mean? What, exactly, is "love"? What, exactly, is "America"? What, exactly, is "Africa" or "Asia"? What, exactly, does a person do that proves that he or she "loves" whatever it is that is "Africa," "Asia" or "America"?

> **Notes:** According to Compensatory Logic, it is best and correct to say, "I will use truth in such a manner as to produce justice, and in such a manner as to produce correctness." This is less confusing and more constructive than saying, "I love America," or "I love Africa," or "I love Asia".

Imitation of Life. Do not use this term the way that the term has often been used.

> **Reason:** During the existence of White Supremacy (Racism), the term "imitation of life" has often been used to describe the conduct of Non-White people who seek to copy the "complete mannerisms" and/or "socio-material customs" of the White Supremacists (Racists). The term "imitation of life" has often been used to help produce the thought that, what is called "life," is whatever it is that White people think, say and do.

Immaculate. Avoid using this word. When others use this word, ask for a detailed explanation that you can easily understand.

> **Notes:** The word "immaculate" has often been used to mean "clean," "pure," and/or "perfect." During the existence of White Supremacy (Racism), it has also been used to associate "cleanliness," "purity," and "perfection" with the word, "white." Indirectly, White Supremacists (Racists) have also used the word "immaculate" not only with "whiteness" in general, but also, with White people. The White Supremacists (Racists) have, directly or indirectly, often associated the words "dirt," "dirty," "dingy," "mud," "soiled," "sullied," "impure," "tarnished," "unclean," etc., with "dark," and/or Non-White people.

Immediate Power. Use this term to apply to the power to destroy, eliminate, and/or kill one or more persons, animals, etc. Most people in the known universe have this power.

Immoral. Avoid using this word. When others use the words "moral" or "immoral," ask for a detailed explanation that you can easily understand. Ask for a detailed explanation of what is "moral" and what is "immoral" in regards to every area of activity, including Economics, Education, Entertainment, Labor, Law, Politics, Religion, Sex, and War/Counter-War. Is something said or done that is supportive of White Supremacy (Racism), "immoral"?

> **Note:** According to Compensatory Counter-Racist Logic, and as long as White Supremacy (Racism) exists, the most powerful act of "immorality" is the practice of White Supremacy (Racism). (See, "Moral"/"Morality").

Important. Use this word with caution. Study the ways that others use the word. According to Compensatory Logic, every person, place, creature, and thing, both known and unknown, is "important." Practice using the word "important," to apply to anything associated with the practice of White Supremacy (Racism), and/or with anything associated with replacing White Supremacy (Racism) with Justice (balance between people).

Impossible. Use this word with caution. Instead, practice using the expression "There is reason to believe _____."

> **Example**: Instead of saying "It is impossible for people to exist without water or air," say, "There is reason to believe that people cannot exist without water or air."

> **Reason:** During the existence of the known universe, many things have happened that were said to be "impossible."

Incentive. Use this word with caution. Study the ways that others use the word. Study the circumstances in which some persons say that other persons do not have "incentive." What, exactly, causes a person to have "incentive"? Why, exactly, is it that a "slave" is often said to have a "lack of incentive"? Is there a "logical reason" for a Victim of White Supremacy (Non-White person) to have the "incentive" to be of service to The System of White Supremacy (Racism)?

In Common. Use this term with caution. Study the ways that others use the term. Ask questions.

Questions: Does "in common," mean the same as "Communism"? If a person has something "in common" with another person, is what they have "in common," therefore, "communistic"? If not, why not? How many "things" or activities must people have "in common" in order to correctly be called a "commune," or to be correctly regarded as "communistic"? What do Non-White people and White people have "in common"? Do the White people who practice White Supremacy (Racism) have anything "in common" with the White people who do not? If so, what? If not, what? Do the Victims of White Supremacy (Non-White people) have anything "in common" with the White Supremacists (Racists)? If they do, what do they have "in common"? Are the White people who have "in common" the practice of White Supremacy (Racism), also "communistic" because of this practice? Are they "Race Communists"? Are they "Race Capitalists"? Are they both?

Incorrect. <u>Use this word</u> to mean the same as the words "not correct." <u>Do not</u>, however, use this word to mean the same as the words "wrong," or "not right."

Reason: In a known universe in which the people do not practice justice (balance between people) or practice correctness (balance between people, creatures, things, etc.), it is reasonable to believe that the people of the known universe do not know and do not understand what is "right," and what is "wrong". Until the people of the known universe show that they know and understand what is "right" and what is "wrong," it is best that they use the terms that are more "mechanical" ("correct" and/or "incorrect") than "spiritual" ("right" and/or "wrong").

Incorrect Sexual Intercourse. <u>Use this term</u>. During the existence of White Supremacy (Racism), use it to mean any and all acts of sexual intercourse that directly or indirectly helps to produce or promote thought speech, and/or action <u>in support of</u> The System of White Supremacy (Racism), and/or helps to produce or promote thought, speech, and/or action <u>against</u> the production of justice (balance between people).

Indecent. <u>Use this word with caution</u>. When others use it, ask for a detailed explanation that you can easily understand. If you choose to use this word, use it to apply to the "arrangement" that White people and Non-White people have with each other during the existence of White Supremacy (Racism).

The System of White Supremacy (Racism) itself can also be correctly described as "indecent." Sexual intercourse and/or "sexual play" between a White person and a Non-White person (during the existence of White Supremacy) is "indecent," and "obscene," and amounts to Direct Racist Aggression by the White person against the Non-White person. Any White person who participates in the practice of White Supremacy (Racism) in any area of activity/existence can be correctly regarded as an "indecent" person. Any Non-White person who is subject to, and/or who cooperates with, any part of The System of White Supremacy (Racism) is also an "indecent" person.

> **Note:** During the existence of White Supremacy (Racism), and according to Compensatory Counter-Racist Logic, there is no way for a person to be "decent," and at the same time, either practice White Supremacy (Racism), or be a Victim of White Supremacy (Racism).

Independent/Independence. Use these words with caution. When others use these terms, ask for a detailed explanation that you can easily understand. Ask questions.

> **Questions:** Is any person, creature, or thing in the known universe truly "independent"? Is everything in the known universe "dependent" on something? Is "dependence" and "independence" a matter of "time," "degree" and "situation"? Does the "existence" of one thing depend on the "existence" of many things, creatures, conditions, etc., that is not the same as the thing itself? Is it possible that everything in the known universe is directly or indirectly "inter-dependent"? Is a hermit truly "independent"? Is any person, creature, or thing that has "needs," truly "independent"?

> **Note:** Words like "independent," "individual," "undivided," "self-supporting," etc., can be confusing and, therefore, should always be used with caution.

Indian. Use this word with caution. When others use the word "Indian," ask for a detailed explanation that you can easily understand. Ask questions.

> **Questions:** What, exactly, is an "Indian"? Are "Indians" the color "red" in appearance? If so, how "red" is "red"? If so, what does the "redness" mean? If so, what should it mean? Are some people who are called "Indians," people who prefer not to be called "Indians"? What, exactly, is

168

an "East Indian," "West Indian," "South Indian," and/or "North Indian"? Can an "Indian" be a White person? If so, how? Can an "Indian" be "White" and "Non-White" at the same time? If so, how? If so, according to whom? What, exactly, is the difference between an "Indian" and a "non-Indian"?

Note: During the existence of White Supremacy (Racism), and, according to Compensatory Counter-Racist Logic, the basic three "Counter-Racist Classifications" for the people of the known universe are: White people, Non-White people, and White Supremacists (Racists).

Indian Blood. Avoid using this term. When others use the term "Indian Blood," ask for a detailed explanation that you can easily understand. Ask people who call themselves "Indians" what the term means. If a "White" person says that he or she has "Indian Blood," ask him or her to explain what he or she means. (See, "Indian").

Questions: What, exactly, is "Indian Blood"? What, exactly, is an "Indian"? What, exactly, is a "non-Indian"? Is the blood of a person who is called an "Indian" redder than the "red" blood of a person who is not an "Indian"? If so, what does it mean? What should it mean – and why?

Indian-Giver. Do not use this term. When other use it, ask for a detailed explanation that you can easily understand.

Note: The term "Indian-Giver" has sometimes been used by White Supremacists (Racists) as a form of criticism of, or insult to, some Non-White people who are called "Indians."

Indian Sub-Continent. Do not use this term. When others use it, ask for a detailed explanation that you can easily understand.

Questions: What, exactly, is an "Indian"? What, exactly, is a "continent"? Why, exactly, is a "continent" called a "continent"? Which persons are correctly authorized to judge that any "place" is a "continent"? What, exactly, is a "sub-continent"? If people are called "Indians" and these "Indians" are said to reside in a "sub-continent," does that mean that the people are a "sub," and/or "subject" people? If so, "sub" and/or "subject" to whom? According to whom? For what purpose?

Notes: According to Compensatory Logic, the people of the known universe reside and/or travel wherever they reside and/or travel. To associate where people "reside" and/or travel with a "continent" or a "sub-continent," is confusing and may help to directly or indirectly support injustice (imbalance between people).

Indivisible. Use this word with caution. Study the ways that others use the word "indivisible," as well as the words "undivided" and "inseparable." Ask questions.

Questions: What, exactly, is "indivisible"? Is there anything in the known universe that cannot be "divided"? Is there anything in the known universe that is not "divided" in some way, form or fashion? Is there anything in the known universe that is not "united" and/or "connected" with something else in some way, form or fashion? Is each person in the known universe, somehow, at all times, "divided" from, and "united" with, all other persons, in some way, form, or fashion?

Ineffective Minority. Use this term to apply to all Non-White persons, collectively, during the existence of the System of White Supremacy (Racism).

Explanation: In a socio-material system dominated by White Supremacists (Racists), those White persons (collectively) who practice White Supremacy (Racism) are, in function, the "Effective Majority". The White Supremacists function as the major and/or majority power. Their power is effective, and the power of their subjects (the Non-White people), are, ineffective. Non-White people function as a comparatively, "Ineffective Minority". They are a "minor" power and they function as minors. They function in the manner of subject children. In comparison to the White Supremacists (the "Effective Majority"), Non-White people are ineffective in their attempts to speak and act as men and women.

Infant/Infantile Person (Racial). Use this term. During the existence of White Supremacy (Racism), use it mostly to apply to: (1) a person who is generally weak, both physically and mentally; and/or (2) a person who, because of physical or mental limitations, is generally incapable of doing willful and deliberate harm to others and, therefore, does not have the ability to be a Racist (White Supremacist).

Inferior. <u>Avoid using this word</u>. <u>Do not use this word to describe any person</u>. When others use this word to apply to a person, ask for a detailed explanation that you can easily understand.

> **Questions:** Are all people "inferior" to each other, at some time, in some way, form or "fashion"? Exactly what purpose does calling a person "inferior" serve? Is a person, at some time, in some way, form or fashion, "inferior" to him or herself? When a person is born, is he or she "inferior" to the way that he or she will be much later? If so, "inferior" how? If so, "inferior" in regards to what?

> **Notes:** The word "inferior" can be used to deceive and/or confuse. The word "inferior" has often been used to apply to people as a reason to mistreat them. How the word "inferior" is used, by whom, and under what conditions, should be studied carefully.

Infinite-Comparative Compensationalism. <u>Use this term</u> to apply to the process of producing those things of constructive value that are missing, but not known and/or not understood to be in existence.

> **Examples**: (1) Speaking and/or acting to produce justice without having experienced justice; (2) Attempting to establish a correct world without knowing and understanding what such a world would be; (3) Producing peace without having the knowledge and/or understanding of the energy used to do so.

Information. <u>Use this word</u> to apply to the revelation and/or presentation of truth or falsehood.

In God We Trust. <u>Use this term with caution</u>. When others use it, ask for a detailed explanation that you can easily understand. When others use the words "God" and "trust," ask for a detailed definition and explanation of what those words mean to that person. Ask for examples. Ask that person if, or how, he or she applies the statement, "In God We Trust" in regards to what he or she does and says in each area of the Nine Areas of (People) Activity.

> **Questions:** In seeking to replace White Supremacy (Racism) with Justice (balance between people), is it correct to "trust" only in "God"? If so, "trust" in "God" by doing what? If not, why not? If in doubt, "trust" in whom, or what, to do what?

171

Initiative. <u>Use this word with caution</u>. When others use it, ask for a detailed explanation that you can easily understand.

> **Questions:** What, exactly, is "initiative"? Is there such a thing as "correct initiative" or "incorrect initiative"? Is it correct for a Non-White person to show "initiative" in trying to replace White Supremacy (Racism) with Justice (balance between people)? Is it correct for all of the people of the known universe to use "initiative" in replacing falsehood, injustice, and incorrectness with peace?

Inner-City/Inner-City Crime. <u>Do not use these terms</u> or any terms similar to these terms. When others use these or similar terms, ask for a detailed explanation that you can easily understand.

> **Reason:** During the existence of White Supremacy (Racism), the term "inner-city" has often been used as a "Racist-Code Term" by White Supremacists (Racists). White Supremacists (Racists) have often used these and similar terms to apply to Non-White people and/or to the place(s) where Non-White people are "assigned" to inhabit by the White Supremacists (Racists).

> **Note:** During the existence of White Supremacy (Racism), it is best and correct to speak of the places where Non-White people are assigned as, "the places where Non-White people are assigned."

Innocent White Person. <u>Use this term</u> to apply <u>only</u> to a White person who, during the existence of White Supremacy (Racism), does not have the will, nor the physical, mental, or spiritual ability (in any way) to think, speak, and act in willful support of The System of White Supremacy (Racism) in any area of activity (Economics, Education, Entertainment, Labor, Law, Politics, Religion, Sex, and War/Counter-War). When others use this term, ask for a detailed explanation that you can easily understand.

Insane/Insanity. <u>Use these words</u> to apply to any behavior that is not supportive of the use of truth in a manner that results in the production of justice, correctness, and/or peace between and among all persons, creatures, things, etc., in the known universe. Study the many ways that others use the words "insane," "insanity," "crazy," "mentally unbalanced," "incompetent," etc. Ask questions.

> **Questions:** Is "insanity" the absence of "peace"? Is The System of White Supremacy (Racism) an "insane" system

of government? Are the White people who practice White Supremacy (Racism) "insane" because of their practice of White Supremacy (Racism), or do they practice White Supremacy (Racism) because they are "insane"? Is it correct to regard all Victims of White Supremacy (Non-White people) as "insane" because being "insane" is a requirement of The System of White Supremacy (Racism)?

Insane Person(s). Use this term to apply to the behavior(s) of those persons who are not supportive of the use of truth in a manner that results in the production of justice, correctness and/or peace between and among all persons, creatures, things, etc., in the known universe. When others use this term, ask for a detailed explanation that you can easily understand.

> **Notes:** During the existence of White Supremacy (Racism) and according to Compensatory Counter-Racist Logic, it is correct to regard both the White Supremacists (Racists) and their Victims (Non-White people) as persons who generally function as "insane persons." Avoid "name-calling." Avoid describing any person as "insane." Choose to ask a person if a specific act is either "sane" or "insane." Compare all answers and all explanations that you receive.

Insensitive Remark(s). Avoid using this term. Instead, use the terms "incorrect remark(s)" and/or, "discourteous remark(s)."

Insubordinate/Insubordination. Use these words with caution. Study, carefully, the ways that others use these words. Ask questions. Is it correct for a person to think, speak, and act in an "insubordinate" manner in regards to his or her interactions with a Racist Suspect (Suspected White Supremacist)? Is it correct for a person to be "insubordinate" to injustice?

> **Notes:** During the existence of White Supremacy (Racism), Racistman and Racistwoman (White Supremacists) often use the word "insubordinate" to apply to Non-White people. They sometimes say that a Non-White person is "guilty" of "insubordination," and then use the word "insubordination" as an excuse to inflict greater mistreatment upon that Non-White person.

Insurgent. Avoid using this word. When others use it, ask for a detailed explanation that you can easily understand. Ask questions. Is a person an "insurgent" when he or she takes direct action to stop someone from doing unjust harm to him or her? Is it correct for all

173

persons to enact an "insurgency" against The System of White Supremacy (Racism)? If not, why not?

Insurrection. Avoid using this word. Study the ways that others use this word. Compare the ways that others use the words "revolution," "riot," "rebellion," "uprising," "pacification," "police action," "mob action," "terrorism," etc. Study the contradictions in the ways that some of these words are used and in how they are defined in different circumstances. Is it correct to promote an "insurrection" against The System of White Supremacy (Racism)?

Intelligence/Counter-Intelligence. Use these terms with caution. When others speak of "intelligence and counter-intelligence," ask for a detailed explanation that you can easily understand. Ask questions.

> **Questions:** What, exactly is "intelligence"? What, exactly, is "counter-intelligence"? Is everything and everybody "intelligent"? "Intelligent," how? When? "Intelligent," as compared with what? Is "counter-intelligence" an "intelligence" that is designed to be greater than another "intelligence," and opposed to that other "intelligence"? Is "intelligence," the absence of "ignorance"? Are all people in the known universe, both "ignorant" and "intelligent" about many things at the same time?

> **Note:** It may be best and correct to avoid using terms like "intelligence versus counter-intelligence" and, instead, use terms like "having and using information constructively," or "having and using information non-constructively".

Intelligence Quotient or "IQ". Use these terms with caution. When others use them, ask for a detailed explanation that you can easily understand. Study all of the ways that the terms are used when associated with Non-White people during the existence of White Supremacy (Racism).

> **Note:** Among the people of the known universe, those White persons who practice White Supremacy (Racism) have proven that they have the necessary "intelligence" to dominate and subjugate the Non-White people of the known universe in all Nine Areas of (People) Activity (Economics, Education, Entertainment, Labor, Law, Politics, Religion, Sex, and War/Counter-War).

Intelligent Black Person. Use this term only to describe or identify a Black person who is not subject to White Supremacy (Racism).

> **Reason:** As long as White Supremacy (Racism) exists, every Non-White person in the known universe is directly or indirectly subject to White Supremacy (Racism). According to Compensatory Counter-Racist Logic, no person can be subject to White Supremacy (Racism) and, at the same time, be correctly identified as "intelligent."

Intelligent Fear (Racial). Use this term to apply to the fear that a Non-White person has of a White Supremacist (Racist) while that Non-White person is speaking and/or acting to replace The System of White Supremacy (Racism) with The System of Justice (balance between people). "Intelligent Fear" is a form of cautious and calculated courage.

International. Avoid using this word. When others use it, ask for a detailed explanation that you can easily understand. Ask questions.

> **Questions:** What, exactly, is a "nation"? Are people, a "nation"? If so, is it possible for a person to interact with other persons in a manner that makes that person an "international" person? If a person functions as an "international person," how can that person, at the same time, be a "national" person? If a person has a thought or an idea that is "international," does that make that person an "international person"?
>
> Is White Supremacy (Racism) an "international" concept, as well as an "international" practice? Is a White Supremacist (Racist) an "international person" who practices White Supremacy (Racism) "internationally"? Do the White Supremacists (Racists) function, collectively, as a "nation," "The White Nation," and/or as "The Internation of White Supremacists (Racists)"?
>
> **Notes:** During the existence of White Supremacy (Racism) and according to Compensatory Counter-Racist Logic, there exists only one functioning "nation" in the known universe. That one "nation" is "The White Nation" and/or "The Nation of White Supremacists" (White Supremacists, collectively). Any and all other "nations," or "internations," or, "international relationships," do not exist. People only pretend or imagine that they exist. The "White Nation" (White Supremacists, collectively) promotes the pretense in various forms of imaging. This

is done for the purposes of promoting greater control of the Non-White people of the known universe through "thought confusion".

Reasons: By the use of pretense and word and picture images, the White Supremacists (Racists) are better able to deceive their Victims (Non-White people) and, thereby, keeping them weak, "divided," and conquered. During the existence of White Supremacy (Racism), no Non-White people can function as a "nation," as "nations," or as "inter-nations." They only function as "collections" or as "arrangements" of people in either "close" or "distant" contact with one another.

International Thug(s). <u>Do not use this term</u>. When others use the term, ask for a detailed explanation that you can easily understand.

Reasons: To use the term "international thug(s)" is to engage in "name-calling." "Name-calling" is an incorrect activity that helps to maintain injustice (non-balance between people). During the existence of White Supremacy (Racism) and according to Compensatory Counter-Racist Logic, there exists no such thing as an "international" person, place, thing, or creature. There exists only one "nation" of people, and that is, "The White Nation" (White Supremacists, collectively). (<u>See</u>, "International").

Interracial. <u>Do not use this word</u>. Study the ways that others use the terms "interracial," "multi-racial," "semi-racial," etc. Instead of using terms like, "interracial," "racial diversity," "racial integration," etc., use the expression "Replace White Supremacy (Racism) with Justice (balance between people)".

Reason: The words "interracial," "multi-racial," "racial integration," "racial segregation," etc., are words that serve no purpose other than to promote greater confusion in the thought, speech, or action that should be designed to replace White Supremacy (Racism) with Justice (balance between people). According to Compensatory Counter-Racist Logic, and as long as White Supremacy (Racism) exists, the word "Race" applies to those persons, collectively, who practice White Supremacy (Racism).

The existence of White Supremacy (Racism) means that no other so-called "Races of people" exist anyplace in the known universe. Within The System of White Supremacy

(The Race Nation), the use of the words "interracial," "inter-race," "multi-race," etc., serves no purpose except to confuse those who seek to replace White Supremacy (Racism) with Justice (balance between people).

Notes: As long as White Supremacy (Racism) exists, there is and can only be one "Race." That "Race" is "The White Race" (The White Nation and/or White Supremacists, collectively). "Race" is Racism. The correct intent should be to replace Racism with Justice.

Interracial Marriage. Do not use this term.

Reason: According to Compensatory Counter-Racist Logic, and as long as White Supremacy (Racism) exists, no "Race" can exist, except "The White Race," and those White persons who have collectively and individually chosen to practice White Supremacy (Racism). Therefore, during the existence of White Supremacy (Racism), the terms "interracial," "interracial marriage," "interracial activity," etc., cannot be applied to any interactions between the people of the known universe. Such terms are confusing, and can only help to cause thought, speech, or action that results in support for the maintenance, expansion, and/or refinement of the practice of White Supremacy (Racism).

Example: A member of The White Race (The Nation of Racists/White Supremacists) cannot "marry" a person who is a "Non-Race" (non-existent "Race"). As long as White Supremacy (Racism) exists, a White person who is a "Race Member" (White Supremacist) cannot "marry" a person who is classified as "Non-White." During the existence of White Supremacy (Racism), all Non-White persons are subject to, and are Victims of, White Supremacy (Racism) - a White person can only pretend to "marry" a person who is "Non-White." Also, as long as White Supremacy (Racism) exists, it is not possible for a Race Person (a member of The White Race) to "marry" or to engage in any act of willful and deliberate sexual intercourse or "sexual play," with a Non-White person, without the White person, by doing so, functioning as a Racist (White Supremacist).

As long as White Supremacy (Racism) exists, a Non-White person cannot be "married," to any person. As long as White Supremacy (Racism) exists, any "interracial sex" (sexual intercourse and/or "sexual play") between a White

177

person and a Non-White person (if the White person participated willfully and deliberately) is an act of Direct Racist Aggression by the White person, against the Non-White person. It is incorrect to say that such acts are "interracial marriages" and/or acts of "interracial sex." All such acts are acts of Direct Racist Aggression against all of the Non-White people of the known universe.

Notes: "Race" is "Racism" and "Racism" and "Race" are one and the same. A person who is a member of a "Race" (based on "color" or "non-color") is a Racist. A Racist is a person who practices Racism. A person who practices Racism has one or more Victims (of mistreatment), who are subject to the Racism being practiced by the Racist. Persons who are Victims of Racism cannot be Victims of Racism and, at the same time, be members of a "Race." There is not, nor can there be, any such thing as an "interracial marriage."

During the existence of The System of White Supremacy, White Supremacy is Racism, and Racism is White Supremacy. The only functional form of Racism that exists in the known universe is White Supremacy. During the existence of White Supremacy, the only people who can function as Racists are those persons who are "recognized" as, and who function as, "White" people.

During the existence of White Supremacy, people who are "recognized" as, and who function as, "Non-White" people, do not and cannot function as "Race People" and/or as Racist(s). If White Supremacy (Racism) did not exist, and a White person married a Non-White person, the marriage could not be correctly called "interracial." It would be a marriage of a "White" person to a "Non-White" person. It would not be a "marriage" or an "attempted marriage" of a "Race Person" to a "Non-Race Person." It would not be a "marriage" of a Racist (White Supremacist) to a person who is a Victim of Racism (Non-White person). It is not possible for a "Race" person to "marry" a person who is a Victim of Racism (Non-White person). A "Race Person" is a Racist, and a Victim of a Racist is a Victim of a Racist.

There is no such thing as two or more "Races" of people, existing in the same universe at the same time. There is no such thing as two people being "members" of "two different Races," getting "married." In the known universe, only one "Race" of people can exist at any time. All other people are "Non-Race" people and/or "Victims of

Race" people. A Racist/Race Member cannot "marry" his or her Victim. He or she can only <u>pretend</u> to marry his or her Victim.

Racism (in the form of White Supremacy) is the <u>most powerful</u> motivating force in the interaction between the people of the known universe. This means that the persons who practice Racism (in the form of White Supremacy) are, at <u>all</u> times, dominant over those Non-White persons who are the Victims of, and the subjects to, the Racism being practiced. Racism does not exist without the practice of Racism being the <u>dominant factor</u> in all interactions between people in all areas of activity (Economics, Education, Entertainment, Labor, Law, Politics, Religion, Sex, and War/ Counter-War).

During the existence of White Supremacy (Racism), a "White" person who engages in willful and deliberate acts of sexual intercourse, and/or "sexual play" with/against a "<u>Non-White</u>" person is, by committing that act, a Racist (White Supremacist). Such acts are not acts of "interracial sex." They are acts of <u>Direct Racist Aggression</u> by the "White" person against the "<u>Non-White</u>" person. Such acts are not the production of "interracial marriage," they are acts of "child abuse". They are expressions of White Supremacy (Racism) against the Victims of White Supremacy [Non-White people] of the known universe. Such acts are not "Race-mixing." They are major expressions of contempt for the minds and bodies of Non-White people.

Intimidate/Intimidation. <u>Use these words</u> mostly to apply to some of the major ways that White Supremacists (Racists) guarantee the domination and general mistreatment of their Victims (Non-White people). When talking with others about the most powerful forms of "intimidation" (among the people of the known universe) say that The System of White Supremacy (Racism) is the most powerful.

Invade. <u>Avoid using this word</u>. Instead, use the term "war-making." When others use the terms "invade," or "invasion," ask them to explain, in detail, exactly what they mean, and ask them to do so in a manner that you can easily understand.

Questions: What, exactly, is an "invasion"? What, exactly, is <u>not</u> an "invasion"? Is an "invasion" the same as "war-making"? Is an "invasion" the same as "Counter-war-making"? Does an "invasion" include killing people? Is it correct to participate in an "invasion" if it means killing people? If so, when? If so, for what reason? Is the existence of White Supremacy (Racism) the same as an "invasion"? Are the Non-White people of the known universe, Victims and/or "prisoners" of an "invasion" by Racistman and Racistwoman (White Supremacists, collectively)?

J

Jap(s). Do not use this word as a means of identifying persons who call themselves "Japanese;" use the word "Japanese" instead. During the existence of White Supremacy (Racism), the word "Jap(s)" has often been used as an insult to the Non-White people who identify themselves as "Japanese." According to Compensatory Logic, it is correct to always call people by the names and/or titles that they ask to be called.

Jesus. Use this word with caution. For purposes of helping to replace White Supremacy (Racism) with Justice (balance between people), do not use any picture, engraving, statue, etc., as an "image" of the person named "Jesus" as told about in a "religious book" called, "The Bible." It is incorrect to use "images" of any kind when such "images" cause or promote non-just or non-correct results.

Jew. Use this word with caution. When others use it, ask for a detailed explanation that you can easily understand. Always ask these questions, and seek the answers from a person who says that he or she is a "Jew."

> **Questions:** What, exactly, is a "Jew"? What, exactly, is not a "Jew"? What, specifically, does a "Jew" do? What, specifically, does a "Jew" not do? Who or what has the power to decide what a "Jew" is, and what a "Jew" is not? What, exactly, are the correct things to say about what a "Jew" is, what a "Jew" does, and/or what a "Jew" does not do?

> **Reason:** During the existence of White Supremacy (Racism) and according to Compensatory Counter-Racist Logic, it is best and correct to minimize all unnecessary conflict with all persons, while seeking to replace White Supremacy (Racism) with Justice (balance between people).

> **Note:** When seeking information about what people do, what people do not do, and what people are trying to do, it is best and correct to learn as many details as possible

in regards to each and every area of activity including Economics, Education, Entertainment, Labor, Law, Politics, Religion, Sex, and War/ Counter-War.

Jewish. <u>Use this word with caution</u>. When others use the word "Jewish," ask for a detailed explanation that you can easily understand. If a person describes him or herself as "Jewish," ask what the word means, and what you can expect him or her to do (or not do) in regards to your interactions with him or her, in all areas of activity. Ask questions. What, exactly, is "Jewish"? What, exactly, is not "Jewish"?

Jewish Blood. <u>Do not use this term</u> except when asking a person who says that he or she has "Jewish Blood." Ask them "what is Jewish Blood"?

Jewish-looking. <u>Do not use this term</u>. Do not attempt to guess or explain what this term means unless you, yourself, know for certain that you are correctly qualified to say what is, and what is not, "Jewish looking." When others use these terms, ask for a detailed explanation that you can easily understand. Ask questions.

> **Questions:** What, exactly, is a "Jewish look"? What, exactly, is a "Hindu look? A "Christian look"? A Confucianist look"? A "Muslim look"? Does a person who is "White," and who says that he or she is "Jewish," look the same as a person who is "Black," and who also says that he or she is "Jewish"? What is the meaning of "look" or "looking"? As applies to what? Hair? Eyes? Nose? Lips? Color? Non-color? Height? Weight? Feet? Arms? Clothes?

Job. <u>Use this word with caution</u>. When others use this word, study the ways that they use it. Do not use the word "job" to necessarily mean the same as the word "duty." Use the word "duty" to generally apply to those things that a person must do in order to end White Supremacy (Racism), and/or in order to produce justice, correctness, and peace.

> **Note:** According to Compensatory Logic, a "job" is anything that a person does in order to accomplish a goal – be that goal correct, or incorrect. A "duty," however, only applies to what a person does that is correct, in order to accomplish a goal that is correct (never incorrect).

Join. Use this word with caution. Avoid using it when speaking or writing about yourself in regards to your interaction with another person or creature. When others use it, ask for a detailed explanation that you can easily understand. Ask questions.

> **Questions:** How, exactly, does a person "join" another person? When and how much interaction of what kind can be said, truthfully, to be the result of a "joining" of one person with another? How close is close? Are White people "joined" with each other? Are Non-White people "joined" with each other? During the existence of White Supremacy (Racism), are most White people "joined" with each other against Non-White people? If so, how? When? How much? In what way? Are White people and Non-White people "joined" to each other in some ways, and not in others?

Judge/Judgment. Use these words to apply to any effective action that results in a "final" decision being made that pertains to a subject or a situation. Always say that every person should seek to be a "judge" in guaranteeing that no person is mistreated, and in guaranteeing that the person who needs help the most (in any situation), gets the most help.

According to Compensatory Logic, every person who thinks, is a "judge" and, as such, makes "judgments."

Jungle. Do not use this word. Instead of the word "jungle" to apply to any place in the known universe, use words that correctly apply to the place. (**Examples**: "Woodlands," "waterlands," "forests," etc.).

> **Reason:** The word "jungle" has too often been used by White Supremacists (Racists) to apply to the places where Non-White people reside. The word is used for the basic purpose of being insulting.

Jurisdiction. Use this word with caution. When others use this word, ask for a detailed explanation that you can easily understand. Study the reasons why others use the word the way that they do. Ask questions.

> **Questions:** During the existence of White Supremacy (Racism), why are "jurisdictions" so-called "located" where they are? Do the White Supremacists (Racists) of the known universe have the greatest "jurisdiction" (decision-

making power) in matters pertaining to the Non-White people of the known universe?

Jury. Use this word with caution. Seek the answers to questions in regards to the many ways in which the word is used.

> **Questions:** What, exactly, is a "jury"? What, exactly, is not a "jury"? What person is the correct person to decide who should, and who will act, as a so-called "jury"? Are the persons who choose a "jury," also a "jury"? Are people who act as a "jury" also acting as "judges"? Do "juries" make "judgments"? During the existence of White Supremacy (Racism), what persons make the most powerful "judgments" about Non-White people? In making "judgments" about Non-White people, are the people who practice White Supremacy (Racism) more powerful than the people who do not practice White Supremacy (Racism)?

Just Doing My Job/Just Doing My Duty. Use these terms with caution. Never say that you are "just doing my duty" unless you are doing or saying something that is designed to best help replace White Supremacy (Racism) with Justice (balance between people), and/or unless you are doing or saying something according to the instructions of "The Creator of the (known and unknown) universe". When acting according to the direct or indirect dictates of White Supremacists (Racists), instead of saying "I'm just doing my job," say, "I'm doing what I was told to do," and when you say this, always make certain that you are telling the truth.

> **Notes:** According to Compensatory Logic, a "job" may be anything that a person chooses to do or is forced to do, be it something that is correct, or something that is incorrect. A "duty," however, is always something that is done that best helps to use truth (that which is), to produce justice (balance between people), and correctness (balance between people, creatures, things, etc.).
>
> It is correct for all people to understand the difference between a "job" and a "duty." During the existence of White Supremacy (Racism) and in "job situations," the Victims of White Supremacy (Non-White people) seldom do what they should do. They do what the White Supremacists (Racists) tell them to do, and/or what the White Supremacists (Racists) "approve" of them doing. Non-White people know that if they do things that Racistman and Racistwoman (White Supremacists, collectively) disapprove of, they will be punished.

It is important to know and understand that Racistman and Racistwoman (White Supremacists, collectively) are very deceitful. In their practice of deceit, they often say things to or about their Victims (Non-White people) that are contradictory. Racistman and Racistwoman (White Supremacists) do not believe in Justice (balance between people), nor do they practice Justice. They teach their Victims (Non-White people) to "believe in" justice, but they do not allow their Victims to <u>practice</u> justice.

Racistman and Racistwoman also speak and act as if they are the only people "qualified" to decide what justice is, and what justice is not. Therefore, since Non-White people are told some things that are correct, and told many things that are incorrect, it is correct for Non-White people to seek to find those things that are correct, try to do them, and when questioned, be able to truthfully say, "I am doing what I was told."

Justice. <u>Use this word</u> to mean balance between people, guaranteeing that no person is mistreated, and guaranteeing that the person who needs help the most, gets the most help. Apply the word "Justice" to a situation in which maximum consideration is given to factors associated with all of the Nine Major Areas of (People) Activity (Economics, Education, Entertainment, Labor, Law, Politics, Religion, Sex, and War/Counter-War). When others use the word "justice," ask for a detailed explanation that you can easily understand.

> **Reason:** According to Compensatory Logic, the word "justice" applies to all of the people of the known universe, and only when they interact correctly with each other at the same time, in all places and in all areas of activity. As such, "Justice" (balance between people) is a total condition. For example, the word "Justice" cannot be correctly used to apply to any situation that exists at the same time that White Supremacy (Racism) exists. It is not possible for "Justice" to exist, and for "injustice" to exist in the same universe, at the same time.

> "Laws" do not, necessarily, produce "Justice" (balance between people). A "law" is anything that is done. If what is done does not produce justice (balance between people), what is done cannot be correctly recognized as a so-called "Law of Justice." Such a "law" is an "anti-justice law." It is correct for all of the people of the known universe who say that they have the "correct intentions," to say that replacing White Supremacy

(Racism) with Justice (balance between people) is one of the major reasons for their existence, as people.

Notes: None of the "laws" that now exist among the people of the known universe have (as yet) resulted in the establishment of "Justice" (balance between people).

Among the people of the known universe, Justice (balance between people) does not exist. It is incorrect to go seeking to "find" justice in any place, and among any people, now existing in the known universe. Justice cannot be "found". It can only be <u>produced</u>. Justice, in order to exist, must be produced and maintained in <u>all</u> areas of activity. To try to produce Justice without involving <u>all</u> of the people in the known universe is to fail to produce Justice. The maintenance of Justice must pertain to all speech and all action by all people in all areas of activity.

"Laws" do not, necessarily, produce Justice. "Laws" (that which is done) either will produce justice, or they won't. It can be correctly said that <u>"laws" change, but justice remains the same</u>. Many "laws" have been produced. Many "laws" <u>are being</u> produced. <u>None</u> of the "laws" produced so far have resulted in a product that can correctly be called "Justice" (balance between people). "Justice" is, as of now, only an "idea," but it is a "great" and correct "idea." It is possible to make into <u>reality</u> every idea, if that idea is correct. The idea of Justice is correct.

Non-justice (non-balance between people) was produced, and is being maintained by people. Justice (balance between people) can be produced by people. It is logical to believe that <u>people</u> can produce justice because the "idea" of justice was "given" to people (presumably, by "The Creator" of people). There is reason to believe that people are not "given" an idea that is correct, and <u>needed</u>, unless those people are "given" the circumstances by which they can make that idea a <u>reality</u>.

There is reason to believe that a correct idea is "given" to people so that at the "correct time," the practical use of the idea becomes the basic "reason" for the very existence of those people, at that time. People who are "given" the "idea" of justice have a choice of making the idea a reality, or not making it a reality. There is reason to believe that once a person is "given" and has "received"

185

the idea of justice, he or she has the <u>duty</u> to think, speak, and act, to <u>produce</u> it. To do so, he or she must make a maximum effort to (1) <u>guarantee</u> that no person in the known universe is mistreated (in any area of activity), <u>and</u> (2) <u>guarantee</u> that in each and every situation, the person who <u>needs</u> help the most, <u>gets</u> the most constructive help.

Important: "Doing justice" does require the cooperation of persons who are "powerful enough" to do what is necessary to produce it. It is correct for all persons to seek the help of persons who are smarter and more powerful than themselves. To ask a person to "do justice" is to ask that person to contribute to the production of that "balance between people" that is necessary in order to achieve peace in the known universe. To ask a person to "do justice," is to ask that person to do what every person should do as long as non-justice (non-balance between people) exists.

Justice Department/Department of Justice. <u>Avoid using these terms</u>. According to Compensatory Logic, the correct use of the word "justice" means a condition of balance between people. A condition of balance between [all] people means guaranteeing that no person is mistreated, and guaranteeing that the person who needs help the most, gets the most help. When others talk about "justice" or talk about "departments" of justice, ask for a detailed explanation that you can easily understand.

Notes: According to Compensatory Logic, justice is "indivisible." Justice is "solid." Justice is "constant." Justice is a total and constructive relationship between all people. It is balance between all of the people of the known universe – not some of the people. It is not possible for justice to exist in one "part" of the known universe without, at the same time, existing in all "parts" of the known universe. It is not possible for one person to "receive justice," and another person to "receive injustice."

The production and maintenance of justice (balance between people), is the duty of every person in the known universe. The only way for a person to be correctly identified as a "department," "agent," "worker," and/or "patriot," in the production of justice, is for that person to have actually <u>produced</u> justice. Since justice (balance between people) does not now exist (any place in the known universe), no person has proven that he or she is correctly qualified to be identified as a "department," "agent," "worker," and/or "patriot," in the production of justice. In addition, when talking about the production of justice, it is important to say that it is impossible for Justice and White Supremacy (Racism) to exist, in the same universe, at the same time.

Justice for All. <u>Do not use this term</u>. Instead, use the word "justice" without adding the words "for all" or "for some," or "for most," etc.

> **Reason:** According to Compensatory Logic, the word "justice" means balance between people, and balance between people means guaranteeing that no person is mistreated, and guaranteeing that the person who needs help the most, gets the most [constructive] help. It is not necessary to use the expression "justice for all." To use this expression may cause a person to think that "justice" can exist without including <u>all</u> of the people (of the known universe). It is not possible to have justice for some people and, at the same time, have injustice for other people. If justice is to be produced, it must include <u>all</u> people. If a person is being mistreated and/or is not getting the help that is needed the most, it means that justice (balance between people) does not exist. (<u>See</u>, "Justice").

Justice is Blind. <u>Do not use this term</u>. Instead, use the term "justice means balance between people." "Justice" means, "guaranteeing that no person is mistreated and guaranteeing that the person who needs help the most, gets the most [constructive] help. When others use this expression, ask for a detailed explanation that you can easily understand. Ask questions.

> **Questions:** What or who, exactly, is "justice"? Is "justice" a person? Is "justice" a person who is blind? What, exactly, is the value in saying that "justice is blind"? Is "justice" a "condition" or a "situation"? If so, what, exactly, are the specific characteristics of that "condition" or "situation"?

> **Note:** According to Compensatory Logic, when talking about justice (balance between people) it is best and correct to say, "justice does not exist - it is the duty of every person to produce it."

Justifiable Homicide. Use this term with caution. Study the ways that others use the term. Ask questions.

> **Questions:** Is it "justifiable" to kill someone in self-defense? Is it "justifiable" to kill a person who is trying to rob you? Is war a reason to kill people? Is war "justifiable"? If so, according to whom? Who is "qualified" to "make war"? Who is "qualified" to make "Counter-War"? Is it "justifiable homicide" for a Victim of Racism (Non-White person) to kill a Racist (White Supremacist)? If so, why? If not, why not? During the existence of White Supremacy (Racism), which White persons are correctly qualified to decide what is or what is not, "justifiable homicide" in matters that involve Non-White people? Which White persons have proven that they are not White Supremacists (Racists)? Is it ever correct for a White Supremacist (Racist) to decide what is or what is not, "justifiable homicide"?

Justified. Use this word with caution. Study the ways that others use the word. Ask questions.

> **Questions:** What, exactly, is "justified"? What, exactly, is "justifiable"? According to whom? When? Where? Is the existence of White Supremacy (Racism) "justified"? Is it "justifiable"? During the existence of White Supremacy (Racism), what persons are correctly qualified to decide what is, and what is not, "justified" in any matter that directly or indirectly involves Non-White people?

K

Kin. Use this word with caution. When others use it, ask for a detailed explanation that you can easily understand.

> **Questions:** What, exactly, makes one person "kin" to another? Are all people "kin" to one another, in some way or another? Are all people not "kin" to one another in some way or another? Are people who are said to be "kin" to one another always "in agreement" with one another? Are White Supremacists (Racists) "kin" to one another? If so, how much "kin"? If so, "kin" in what ways? Are Victims of White Supremacy (Non-White people) "kin" to one another? If so, how much "kin"? If so, "kin" in what way? Can a person express "kinship" to a creature that is not a person? Can a person be "kin" to another person, and at the same time not function as "kin" to that

188

person? Is it possible to be "kin," and not express "kinship"? If so, what is the true "value" of such "kin," without "kinship"?

Note: During the existence of White Supremacy (Racism), correct "kinship" is that combination of thought, speech, and action that best helps people to replace White Supremacy (Racism) with Justice (balance between people).

Kinky/Kinky Hair/Kinky Sex. Do not use these words to apply to anything that a person is, has, says, or does. When others use the word "kinky" to apply to a person, ask for a detailed explanation that you can easily understand. Ask questions.

Questions: What, exactly, is a "kink" (when applied to a person)? Why is some hair called "kinky," but an elbow is not? Is it because someone said that an elbow is "natural," but that a "kink" in a person's hair is "not natural"? Is a "bend" the same as a "kink"? Is a "curl" superior to a "kink"? Is an "angle" the same as a "kink"?

During the existence of White Supremacy (Racism), why is the hair of many Non-White people described as "kinky," and incorrect sexual activity, also described as "kinky" ("kinky sex")? Do Non-White people have "kinky" hair? If they do, is it incorrect to have it? Incorrect, according to who? If so-called "kinky sex" is "incorrect sex," is not "kinky hair" "incorrect hair"? If so, according to whom? Is so-called "straight hair" better than "kinky" hair? If so, why? If so, according to whom? If so, what makes it "better"? Is not the term "kinky sex" a tricky way for White Supremacists (Racists) to say that "kinky hair," "kinky behavior," "kinky sex," and Non-White people, are "closely related"? Exactly what makes a sex act "kinky"? Can such "kinks" be "measured"? If so, what, exactly, would the "measurement" mean?

What about hair, as related to sex, and "kinks"? If a male person touches the hair of a female person, and one or both persons have "kinky" hair, can this act of touching be correctly called "kinky sex"? If "kinky hair," "kinky sex," and Non-White people so-called "go together," does this mean that "straight hair," and "straight sex," and White people also, "go together"? If so, what, exactly, is "straight sex"? Is there a "sex" that can be correctly called "crooked sex"?

Notes: It is best and correct to call hair, "correct hair" or "incorrect hair." It is best and correct to call "sex" male or female, or male "with" female. It is best and correct to call sexual intercourse, "sexual intercourse." It is best and correct to call sexual play, "sexual play." "Correct hair" is any hair that serves a correct purpose. Everything that each person does is either constructive, or non-constructive.

L

Labor/Laborer. <u>Use these words with caution</u>. When others talk about "labor" and/or "laborers," ask for definitions and for detailed explanations that you can easily understand. Ask questions.

> **Questions:** What, exactly is "labor"? What, exactly, is a "laborer"? Is "work," the same as "labor"? What kind of "work" is the same as "labor"? Is a "manager" the same as a "laborer"? Is a "laborer" the same as a "manager"? Does a "laborer" also "manage" his or her "labor"? Does a "manager" also "labor" at the task of "management"? Is a "manager," a "worker" or a "laborer"? Does a "manager" do any "work"? Does a "laborer" also "manage" to do "work"? Does every person do some "work"? Does every person do some form of "labor"? Does every person "manage" by doing something that can be correctly called "labor" and/or "work"?

> **Notes:** In order to promote the production of justice (balance between people), it is correct to talk, and/or to exchange views with others about every detail of what is, and what is not, "labor," a "laborer," "work," a "worker," and what it means to "manage," and/or to function as, a "manager."

Labor (Skilled/Unskilled). <u>Do not use these terms</u>. When others use these terms, ask for a detailed explanation that you can easily understand. Study the ways that the terms are sometimes used in a manner that results in confusion. Study the ways that both terms have been used in a manner that has helped to promote injustice (non-balance between people). Ask questions.

> **Questions:** Is every form of labor "skilled" labor? Is every form of labor "unskilled" labor? Is every form of labor both "skilled" and "unskilled"? How, exactly, can any labor that produces a constructive result be correctly

regarded as "unskilled"?   What, exactly, is a "skill"? What, exactly, is an "un-skill" or "non-skill"?

What, exactly, is "common labor"?   Does a "common laborer" have anything "in common" with an "uncommon laborer"?   If they do, does that mean that "common laborers," and "uncommon laborers" are "communistic"? Is a "common laborer," a "skilled laborer"? If "common labor" does not require "skill," how can the result of the "labor" be of any constructive value?   If "labor" accomplishes something of constructive value, how can it be correctly called "unskilled labor"? If a person who did it, and knew how to do what was done, was the person "skilled" in doing what was done?

Reason: All "labor" accomplishes something, if no more than revealing that there may be a better way of accomplishing that something.   Therefore, all "labor" is "skilled labor" and, at the same time, all "labor" is "unskilled labor."

Notes: White Supremacists (Racists) call labor either "skilled," or "unskilled," in order to say that the labor (work) of White people is of greater value ("skilled" labor) than the labor (work) of Non-White people ("unskilled" labor).

During the existence of White Supremacy (Racism), Racistman and Racistwoman (White Supremacists, collectively), speak and act to mistreat Non-White people, both individually and collectively by "classifying" many of them as so-called "laborers," "common laborers," "low-class laborers," "unskilled laborers," etc.

Labor Union. Use this term with caution. When others use it, ask for a detailed explanation that you can easily understand.   Ask questions.

Questions: What, exactly, is "labor"? What, exactly, is a "union"? What, exactly, is a "union of labor" for? What, exactly, is a "union of labor" against? Is the only correct purpose for a "union" of people is to produce justice? Does "justice" mean, "balance between people"? Does "balance between people" mean, guaranteeing that no person is mistreated, and guaranteeing that the person who needs help the most, gets the most [constructive] help?

If "labor" is "work," and two or more people are "working" to produce justice, does that mean that those people are a "union for justice" – a "justice union"? If true, is it best and correct to use the term "justice union" (people working to produce balance between people), rather than use the term "labor union"? What, exactly, is "labor"? Is "labor" the same as "work"? What, exactly, is "work"? Is "work" "united"? If so, "united" with what? "United" against what? "United" in order to accomplish what? Do all people "labor"? What people, if any, do not "labor"? What people's "labor" is not "united"? During the existence of White Supremacy (Racism), are the White Supremacists (Racistman and Racistwoman, collectively), the smartest, most powerful, and most "unionized" people in the known universe?

Note: The System of White Supremacy (Racism) is a "labor union" that has proven to be far more powerful than any of the so-called "unions of labor," of all of the Non-White people in all of the known universe.

Lackluster. <u>Do not use this word</u>. Instead, use the word "incorrect."

Reason: During the existence of White Supremacy (Racism), the word "lackluster" may help to promote the thought that things or persons that are "dark" in appearance, (because they are "dark"), are not of, "correct quality."

Lady. <u>Use this word</u> to apply to all White and Non-White female persons.

Reason: During the existence of White Supremacy (Racism), many female persons have been called by the names and/or titles of "bitch," "cow," "rat," "slut," "wench," etc. It is non-just and incorrect to use such names and/or titles to apply to <u>any</u> person. It is, at all times, correct to apply the title of "lady" to every female person. A female person is, at all times, a "lady," (a "nice lady," a "rude lady," a "tall lady," a "nervous lady," a "vulgar lady," etc.), but always a "lady." Terms like "the ugly lady," or, "my old lady" should not be used. When in doubt about the use of the word "lady" being used in an insulting manner, it is best and correct to simply say, "a lady" or, "the lady."

Ladymate. Use this term instead of the terms "girlfriend" or "wife" when referring to an "intimate" mutual female [sexual] companion during the existence of White Supremacy (Racism).

Land-Owner/Land Ownership. Avoid using these terms. If allowed to do so by the White Supremacists (Racists), use instead, the terms "land user(s)," "land possessor(s)," and/or "land possessorship." When others use the terms "land owner," and/or "land ownership," ask for a detailed explanation that you can easily understand.

> **Questions:** What, exactly, qualifies a person to "own" land, water, air, sunshine, day, night, morning, darkness, sky, etc.? What person(s) are correctly qualified to say who is, and who is not, qualified to "own" land? If a person is "owned" by another person, can it be truthfully said that the person who is "owned" is a "landowner"? Do White Supremacists (Racists) "own" their Victims (Non-White people)? If they do, what, exactly, do their Victims (Non-White people) "own"? Are "domination" and/or "subjugation" the same as "ownership"? Is "possessing," the same as "owning"?

> Does every person truly "own" anything that involves help, or support from, or cooperation with, any other person(s) in order for the thing "owned" to be of "productive value"? Which person(s) can correctly qualify for "ownership" of the clouds in the sky, and/or of the "sky" itself? One person? No person? Every person?

> Since White Supremacy (Racism) is non-just and incorrect, can a White Supremacist (Racist) correctly claim "ownership" of any land, any place in the known and unknown universe?

Land Reform. Avoid using this term. Instead, use terms like "the correct use of land." When others use this term, ask for a detailed explanation that you can easily understand.

> **Reason:** The term "land reform" is sometimes used in a manner that helps to promote confusion, and/or the mistreatment of people through deception. Terms like, "land reform," "land ownership," "land boundaries," and/or "eminent domain," should require an easily understood explanation.

> **Note:** During the existence of White Supremacy (Racism) Racistman and Racistwoman (White Supremacists,

collectively), dominate and control the use of land by dominating and controlling the Non-White people who "occupy" the land.

Law. Use this word with caution. Use the word "law" to mean anything that has an "effect." Use it to mean anything that is done by a force, a person, a creature, or a thing that results in an "effect." Use this word to mean, generally, anything that is done. When others use the word "law," study how they use the word. Ask questions.

> **Questions:** What, exactly, is a "law"? What, exactly, is not a "law"? Is a "written" law truly a "law" if it does not result in doing what the "written law" describes as "being done"? Is there truly a "law" against the practice of White Supremacy (Racism) if White Supremacy (Racism) is being practiced?

> **Notes:** Words that are called "laws" and that are said to be used to produce "justice" (balance between people), are not "laws" until they result in the establishment of justice. Written or spoken words only have the effect of being "word-law" if they result in the effect that they were intended to have, or not to have. Written or spoken words may be intended to produce justice (balance between people), or they may be intended to maintain injustice (non-balance between people). Words are often used to serve as tools for producing effects ("laws") on the thought, speech, and action of people (or creatures) in such a manner that the "law," the "effect" and the "result" are, at all times, one and the same.

According to Compensatory Counter-Racist Logic, the most powerful political and socio-material "laws" now in existence among the people of the known universe are the "laws" that, directly or indirectly, resulted in the existence of The System of White Supremacy (Racism). No "laws" (effects) produced by people have yet proven to be more powerful than the "laws" (effects) that maintain The System of White Supremacy (Racism).

"Laws" do not, necessarily, produce Justice. "Laws" (that which is done), either will produce Justice or they will not. It can be correctly said that "laws" change, but Justice remains the same. Many "laws" have been produced; many "laws" are being produced. None of the "laws" produced so far have resulted in a product that can be correctly called "Justice" (balance between people).

"Justice" is, as of now, only an "idea," but it is a "great" and correct "idea." It is possible to make into reality every idea, if that idea is correct. The idea of Justice is correct.

Non-justice (non-balance between people) was produced and is being maintained by people. Justice (balance between people) can also, be produced, by people. It is logical to believe that people can produce Justice because the "idea" of Justice was "given" to people (presumably, by "The Creator" of people). There is reason to believe that people are not "given" an idea that is correct, and needed, unless those people are "given" the circumstances by which they can make that idea a reality.

There is reason to believe that a correct idea is "given" to people so that, at the "correct time," the practical use of the idea becomes the basic "reason" for the very existence of those people, at that time. People who are "given" the "idea" of Justice have a choice of making the idea a reality, or not making it a reality. There is reason to believe that once a person is "given," and has "received" the idea of Justice, he or she has the duty to think, speak, and act to produce it. To do so, he or she must make a maximum effort to guarantee that no person in the known universe is mistreated (in any area of activity), and guarantee that in each and every situation, the person who needs help the most, gets the most constructive help.

Important: "Doing Justice" requires the cooperation of the persons who are "powerful enough" to do what is necessary to produce it. It is correct for all persons to seek the help of persons who are smarter and more powerful than themselves. To ask a person to "do Justice" is not a request for "personal" gain only. To ask a person to "do Justice" is to ask that person to contribute to the production of that "balance between people" that is necessary in order to achieve "peace" in the known universe. To ask a person to "do Justice" is to ask that person to do what every person should do as long as non-Justice (non-balance between people) exists.

Law-Abiding/Law-Abiding Citizen. Use these terms with caution. When others use these terms, ask for a detailed explanation that you can easily understand. Ask questions.

Questions: What, exactly, is a "law-abiding citizen"? What, exactly, is not a "law-abiding citizen"? When? "Abiding" by which laws? When? "Abiding" by how many "laws"? When? "Abiding" by some "laws"? All "laws"? At all times? How many "laws" exist? Is any person in the known universe [truly] "law-abiding"? Does a "law-abiding" person ever "violate" any "law"? If a "law-abiding" person "violates" one "law," how can he or she ever, truthfully, be called "law-abiding"? If a "law" is whatever it is that a person does, does that mean that every person is "law-abiding"?

Note: To minimize the promotion of false information and confusion, it is best and correct to avoid describing any person in the known universe as "law-abiding."

Law, against the. Use this term with caution. Study the ways that others use the term.

Questions: During the existence of White Supremacy (Racism) what makes a "law" among people a "law" among people? Are some "laws" stronger than other "laws"? Do some "laws" make other "laws" - "laws" that are non-existent? Can a "law" be a "law" if it does not function as a "law"? How can a "law" against White Supremacy (Racism) exist at the same time that White Supremacy exists? If White Supremacy (Racism) exists, can it be truthfully said that there exists a "law" against White Supremacy (Racism), and that White Supremacy (Racism) is, truthfully, "against the law"? What, exactly, is a "law"? Is a "law," in truth, anything that is done? Is it true that, during the existence of White Supremacy (Racism), White Supremacy (Racism) is "the law"?

Law and Order. Avoid using this term. Study the ways that others use the term. What, exactly, is "law and order" and what, exactly, is its purpose? Whose "law"? Whose "order"? In order to accomplish what? To avoid confusion, it is best and correct to be more specific by saying, "Use law in a manner that best promotes the production of justice (balance between people), and correctness (balance between people, creatures, things, etc.)".

Notes: The term "law and order" has often been used to mean a way of so-called "justifying" the forcing of people to "cooperate" with the maintenance of a non-just situation. Many people have done many incorrect and non-just things, and explained it all away by saying that they did those things for the purpose of maintaining "law and order." According to Compensatory Logic, a "law" is anything that is done.

Law (Compensatory Counter-Racist). Use this term to apply to a word or deed and/or a combination of words or deeds that have proven effective in ending The System of White Supremacy (Racism).

Law of Counter-Racist White Credibility. Use this term to apply to the requirement that a White person who is able to practice White Supremacy (Racism) be suspected of being a White Supremacist (Suspected Racist) unless he or she has proven to each and every Victim of White Supremacy (Non-White person) that he or she is not now, nor has ever been, a White Supremacist (Racist).

Law (Court of). Use this term with caution. When others use it, ask for a detailed explanation that you can easily understand.

> **Questions:** What, exactly, is a "court of law"? What, exactly, is a "court"? What, exactly is a "law"? Is a person a "court"? Is an act a "law"? Is a "law" anything that is "done"? Does each person, each day, "examine facts"? Does each person, each day, all day, make "judgments" during his or her entire existence in the known universe? If so, does that mean that each person functions as a "Court of Law"?

> **Note:** During the existence of The System of White Supremacy (Racism), those White persons in the known universe who practice White Supremacy (Racism), function, collectively, as the greatest and most powerful "lawyers," "law-makers," "law-breakers," and "Courts of Law" in the known universe.

Law (of the Jungle). Do not use this term.

> **Reason:** There is no logical or constructive reason for using this term. According to Compensatory Logic, there exist only two types of "laws" in the known universe - correct law, and incorrect law.

> **Notes:** Correct law is law (collective acts) that results in justice (balance between people) and correctness (balance between people, creatures, things, etc.). Incorrect law is law (collective acts) that results in non-justice (non-balance between people) and non-correctness (non-balance between people, creatures, things, etc.).

During the existence of White Supremacy (Racism), the White Supremacists (Racistman and Racistwoman), enjoy doing and saying things to belittle Non-White people. The use of the term "law of the jungle" is mostly used for the enjoyment of White Supremacists (Racists), because the term is often applied to the vicious, savage, and terrifying behavior of some of the people and creatures in areas in which "very dark people" inhabit. Since many of the Non-White people of the known universe have inhabited areas that are thick with many trees (forests, wood and water-lands, etc.), the White Supremacists (Racists) choose to say that these Non-White people are "savages" who practice the so-called "law of the jungle."

The White Supremacists (Racistman and Racistwoman, collectively), say, and/or imply, that the Non-White people who inhabit these lands of many trees, creatures, and sometimes much water, are, somehow, inferior. The people who inhabit such lands are sometimes belittled as being "more savage" than White people, and are not as so-called "civilized" as the White people who have produced "civilized law" (as opposed to the "law of the jungle").

Law (Taking into Your Own Hands). Do not use this term. Instead, describe what was done or not done, and by whom. Ask questions about the ways that others use the term.

> **Note:** According to Compensatory Logic, a "law" is anything that is done (while what is done, is done).

Law (Under Color Of). Avoid using this term. When others use it, ask for a detailed explanation that you can easily understand. What, exactly, is so-called "color of law"? Does "law" have a "color"? If so, what "color"? How, exactly, is a so-called "color" of law under? Should something (or someone) of "color" be "under"? Instead of using the term "under color of law," why not use the term "incorrect law," or "correct law"?

Law-Maker/Law-Making. Use these terms to apply to persons, creatures, things, etc., in any situation where something is being done that is effective.

Law Man/Law Woman. Avoid using these terms. Instead use the terms, "law enforcement officer," and/or "law enforcement person." Also, keep in mind that a law enforcement officer, or law enforcement person are not, necessarily, a "police officer." A "police officer" is a person who, at all times, speaks, and acts in a manner that always results in justice (balance between people) being produced and/or maintained. A "law enforcement officer," however, is a person who enforces a "law" in such a manner as to make that "law" effective. The "law" (act) that is "enforced," however, may or may not help to produce justice.

In a known universe in which justice (balance between people) does not exist, no person can truthfully claim to be, or be correctly regarded as, a "police officer." No "law" among the people of the known universe has, as yet, resulted in the establishment of justice (balance between people). Therefore, in a known universe in which justice does not exist, all persons (for better, or for worse) can only be correctly described as "law enforcement officers," "law enforcement persons," and/or as "agents" of "law(s)."

> **Notes:** According to Compensatory Counter-Racist Logic, it is impossible for a White Supremacist (Racist) to be a "police officer," or for a "police officer" to be a White Supremacist (Racist). The correct term for a "law-enforcement officer" who practices White Supremacy (Racism) is a "Suspected Race Soldier," "Suspected Racist," and/or "Suspected White Supremacist."

Lawyer. Use this word to apply to any person who speaks and/or acts in a manner that results in one or more persons being influenced to speak, and/or act in the manner intended by that person. (See, "Law," "Law-Maker" and "Law-Man").

Lazy. Use this word with caution. During the existence of White Supremacy (Racism) the word "lazy" has often been used by Racistman and Racistwoman (White Supremacists, collectively), to describe the so-called "nature" of most, or many, of the Non-White people of the known universe. What they say is sometimes true, but most of the time, is not true.

> **Notes:** According to Compensatory Counter-Racist Logic, any people who are subject to unjust "Masters" should be expected to be called "lazy" in doing anything that is of benefit to those Masters. With regard to The System of White Supremacy (Racism), it could be said that the White Supremacists (Racists) have proven that they are "lazy" about replacing The System of White Supremacy (Racism), with The System of Justice (balance between people). When any person is regarded as "lazy," it is correct to seek to know and understand why.

Leader [Racial]. Use this word with caution. Do not use it to describe, identify, and/or apply to any Non-White person who is subject to White Supremacy (Racism). During the existence of White Supremacy (Racism), practice using the word "leader" to describe, identify, and/or apply to all White persons who practice White Supremacy (Racism). During the existence of White Supremacy (Racism), practice using the word "spokesperson" (a person who speaks) to apply to any Non-White person who speaks with the intention of producing those actions and reactions that will result in White Supremacy (Racism) being replaced with Justice (balance between people).

> **Reason:** During the existence of White Supremacy (Racism), the White people who practice White Supremacy (Racism) are, directly and/or indirectly, the "leaders" and the functional "Masters" of all of the Non-White people in the known universe. The White Supremacists (Racists) "lead" and "master" all of the Non-White people, in all areas of all activity, including Economics, Education, Entertainment, Labor, Law, Politics, Religion, Sex, and War/Counter-War. Since this is true, it is only the White Supremacists (Racistman and Racistwoman, collectively), who are, truthfully (if unjustly) "qualified" for the title of "leader" in regards to the behavior of Non-White people.

> **Notes:** According to Compensatory Counter-Racist Logic, no person can be subject to White Supremacy (Racism), and be a "leader" of Non-White people at the same time. A person who is subject to White Supremacy (Racism) can only function as a "spokesperson" (a person who speaks) either for or against White Supremacy (Racism) – if he or she is "allowed" to speak. Within The System of White Supremacy (Racism), all of the "leaders" of Non-White people are White people.

Learning Date. Use this term to apply to the only type of non-sexual intercourse "date" (meeting of a Non-White male with a Non-White female) that is agreed upon for the purpose of each becoming constructively acquainted with each other, but only through the process of learning how to consistently do something (with each other) that is of an agreed-upon constructive purpose.

Examples of what to do on a "learning date":

1.   Exchange views about methods of producing justice and correctness (balance between people, creatures, things, etc.), and/or about "codifying" methods of replacing The System of

White Supremacy (Racism) with The System of Justice (balance between people), in all areas of activity.

2. Learn how to build, produce, repair, clean, and/or use something of constructive value to be used for a constructive purpose.

3. Learn as much as possible, about everything that can be known, about each other, before any act (first act) of sexual intercourse and/or "sexual play." Learn about each other by asking and answering many, many, questions, in great detail, with all secrets revealed, and with no information withheld. Do, however, avoid saying anything in a manner that promotes gossip or any other forms of unjust harm to self or others.

Left/Leftist/Left-Wing. Do not use these terms to describe any people, or persons, and/or to describe any "group" of people or persons. When others use these terms, ask them to explain, in exact detail, what they mean. Also, ask them to explain, in exact detail, what they mean when they use terms such as "right," "rightist," "right-wing," "right of center," "left of center," "center," etc.

Write or record the answers and explanations that such persons give to you. Study these answers and explanations. Look for contradictions. Look for similarities. Seek to detect any "answer" or "explanation" that seems to produce or promote confusion. Instead of using terms like "leftist," "rightist," etc., use terms that describe what people actually do (in every area of activity), and describe what is done, as being either "correct," or "incorrect."

Legal. Use this word with caution. Study very carefully the many, many, ways this word is used by others. Be aware of when, how, and where the word is used – and by whom. Study how the question of what is "legal," and what is not, is asked by some people, only when it is convenient or when it is to their advantage to do so.

> **Questions:** Is White Supremacy (Racism) "legal"? If White Supremacy (Racism) is not "legal," is White Supremacy (Racism) a "crime"? If White Supremacy (Racism) is a "crime," is a White person who practices White Supremacy (Racism), a "criminal"? Does White Supremacy (Racism) cause people to be unjustly killed? Are all of the White people who participate in The System of White Supremacy (Racism), also "legally" to blame for the deaths of Non-White people who are unjustly killed because of the existence of The System of White Supremacy (Racism)? Is it "legal" to kill the people

[White] who practice White Supremacy (Racism) when they do so in such a manner as to cause Non-White people to be killed, maimed, raped, dislocated, and/or in other ways, mistreated, and/or forced, trained, or enticed to mistreat each other?

Legal Assistance/Legal Assistant. Use these terms to mean "assistance" of any kind that is helpful in accomplishing something that is involved with "law," "law-making," "law interpretation," etc. That "assistance" may be no more than one person telling another person the date that something must be done, or must not be done. A "legal assistant" may be a person who informs a person about any "law," "law-making," or "law interpretation," etc.

According to Compensatory Logic, such information can be correctly called "legal assistance." The person who gives the information can be called - correctly, at that time, an "attorney" if only with regard to the "legal" information (or advice) that is presented at that time.

Legal-Mate. Use this term in place of the term "married [person]" when referring to yourself, and/or other Non-White person during the existence of White Supremacy (Racism).

Legal-Mated/Legally-Mated. Use these terms instead of the term "married" when referring to any two or more Non-White persons who are in a so-called "marital" or "marriage" situation during the existence of White Supremacy (Racism).

Liable/Liability. Use these terms with caution. Study the many ways that others choose to use the terms. Study how others choose not to use these terms. Ask questions.

> **Questions:** If a person is "guilty" of something, should that person always be made "liable" for what he or she is "guilty" of? Is it correct to judge a person "liable" for what another person is "guilty" of? If so, when? Under what circumstances? In regard to what? During the existence of White Supremacy (Racism), are the White Supremacists (Racists) correctly "liable" when their subjects (Non-White people) do things that they should not do? Should a smart and powerful people who are "in charge" of a weak and/or stupid people, be held "liable" for the incorrect speech or action of those weak and/or stupid people?
>
> Is it correct for every person who is "guilty" of committing an incorrect act, be held "liable" for having committed the

act? If so, when? If so, what person? If so, what act? If so, under what exact circumstances? Is it correct for a Victim of White Supremacy (a Non-White person) to be made "liable" for "allowing" him or herself to be a Victim of White Supremacy? If not, why not? If it is correct to make the victim "liable," what is the correct "penalty" that the victim should suffer? Is it correct for the Victim of White Supremacy (a Non-White person) to be blamed for being a victim? Is it correct to blame the White Supremacists (Racists) for making the Non-White person a victim? Who should be judged "liable"? The Victim? The White Supremacists (Racists)? Both? Neither?

Are children "liable" for what they do, or are their parents "liable"? Are the Non-White people who are subject to White Supremacy (Racism) the "illegitimate children" of the White Supremacists (Racists)? In a System of White Supremacy (Racism), are the White Supremacists (Racistman and Racistwoman, collectively), the "Master-Parents (Race-Parents)" of all of the Non-White people of the known universe?

Liberal (Racial). Use this term to mean a White person who speaks and/or acts to maintain White Supremacy (Racism) by using a greatly refined form of deceit. The deceit that is used by such persons is so refined that it is usually very acceptable, comfortable, and satisfying to the Victims (Non-White people). Also, use it to mean any White person who seeks to maintain White Supremacy through the use of greatly refined deceit.

> **Explanation**: In a socio-material system dominated by White Supremacy (Racism), a Liberal is a refined White Supremacist (Racist). The Liberal Racist, both male and female, is oftentimes characterized by the following:
>
> 1. Handling, lending, and/or granting money for curing specified physical and/or social ills among Non-White people, while making certain that none of the money is used effectively against White Supremacy (Racism).
>
> 2. Moving among Non-White people as teachers of subjects that are interesting, but not effective in helping Non-White people to eliminate Racism and/or in produce justice and correctness.
>
> 3. Providing and encouraging various forms of entertainment that have the effect of diverting the attention of Non-White people away from serious

matters such as Economics, Education, Politics, etc.

4. Working closely with Non-White people in a manner that he or she can watch and study them, and control their thinking more directly and efficiently.

5. Making suggestions to Non-White people that are attractive, but are functionally designed to indirectly make Non-White people render better service to The System of White Supremacy (Racism).

6. Using religion as a means of division and deception and to gain greater influence over their Victims (Non-White people).

7. Using sex and/or anti-sex in any form that increases the influence of the White Supremacists over the sexual conduct of their Victims. Liberal Racists (both male and female) promote Racism by engaging in sexual activity with (against) Non-White people. The liberal Racistwoman is skilled in promoting damaging influence among Non-White people through the lustful presentation and use of her body.

8. Using Non-White people to fight any people, White or Non-White, in such a manner that White Supremacy (Racism) is made stronger.

9. Presenting themselves to Non-White people as being people who are not really White in a racial sense, but who are "Christian," "Jew," "Muslim," "Marxist," "Aristocrat," etc.

They do this to confuse Non-White people. They do this to eliminate the question of whether a so-called "Liberal" is, or is not, a White Supremacist (Racist). They do this as a means of evading discussion of Racism, as it pertains to them. The so-called "Liberal Racist" will use some Non-White people to do harm to some White people, if he or she judges it to be necessary to help maintain, expand, and/or especially refine the practice of White Supremacy (Racism). The so-called Liberal Racist is an up-to-date Racist. Liberal Racists avoid petty and/or nit-picking forms of Racism.

Liberal Racists will kill and/or intimidate those White people who practice more direct and obvious forms of Racism, with the intention of getting all White people to practice Racism in a form that is more refined. The Liberal White Supremacist considers him or herself to be smarter than other White

Supremacists. The Liberal White Supremacists make plans for a world in which the Victims of White Supremacy (all Non-White people) will come to enjoy White Supremacy so much that they will never wish to exist in any way other than as subjects to the White Supremacists (Racists).

Note: The so-called "Liberal Racist" and "Conservative Racist" both have the same goal – to be "liberal" in the "conservation" of The System of White Supremacy (Racism).

Liberal/Liberty/Libertarian. Avoid using these terms. Use, instead, the terms "correct," "correct activity," "correct speech," "correctness," "correct conditions," "correct intentions," etc. When others use these terms, ask for a detailed explanation that you can easily understand. Ask questions.

> **Reason:** The words "liberal," "liberty," "libertarian" and "liberated," like the words "free," and "freedom," have been used in many ways that promote confusion. The use of these words often produces more questions than answers. When confusion is produced, it is best and correct not to use the terms, "Liberal," "Liberty" or "Libertarian" at all.

> **Questions:** Who, in the known universe, is "liberated"? "Liberated," from what? By whom? According to whom? Is being "liberated," the same as being "freed"? What is "free"? Who is "free"? "Free" from what, to do what? "Free" to dominate? "Free" to "liberate" others? Is "freedom" the same as "liberty"? "Liberty" to do what? "Liberty" by whom, for whom and/or against whom? What, exactly, is a so-called "libertarian"? How "liberal" is a "libertarian"? Is "liberty" limited? If it is, limited by whom? – a "libertarian"? If "liberty" is limited, how can it be "liberty"?

> What, exactly, is a "liberated person"? What, exactly, does a "liberated person" do in each area of activity (Economics, Education, Entertainment, Labor, Law, Politics, Religion, Sex, and War/Counter-War)? Is a "liberated person" a person who does whatever he or she wants to do, whenever and wherever he or she wants to do it? (See, "Liberal" (Racial).

Lie. Use this word to apply to speech and/or action with the intention of promoting falsehood, confusion, deception, etc.

Life. Use this term to apply to: (1) Any condition/situation of existence in which there is justice, correctness and peace; and (2) a condition/situation of existence in which there is a total absence of fighting, killing, hatred, jealousy, greed, intimidation, discourtesy, mistrust, lust, theft, etc. When others use this word, ask for a detailed explanation that you can easily understand.

> **Suggestion:** Since the word "life" has often been used in many different ways that have resulted in confusion, it may be best to use the word "existence" instead. For example, a person could say, "I have, as of now, a very interesting existence," rather than saying, "I have, as of now, a very interesting "life.""

Life, Liberty and the Pursuit of Happiness. Avoid using this term. Instead, use the expression, "Use truth in such manner as to produce justice (balance between people) and correctness." When others talk or write about "life," "liberty," and "happiness" ask for a detailed explanation that you can easily understand. Ask questions.

> **Questions:** What, exactly, is "life"? Is "life" the same as "existence"? Is "existing" the same as "living"? What, exactly, is "liberty"? Is it correct for a person to be "at liberty" to "pursue happiness" in any way that he or she chooses?

> **Note:** During the existence of White Supremacy (Racism), and according to Compensatory Counter-Racist Logic, it is best and correct to "pursue happiness" by thinking, speaking, and acting to replace White Supremacy (Racism) with Justice (balance between people).

Lighten Up. Do not use this term. Use, instead, the term, "lessen the weight."

> **Reason:** During the existence of White Supremacy (Racism) the word "lighten" used with the word "up," sometimes has the effect of causing a person to think of "lightness" with "whiteness," "whiteness" with "White people", "White people" with being "up," as "opposed" to "down," and "down," as associated with "dark," "darkness," and/or "dark people," as being the opposite of "light," "bright," "White" and/or "up" people.

Lighter Shades of Black (Racial). Use this term as a racial term referring to Non-White people who, visually, may appear to be Brown, Beige, Red, Rust, Tan, Yellow, etc.

Examples:

Yellow	=	very light Black
Red	=	lighter Black
Brown	=	light Black
Black	=	dark-dark

Light-Hearted. Do not use this term. Instead, use the terms, "cheerful thinking," "cheerful thoughts," "cheerful acts," etc.

> **Reason:** The word "light" is often directly associated with the word "bright," which is often associated with the word "white," which is often associated with the word "right," or the word "good." During the existence of White Supremacy (Racism), all of the aforementioned words are often deliberately used by Racistman and Racistwoman (White Supremacists, collectively), in such a manner as to associate "rightness," "righteousness" and/or "goodness" with White Supremacy (Racism).

Like. Use this word with caution. Use it mostly to say that one thing (person, etc.), is similar to another. Do not use the word "like" in the following manner, "He likes me." "That White woman likes Black people." "I like her a lot." In other words, do not say that you "like" yourself. Instead, say, "I get comfort from my appearance." "I am comfortable when I am with (or near) that person". "I have reason to believe that she is comfortable with me, most of the time," etc. When others say that they "like" you or that they "like" another person, ask them to explain, in detail, exactly what they mean.

> **Reason:** People often say that they "like" another person. Sometimes the ways that people show what they mean using the word "like," produces or promotes confusion. The expression "I like you," often leads to misunderstanding and disappointment, and sometimes, great anger. What the word "like" means to one person, may not be the same to another person. Therefore, it is best and correct to practice being very specific. Instead of saying, "I like you," or "they like me," it may be better to say, "I think she attracts me to her because_____," or "I often agree with what he says about justice," or "I enjoy going some places with her, but I do not enjoy visiting her Aunt." The use of the word "like," often fails to produce correct communication in matters of great importance.

> **Notes:** During the existence of The System of White Supremacy (Racism), and according to Compensatory Counter-Racist Logic, there is no "reason" for any person

to "like" Black people. There is no "reason" for any person to "like" White people. The people of the known universe have too many flaws for there to be a "reason" to "like" them. The people of the known universe are not "in balance" with each other, nor are they "in balance" with themselves as individual persons. It is not necessary, however, for people to wait until they "like" each other, or wait until they "like" themselves as individuals, before doing things of constructive value. It is not necessary to "like" people before being willing to do what can be done to produce justice and correctness.

Lily-White (Racial). <u>Do not use this term</u>. When speaking or writing about any person or any place, do not describe them as being "lily-White." When speaking or writing about people in regards to color and/or non-color, use the terms "White," "Non-White" and/or "White Supremacists (Racists)." Study the ways that others use the term "lily-White – particularly when they apply it to people.

> **Note:** During the existence of White Supremacy (Racism), the term "lily-White" has often been used to imply that a White person is not only "white" in appearance, but also "clean," "pretty," "beautiful," "pure," "unspoiled," and/or in other ways, "non-contaminated" by any person or thing that is "dark" in appearance, or in so-called "essence."

Little White Lies. <u>Do not use this term</u>. Instead, use the words "lies," "falsehoods," etc. When others use this term, ask for a detailed explanation that you can easily understand.

> **Questions:** What, exactly, is a "white lie"? What, exactly, is a "black lie," "gray lie," "orange lie," "purple lie" or "green lie"? What "color" is a lie? According to whom? For what practical reason? Does a lie need to have a "color," and/or does a lie "need" to have a "non-color"? If so, why? If so, according to whom?

> **Notes:** According to Compensatory Counter-Racist Logic, it is correct to believe that the use of the term "White lies" help White Supremacists (Racistman and Racistwoman, collectively), to associate the word "white," and/or the idea of "whiteness," with people, actions, places, creatures, things and/or thoughts that are harmless, beneficial, or the so-called, "lesser of two evils."

Living. Use this term to apply to the complete absence of falsehood, non-justice, and incorrectness, at all times, in all places, in all areas of activity.

> **Notes:** A person, and/or being, does not and cannot live, and/or is not making a living, while dominated by or affected by the existence of falsehood, non-justice, and/or incorrectness, at any time, in any place, in any area of activity. Persons who function in subjugation to White Supremacy (Racism) do not live; such persons only exist. (See, "Life," "Death," "Existence," and "Non-Existence").

Living in Sin. Avoid using this term during the existence of White Supremacy (Racism). Apply it mostly to one or more of the following acts:

(1)   Being hypocritical;

(2)   Telling lies and/or willfully and deliberately refusing to promote truth in a manner that produces justice and correctness;

(3)   Not trying to find truth, and use truth in a manner that produces justice and correctness;

(4)   Not trying to eliminate Racism (White Supremacy); and/or

(5)   Practicing Racism, or cooperating with those who do. (See, "Sinner").

Living Together. Do not use this term. When others use the term, ask them to explain, in detail, exactly what they mean – and what they do not mean. Ask them to explain, exactly, what is "living" and what is "together."

> **Questions:** Is so-called "living" the same as "working," or "playing"? Is "living together" the same as "working together," or "playing together," or "praying together," or "staying together," or "traveling together," or "dancing together," or "sleeping together," or "dining together"? If two or more people fight each other, is it correct to say that they also "live" with each other, or that they "live together"? How "together" is "together"? How much "togetherness" is required for two or more people to "qualify" for "living"? How much "living" is required for two or more people to "qualify" for "togetherness"? How much "distance" is required to "exist" between one person and another before it can truthfully be said that those persons are not "living together"?

Logic. Use this term to apply to the process and/or the production of the correct answers to every question that pertains to the "who," "what," "when," "where," "why" and "how" of whatever needs to be known and understood, or should be known and understood, including the "causes" and the "effects."

Use this term during the existence of Racism (White Supremacy) mostly to mean the same as the words "Compensatory Counter-Racist Logic." Use "Compensatory Counter-Racist Logic" to apply to any thought, speech, or action that is produced for the following purposes:

(1) To make up (compensate) for the lack of understanding of truth (that which is).

(2) To make up (compensate) for the lack of understanding of how to use truth (that which is) in a manner that will best produce justice and correctness (balance between people).

(3) To make up (compensate) for the lack of understanding of the need for the will, and the ability to "codify" the process of ending The System of White Supremacy (Racism), and replacing it with Justice, and correctness, in all areas of activity (Economics, Education, Entertainment, Labor, Law, Politics, Religion, Sex, and War/Counter-War.

> **Note:** The term "The Logic" is a shortened way of saying "Compensatory Counter-Racist Logic," and should always be used in a manner in which both terms are understood as having the same meaning.

Long/Long Time/Long While. Use these terms with caution. Study, in detail, the many ways that others use these terms. Ask questions.

> **Questions:** How "long" is "long"? "Long," as compared with what? When? What, exactly, is a "long time"? What, exactly, is "time"? Can "time" be "long"? What, exactly, is the difference between the "long ago" of "yesterday," and the "long ago" of ten thousand years? Is a person who "died" a minute ago as "dead" as a person who "died" ten thousand years ago? Is something that is "too long" according to one person's judgment, not "long enough" according to the judgment of another person?

> **Note:** It is correct to use the words "long," "short," "limited," "old," "young," and "extended," in such a

manner as to always result in the truth (that which is) being used to best promote the production of justice (balance between people), and correctness (balance between people, creatures, things, etc.).

Longest Journey, The. Use this term to mean the period from the beginning of Racism (White Supremacy) and/or of injustice (non-balance between people), to the end of Racism (White Supremacy) and/or of injustice (non-balance between people), in regards to the people of the known universe. Use it also to mean everything said and done that helps to maintain The System of White Supremacy (Racism), plus everything said and done to try to end it.

Look on the Sunny Side. Do not use this expression when talking about an idea, concept, etc., that is not directly associated with the sun itself. Instead, use the expression "look and see correctly."

> **Reason:** The term "look on the sunny side" is sometimes used to mean the opposite of the term "look on the dark side." During the existence of White Supremacy (Racism), the words "dark side" is often used in a manner that causes people to think of "darkness" as being associated with "evil." During the existence of White Supremacy (Racism), the White Supremacists (Racists) practice the concept of making people think that "dark" people, like many "dark" creatures or things, are "evil," incorrect, dangerous and/or valueless.

Lord/Lords. Use these words with caution. When others use these words as titles for themselves, and/or as titles for other existing persons, ask them to explain their reasons for doing so. Ask questions. Is a "Lord," a "God"? Is a person who is called by the title of "Lord" also "entitled" to be regarded the same as a "God"?

Love. Use this word with caution. Do not use this word to describe any condition that now exists between the people of the known universe. Instead, use terms like "affection," "affectionate," "caring," "concerned," "considerate," "cooperative," helpful, "supportive," etc., to apply to speech and action between persons, creatures, and/or things that produce a constructive result. Do not use the word "love" to apply to such speech or action. When others use the word "love," ask for a detailed explanation that you can easily understand. When people say that they "love" someone or that someone "loves" them, it is correct to ask those people to explain, exactly, and in detail, what they mean. Ask questions.

Questions: Why is the word "love" used to apply to circumstances where people are either mistreating each other, or where people are deliberately not trying to help people who need help the most?   Can there be "love" where there is no justice?   Can "love" exist in the absence of correctness?   How, exactly, does one person "prove" his or her "love" for another person?   What is the exact "test"?   Which persons are so-called "worthy" of "love"? When? How many? Under what conditions? Is it correct for a person to "love" everybody?   If so, how should that "love" be expressed?   What, exactly, are the ways to express "love" for a person in each and every area of activity (Economics, Education, Entertainment, Labor, Law, Politics, Religion, Sex, and War/Counter-War)?

What, exactly, is "love"?   How, exactly does a person prove that he or she "loves" another person?   Is "romance" the same as "love"?   What, exactly, is the difference between "love," and "friendship"?   Is "friendship" a part of "love," and if it is, how is friendship expressed during a "love" relationship? Is it correct for a person to "love" <u>every</u> person? Is it correct for a person to do harm to any person that he or she "loves"? Is it correct for a person to do harm to any person that he or she <u>does not</u> "love"?   Can "love" produce mistreatment? Can "love" exist without justice?

Is it ever correct to express "love" for a person by killing that person?   When?   For what "reason," and/or under what condition?   Is "love" conditional?   If so, what does that mean?   Is "love" so-called "limited" or "unlimited"? Are there different "degrees" of "love"?   If so, how many "degrees" does "love" require in order to "qualify" as "love"?   Is it correct for a person to "love" all persons "equally"? If it is correct, how must this "love" be shown/ expressed/practiced?   Why is sexual intercourse sometime called "making love"?   Is it correct to associate acts of sexual intercourse and/or "sexual play" as a "test" of the existence, or of the non-existence, of "love"?   Is it correct to regard sexual intercourse or to regard the absence of sexual intercourse as being "proof" (or non-proof) of the existence of "love"?

Love (making). <u>Avoid using this term</u>. Particularly, do not speak or act as if "love" is produced through sexual intercourse. Do not call sexual intercourse "making love." Call sexual intercourse, "sexual intercourse." When others use it, ask for a detailed explanation that you can easily understand.

Questions: What, exactly, is "love"? What, exactly, is not "love"? What areas of activity are involved in "proof" of love? To "make love," is it necessary to show caring, affection, and willingness to sacrifice? When? How? How "much"? Is there more than one "set of laws" that define what "love" is, and what "love" is not? How, exactly, does one person "prove" that he or she "loves" another person? How, exactly, does a person "prove" that he or she "loves" him or herself? Is it possible that "love" means whatever a person who uses the word "love" says that it means? What person in the known universe is best qualified to say, truthfully, what "love" is, and what it is not? Is it correct to ask persons what they mean when they use the term "making love"?

What, exactly, is the "procedure" for "making love"? After "love" has been "made," what, exactly, is the "proof" that it was "love" that was "made"? What is the result of "love-making" in regards to its effect on Economics, Education, Entertainment, Labor, Law, Politics, Religion, Sex, and War/Counter-War? Does sexual intercourse produce "love"? Does "love" produce sexual intercourse? Is "love" and sexual intercourse one and the same? During the existence of White Supremacy (Racism) how can a person, truthfully, define "love" between a White person and a Non-White person? Is ending White Supremacy (Racism) and producing Justice (balance between people) one of the greatest expressions of "love"?

Notes: According to Compensatory Logic, "love" and "justice" (balance between people) function as one and the same. Without justice, there is no "love." Without "love," there is no justice. Without justice, there can be "attention," there can be "affection," or "caring" or "concern," but if there is no justice, there is no "love".

Low/Low as Dirt/Low Class/Low Down, etc. Do not use these terms to describe the so-called "status," "rank," position," etc., of any person. Instead, use the terms "incorrect position," "subjugated position," "non-favored person," "unfavorable position," etc. When others describe people as "low," "low as dirt," "low class," "low down," etc., ask for a detailed explanation that you can easily understand.

Questions: What, exactly, is the purpose for saying that a person is "low" or "low-down"? What, exactly, is the constructive value in saying that a person is "low as dirt"? If one person is regarded as "low-down," why is another person regarded as "high-up"? How "high" can a person be if that person eats food that is produced in the "dirt"? What, exactly, is incorrect about "dirt"? Are people and "dirt" closely associated? Is the expression "low as dirt," an expression often promoted as the result of White Supremacists (Racists) thinking?

Is "dirt" associated with being "low" because it is generally thought of as being not only "underfoot," "undesirable," and/or "useless," but "dark" – like "dark" people? Do the White Supremacists (Racists) associate "dirt" with "dark" (Non-White) people, and "dark" people with "dirt"? Do the White Supremacists (Racists) think of "dark" people and "dirt," as "lowly" items to be used for the convenience of the White people of the known universe?

Is it true that in The System of White Supremacy (Racism), the people who are most often regarded as "low-in-status" are, most often, people who are Black or "dark" in appearance? Is there reason to believe that words like "low," "low-down," "low-as-dirt," "dirty linen," "dirty-image," and "mud-slinging" are words that have been made popular by White Supremacists (Racists) in order to associate all that is said to be "unworthy," with "dark" (Non-White) people?

Notes: During the existence of The System of White Supremacy (Racism), the term "low-class," when used by White Supremacists (Racists) usually applies to some White people. White people who believe in White Supremacy (Racism) do not regard Non-White people as being "high-class," "middle-class," or "low-class." White people who believe in White Supremacy (Racism) regard all Non-White persons as being in a "Non-White class." During the existence of White Supremacy (Racism), the "Non-White class" includes any and all persons in the known universe that the White Supremacists (Racists) "classify" as "Non-White."

Lynch/Lynching (Racial). Use these words. During the existence of White Supremacy (Racism), use these words to mean the mistreatment of, and/or the non-just killing of any Non-White person, by a White person, during the existence of White Supremacy (Racism). When others use these words, ask for a detailed explanation of what they mean, and/or study the ways that the words are used, or not used.

M

Majority. <u>Use this word with caution</u>. When others use this word, ask for a detailed explanation that you can easily understand.

> **Questions:** What, exactly, is a "majority"? What, exactly, is a "minority"? Who is "major"? "Who is "minor"? In regards to what? As compared with what? When? Where? How? Can a "majority" sometimes be one person among many? Can one person with superior power actually function as a "majority" power over or against persons who, at that time and place, are powerless?

> **Notes:** During the existence of White Supremacy (Racism), according to Compensatory Counter-Racist Logic, as long as White Supremacy (Racism) exists, the "Effective Majority" ("Power Majority") among the people of the known universe, are, collectively, those White persons who practice White Supremacy (Racism).

> "The Majority" is not a matter of the *number* of people, but a matter of *which* people dominate other people. White Supremacists (Racistman and Racistwoman, collectively), do not, functionally, use the words "majority" or "major" to apply to numbers of White people, in their interactions with Non-White people. They do, however, deceive Non-White people by causing Non-White people to think, speak, and/or act as if the words "majority" and "minority" are words that are used to measure the so-called power or value of people based on the number(s) and location(s) of those people.

> During the existence of White Supremacy (Racism), the words "majority" and "minority" apply to who dominates whom. To a White Supremacist (Racist), the word "majority," when applied to the people of the known universe, means being powerful and supreme (White power and White Supremacy). To a White Supremacist (Racist), power and supremacy means White people having major power over all of the Non-White people of the known universe, in all areas of activity, including Economics, Education, Entertainment, Labor, Law, Politics, Religion, Sex, and War/ Counter-War.

Majority (Racial). <u>Do not use this term</u>. Instead, use "Racists", "Racistman and Racistwoman", and "White Supremacists".

Notes: During the existence of White Supremacy (Racism) the use of the term "racial majority" only serves to promote confusion among and between the Victims of White Supremacy (Non-White people).

During the existence of White Supremacy (Racism), the terms "racial majority," and/or "racial minority," may or may not apply to the total number of White people as compared with the total number of Non-White people, and/or may or may not apply to a comparison between the power of White Supremacists (Racists), as opposed to the powerlessness of the Victims of White Supremacy (Non-White people).

Malicious. Use this word. During the existence of The System of White Supremacy, use it mostly to apply to the basic intent of many White people, toward most Non-White people in regards to all areas of activity.

Note: According to Compensatory Counter-Racist Logic, there is reason to believe that, without a basic "malicious" intent of many White people, The System of White Supremacy (Racism) would not exist.

Man. Use this word to apply to any male person who is "classified" as, and who functions as, a White male person, and who has the ability to function as a White Supremacist (Racist), some, all, or most of the time, during his existence in the known universe, and who has participated, either directly or indirectly in support of The System of White Supremacy (Racism). During the existence of White Supremacy (Racism), do not use the word "man" to apply to any Non-White person who is "classified" as, and/or who functions as, "Non-White".

Reason: During the existence of White Supremacy (Racism), and according to Compensatory Counter-Racist Logic, it is not possible for any person to be a "man" if that person is functionally classified as "Non-White."

"Men" are not subject to White Supremacy (Racism). "Men" do not submit to or cooperate with persons who practice White Supremacy (Racism) unless those "men" are "White" persons. Therefore, all "Non-White" persons who submit to, and/or who cooperate with, White persons who practice White Supremacy (Racism), are Victims of, and/or are subject to, White Supremacy (Racism). The only people in the known universe who exist as Victims of, and/or in subjugation to, The White Supremacists (Racistmen and Racistwomen, collectively) are "Non-White" males. None of these Non-White males function as "men". All of them function as "boys."

Note: "Boys" are subject to, and dependent upon, "men." During the existence of White Supremacy (Racism), all of the "men" in the known universe are White. (See "Baby Boy").

Man Friday (my). Do not use this term.

Reason: "Friday" was said to be the name of a Black male person who could be absolutely depended upon to do whatever his White "overseer" wanted done. The use of the term "my man Friday" does little other than help to promote the thinking that the practice of White Supremacy (Racism) is not only a comfort and convenience, but also a "natural" and correct means of accomplishing any desired goals.

Manager/Management. Use these words. During the existence of White Supremacy (Racism) use these words to apply only to those White male or female persons who practice White Supremacy (Racism) in one or more of the following areas of activity (Economics, Education, Entertainment, Labor, Law, Politics, Religion, Sex, and War/Counter-War).

Do not use the words "man," "manager," or "management" to apply to any person who is Non-White. During the existence of White Supremacy (Racism), instead of using these terms to apply to Non-White persons, practice (when you can do so without promoting conflict and confusion), using one or more of the following: administrator, advisor, arranger, director, executive facilitator, management assistant, officer, official, person, and/or spokesperson.

Reason: As long as White Supremacy (Racism) exists, it is incorrect to say that any Non-White person is a "man," "manager," etc. During the existence of White Supremacy (Racism), a Non-White person is subject to the power of Racistman and Racistwoman (White Supremacists, collectively). Non-White people who are subject to (the dictatorship of) White Supremacists (Racists), are not qualified for the titles of "man," or "manager," or "management," etc. Non-White people who are subject to (the dictatorship of) White Supremacists (Racists) are forced to be, and to function as "children". During the existence of White Supremacy (Racism), only White persons are allowed to function as a "man," "manager," "management," etc.

Note: According to Compensatory Logic, it is correct to minimize unnecessary conflict by not "name-calling." Therefore, if any person shows that he (or she) prefers to be called by the titles of "manager" or "management," etc. it is correct to call him or her by those titles.

Man's Shadow/Shadow of a Man. Use these terms to apply to any Black and/or Non-White male person who exists any place in the known universe at the same time that White Supremacy (Racism) exists.

Reason: As long as White Supremacy (Racism) exists, no Non-White person is, or can be, a "man." As long as White Supremacy (Racism) exists, every Non-White person is subject to the power of those White people who participate in the practice of White Supremacy (Racism). Therefore, as long as White Supremacy (Racism) exists, every Black male person is required to function as a "boy." A "boy" is subject to, and/or is dependent upon, a "man".

During the existence of The System of White Supremacy (Racism) all Non-White male persons function as or "within" the so-called "White Man's Shadow." A Non-White male person, under such a condition, is only a "Shadow of a Man." He is only a "Man's Shadow." A "Man's Shadow" only acts when "The Man" acts. Most of the time, such a "Shadow Person" acts in a manner that is "greatly distorted." Such a "Shadow Person," like any shadow of a person, creature, or thing, performs in a manner that is aimless, and/or meaningless when compared with the person, creature, or thing, that "makes" the shadow. A shadow, or a "Shadow Person," has no motivation of its own. A shadow only acts when the "Shadow-Maker" makes it act. The "Shadow Person" (Non-White person) only acts (or reacts) when the "Shadow-Master" (White Supremacist) makes him act (or react). The "Shadow Master" (White Supremacist) can also "arrange" for the "Shadow Person" to "appear" or "disappear."

Marriage/Married. Use these words with caution. During the existence of White Supremacy (Racism), do your best to avoid using the words "marriage" or "married" to apply to any Non-White person.

Instead, in most so-called "marital situations" as it pertains to Non-White persons (male with female), try using the following" "care-mated," choiced," "chosen," "favored," "intimated," "intimates," "mates," "mated" "soul-mated," ladymated," "gentlemated," etc.

Other words can be used to apply to those Non-White persons in a so-called "marital situation" if the words used are acceptable to those involved in the situation. In addition, it is correct to study, in detail, all of the ways that others use the words "marry," "married," and/or "marriage." Study the definitions for such words, and compare definitions of such words with what people actually do to "qualify" for the definitions.

> **Reasons:** "Marriage" is a <u>means</u> toward an <u>end</u>. During the existence of White Supremacy (Racism), the "marriage" of a White person is a <u>means</u> by which a White person, directly or directly, supports the "end" result. The "end result" is marital thought, speech, and action in greater support of the System of White Supremacy (Racism).
>
> During the existence of White Supremacy (Racism), the so-called "marriage" of a <u>Non-White person</u>, regardless of intent, either has the <u>effect</u> of giving greater support for the System of White Supremacy (Racism), or the <u>effect</u> of giving greater support for helping to <u>end</u> The System White Supremacy (Racism). During the existence of White Supremacy (Racism), the so-called "marriages" of Non-White persons – either to <u>each</u> other or to White persons – has, so far, only proven to be of service in greater support of the System of White Supremacy (Racism).
>
> These so-called "marriages" <u>have</u> <u>not</u> resulted in justice (balance between people), nor have they resulted in services to any "God" other than to the so-called "Great White Father" and "Great White Mother" (Racistman and Racistwoman and/or White Supremacists, collectively). These so-called "marriages" have proven to be subject to the direct or indirect control of Racistman and Racistwoman. During the existence of White Supremacy (Racism), all <u>Non-White</u> people function as the "illegitimate subject-children" of Racistman and Racistwoman (White Supremacists, collectively). As "children," Non-White people are directly or indirectly dependent upon the decisions made by Racistman and Racistwoman (White Supremacists, collectively). This means that <u>Non-White</u> people are "required" to function

in a child-like manner, in all areas of activity, including sex and marriage. Marriage can only exist between men and women – not between "children".

During the existence of White Supremacy (Racism) and according to Compensatory Counter-Racist Logic, Non-White persons are not allowed to function as "married" people. The White Supremacists (Racists), do not allow Non-White persons to function as "married" people. They do this by dominating what Non-White people do, and not do, in all areas of (people) activity - Economics, Education, Entertainment, Labor, Law, Politics, Religion, Sex, and War/ Counter-War.

According to Compensatory Counter-Racist Logic, a person cannot be subject to White Supremacy (Racism) and, at the same time, be a "partner" in a "true marriage." A Black male person who is subject to White Supremacy (Racism) cannot, at the same time, *function* as a "husband". He can only *pretend* to function as a "husband" according to the dictates of Racistman and Racistwoman (White Supremacists, collectively).

A Black female person who is subject to White Supremacy (Racism) cannot, at the same time, *function* as a "wife." She can only *pretend* to function as a "wife" according to the dictates of Racistman and Racistwoman (White Supremacists, collectively).

It should also be known and understood that Racists (White Supremacists) do not allow their Victims (Non-White people) to be "financially independent." It is Racistman and Racistwoman (White Supremacists, collectively) who directly or indirectly control all the money, and/or the "value" of all money that is possessed, and/or produced, by Non-White people.

Notes: During the existence of White Supremacy (Racism), and according to Compensatory Counter-Racist Logic, it is correct for Non-White people (both male and female) to believe that Racistman and Racistwoman (White Supremacists, collectively), are the "Masters" of all money and finance in any so-called "marital arrangement" that involves Non-White people. It is incorrect to pretend that this is not true.

As long as White Supremacy (Racism) exists, the definition of, and the so-called "standards" for, "marriage" (as it applies to Non-White persons), should be substantially different from the definition and "standards" for "marriage" as it applies to White persons.

Because of the existence and effects of White Supremacy (Racism) on the interactions between Non-White males and Non-White females, the definition and "standards" for "marriage" or "mate-ship," as it applies to Non-White persons should not only be different, but should be the most honest, true, and constructive form of male-female interaction ever produced in the known universe.

Avoid using the term "married" when making reference to any Non-White person during the existence of The System of White Supremacy (Racism), and try using one or more of the terms, "mated," "gentlemated," "ladymated," "legal-mated" and/or "legally-mated," "formal-mated," "informal-mated," "mutual-mated," "religion-mated," "spirit-mated," "choice-mated," "chosen-mated," "care-mated," 'share-mated" etc.

Marriage (Compensatory Counter-Racist). Use these terms to apply to the commitment a Non-White male and a Non-White female make, to each other, to do all they can to be of constructive help to each other in all areas of activity, with no restrictions in regard to sexual intercourse and/or sexual play (except for considerations of disease prevention and pregnancy prevention).

> **Notes:** During the existence of The System of White Supremacy (Racism) and according to Compensatory Counter-Racist Logic, no Non-White person can claim, correctly, that he or she is "married". All so-called "marriages" by Non-White persons are, at best, "non-balanced arrangements" dominated by Racistman and Racist-woman (White Supremacists, collectively).

Massacre. Use this word with caution. When others use it, ask for a detailed explanation that you can easily understand. Ask questions.

> **Questions:** What, exactly, is a "massacre"? Is a "massacre" the same as a "war"? Is a "massacre" the same as "murder"? Is a "massacre" a "crime"? If it is, is "war" a "crime"? When White people willfully and deliberately kill Non-White people in order to (directly or

indirectly) establish, maintain, expand, and/or refine White Supremacy (Racism), is it correct to call such killing a "massacre"?

Notes: Study the "peculiar" ways that some White people often apply the word "massacre" to the killing of White people, particularly when White people are killed by Non-White people.

Mass Murder. Avoid using this term. When others use it, ask for a detailed explanation that you can easily understand.

Questions: Is "war" a form of "mass murder"? If so, why? If not, why not? Is "mass murder" the killing of two people? Three people? Five hundred people? When? Where? For what? By whom? Against whom? Was an "innocent person" [who was] killed during a "war," "murdered"? What, exactly, is an "innocent person" during a "war"? How many people make up a "mass"? Is every White Supremacist (Racist) guilty of "mass murder"?

Masses, The. Do not use this term. Use, instead, the term "the people," and explain which or describe what people you are talking about and in regards to what. During the existence of White Supremacy (Racism), always use the term "the people" to apply to any and all people other than those (White) people who practice White Supremacy (Racism). When others use the term "the Masses," ask for a detailed explanation that you can easily understand.

Master Capitalist/Communist - Supreme Capitalist/Communist. Use these terms to apply to:

(1)   A White person who practices White Supremacy (Racism) and who, by word or deed, makes common cause with other White persons who do the same;

(2)   A Race Capitalist;

(3)   A Race Communist;

(4)   A White person who capitalizes on the subjugation of Non-White people by practicing White Supremacy (Racism), and who makes common capital with those White persons who do the same;

(5)   A White person who practices Racism (White Supremacy) and willfully maintains membership in, and/or gives direct or indirect support to, the strongest and most effective "capital-

communist," and/or "community-type" system in the known universe - the "White Nation" and/or "White Community";

(6)   A White person who is a Racist (White Supremacist), and who maintains a common bond of social and/or material interests with all other Racists (White Supremacists) in the known universe;

(7)   A Race Communist/Capitalist;

(8)   A member of the Master Commune (White Supremacists, collectively);

(9)   A White person who is a member of the Universal Master Community, and/or Universal Supreme Community; and/or

(10)   Any White Supremacist (Racist).

Master Child Abuser. Use this term to apply to a White Supremacist (Racist).

> **Explanation**:   In a world social and material system dominated by White Supremacy (Racism), in order to survive, all Non-White people must function in a manner that is comparatively "child-like".   They are forced to speak and act in a manner that is both childish and subordinate, all of the time, in all areas of activity, including Economics, Education, Entertainment, Labor, Law, Politics, Religion, Sex, and War/Counter-War.
>
> Since White Supremacy is the dominant form of non-justice in the known universe, those White persons who practice White Supremacy are the greatest and most masterful abusers of children in the known universe. Therefore, any person who practices White Supremacy is a "Master Child Abuser".

Master Crime Families (Racists/White Supremacists).   Use this term to apply to the most powerful "associations" of large numbers of White Supremacists (Racists) men and women, who, because of their direct support for each other, from different locations, give them greater and more focused power to practice White Supremacy (Racism) in a more coordinated manner. These "Master Criminals" of the known universe have proven to be the smartest, most sophisticated, and most powerful of the criminals in the known universe. One way to talk about them in general conversation is to speak of them according to their current basic "location."

> **Examples:** "The Master Crime Families in the East," "The Master Crime Families in the West," "The Master

Crime Families in this area of the world," "The Master Crime Families in other areas of the world," "The Race-Master-Criminals south of where we are," etc.

Notes: The Master Crime Families often act in violent, competitive conflict with each other when deciding the best methods for conducting the "business" of White Supremacy (Racism), by choosing which "benefits" for which "family members." When they do so, it is important that Non-White people ask all of the Master Crime Families (White Supremacists collectively) to keep Non-White people out of harm's way during these disputes. It is also correct for Non-White people not to expect these Master Crime Families to protect them from harm.

When making remarks about the Master Crime Families, it is incorrect to use the names or titles of any so-called "countries" or "nations" (as being Racist) except, "The White Nation," "The Race Nation," "The White Supremacists," "Racistman and Racistwoman," "The System of White Supremacy (Racism)," "The System," "The Master Suspects," "The Usual Suspects," etc.

Master Criminal (Racial). <u>Use this term</u> to apply to a White Supremacist (Racist).

Explanation: Those White people who practice Racism are the Masters of Non-White people in all areas of activity. Since Racism (White Supremacy) is the greatest and most effective form of injustice among the people of the known universe, it is, therefore, the greatest and most effective crime. Since those White people who practice Racism are also the Masters of all Non-White people in all areas of activity, then all White people who practice Racism are "Master Criminals".

Master Organization, The. <u>Use this term</u> to apply to those White people, collectively, who practice White Supremacy (Racism).

Explanation: The White people who have chosen to practice White Supremacy (Racism) are so organized and so masterful, that they are, collectively, more powerful than any other category or classification of people in the known universe.

Master Race. Use this term to apply to: (1) White Supremacists, collectively; (2) those White persons, collectively, who are the Masters in the practice of Racism (White Supremacy); and (3) the only "Race" of people in the known universe which is based on the domination and mistreatment of people because of a "skin color" classification.

Master-Racket/Master Racketeer(s). Use these terms to mean the same as "White Supremacy (Racism)," and "White Supremacists (Racists)."

> **Reason:** During the existence of White Supremacy (Racism), there are no "rackets," "racketeers," and/or "organized criminals" more powerful than those White people of the known universe who participate in The System of White Supremacy (Racism). Such White persons, collectively, are the "Master Racketeers". The System of White Supremacy (Racism) is the "Master Racket".

Master Security Risk. Use this term to apply to a White Supremacist (Racist).

> **Explanation**: Security is the result of truth that is used in a manner that produces justice and correctness. Racism is the greatest threat to truth being used to produce justice and correctness. Racism, in the form of White Supremacy, is the greatest motivating force by people, among the people of the known universe.
>
> The White people who practice White Supremacy are the functional "Masters" of all of the people of the known universe who are classified as Non-White. The White Supremacists (Racists) are, therefore, the "Master Security Risk" of the known universe.

Master Terrorist. Use this term to apply to:

(1)   A White Supremacist (Racist);

(2)   Any White person, while practicing White Supremacy (Racism) in any one or more areas of activity; and/or

(3)   Any White person who practices White Supremacy in such a manner that one or more Victims (Non-White persons) are made to experience great fear, panic, dread, alarm, dismay, horror, etc.

225

Explanation: White Supremacists (Racists) are the "Masters of Terrorism". More Non-White people fear them more than they fear any other force in the known universe.

Master-Universal Subversive Elements. Use this term to apply to the White Supremacists (Racistmen and Racistwomen, collectively) who act as the people of the known universe who are the smartest, most powerful and most malicious, and who have chosen to promote injustice by using the most destructive features of "Capitalist," "Communist," "Fascist," "Socialist" and/or any other socio-material concept.

Maximum Emergency Compensatory Action. Use this term to mean:

(1) The willful and deliberate elimination of one or more Racists (White Supremacist), through death, and the willful and deliberate elimination of self, through death, by a Victim of Racism (Non-White person), acting alone, according to a detailed plan and acting only after he or she has judged that he or she can no longer endure the effects of Racism, and/or is no longer able to effectively promote the production of justice, except by eliminating one or more Racists, as well as eliminating him or herself, as a subject of the Racists.

(2) Swift, efficient, surprise execution of one or more Racists (White Supremacists), by an individual Victim of Racism, acting openly and alone, at a time and place of his or her own choosing, continuing to execute as many Racists as possible, without respite or surrender, until he or she is forced to eliminate self, rather than be eliminated or captured by others.

Use this term whenever the term Maximum-Emergency Compensatory Justice becomes confusing, and/or promotes disagreement about whether an act of Maximum-Emergency Compensatory Justice did or did not, in truth, actually *produce* justice (balance between people). If the evidence shows that an act of "Maximum Emergency Compensatory Justice" did not actually *result* in justice being produced, then the act did not qualify for the title "Maximum Emergency Compensatory Justice." The act qualified for the title "Maximum Emergency Compensatory Action."

Notes: Maximum-Emergency Compensatory Action is enacted only under prolonged conditions of extreme and practically hopeless deprivation and acute suffering of injustice caused and/or promoted by those White persons who practice White Supremacy (Racism). According to Compensatory Counter-Racist Logic, the word "justice" only applies to the actual guarantee that no person in the known universe is mistreated, and the actual guarantee that the person in the known universe who is most in need of constructive help, actually receives that constructive help.

It can be argued, however, that the person who enacts what is called "Maximum-Emergency Compensatory Justice" intended the enactment to result in the establishment of justice. However, the only person in the known universe who would know what the intent was, would be the person engaged in the enactment. Since that person would no longer exist, no other person can truthfully say what the intention was or was not. According to Compensatory Counter-Racist Logic, it is useless and non-correct to argue about whether a specific act was "Maximum Emergency Compensatory Justice," or "Maximum Emergency Compensatory Action," or was neither, or was both.

It is important to know and understand that if the person who had the intent of enacting Maximum-Emergency Compensation Action, did harm to any Non-White person, or to any White person who was not a White supremacist (Racist) or Suspected White Supremacist (Racist Suspect), during the attempted enactment, the enactment did not qualify for the definition of Maximum-Emergency Compensatory Action.

According to Compensatory Counter-Racist Logic, no person is correctly qualified to comment on any specific act that appears to be "Maximum-Emergency Compensatory Action. Any person can explain (but not define) what Maximum-Emergency Compensatory Action is or is not, and only according to The United-Independent Compensatory Code/System/Concept.

Maximum Racist Aggression. Use this term to mean:

(1)   Anything willfully and deliberately said or done by a White person, under conditions dominated by White Supremacy (Racism), that results in a Non-White person being (non-justly) deceived.

(2)   Anything willfully and deliberately said or done by a White person, under conditions dominated by White Supremacy, that results in a Non-White person being deprived of something that he or she must have in order to produce justice and/or correctness.

(3)   Any willful, deliberate and mutual act of sexual intercourse, and/or "sexual play," between a White person and a Non-White person, during any period in which any person is subject to White Supremacy (Racism), any place in the known universe.

> **Note:** All White persons who participate in, and/or who directly or indirectly help to promote such acts, are guilty of "Maximum Racist Aggression".

Maximum Racist Insult. Use this term to apply to any act of sexual intercourse, and/or "sexual play" by a White person with/against a Non-White person under any condition, directly or indirectly dominated by White Supremacy (Racism).

Media, The. Do not use this term. Instead say, "Some people have said _____". When others use the term, ask for a detailed explanation that you can easily understand, and ask if the term includes everything that any person says to any other person, about anything.

> **Note:** According to Compensatory Logic, "The Media" is, generally speaking, any person who buys, sells, gives, or receives information of any kind, at any time.

Medical Care. Use this term to apply to anything that is said or done that helps a person to think, speak, and act in a constructive manner in any one or more areas of activity: Economics, Education, Entertainment, Labor, Law, Politics, Religion, Sex, and War/Counter-War. Study the ways that others use the terms, "medicine," "medical," "medical care," "health," "health care," "physical," "mental," "non-medical," "sick," "well," etc.

> **Note:** According to Compensatory Logic, there is reason to believe that what is sometimes called correct "health care" is the combination of things done that results in justice and correctness in all areas of activity.

Meeting (constructive). Use this term to mean any "meeting" of people that results in things done that helps to guarantee that no person is mistreated, and/or helps to guarantee that the person who needs help the most, gets the most help.

Meeting (non-constructive). Use this term to mean any "meeting" of people that <u>results</u> in things done that <u>do not</u> guarantee that no person is mistreated, and/or that <u>does not</u> result in a guarantee that the person who needs help the most, gets the most help.

Mental Patient. Use this term to mean any person who receives help in thinking, speaking, and/or acting in a constructive manner, in any one or more areas of activity. Study the ways that others use the term "mental patient."

> **Note:** During the existence of White Supremacy (Racism) and according to Compensatory Counter-Racist Logic, it is correct to regard all of the people who practice White Supremacy (Racism) and all of the people who are subject to White Supremacy (Racism), as "mentally-ill" people.

Mentor. Use this term to apply to the following (during the existence of White Supremacy/Racism):

(1) A person who has not told a lie.

(2) A person who has not made a mistake.

(3) A person who has not mistreated any person or any creature, or who has not refused to help the person who was most in need of help.

(4) A person who has not practiced White Supremacy (Racism) in any one or more areas of activity, and who is not a Victim of White Supremacy (Racism), in any one or more areas of activity.

(5) A "Code" for correct thought, speech, and action that applies to all areas of activity/existence, including Economics, Education, Entertainment, Labor, Law, Politics, Religion, Sex, and War/Counter-War.

(6) The Creator of all things, creatures, people, etc.

Mercy. Use this word with caution. Study the ways that others use the word "mercy." Study the ways that others use the term "justice with mercy." How, exactly, is "mercy" measured correctly? Is it possible for "mercy" to exist, and The System of White Supremacy (Racism) to exist, in the same universe at the same time? Is "mercy" a correct "substitute" for justice (balance between people)? Is there any correct "substitute" for justice (balance between people)?

> **Note:** During the existence of White Supremacy (Racism), and according to Compensatory Counter-Racist Logic, it

is incorrect to expect to receive "mercy" from anyone, at any time, for any reason.

Merit. <u>Use this word with caution</u>. Study the ways that others use the word "merit." How does the word "merit" relate to the word "worthy"? Is any person "worthy"? Is every person "worthy" of "merit"? If so, what kind of "merit"? How much "merit"? "Merit" in what form? "Merit" by whom? "Merit" given for what ultimate purpose?

> **Notes:** During the existence of White Supremacy (Racism), and according to Compensatory Counter-Racist Logic, only those things that people do that directly or indirectly help to replace White Supremacy (Racism) with Justice (balance between people) are "worthy" of "merit" to the people of the known universe. All "merit" for what people do that is of constructive "worth," should be recognized as the result of the work of "The All-Power", "The Supreme Force," "God," "The Great Spirit," "The Source," etc.

Middle-America/Middle-American. <u>Do not use these terms</u>. Instead, use the terms "White people," "Non-White people," and "White Supremacists (Racists)." Study the ways that others use these terms. Ask questions.

> **Reason:** During the existence of White Supremacy (Racism), and according to Compensatory Counter-Racist Logic, there is no person, no place, or no thing, that can be correctly called "America," "American," "Middle-America," "Middle-American," etc. "America and/or American" is not a "place" or a person. An "American" is not a person "placed" in the "middle" of a "place" ("Mid-America," etc.).
>
> According to Compensatory Logic, an "American" is, and must be: (1) a person who does not mistreat anyone, (2) a person who does not allow anyone to be mistreated; and (3) a person who helps that person who is most in need of help. The evidence shows that no such person now exists, any place in the known universe. The evidence shows that, so far, a person who correctly qualifies for the title, "American," is yet to be produced. The definition for an "American," is the exact same as the definition for "African," and "Asian." According to Compensatory Counter-Racist Logic, this means that people who can be correctly called "American," "African," or "Asian," do not exist. During the existence of White Supremacy (Racism),

the major correct titles for the people of the known universe (collectively) are:

- White people (non-Racist) White people who are not able to practice White Supremacy and who are not able to stop other White people from practicing White Supremacy.

- Non-White people ("Black," "Brown," "Red," "Yellow," "Tan," etc.).

- White Supremacists (Racistman and Racistwoman, and/or those White people who directly or indirectly dominate, unjustly, the Non-White people of the known universe based on factors associated with the "Non-White" classification.

Notes: According to Compensatory Counter-Racist Logic, it is impossible for a person to be an "American" and, at the same time, either practice, or be the Victim of, the practice of White Supremacy (Racism). If this were not true, what would be the justifiable reason for anyone wanting to be an "American"?

Middle-Class/Middle-Class Values. Do not use these terms. Instead, use the terms "Power Class" (those White persons who practice White Supremacy"); and "Power-less Class" (the Non-White people of the known universe during the existence of White Supremacy).

Reason: During the existence of White Supremacy (Racism), and according to Compensatory Counter-Racist Logic, it is meaningless and confusing to use terms like "high-class," "middle-class," "middle-class values," "low-class," "upper middle-class," "Black middle-class," etc. As long as the practice of non-justice (non-balance between people) is the greatest influence among the people of the known universe, it is incorrect to describe any people as "high class," "middle-class," "low-class," etc.

Since all of the people of the known universe help to support the practice of non-justice (non-balance between and/or mistreatment of people), then the only "class" differences between people are that some are "powerful," and some are, by comparison, "powerless." In addition, those White persons who have proven that they do not participate in the practice of White Supremacy (Racism) are also in the "powerless class."

Notes:

(1) As long as White Supremacy (Racism) exists, all of the White people who practice White Supremacy (Racism) are "members" of the "Power<u>ful</u> Class".

(2) As long as White Supremacy (Racism) exists, all of the White people who do not practice White Supremacy (Racism) are "members" of the "Power<u>less</u> Class."

(3) As long as White Supremacy (Racism) exists, all of the Non-White people of the known universe are the Victims of White Supremacy and, as such, are "more powerless" than the White people who are "powerless."

(4) As long as White Supremacy (Racism) exists, no White person is, or can be, a Victim of Black or Non-White Supremacy. "Black Supremacy" or "Non-White Supremacy" does not exist any place in the known universe.

(5) As long as White Supremacy (Racism) exists, no White person is, or can be, a Victim of "White" Supremacy. He or she can only be a Victim of non-justice (non-balance between people).

(6) During the existence of White Supremacy (Racism), all of the people of the known universe participate in the practice of non-justice (non-balance between people).

(7) During the existence of White Supremacy (Racism), it is the White Supremacists ("The Powerful Class"/"Racist Class") who do the most to maintain, expand, and refine the practice of non-justice (non-balance between people).

(8) During the existence of White Supremacy (Racism), the one basic "value" of the "Powerful Class" is White Supremacy (Racism).

(9) During the existence of White Supremacy (Racism) the three basic values of the "Powerless Class" are: (1) "survival," (2) "comfort," and (3) "showing-off".

Middle-East/Middle-West. Avoid using these terms. Instead use terms like "east of where we are now," "west of where we are now," "east of here," "west of where they are," etc. Study the ways that others use the terms "East," "West," "North," "South," "Middle-East," "Middle-West," "The Mid-West," "Western Culture," "Eastern Culture," "Country and Western," "Western clothing," "Eastern attire," "Country and Western music," "Middle-Eastern cooking," "Southern cooking," "Out West," "The Western World," etc. When others use terms like the aforementioned, ask for a detailed explanation that you can easily understand.

> **Note:** White Supremacists (Racists) sometimes use words that seem to mean that they apply to a "place" or to a "direction" when, in truth, they are using those words to identify the activities of White people, and/or the activities of Non-White people.

Migrant/Immigrant. Avoid using these terms. Instead, use terms like the following: (1) travelers, (2) travelers seeking better conditions, (3) travelers looking for constructive employment, (4) travelers trying to produce justice, (5) travelers seeking excitement, (6) travelers seeking to mistreat people, etc. Study the ways that others use the words "migrant," "immigrant," "explorer," "adventurer," "pioneer," "pilgrim," "aggressor," "developer," "missionary," "conqueror," "invader," "settler," "intruder" etc.

> **Notes:** During the existence of White Supremacy (Racism), the White Supremacists (Racistman and Racistwoman, collectively), use many words to apply to the movement(s) of people. They use these words in such a manner as to justify White Supremacists (Racists) going any place that they choose to go, and doing anything (against Non-White people) that they choose to do.
>
> The White Supremacists (Racists) also use words that they apply to the movement(s) of Non-White people in a manner that is intended to cause people to think that Non-White people should only be where the White Supremacists (Racists) say that Non-White people should be, and that Non-White people should only move where the White Supremacists (Racists) say that they should move. In addition, the White Supremacists (Racists) use words that they cause to mean that White Supremacists (Racists) can and should go wherever they choose to go, and be wherever they choose to be, regardless of what Non-White people think, say, or do.

Militant. <u>Avoid using this word</u>. When others use it, ask for a detailed explanation that you can easily understand.

> **Questions:** What, exactly, is a "militant"? What, exactly, is not a "militant"? Is it correct to say that a "militant" is any person, creature, or "spirit" that is willing to "fight"? If so, what, exactly, is "fighting"? What, exactly, is not "fighting"? Are there different ways to "fight"? How many different ways can a person be a "militant"? Is it ever correct for a person to be a "militant"? If so, when? Where? How? As it pertains to what? Is defending oneself from being mistreated, the same as being "militant"? What is the difference between being "civil," and being "militant"? Is a "civil war" a "militant" activity? If so, how can it be "civil," and "militant," at the same time? If so, how can a "war" be "civil" ("civilized")? Is telling the truth, the same as being "militant"? Is a law enforcement officer "militant"? Is a person "militant" if he or she kills another person in self-defense? Is a White Supremacist (Racist) "militant"? Is a person who seeks to replace White Supremacy with Justice a "militant"?

Military/Military Law/Military Target/Militia. <u>Use these terms with caution</u>. When others use these terms, ask for a detailed explanation that you can easily understand. Ask them to explain the true differences between what is, and what is not, "military," "civil," "civilian," "combative," "combatant," "non-combatant," "militia," "military support," "civilian support," "fighting," "military law," "civil law," "hostile action," "political action," "self-defense," "police action," "military action," etc. Ask many questions, and compare the answers received for one question, with the answers received for other questions.

> **Questions:** What, exactly, is the difference between "military law," and "civil law"? What, exactly, is the purpose of "military law"? What, exactly, is the purpose of "civil law"? Does "military law," "civil law," and "religious law," serve the same purpose? Is "civilian support" for the "military" the same as "military support"? If so, why and how? If not, why not? Is helping a person to get a weapon to kill a person, the same as helping to kill the person who was killed? Is killing a person a "military" act, or a "civil" act?
>
> What, exactly, is the difference between a "military target," and a "civilian target"? What, exactly, is a "military weapon"? Is killing or maiming a person with a "military weapon," a "military act"? Was the person who

was killed, killed as a result of "military activity"? What, exactly, is the difference between "war," "civil-war," "military-war," "militia-war," and any form of people fighting or killing people? What, exactly, is an "army"? What, exactly, is not an "army"? Is a cook in an "army" a "civilian"? A "militia-person"? Is a "militia-person" the same as "civilian"? Is a "civil-servant," who is also a "member" of a "militia," also a "militant"?

What, exactly, is a "non-combatant"? When? Where? Under what circumstances? According to whom? Is a person who deliberately kills another person during a "civil disturbance," a "non-combatant"? Is he or she a "militant"? What, exactly, is the "difference" between "civilian clothes"? Is a naked person a "militant"? Is a White person who willfully and deliberately engages in sexual intercourse with a Non-White person during the existence of White Supremacy guilty of an act of "militant/military/Racist Aggression"?

Mind Rape (Racial). Use this term to apply to what happens against all of the Non-White people of the known universe when they directly or indirectly are taught, led, and/or influenced by White Supremacists (Racistmen and Racistwomen, collectively), particularly in regards to the support for White Supremacy (Racism) in matters involving sex and/or anti-sex.

> **Notes:** Sex is any interaction between a male and female person that may or may not include sexual intercourse and/or "sexual play." Anti-sex is any *pretended* "sexual" act between two or more males with each other, or two or more females with each other. According to Compensatory Counter-Racist Logic, every Victim of White Supremacy (Non-White person) is a victim of "mind-rape" by both Racistman and Racistwoman (White Supremacists, collectively). This "mind-rape" not only applies to the area of sex and anti-sex, but also to every other area of activity, including Economics, Education, Entertainment, Labor, Law, Politics, Religion, and War/Counter-War.

Minor/Minority. Use these words with caution. When others use the words "minor" or "minority" to apply to descriptions of people, ask for a detailed explanation that you can easily understand. Instead, use, "Victims of White Supremacy" and/or "Non-White people." Ask questions.

Questions: Are Non-White people a "minor" people? Are Non-White people a "minority" people? If so, what makes Non-White people a "minor" or a "minority"? When? Where? According to whom, or what? "Minor" or "minority," in order to "accomplish" what? Is a child a "minor"? Is a "minority-person" a "child-like" person? Is a "minority-person" a helpless, powerless, and/or defenseless person? Are Victims of White Supremacy (Non-White people) "minor" people? If so, "minor" as compared to what? If so, "minor" as compared with whom? Is being a "minor-person" the same as being in a "minority-position"? Does "minority" mean the same as having "minor" power, as compared with those persons, creatures, etc., that have "major" power? Does being a "minor" mean being subject to, and/or being dependent upon, those who are not "minor"? Are all persons directly or indirectly "dependent" upon each other? If so, how? If so, in regards to what?

Is a "majority" dependent upon a "minority"? Is a "minority" dependent upon a "majority"? If so, when? Where? Why? For what? Does a greater number of people always make a "majority"? If a person is power<u>less</u>, does that make that person a "minor" when compared with a person who is power<u>ful</u>?

Reasons: During the existence of White Supremacy (Racism), the use of the term "racial minority" only serves to promote confusion among and between the <u>Victims of White Supremacy</u> (Non-White people). During the existence of White Supremacy (Racism), the terms "racial <u>minority</u>," and/or "racial <u>majority</u>," may or may not apply to the total number of <u>White</u> people, as compared with the total number of <u>Non-White</u> people, and/or they may or may not apply to a comparison between the <u>power</u> of White Supremacists (Racists) as opposed to the power<u>less</u>ness of the Victims of White Supremacy (Non-White people).

Notes: According to Compensatory Counter-Racist Logic, and during the existence of White Supremacy (Racism), those White people of the known universe who practice White Supremacy (Racism) are, collectively, The "Majority" Power when compared with the Non-White people of the known universe (The "Minority Power") - people whose power is less than the power of the White Supremacists (Racists).

Miscegenation. <u>Do not use this word</u>. When others use this word, ask for a detailed explanation that you can easily understand.

> **Notes:** During the existence of White Supremacy (Racism), the word "miscegenation" serves no constructive purpose. The use of the word, at best, only helps to support and add strength to the practice of White Supremacy (Racism).

Misconduct. <u>Use this word</u> mostly to apply to anything said or done that does not help to promote the use of truth (that which is) in a manner that best helps to produce justice (balance between people), and in a manner that does not help to promote the production of correctness (balance between people, creatures, things, etc.).

Use the word "misconduct" to apply to anything and everything that any person does or says that directly or indirectly helps to maintain, expand, and/or refine The System of White Supremacy (Racism), in any one or more areas of activity (Economics, Education, Entertainment, Labor, Law, Politics, Religion, Sex, and War/Counter-War).

Misfitted Person [Racial]. <u>Use this term</u> to apply to any Non-White person who is subject to White Supremacy in any one or more areas of activity.

Misfitted and/or Zeroistic Speech or Action. <u>Use this term</u> to apply to anything said or done by a Non-White person, while existing in subjugation to White Supremacy, that is not said or done in such a manner as to be effective in the elimination of White Supremacy.

Misfitted and/or Zeroistic Thinking. <u>Use this term</u> to apply to any thinking and/or thought by a Non-White person while existing in subjugation to White Supremacy, that does not promote speech and/or action that is effective in the elimination of White Supremacy.

Mismarriage. <u>Use this term</u> to mean any so-called "marriage," "mate-ship," "marital-situation," etc., between persons that includes a <u>Non-White</u> person during a period when that Non-White person is directly or indirectly subject to The System of White Supremacy (Racism). Use the term "mismarriage," and/or "Racemarriage" to mean any "marriage" that includes a <u>Non-White</u> person during the existence of White Supremacy (Racism).

> **Notes:** During the existence of White Supremacy (Racism), Non-White people are not allowed to <u>be</u> "married" - Non-White people are only allowed to <u>pretend</u>

that they are "married." During the existence of White Supremacy (Racism), Non-White people are only allowed to function in "mate-ship arrangements" ("mismarriages"). During the existence of White Supremacy (Racism), these "mate-ship arrangements" ("mismarriages") are directly or indirectly subject to and controlled by, Racistman and Racistwoman (White Supremacists, collectively). Non-White persons who are "married" within The System of White Supremacy (Racism) are, according to Compensatory Counter-Racist Logic, "Race-mated."

Miss America/Mr. America. Do not use either of these terms for the purpose of truthfully identifying any person, creature, or thing, now existing in the known universe, as long as White Supremacy (Racism) or any other form of non-justice (non-balance between people) exists anywhere in the known universe.

> **Reason:** During the existence of White Supremacy (Racism), and according to Compensatory Counter-Racist Logic, the basic correct definition for "America," "American(s)," "Africa," "African(s)," "Asia," and "Asian(s)," is: (1) a person who does not mistreat anyone; (2) a person who does not allow anyone to be mistreated; and (3) a person who helps the person who is in need of the most help.
>
> According to Compensatory Logic, the definition for the aforementioned terms (collectively) is the exact same basic explanatory definition for a person who practices justice (balance between people). The compensatory correct definition for "Justice" is: (1) a condition in which no person, anywhere, is mistreated, and (2) a condition in which the person who needs help the most, gets the most help. Since it is not possible for Justice (balance between people) to exist and White Supremacy (Racism) to exist in the same universe, at the same time, there are no people in the known universe who correctly qualify for the title of "America," "Americans," "Africa," "Africans," "Asia," or "Asians," or for the title of "Miss America," "Mr. America," "Mr. Africa," "Miss Asia," etc.
>
> **Note:** As long as non-justice (non-balance between people) exists in the known universe, "Americans," "Asians," and "Africans," do not exist, and are yet to be produced.

Mistake. Use this word with caution. Study the ways that others use the word. Study the ways that others do not use the word. Ask questions. Is The System of White Supremacy (Racism) a "mistake"? Is it a "mistake" to use time and energy doing things other than speaking and acting to replace White Supremacy (Racism) with Justice (balance between people)?

> **Note:** During the existence of White Supremacy (Racism), and according to Compensatory Counter-Racist Logic, it is correct to call The System of White Supremacy (Racism), "The Master Mistake."

Mistreat/Mistreatment. Use these words to apply to anything that is said or done, either directly, or indirectly, that results in incorrect harm to one or more persons or creatures.

> **Notes:** During the existence of White Supremacy (Racism), and according to Compensatory Counter-Racist Logic, the White Supremacists (Racistmen and Racistwomen, collectively) are the smartest and most powerful people in the known universe. Therefore, according to Logic, they are the people who are best able to guarantee that no people are mistreated. They can do this if they choose to do so. They cannot do so if they try to do so as White Supremacists (Racists). They can only do so as "White" people who are opposed to White Supremacy (Racism), and who are dedicated to producing justice (balance between people). As White Supremacists (Racists), those White persons who have chosen to continue being White Supremacists (Racists) are the Greatest Mistreaters of the Non-White people in the known universe. Use the term "Mistreatment of People" to apply to the many ways that the people of the known universe interact with each other in a non-constructive manner, particularly during the existence of The System of White Supremacy (Racism).

Mistreatment, Comforting. Use this term to apply to any form of mistreatment that is designed or intended to "help" a victim of mistreatment to find "comfort" in the manner or style in which he or she is being mistreated.

> **Notes:** White Supremacists (Racistmen and Racistwomen) are often extremely skilled in knowing how to make their Victims (Non-White people) very "comfortable" in receiving mistreatment. The White Supremacists (Racists) do this mostly by using deception in a manner that causes their Victims to think that they are being "benefited," when, in truth, their Victims are

being non-justly deprived of, or being prevented from, gaining something of constructive value.

Mixed-Blood/Mixed Race. Do not use these terms. When others use them, ask for a detailed explanation that you can easily understand. Ask questions.

> **Questions:** What, exactly, is "mixed-blood"? Is not all blood "mixed"? If so, "mixed" with what? If blood is not "mixed," how can it be "blood"? What, exactly, is "blood"? What, exactly, is not "blood"? What, exactly, is a "Race"? What, exactly, is not a "Race"? What, exactly, is a "mixed-Race"? What, exactly, is not a "mixed-Race"? Is "Race" and "Racism," one and the same? If being a "member" of a "Race" is not for the purpose of practicing Racism, then what exactly, is the constructive (or destructive) "value" in being a "member" of a "Race"? If "Race" and "Racism" are one and the same, how can "Racism" be "mixed" with non-Racism?

> How can a person be a "member" of a "Race," and not be a member of a "Race," at the same time? How can a person be a "Racist," and not be a "Racist," at the same time? What, exactly, is "Racism"? Is "Racism" the same as White Supremacy? If White Supremacy is "Racism," and "Racism" is White Supremacy, how is it possible for any other form of "Racism" (i.e., "Black supremacy," "Non-White Supremacy," etc.), to exist in the same universe, at the same time?

> **Note:** During the existence of White Supremacy (Racism), and according to Compensatory Counter-Racist Logic, and "racially speaking," there are only three categories of people in the known universe: White people, Non-White people, and White Supremacists (Racists).

"Mmmmmm". Use this (sound) in the form of an almost quiet humming, or "ummmm"-ing sound, as a way of responding to remarks (statements) whenever you prefer not to express a response of any kind, other than a short "ummmm"-ing sound. The sound, itself, should be used to be *intentionally* "meaningless." The sound, itself, could mean that the person making the sound is choosing to do nothing else other than think about the remarks being made.

Mob/Mobster, etc. Avoid using these words. When others use these words, ask for a detailed explanation that you can easily understand. Ask questions.

Questions: What, exactly, is a "mob"? What, exactly, is a "mobster"? What, exactly, does a "mob" do? Is a "mobster" the same as a "gangster"? If so, in what ways? What, exactly, do "mobsters," and/or "gangsters" do? What do they do in regards to Economics, Education, Entertainment, Labor, Law, Politics, Religion, Sex, and War/Counter-War?

How many "mobsters" make a "mob"? Is every White Supremacist (Racist) a "mobster"? Is every "mobster" a criminal? Is White Supremacy (Racism) a "crime"? Are those White persons who practice White Supremacy (Racism), the most efficient, the most brutal, the most powerful, and the smartest of all of the "mobsters" in the known universe?

Modern. Use this word with caution. When others use it, ask them to explain, in detail, exactly what they mean. Does "modern" mean "different"? If so, how "different"? Does it mean, "improved"? If so, "improved" how?

> **Note:** "Different" and/or "new" do not, necessarily, mean the same as "improved," or "better."

Money. Use this word to apply to any person, creature, or thing that is used in exchange for whatever is regarded as being the same value, or of greater value, in the exchange. When others use this word, ask for a detailed explanation that you can easily understand.

> **Note:** During the existence of White Supremacy (Racism), the White Supremacists (Racistmen and Racistwomen) have the greatest control of the value of all of the "money" that is directly or indirectly associated with the Non-White people of the known universe.

Money Masters. Use this term to mean the White Supremacists (Racists) of the known universe.

> **Reason:** As long as The System of White Supremacy (Racism) exists, Racistman and Racistwoman (White Supremacists, collectively) will control the value of all of whatever is used as "money" by the Non-White people of the known universe. This means that, as long as White Supremacy (Racism) exists it is the White Supremacists (Racists) who are the "masters" of money. They are the "masters" of money because they are also the "masters" of all of the Non-White people, including those who have

money, those who do not have money, and/or those who are in need of money. People who dominate other people also dominate whatever it is that those other people have, including the "value" of whatever it is that those other people have.

Notes: The White Supremacists (Racistman and Racistwoman, collectively) speak and act to guarantee that Non-White people do not have enough of what is needed that will allow them to be able to depend on each other. The White Supremacists (Racists) make sure that Non-White males and Non-White females cannot help themselves – or each other - to get what is needed without them being forced to get what is needed only by directly or indirectly submitting to the will of the White Supremacists (Racistman and Racistwoman, collectively).

In money matters, the White Supremacists (Racists) deceive many Non-White males and Non-White females by making them believe that they can support and defend each other financially, without the direct or indirect approval of Racistmen and Racistwomen (White Supremacists). They often do this by promoting the illusion of Non-White males and Non-White females being able to protect each other through the so-called "institution of marriage." During the existence of White Supremacy (Racism), all "marriage-arrangements," and "family arrangements" that involve Non-White persons are subject to the will of the White Supremacists (Racistmen and Racistwomen).

Monkey on His Back. Do not use this term. Instead, say, "He has a problem that needs to be eliminated."

Reason: During the existence of White Supremacy (Racism), White Supremacists (Racistman and Racistwoman, collectively), have often expressed that monkeys, apes, and other so-called "lesser-creatures" are more "akin" to Non-White people than they are to White people. White Supremacists (Racists) often say, or imply, that the Non-White people of the known universe are similar in appearance, behavior, and intelligence, to monkeys, apes, gorillas, etc. Therefore, terms like "monkey on his back," "monkey business," "going ape," "acting like a monkey," etc., should not be used.

Monster and/or Monstrosity Behavior. Use these terms to apply to any greatly destructive behavior by any persons, White or Non-White, who, during the existence of White Supremacy (Racism) results in the mistreatment of people, or creatures, and/or the incorrect use of things, in regards to one or more areas of activity.

Use these terms to apply to the general behavior of a Non-White person who, for whatever reason, is subject to, and/or is a Victim of, White Supremacy and who, for whatever reason, willfully and deliberately does major unjust harm to any person. Use the term "monstrosity behavior" to apply to the general behavior of a Non-White person who, for whatever reason, is subject to, and/or is a Victim of, White Supremacy and who, for whatever reason, does not have the will, and/or the ability to end White Supremacy (Racism).

Use these terms to describe the general behavior of all Non-White people while they are subject to The System of White Supremacy (Racism). Also, use these terms to sometimes explain that, in The System of White Supremacy (Racism), all Non-White people are, from birth, systematically "trained" and/or forced to think, speak, and act in the manner of "monsters" and/or "monstrosities".

> **Notes:** During the existence of White Supremacy (Racism), all of the Non-White people and all of the White people, including the White Supremacists (Racists), function, at all times, in a manner that is the same as, or similar to, "monsters" and/or "monstrosities." It is incorrect, however, to use these terms as unasked titles and/or names to apply to particular individual persons. It is incorrect to "name-call" any person. It is, at all times, correct to call persons only by the names and/or titles that person chooses for you to call them.
>
> It is best and correct to use the terms "monster behavior" and/or "monstrosity behavior" only when speaking of the behavior of people in general (particularly Non-White people), during the existence of White Supremacy (Racism). As long as White Supremacy (Racism) exists, it is incorrect to expect any people in the known universe to behave in any manner other than that of "monsters" and/or "monstrosities." It can be correctly said that The System of White Supremacy (Racism) produces only two basic forms of behavior in Non-White people – that of "monsters" and "monstrosities."
>
> One of the basic "requirements" of Racistman and Racistwoman (White Supremacists, collectively) is that their Victims (Non-White people) interact with all people, all creatures, and all things in the manner of "monsters" and/or "monstrosities."

Moral/Morality.   Avoid using these words.   When others use the words "moral," "morality," "moral person(s)," "Moral Majority," etc., ask for a detailed explanation that you can easily understand.

> **Questions:**   What, exactly, is a "moral person"?   What, exactly, is "moral"? What, exactly, is "morality"? What, exactly, makes a person "moral"? What, exactly, are the qualifications for being "moral" in each of the Nine Major Areas of (People) Activity?

> **Notes:**   During the existence of White Supremacy (Racism), the terms "moral," "morality," "moral person," "moral society," etc., are difficult to define in a manner that reveals truth (that which is). The use of these words can usually be employed to produce or promote confusion. Many people use these terms in such a manner as to dominate and mistreat other people. Many people use these terms in such a manner as to pretend to produce justice (balance between people), while, in truth, continuing to practice non-justice (non-balance between people).

Moral Majority, The. Do not use this term. The word "moral" has been used in many ways. The result has been confusion and the mistreatment of people. When others use this or similar terms, ask for a detailed explanation that you can easily understand.

> **Questions:**   What, exactly, is the so-called "Moral Majority"? Where is it? Who is it? What makes it "moral"? Based on what? What, exactly, does a "Moral Majority" do in each area of activity? Can a White Supremacist (Racist) be a "moral person"? During the existence of White Supremacy (Racism), who, exactly, are the "moral people" of the known universe? Where, exactly, is the "proof" of the existence of a "moral person," and/or of a "Moral Majority," in the known universe?

Moslem/Muslim. Use these words only to describe and/or to identify those persons who describe, and/or who identify themselves, as "Moslems" or "Muslims." When people identify themselves as "Moslems" or "Muslims," ask them to tell you what they are "required" to do as "Moslems" or "Muslims." Ask them what they are "required" to do, and not do, in each area of activity, including Economics, Education, Entertainment, Labor, Law, Politics, Religion, Sex, and War/Counter-War, and seek answers that you can easily understand. Avoid conflict. If you are not a "Muslim" or "Moslem," do not argue about what a "Muslim" or "Moslem is, or is not, when talking to persons who say that they are "Muslims" or "Moslems."

Note: During the existence of The Religion of White Supremacy (Racism), it is correct to avoid arguments about or against any religion other than The Religion of White Supremacy (Racism).

Mother/Motherland/Fatherland. Use the words "mother" or "father" with caution. When others use the words "motherland," or "fatherland," ask for a detailed explanation that you can easily understand. When you choose to use these words, always explain that you are talking about every part of the known and unknown universe. During the existence of White Supremacy (Racism), use the terms "Race-Mother" or "Race-Father" to describe those White persons (collectively), who practice White Supremacy (Racism).

> **Notes:** During the existence of White Supremacy (Racism) and according to Compensatory Counter-Racist Logic, the Non-White people of the known universe can and do function as "large-size" or "small-size" "children". As children, they are allowed to produce offspring, but they are not allowed to function as "fathers," or as "mothers."
>
> During the existence of White Supremacy (Racism) the White people who practice White Supremacy (Racism) are the functional "mothers" and "fathers" of the Non-White people ("children") of the known universe. As such, the White people who practice White Supremacy (Racism) can be correctly described, collectively, as the "Race-Mothers," "Race-Fathers," "Great White Mother," "Great White Father," "Master-Mother," "Master-Father," etc.
>
> During the existence of White Supremacy (Racism) all of the Non-White people of the known universe function directly or indirectly as the illegitimate "subject-children" of White Supremacists (Racistman and Racistwoman, collectively). As the powerless and abused "child subjects" of Racistman and Racistwoman (White Supremacists, collectively), the Non-White people of the known universe are continuously raped by Racistman and Racistwoman in all areas of activity.

Motivational Speaker. Use this term to apply to any person who says something that has an effect on the behavior of one or more persons, creatures, or things.

> **Note:** During the existence of White Supremacy (Racism) those White persons who have chosen to practice White

Supremacy (Racism) have proven to be the most powerful "Motivational Speakers" of all of the people of the known universe.

Mud. Use this word with caution.

Mud (down in the). Use this term with caution. Use it only to describe something or someone that is actually "down" in actual mud. Do not use this term to mean the same as something or someone being in socio-material circumstances that are generally regarded as "degrading."

> **Reason:** During the existence of White Supremacy (Racism), the expression "down in the mud" is, indirectly, used by White Supremacists (Racists) to promote thoughts of "dark" people and "mud" being somehow, "degrading," unworthy, and/or non-constructive. White Supremacists (Racists) sometimes associate "degrading circumstances" with mud. Because the color of mud is dark, the "degrading circumstances" are then, indirectly associated with Non-White people, who are similar to mud in appearance.

Mud (your name is). Do not use this term.

> **Reason:** During the existence of White Supremacy (Racism), the name and color of mud has often been associated with Non-White people, and the color "dark brown" or "black" has often been used in a derogatory manner. Other expressions that have been used, but should not be used, are "down in the mud," "treated like dirt," "mired in misery," "mud-slinging politicians," etc. Because of "color," the White Supremacists (Racists) of the known universe have chosen to say derogatory things about dirt, mud, or clay, because dirt, mud and clay, are "dark" like Non-White people.

> **Notes:** There is nothing incorrect about dirt, mud, or clay. Dirt, mud, and clay are essential to making the universe as it should be. The colors of dirt, dust, mud, and clay are the colors that they should be. The color and/or the "shades" of color that Non-White people are ("Black," "Brown," "Yellow," "Red," "Tan," etc.), are the colors that Non-White people should be. None of these colors should be used in a derogatory manner. (See "The Mud Race(s)," "Mud-Slinging").

Mud-People, The. <u>Do not use this term</u>. Study the ways that others use this term.

Mud-Race(s), The. <u>Do not use this term</u>. Study the ways that others use these words and word-terms. Ask yourself and others the reason that the word "mud" is often used in a manner that is intended to be derogatory when associated with a person.

> **Reason:** During the existence of White Supremacy (Racism), the words "mud," and "dirt" are often used in a manner intended to be insulting. Those White people who believe in and who practice White Supremacy (Racism) sometimes, deliberately, associate the words "dirt," "dirty," "mud," "muck," "smutty," "mire," etc., with people who are classified as "Black," "dark," and/or "Non-White." The White Supremacists (Racistman and Racistwoman, collectively) sometimes associate "mud" or "dirt" with "filth" or "poison." They deliberately do this because "mud" or "dirt" is similar in "color" and "appearance" to many Non-White people. In The System of White Supremacy (Racism), a so-called "joke" that is disapproved of, is sometimes described as "dirty" or "smutty." "Down-in-the-mud," or "your name is mud," are also used as "slang" expressions that are used to mean that a person is, or should be, in unfortunate circumstances. So-called "muddled-thinking" is regarded as "poor" or "inferior" thinking.
>
> Mud-Race(s) is a term that White Supremacists (Racists) sometimes use to associate the color of mud with the color of "dark" (Non-White) people. They do this in such a manner as to promote the thinking that mud is dark and worthless, and, therefore, "mud-colored" people are also worthless (and/or ugly). White Supremacists (Racists) sometimes speak and write as if dirt, mud, muck, soil, and so-called "mud-slinging" are all unpleasant and are all to be avoided because, according to them, they are "dark and ugly."
>
> White Supremacists (Racists) prefer to associate many things that are "black," "brown," "tan," and/or "dark," with people who are "dark" (Non-White), and, therefore, as such, are "things" to be trampled on, despised, disdainfully avoided, and/or only put to use as some "necessary evil." In the thinking of a White Supremacist (Racist), "mud," and so-called "mud-colored people" are things like the "darkness of space" – to be "feared," "detested," "explored," and "conquered".

Notes: "Mud" is dirt mixed with water. "Mud" nourishes the things that grow in the known universe. The "color" of mud is a correct and constructive color. The "color" that is assigned to any person, creature, or thing by The "Originator of Color" is always correct. This includes the "color" of mud, as well as so-called "mud-colored" people.

Mud-Slinging. Do not use this term to mean the same as the act of making hurtful and/or insulting remarks. Do not use the term "mud-slinging" as a "slang" term. Use the term to mean only the "slinging" of actual mud (dirt mixed with water). When others use this term, ask for a detailed explanation that you can easily understand. Also ask the reason why the word "mud" was chosen to be used in the manner explained.

Reason: White Supremacists (Racists) sometimes use this term to mean the same as saying something to insult, and/or to do harm to a person's "feelings" (emotions). White Supremacists (Racists) sometimes choose to use the word "mud" in this manner because of the color of mud – "tan," "brown" or "black." They also, in this manner, associate the color of mud with the color of "dark" and/or Non-White people. Therefore, the "slinging of mud," according to Racist (White Supremacist) thinking and intentions, means to say things to or about a person that renders that person "dark," and thereby making that person unworthy and/or despicable.

Muddle Along/Muddled Thinking/Muddle-the-Water. Do not use these terms. (See, "The Mud Race(s)," "Mud-Slinging").

Mulatto. Do not use this term or any similar term. Instead, use the terms "White people," "Non-White people," and/or "White Supremacists (Racistman and Racistwoman).

Reason: Words like "mulatto," "half-White," "mixed-race," "part-White," etc., serve no constructive purpose when applied to any people in the known universe. The use of such terms only help White Supremacists (Racistman and Racistwoman, collectively), to maintain, expand, and/or refine the practice of White Supremacy (Racism). The basic effect of the use of such terms between and/or among Non-White persons is to produce confusion, conflict, and hostility.

Multi-Race/Multi-Racial. Do not use these terms. When speaking or writing about the existence of any so-called "Race" of people, always say that there is only one "Race"- "The White (Supremacist) Race."

Reason: During the existence of White Supremacy (Racism), according to Compensatory Counter-Racist Logic, and, as long as White Supremacy (Racism) exists: White Supremacy is Racism, and Racism is White Supremacy. All of the White people who practice White Supremacy, are, collectively, the only "Race," and the only "Racists" that exist in the known universe. White people who do not participate in the practice of White Supremacy (Racism) are "non-Race White people" and/or "non-Racist White people". The Non-White people of the known universe are also "non-Race" and/or "non-Racist" people.

Notes: According to Compensatory Counter-Racist Logic, Non-White people of the known universe are subject to, and are the Victims of, The Race People (White Supremacists, collectively). No Non-White people are members of a "Race." During the existence of White Supremacy (Racism) the Non-White people of the known universe may or may not function as "club people," "fraternity," "sorority," "gang," "group," "party people," etc., but the Non-White people of the known universe do not, and cannot, function as "Race People" and/or as "Racist People," as long as White Supremacy (Racism) exists - they can only function as Victims of White Supremacy (Racism). The only way for a Non-White person to avoid being a Victim of White Supremacy is for White Supremacy not to exist.

Mutant. Use this word with caution. When others use it, ask for a detailed explanation that you can easily understand.

Questions: What, exactly, is a so-called "mutant"? What, exactly, is not a "mutant"? Are all people "mutants"? Exactly which persons, if any, are not "mutants"? Does every person, in some way, "mutate" with the food and drink that he or she puts into his or her body? Are the offspring of a male person and a female person, "mutants"?

Is being a "mutant" an incorrect person to be? Is it correct for a "mutant" to exist? Is anything that is not "original," a "mutant"? Is everything that is "created," a "mutant" of a "creative thought" produced by its "Creator"? Are every person's thoughts, speech, and actions, a "mutation" of the thoughts, speech, and actions of other persons? Is every person a "mutant" of a male and female person?

Mutual Mates/Mutually Mated. Use these terms to apply to the intimate arrangement between Non-White persons who are "married" to each other, while subject to The System of White Supremacy (Racism). When it is possible to do so, without being insulting, discourteous, and/or without promoting conflict, avoid saying that any Non-White person is "married" to any person. Describe all "marriages" that involve Non-White persons with terms like "mutual arrangements," "mutual mate-ship," "intimate arrangement(s)," "intimately mated," etc.

> **Reason:** According to Compensatory Logic, "marriage" is a mutual and harmonious relationship between a male and a female. All of the Non-White people in the known universe are directly or indirectly subject to the power of the White Supremacists (Racistman and Racistwoman). While subject to the power of White Supremacists (Racists), Non-White males and females can have a "mutual arrangement" with each other, but they cannot have a "harmonious" relationship.
>
> A "mutual arrangement" means that two or more people have made some "agreement" with each other. A "harmonious" relationship is stronger and more difficult to describe than a "mutual arrangement" and/or a "mutual agreement."
>
> A "harmonious" relationship means that two or more persons, at all times, interact with each other in a manner that proves that their major reason for existence is the most important value in their interaction with each other. This means that when there is conflict of any kind, this major reason for existence keeps their "mutual" interaction in "harmony" (in balance) with each other. According to Compensatory Logic, the major reason for the existence of all people during the existence of non-justice is to replace non-justice with Justice.
>
> During the existence of White Supremacy (Racism), the Non-White people who are subject to White Supremacy (Racism) are prevented from interacting with each other in "harmony" because of the destructive effects of White Supremacy (Racism). These destructive effects are confusing, divisive, and frustrating.

According to Compensatory Counter-Racist Logic, and during the existence of White Supremacy (Racism), the White Supremacists (Racistman and Racistwoman, collectively), speak and act to guarantee that Non-White males and females are not able to have dominant control over their interactions with each other in <u>any</u> area of activity, including Economics, Education, Entertainment, Labor, Law, Politics, Religion, Sex, and War/Counter-War.

"<u>Harmony</u>" can only exist in the absence of confusion. When confusion is the dominant force in the interactions between people, there is no "harmony" between those people. A "marriage" must have "harmony." A so-called "marriage" that does not have "harmony" is a "non-marriage," and/or a "play-marriage." Such "marriages," are, at best, "mutual arrangements."

According to Compensatory Counter-Racist Logic, no person can be subject to White Supremacy, (Racism) and be "married" at the same time. During the existence of White Supremacy (Racism), White people can be, and are, "married" – but only to each other. The System of White Supremacy (Racism) is designed to support White persons in regards to their marriages to each other, as long as they are not effectively attempting to replace White Supremacy (Racism) with Justice (balance between people).

Also, according to Compensatory Counter-Racist Logic, a White person who is "married," (or not "married") to a Non-White person, and who engages in willful and deliberate (or mutual) sexual intercourse with that Non-White person, is guilty of practicing White Supremacy (Racism) in its most destructive form.

The Non-White person who submits to, and/or who cooperates with, those White persons who engage in willful, deliberate, and/or mutual sexual intercourse or "sexual play" with Non-White persons, are the Victims of all White persons who participate in the practice of White Supremacy (Racism).

Notes: While subject to White Supremacy (Racism), a Non-White male and female can "mutually agree" on many things. They are prevented from making their mutual agreements "harmonious" because Racistman and Racistwoman (White Supremacists, collectively) cause confusion in all that Non-White males and females do, or attempt to do. Racistman and Racistwoman do this, both directly and indirectly by controlling whatever Non-White males and Non-White females do in each area of activity, including Economics, Education, Entertainment, Labor, Law, Politics, Religion, Sex, and War/Counter-War. It is Racistman and Racistwoman (White Supremacists, collectively) who decide what a Non-White male and Non-White female can and cannot do in regards to each other, in all areas of activity.

A Non-White male and Non-White female cannot produce "harmony" with one another while subject to White Supremacy (Racism). Therefore, they can only function as "mutual mates" - they cannot function as "married" people. Non-White persons who are "mutually-mated" during the existence of White Supremacy (Racism) can best be described as "mutualized" and/or "intimately-mutualized."

My Rights. Do not use this term. Instead, use the term "my duties."

> **Reason:** During the existence of White Supremacy (Racism), and according to Compensatory Counter-Racist Logic, it is confusing when one uses the terms "my rights," "your rights," "our rights," "civil rights," "property rights," etc. It is best and correct to use the terms "my duties," "your duties," "our duties," "the duties," "correct duties," etc. The words "duty" or "duties" must always directly or indirectly apply to the use of truth (that which is) in such a manner as to produce justice (balance between people), and correctness (balance between people, creatures, things, etc.). During the existence of White Supremacy (Racism), it is the duty of every person to think, speak, and act to replace White Supremacy (Racism) with Justice (balance between people), in all areas of activity.

> **Notes:** The use of the term "my rights" sometimes has the effect of meaning that a person is demanding a "gift." Therefore, it is best and correct for a person to say "my duty" to produce justice, rather than say, "my right" to produce justice. Producing justice should be regarded as a duty. The duty of producing justice is a "benefit" as well as a duty. The fact that justice also produces "benefits" should not be regarded as a reason to be resentful of one who works to produce justice.

N

Nation. <u>Use this word with caution</u>. During the existence of White Supremacy (Racism) always say that, "No other nation (of people) exists in the known universe except "The White Nation," "Nation of White Supremacists" and/or "The Race-Nation".

> **Reason:** In a known universe in which all of the Non-White people are directly or indirectly dominated by White Supremacists (Racistman and Racistwoman), only those White people who practice White Supremacy (Racism) can and do function as a "Nation." All other persons are either individual White people who do not practice White Supremacy (Racism), or they are the Non-White people who are subject to The White Nation.

> **Questions:** What, exactly, is a "nation"? Why has the word "nation" been used in many ways that are confusing? How many people make a "nation"? Can one person be a "nation"? What is it that people do that makes those people a "nation"? Do things make a "nation"? If so, what things? How many things? What is it that people do with things and with each other that make those people a "nation"? Is it possible for a "nation" to be "in" or "inside" another "nation"? Can a "nation" be subject to a "nation" and, at the same time, be a "nation"?

> What, exactly, is a "country"? Is a "country" the same as a "nation"? What, exactly, is a "state"? Is a "state" necessarily a part of, or "member" of a "nation"? How many people make a "state"? How many "states" make a "nation"? Can one person be a "state"? What, exactly, is an "independent state"? What, exactly, is an "independent nation"? What, exactly, is an "independent person"? If a "nation" is "independent," what makes it so? If a "nation" is not "independent," is it really a "nation"?

> **Notes:** According to Compensatory Counter-Racist Logic, and during the existence of White Supremacy (Racism), no person who is classified as "White," and/or who functions as a White person can be a Victim of White Supremacy, nor can he or she be a Victim of "Non-White Supremacy". During the existence of White Supremacy (Racism), "Non-White Supremacy," or "Black Supremacy," does not and cannot exist. During the existence of White

Supremacy (Racism), all Non-White people are Victims of White Supremacy. Any White person who is mistreated by any person (whether White or Non-White) is a Victim of <u>mistreatment</u> – not a Victim of "Non-White Racism."

National Defense/National Security. <u>Do not use these terms</u>. Use, instead, the expressions "production of justice" and/or "production of balance between people."

> **Reason:** The terms "national defense" and/or "national security" have often been used in a manner that produces confusion. They have too easily been used in a manner that has resulted in people doing things that were non-constructive. In the absence of justice (balance between people) among and between the people of the known universe, the use of the terms "production of justice," and/or "production of balance between people" are better than the use of the terms "national defense," "national security," "national interest," etc.

> **Note:** During the existence of White Supremacy (Racism), and according to Compensatory Counter-Racist Logic, the only "nation" in the known universe is, "The White Nation" ("The Nation of White Supremacists").

Nationalism. <u>Use this word with caution</u>. During the existence of White Supremacy (Racism), use this word to apply to "The White Nation," "The Race Nation," "The Nation of White Supremacists" (White Supremacists, collectively). When others use the words "nation," "nationalism," etc., ask for a detailed explanation that you can easily understand. Ask them to explain, in detail, the correct purpose for the existence of a "nation," and the correct purpose for the existence of the concept of "nationalism."

Native(s). <u>Avoid using this term</u>. When others use it, ask for a detailed explanation that you can easily understand. Ask questions.

> **Questions:** What, exactly, is a "native"? What makes a "native" a "native"? Is everyone and everything a "native" of the universe? Is everyone and everything associated with everything that is a part of the universe, both known and unknown, a "native"? What, exactly, is a "place"? How much of a "place" is a "place"? Is the universe a "place"?

> Is a person a "native" of the womb of a female? If so, is that person also a "native" of the "universe" in which that

womb "originated"? Are some "natives" treated as if they are "foreigners"? If so, how can a person be a "native" and be correctly treated (or mistreated) as a "foreigner"? Where is a person "from"? Is every person "from" every "place" where he or she is at that very moment? What is the meaning of the word "from"? Is a person "from" every place that he or she has ever been? Is a person "from" every place that he or she has never been? Is every person in the known universe a "native" of both "every place" and, at the same time, a "native" of "no place"?

Note: According to Compensatory Logic, it is correct to avoid using the word "native" to apply to any person in the known universe unless a person knows and understands the "origin" of all things, all persons, and all creatures.

Native American(s). Avoid using this term. Do not use it to apply to any person in the known universe unless the term is the choice of each person to whom the term applies, and/or is said to apply. When others use the term, ask for a detailed explanation that you can easily understand.

Questions: What, exactly, is a "native"? What, exactly, is an "American"? During the existence of White Supremacy (Racism), are the White Supremacists (Racistman and Racistwoman) the people who have the most power to decide who is, and who is not, a "Native American," "Non-Native American," "Indian," "Part-Indian," etc.?

Reason: Being called a "Native," may or may not be correct. Being called an "American" is confusing, and has no correct basis for belief. According to Compensatory Counter-Racist Logic, it is not possible for "Americans" to exist and White Supremacists (Racists) to exist in the same universe, at the same time. "Americans" are people who do not mistreat people, who do not allow people to be mistreated and who, at all times, helps the person who needs help the most.

In a known universe in which people continue to be mistreated, "Americans" do not exist. There is no evidence that "Americans" exist. "Americans" are yet to be produced. What does exist, are White people who practice White Supremacy, White people who do not practice White Supremacy (White Supremacists), and Non-White people (Victims of White Supremacy).

Note: The so-called "American Dream," or the "American Reality" are concepts that are, so far, productive of confusion. Both terms seem to be difficult to define in a manner that is easily understood – particularly by those who are White Supremacists (Racists), and those who are the Victims of The White Supremacists (Non-White people).

Natural/Unnatural. Use these terms with caution. When others use these terms, ask for a detailed explanation that you can easily understand. Ask questions.

> **Questions:** What is "natural"? What is "unnatural"? What is "natural," and "unnatural," as it pertains to interactions between people in each area of activity (Economics, Education, Entertainment, Labor, Law, Politics, Religion, Sex, and War/Counter-War)? Is the existence of White Supremacy (Racism) "natural" or "unnatural"? Is being a Victim of White Supremacy "natural" or "unnatural"?

> **Notes:** The smartest and most powerful people of the known universe have often proven they have the ability to make acts and/or conditions appear to be something other than what they are. It is not always easy, and sometimes extremely difficult, to be able to discover what is, or is not, "natural" or "unnatural."

Natural War and/or Counter-War. Use these terms to apply to effective speech and/or action against falsehood, non-justice, incorrectness, and effective speech and/or action against Racism (White Supremacy).

Negative/Negative Attitude/Negative Thinking. Do not use these terms to mean the same as "incorrect" or "non-constructive." If something is being done that is not correct or not constructive, say that it is "not correct" or "not constructive." Use terms like, "incorrect," "incorrect thoughts," "incorrect deeds," "incorrect conclusions," etc. Do not say things like, "Don't be so negative" or, "You have a negative attitude."

> **Reason:** The word "negative" has been used to mean "undesirable," "useless," "unwanted," "no longer needed," "incorrect," etc. It has also been associated with "darkness" and/or with the expressions "dark and unwanted" or "dark and disposable."

A "negative" portion of a photographic item process is sometimes called a "negative" because it is dark in appearance, and/or because it is "undeveloped." Because the word "negative" is associated with the word "dark" (in matters of some photographic processing), the White Supremacists (Racists) have directly or indirectly caused the word "negative" to also be associated with "black," "dark," and "undeveloped" and/or "primitive" people.

Notes: A better title for the "dark" portion of a photographic production process would be the term "Foundation Photograph," or "Original Print." It should be called this or a similar term because they are the photographs from which (the other) similar photographs are made. The word "developed" in the photographic process should be replaced by the word "processed." It is best and correct to stop using the word "negative." Instead, it is best and correct to use the words "no," or "incorrect," or "non-constructive".

Negress/Negro/Negroid/Nigger, etc. Do not use these terms as insulting names and/or titles directed toward individual persons. Do not use these terms for the purpose of "name-calling." Do not use these terms with the intention of being discourteous, or in such a manner that the effect is to belittle, rather than to constructively inform.

Suggestion: When exchanging views about the use of the word "Nigger," limit your remarks to the following two questions: (1) "What is a Nigger"? and (2) "What is the correct thing to do 'about', 'with', "for and/or against a 'Nigger' in regards to each area of people activity (Economics, Education, Entertainment, Labor, Law, Politics, Religion, Sex, and War/Counter-War")? If you or some other person is called a "Nigger" ["name-calling"], sometimes the best and correct response is silence.

Notes: During the existence of White Supremacy (Racism) and according to Compensatory Counter-Racist Logic, the words "Negress," "Negro," "Negroid," "Negression," "Nigger," etc., can serve no constructive purpose except to "identify" Non-White persons as Victims of White Supremacy (Racism).

Negro Fun and/or Niggerized Fun. Use these terms to apply to anything said or done by Non-White people under White Supremacy that is for the purpose of showing off to each other, mistreating each other, or directly or indirectly poking fun at each other's weaknesses and/or misfortunes.

Negroism and/or Niggerism. Use these terms to apply only to the victimization of Non-White people by White Supremacists (Racists). Do not use these terms to apply to any specific person, unless asked to do so by that specific person. (See, "Negress"/"Negro"/ "Negroid"/"Nigger").

Neighbor/Neighborhood. Use these words with caution. Study how others use these words. Ask yourself and/or others questions.

> **Questions:** What, exactly, is a "neighbor"? What, exactly, is a "neighborhood"? Is a "neighbor" a person who is "located" near another person? "Located" how? "Located" in what way? How "near" does a person have to be to another person in order to be a "neighbor"? How "far" from another person does a person have to be not to be a "neighbor"? Can a person be a "neighbor" and, at the same time, be "far away"? When, exactly, is a "neighborhood" so-called "divided"? If a "neighborhood" is "divided," how can it be "divided" and, at the same time, be a "neighborhood"? Can a "neighborhood" be "divided" by a river?

Neo-Colonialism. Avoid using this term. When others use it, ask for a detailed explanation that you can easily understand.

> **Questions:** What, exactly, is "neo-colonialism"? What, exactly, is "colonialism"? Is The System of White Supremacy (Racism) a form of "colonialism"? What, exactly, is a "colony"? What, exactly, is not a "colony"? During the existence of White Supremacy (Racism), are all of the Non-White people of the known universe a "colonized" people? If so, why? If not, why not?

> **Notes:** During the existence of White Supremacy (Racism) and according to Compensatory Counter-Racist Logic, it is best and correct not to use the words "colonialism," or "neo-colonialism" to apply to any situation involving White Supremacists (Racists). Instead, it is best and correct to use the term "White Supremacy (Racism)".

Neo-Fascism/Neo-Nazism/Neo-Racism, etc. Do not use these terms. Instead, use the term "White Supremacy (Racism)" and always use it to mean the same as "fascism," "Nazism," and/or so-called "Neo-Nazism" and do this as long as White Supremacy (Racism) exists. Whenever others use these terms, ask for a detailed explanation that you can easily understand.

Neutral/Neutrality. Do not use these words to apply to any person and/or to any condition dominated by The System of White Supremacy (Racism). When others use these terms, ask for a detailed explanation that you can easily understand.

> **Notes:** During the existence of White Supremacy (Racism) and according to Compensatory Counter-Racist Logic, all of the people of the known universe are either practicing White Supremacy (Racism), or they are not practicing White Supremacy (Racism) – either because they choose not to, or because they can't. The only people who can't practice White Supremacy (Racism) are all persons who are Non-White, and any White persons who, because of physical or mental inabilities, cannot willfully and deliberately participate in doing harm to others.

> **Questions:** Do "geographical boundaries" make people "neutral"? Does material move across "geographical boundaries"? Do people move across "geographical boundaries"? If they do, how can either materials or people be "neutral"? Are all of the materials and all of the people of the known universe somehow, directly or indirectly, interactive? Do they affect one another? If they do, how can they be neutral? Can a person who is not dead, and who can and must make choices that involve others, be a person who is "neutral"?

New World/Old World/Third World, etc. Do not use these terms. When others use them, ask for a detailed explanation that you can easily understand.

> **Questions:** What, exactly, is the "world"? How much, of what, is required to be a "world"? Are the "world" and the "universe" one and the same? If not, how many "worlds" make a "universe"? What person is correctly qualified to say what is and what is not a "world"? Is The System of White Supremacy (Racism) "The Old World" or "The New World"? Is it the "Third World" or the "Tenth World"? How much of the "world" is dominated by the White Supremacists (Racistman and Racistwoman)? How "new" is "new"? How "old" is "old"? During the existence of White Supremacy (Racism), what is the "value" of these terms?

Note: During the existence of White Supremacy (Racism), and according to Compensatory Counter-Racist Logic, there is no reason to believe that the use of terms like "The Old World" or "The New World," are necessary in helping to do what needs doing.

Nice (facial) Features. <u>Avoid using this term</u> except for saying that a person's "facial features" are basically doing the job that "facial features" are designed to do. When others use this term when describing a person's face, ask for a detailed explanation that you can easily understand. Ask questions.

> **Questions:** What, exactly, are "nice facial features"? Why are some "facial features" of persons described as "nice" and some are not? What, exactly, are the qualifications for "nice facial features"? What persons are correctly qualified to know and say?

> **Note:** During the existence of White Supremacy (Racism), the White Supremacists (Racistman and Racistwoman, collectively), of the known universe think, speak, and act as if the best, correct, "nice," and/or "most beautiful" facial features are those of White people.

Nice/Nice Person. <u>Use these terms</u> only to apply to persons, places, creatures, and situations that you regard as "pleasing" to you, and/or as having a "pleasant effect" on the way that you think, speak, or act. Use the terms "nice" or "nice person" to apply to any or all persons (White or Non-White) who, for whatever reason, are "pleasing" to you. Do not, however, say that any person is a "good" person.

Do not think, speak, or act as if a "nice person" is one who believes in justice (balance between people) because he or she says or does something that you regard as "nice" or "pleasing." Do not confuse being "nice" with being "just," "correct," "good," "honest," "loyal," "trustworthy," "loving," and/or with having the correct intentions. When others use the terms "nice" and/or "nice person," ask for a detailed explanation that you can easily understand.

> **Note:** A White person can be a Racist (White Supremacist) and, at the same time, say and do many things that can be correctly described as "nice" (pleasing, pleasant, comforting, satisfying, etc.), but not "good," or "just".

Nigger. <u>Use this word with caution</u>. Do not use it to apply to any specific person. Use it only to apply to Non-White people in general, and/or to yourself in particular. Use it to apply to the Non-White people of the known universe only while they are subject to White Supremacy (Racism). Do not use it when you have reason to believe that using it will produce or promote greater conflict or confusion among or between Non-White persons. When White people use the word "Nigger," ask for a detailed explanation that you can easily understand. When in doubt about using or not using this word, use instead the terms, "The Pitiful Person" and/or "The Pitiful People" (to apply to Non-White people, in general) during the existence of White Supremacy (Racism). Do not, under any circumstance, use the word "nigger" to "name-call," insult, or embarrass anyone, at any time.

> **Correct usage**: "Racistman and Racistwoman are determined to have us function forever as Niggers."

> **Incorrect usage**: "That nigger that we voted for is not doing the job that we asked him to do."

> **Note:** During the existence of White Supremacy (Racism), and according to Compensatory Counter-Racist Logic, the Compensatory-Functional Definition of a "Nigger," is any Non-White person who is directly or indirectly subject to The System of White Supremacy (Racism) in any one or more areas of activity (Economics, Education, Entertainment, Labor, Law, Politics, Religion, Sex, and War/Counter-War).

Nigger-Lover. <u>Do not use this term</u>. When others use it, ask them to explain, in detail, exactly what they mean. Ask them to explain in a manner that you can easily understand. Ask them to define exactly what a "Nigger" is, and exactly what a "Nigger" is not. Ask them to explain what "love" is and to explain what is the exact "proof" of a person showing so-called "love."

Nightmare. <u>Do not use this term</u>. Use, instead, the terms "dreamfear," "feardream," "sleepscare," and/or "disturbing dream."

> **Reason:** During the existence of White Supremacy (Racism), this term may cause people to think in such a manner as to associate a "disturbing dream" with a "dark" creature, person, and/or thing. Therefore, during the existence of White Supremacy (Racism), it is best and correct not to use any word that a Victim of White Supremacy (Non-White person) has reason to believe will

help to promote the maintenance, expansion, and/or refinement of the practice of White Supremacy (Racism).

Nine Major Areas of (People) Activity, The. Use these terms with caution. According to *The United-Independent Compensatory Code/System/Concept*, always use with Compensatory-Functional Definitions and explanations that are specifically designed to best help produce thought, speech, and action intended to result in the replacement of The System of White Supremacy (Racism) with The System of Justice (balance between people). The Nine Major Areas of (People) Activity are: Economics, Education, Entertainment, Labor, Law, Politics, Religion, Sex, and War/Counter-War. When others use one or more of these terms, ask for a detailed explanation that you can easily understand.

No Man's Land. Do not use this term. When others use it, ask for a detailed explanation that you can easily understand. This term is confusing.

> **Questions:** What land "belongs" to what man? Who is correctly qualified to decide which land "belongs" to which man? How much land can a man "occupy"? When? Where? How? Based on what "qualifications"? Can a man truly "possess" land, or can he only "possess" people who "occupy" land?

Non-African/Non-American/Non-Asian. Use these terms to apply to speech and action by persons that does not result in the establishment of The System of Justice (balance between people) in all areas of activity, including Economics, Education, Entertainment, Labor, Law, Politics, Religion, Sex, and War/Counter-War.

> **Notes:** During the existence of White Supremacy (Racism), and according to Compensatory Counter-Racist Logic, "Africans," "Americans," and "Asians" are all one and the same "concept" of people behavior that has not yet been put into practice. "Africans," "Americans," and "Asians," are people who practice justice. They are people who, at all times, speak and act in such a manner as to guarantee that no person is mistreated, and guarantee that the person who needs help the most, gets the most help. No such people exist. It is the duty of every person in the known universe to become an "African," an "American," or an "Asian" (a person who practices justice).

Non-Black Person. Use this term to apply to a White person, but avoid using it during the existence of White Supremacy (Racism).

> **Reason:** During the existence of White Supremacy (Racism), and according to Compensatory Counter-Racist Logic, it is correct to emphasize the true power arrangement between Non-White people, White people, and White Supremacists (Racists). As long as White Supremacy (Racism) exists, the Non-White people of the known universe will, by comparison with White people, have less power. To think correctly about this power and powerless arrangement between White people and Non-White people, it is best and correct to say that White people are "White," and that people who function as "Black," "Brown," "Red," "Yellow," "Tan," etc., are "Non-White".

Non-Existence. Use this term to apply to "non-function" or, the "absence of function".

Non-Human Being/Non-Humane Being. Use these terms to apply to any person in the known universe who, for any reason, does not practice justice and correctness at all times, in all places, in all areas of activity, including Economics, Education, Entertainment, Labor, Law, Politics, Religion, Sex, and War/Counter-War.

> **Notes:** According to Compensatory Logic, no person in the universe "qualifies" for the title of "human being" and/or "humane being" if he or she does not practice justice and correctness at all times in all areas of activity. He or she only "qualifies" for the basic title of a "being," a "non-human being" and/or a "person".

Non-Justice. Use this term to apply to: (1) imbalance between people; and (2) circumstances within the known universe wherein any person is being mistreated, and/or any person is not receiving the most constructive help as it is needed.

Non-Justice (The Masters of). Use this term to apply to all White persons who practice White Supremacy (Racism).

Non-Just People. Use this term to apply to: (1) any people who exist during a period when injustice exists any place in the known universe and (2) all of the people now existing in the known universe.

Non-Organized Unification. Use this term to apply to two or more persons, thinking, speaking, and/or acting in a prescribed manner, to accomplish the same basic objective, except with each person functioning independently of the other, in regard to the time and/or place of any particular speech, and/or action chosen. *The United-Independent Compensatory Code/System/Concept (for Victims of Racism (White Supremacy)* is a prime example of "Non-Organized Unification".

Non-Person/Nothing Person. <u>Use these terms</u> only to apply to <u>yourself</u>, if you choose to do so. <u>Do not use these terms</u> to apply to other persons unless those persons ask you to do so. When others use these terms, ask for a detailed explanation that you can easily understand.

> **Reason:** According to Compensatory Logic, every "person" is a person. Every "person" is a special person. Every "person" is a very important person. Every "person" is the sum total of everything, and nothing. Every "person" is the sum total of nothing, and everything. There is no "person" exactly like any other person in the entire universe.

Non-Profit. <u>Avoid using this term</u>. When others use this term, ask them to explain, in detail, exactly what they mean – and what they do not mean. What is "profit"? What is "non-profit"? Is not everything that is done intentionally, done for profit?

Non-Race. <u>Use this term</u> to apply to any person who has proven that he or she is not a member of the "White Race," "The White Nation," "The Race Nation," and/or is not a White Supremacist (Racist), or a White person who, in any manner, functions in support of The System of White Supremacy (Racism).

> **Notes:** During the existence of White Supremacy (Racism), and according to Compensatory Counter-Racist Logic, there exists only one "Race" of people in the known universe (based on "color"/"non-color"). That "Race" is "The White Race" (White Supremacists and/or Racistman and Racistwoman, collectively). The basic function of "The White Race" is to practice Racism (White Supremacy). The basic function of The System of White Supremacy (Racism) is to guarantee "benefits" to the White people of the known universe through the systematic mistreatment of the Non-White people, at all times, and in all areas of activity.

Non-Racial. <u>Avoid using this term</u>. When others use this term, ask for a detailed explanation that you can easily understand. During the existence of White Supremacy (Racism), what is or can be "non-racial," if it directly or indirectly involves interaction(s) between the people of the known universe? Are not all of the people in the known universe directly or indirectly involved in something that is "racial"? Does not the existence of White Supremacy (Racism) affect all people, either directly or indirectly?

> **Note:** During the existence of White Supremacy (Racism), and according to Compensatory Counter-Racist Logic, it is correct to blame the White Supremacists (Racists) for all things that the Victims of White Supremacy (Non-White people) do and say that is non-constructive.

Non-Racists. Use this term to apply to: (1) those White persons who do not practice White Supremacy (Racism), at any time, in any place, in any area of activity, including Economics, Education, Entertainment, Labor, Law, Politics, Religion, Sex, and War/Counter-War; and (2) all Non-White people during the existence of White Supremacy (Racism).

> **Note:** During the existence of White Supremacy (Racism), only a White person can function as a Racist. White Supremacy is Racism, and Racism is White Supremacy.

Non-Truth. Use this term to mean, "That, which is not true".

Non-Violence. Use this term to mean the complete absence of all forms of violence – including the unjust and incorrect results of deceit (indirect violence). Use the term "non-violence" only to apply to the interactions between the people of the known universe when none of them are doing harm to each other in any area of activity. Use the term "non-violence" to apply only to a world in which there exists no injustice, and no incorrectness, in any area of activity or existence. When others use this term, ask for a detailed explanation that you can easily understand.

> **Notes:** It is correct to regard any action that is effective in helping to replace White Supremacy (Racism) with Justice (balance between people) as "counter-violence." During the existence of White Supremacy (Racism) and according to Compensatory Counter-Racist Logic, the best and correct way to explain "the basics" about "non-violence," "violence" and/or "counter-violence" is as follows:

- "Non-violence" is the complete absence of violence, of any kind, against any person, creature, place, thing, etc.

- "Violence" is any form of harm done to a person, creature, place, thing, etc., for reasons that are non-just and/or non-correct.

- "Counter-violence" is a form of correct counter-activity enacted against those persons, creatures, things, etc., who are enacting "violence" against any person, creature or thing.

- The existence of The System of White Supremacy (Racism) is, by functional definition, a condition of violence against the Non-White people of the known universe, in every area of activity, including Economics, Education, Entertainment, Labor, Law, Politics, Religion, Sex, and War/Counter-War.

Non-White Person. Use this term to apply to any person who is not "classified" as "White," and who is not treated as "White" by those persons who are "classified" as "White," or by those persons who generally function as "White" and who are "accepted" as "White," and/or by White Supremacists (Racists), during the existence of White Supremacy (Racism).

Notes: During the existence of White Supremacy (Racism) and according to Compensatory Counter-Racist Logic, the three correct so-called "racial classifications" and "counter-racist classifications" that apply to the people of the known universe are:

1. Non-White people - People "identified" as "Black," "Brown," "Red," "Yellow," etc., and/or other than "White."

2. White people - People who are "classified" as "White," and who are "accepted" as "White" by "White" people, but who do not function as White Supremacists (Racists).

3. White Supremacists (Racists) - People who are "classified" as "White," who "function" as "White," and who "function" as White Supremacists (Racists), either directly or indirectly in any one or more areas of activity.

266

The term "Non-White People" is generally used or considered:

1.   A "catch-all" term maliciously used by White Supremacists (Racists) to identify all people who are not classified as White, and/or who are not to be permitted to generally function as White, in any one or more areas of activity.

2.   Any people, classified (by White people) as "Black," "Brown," "Red," "Yellow," "Tan," and/or "Non-White," and who are regarded or treated as such, and/or subjugated because of factors associated with such classification.

3.   Any people who are generally or specifically considered to not be White by those people who consider themselves to be White, and who practice White Supremacy (Racism) on the basis of that consideration.

Explanation: The people of the known universe who call themselves "White," call all other people Non-White. Since the "Non-White" classification is not the opposite of the "White" classification, the two terms are, therefore, not of equal value. The classification that is the opposite of the "White" classification is the classification "Black".

"Black" people are Black people. "White" people are White people. "White" people are also people who are "Non-Black". "Black" people are also people who are "Non-White". "Brown," "Red," "Tan," and "Yellow" people, are "shades" of "Black" people.

Normal. Use this word with caution. When others use the word (as it applies to some or many circumstances), ask for a detailed explanation that you can easily understand. Ask questions.

Questions: What, exactly, is "normal"? What, exactly, is not "normal"?   What, exactly, is "abnormal" or "sub-normal"? Is "normal" the same as "just"? Is "normal" the same as "correct"? If not, why not? What, exactly, is "normal" in the areas of Economics, Education, Entertainment, Labor, Law, Politics, Religion, Sex, and in War and/or Counter-War? What, exactly, is "normal behavior" in matters of Race, Racism and Counter-Racism? What, exactly, is "normal" in the behavior of White people, and Non-White people, during the existence of White Supremacy (Racism)? What, exactly, should this "normal" behavior be?

Note: The System of White Supremacy (Racism) causes "abnormal" behavior in people to be "normal" – but only if such behavior helps to support the practice of White Supremacy (Racism).

Normal Person. Avoid using this term. When others use it, ask them to explain, in detail, exactly what they mean.

> **Questions:** What, exactly, is a "normal person"? During the existence of White Supremacy (Racism) is a "normal" White person the same as a "normal" Non-White person? Are both persons "equally normal"? If so, what is the "value" of their being "equally normal" and where is the proof of them being "normal" and "equal"? Is it correct to be "normal" in a situation that is incorrect? Is injustice a "normal" situation that is supported by or allowed to exist by people who are "normal persons"? If the existence of White Supremacy (Racism) is "normal," is a person who speaks and/or acts to end White Supremacy (Racism), a "normal person," or an "abnormal person"?

Number One (Racial). Use this term to apply to any White person who practices White Supremacy (Racism).

> Explanation: The White people who practice White Supremacy (Racism) are the smartest and most powerful people in the known universe. They are first (number one) in knowledge, and first in direct power by people, over all people classified as Non-White, in all areas of (people) activity.

O

Oath (under). Use this term with caution. When others use this term, ask for a detailed explanation that you can easily understand.

> **Questions:** What, exactly, is an "oath"? What, exactly, is not an "oath"? Is it correct to punish a person for violating an "oath"? If so, which "oath"? How many "oaths," and as pertaining to what? Is it correct for every person to speak an "oath" that he or she will always do everything that he or she can do to replace The System of White Supremacy (Racism) with The System of Justice (balance between people)? Is it correct to trust a person who has spoken an "oath" and then violated that "oath"?

Obscene/Obscenity. Use these terms with caution. Use them to apply to anything that is said or done and/or that is not said or done, that result in The System of White Supremacy (Racism) not being replaced with The System of Justice (balance between people). Use these terms mostly to apply to The System of White Supremacy (Racism), itself. Say, "White Supremacy (Racism) is the Greatest Obscenity," or "There is nothing more obscene than the effects that White Supremacy (Racism) has on those who practice it, and those who are the Victims of it."

When others use terms like "obscene," "obscenity," "indecent," "vulgar," "profane," etc., ask for a detailed explanation that you can easily understand, and ask if all of these terms apply to the practice of White Supremacy (Racism), more than they do to any other activity.

> **Notes:** During the existence of White Supremacy (Racism) and according to Compensatory Counter-Racist Logic, the greatest and most destructive expression of White Supremacy (Racism) as an "obscenity," is through acts of sexual intercourse, "sexual play," and/or through the promotion of anti-sexual (so-called "homo-sex" or "lesbianism") between White persons and Non-White persons. As long as White Supremacy (Racism) exists, all such acts are the most vulgar, profane, and indecent specific acts of Direct Racist Aggression that is or can be committed by White people against the Non-White people of the known universe.

Occident/Occidental. Avoid using these terms. When others use these terms, ask for a detailed explanation that you can easily understand.

> **Questions:** What, exactly, is an "occidental" person? Is it a "White" person? Is it a bird? A rock? A tree? Is it a "combination" of "religions"? What, exactly, makes a so-called "occident" different from something or someone that is not an "occident" or "occidental"?

Off-Color. Do not use this term. When others use it, ask for a detailed explanation that you can easily understand. What, exactly, is a so-called "off-color" remark? How does an "off-color" remark differ from an "on-color" remark? What, exactly, is an "on-color" remark? How can a person know the "color" of a remark? What is the purpose of deliberately associating "color" with a remark, without the remark itself being associated with what is regarded as "color"?

Official/Official Business/Unofficial Business. Use these terms with caution. When others use these terms, ask for a detailed explanation that you can easily understand.

> **Questions:** What, exactly, makes something or someone "official"? What, exactly, makes someone or something, "unofficial"? What, exactly, is "business"? What, exactly, is the difference between "business" that is "official," and "business" that is "unofficial"? What, exactly, is "official business," and "unofficial business," in each area of activity (Economics, Education, Entertainment, Labor, Law, Politics, Religion, Sex, and War/Counter-War)? Who decides what is and what is not, "official"? Based on what "qualification"?

> **Note:** During the existence of White Supremacy (Racism) and according to Compensatory Counter-Racist Logic, it is correct to regard as "official business," all speech and action that is designed to help replace White Supremacy (Racism) with Justice (balance between people) in any one or more areas of activity.

Official and/or Master Lynch Force. Use these terms to apply to any one or more White persons who speak and/or act in any manner that directly or indirectly helps to establish, maintain, expand, and/or refine White Supremacy (Racism).

Off-White/Half-White/Part-White, etc. Do not use any of these or similar terms to apply to any persons, creatures, things, etc. Instead, use the term "White" (the absence or lack of color), or "Non-White" (the presence of color or "shades" of color - "black," "brown," "red," "yellow," "tan," "orange," "green," "purple," etc.).

When others use terms like "off-White," "half-White," etc., ask for a detailed explanation that you can easily understand. When talking to people and you are confused about them being "White" or "Non-White," ask them, "Are you "White" or "Non-White"? Continue to ask that question until the answer that you receive is either "White," or "Non-White" – or until the person decides not to answer the question.

If a person who appears "White," but is not willing to say that he or she is "White," or "Non-White," and if you have reason to believe that he or she is "White," (and not "Non-White), it is correct to think, speak, and act as if he or she is a Racist Suspect (Suspected White Supremacist). In addition, explain to him or her the reason you asked if they are "White" is because many people who are "Non-

White" appear to be "White." As long as White Supremacy (Racism) exists, it is important to know and to understand the difference.

Notes: During the existence of White Supremacy (Racism) and according to Compensatory Counter-Racist Logic, it is best and correct for every Victim of White Supremacy (every Non-White person) to suspect that any White person is a White Supremacist (Racist) if that White person is physically and mentally able to practice White Supremacy (Racism), and if that White person has not proven to every Victim of White Supremacy (Non-White person) that he or she is not a White Supremacist (Racist).

Old Person (Racial).   Use this term to apply to the following conditions: (1) Any person who loses the will to think, speak, and/or act to find truth, and to use truth to produce justice and correctness; and (2) Any person who loses the will to think, speak and/or act to eliminate Racism (White Supremacy).   Study the ways that others use the term "old" person.

On Automatic (Racial).   Use this term to apply to all of the *effects* that the System of White Supremacy (Racism) has on its Victims (Non-White people) by causing its Victims to ("automatically") say and do things again, and again, and again, that do not produce constructive results.

Notes: White Supremacists (Racists) make it their business to train their Victims (Non-White people) to react to every situation in a manner that causes their Victims to do more harm to themselves than they do to the System of White Supremacy (Racism). A skilled White Supremacist (Racist) takes great pride in his or her ability to predict, with great precision, what it is that a Non-White person will do, or say, and will not do, or say, in most, or all, situations.

A skilled White Supremacist (Racist) usually knows exactly what a Non-White person is thinking about. They usually know what to do, or say, to a Non-White person, or about a Non-White person, the things that will make that Non-White person be calm, be sad, be happy, or be ferociously angry. All of these reactions are designed to be for the benefit of The System of White Supremacy (Racism).

The White Supremacists (Racists) make a precise study of a Non-White person's strengths and weaknesses. They usually make sure that they know more about that Non-White person than that Non-White will ever know about them (the White Supremacists/Racists).

The White Supremacists (Racists) are usually The Masters in the science of getting a Non-White person to talk about their "personal feelings" in regards to any or all topics – in all the Nine Areas of (People) Activity (Economics, Education, Entertainment, Labor, Law, Politics, Religion, Sex, and War/Counter-War).

They are usually the Masters at getting Non-White people to do things out of "emotion," rather than the use of Logic.

Suggestions:

(1) Stop being "on automatic" (in support of The System of White Supremacy/Racism);

(2) Be a keen observer of what others are doing and saying. Listen to others, but always try to say no more than is necessary.

(3) When speaking, always do your best to put everything you say in the form of a question. Make a record of the answers you receive.

(4) Be calm. Take notes. Never express anger or use curse words or profanity towards others.

(5) Always, always, think, think, and think again before speaking, writing, and/or acting.

On the Bright Side/Lighter Side. Do not use these (or similar) terms as expressions that mean thoughts or deeds that are somehow supportive of thought, speech and/or action that is correct or "good" or "right," etc., as opposed to thought, speech and/or action that is "dark" (like some people are "dark"). When others say things like "Let's look on the bright side of this arrangement between Non-White people and White people," ask them why they used the words "bright side."

> **Notes:** During the existence of White Supremacy (Racism), words like "bright," "brighter," "brilliant," "fair," "light," etc., are often used in a manner that directly or

indirectly promotes the thought that "goodness," "correctness," "righteousness," etc., are all values that are directly or indirectly associated with White people (and not Black and/or Non-White people). When talking about things done or not done, it is correct to use the terms "correct" or "incorrect," rather than terms that imply "lightness" or "darkness."

On Top. <u>Use this term with caution</u>, particularly when talking or writing about "positions" of people in their relationships or "arrangements" with each other. Study the ways that others use this expression.

> **Reason:** It is incorrect for people to glorify being "on top" of other people. The domination of people should not be equated with progress.

> **Questions:** What is meant by being "on top" of the world? What person(s) should be recognized as being qualified to be "on top" of other people? What should being "on top" mean? For what purpose? Is it correct to be "on top" if people are being mistreated in the process?

One Zero (1/0). <u>Use this term</u> as a way of reminding yourself and others that every person in the known universe is, at all times, "everything" (one) and "nothing" (zero). Therefore, no person should, at any time, think, speak, and/or act as if he or she is of more or less "value" (as a person) than any other person. Always remind yourself and others that, according to Compensatory Logic, "everything" came from "nothing" and therefore, "nothing" is a "part" of "everything" and "everything" is a "part" of "nothing."

It is logical and correct for every person to keep in mind that he or she should not be ashamed or arrogant in matters pertaining to his or her assigned reason for existence by his or her "Creator".

> **Notes:** One-Zero (1/0) is (at the same time) "one," and "nothing," and both "one" and "nothing" are of "equal value" in regards to the interactions of all that is "in" and all that is "out" of the known and unknown universe. Therefore, all that "is" is an equal part of all that "isn't." All that "isn't" is what gives "awareness value" to all that "is."

Open-Airism and/or Universalism. <u>Use these terms</u> to apply to a method of thinking, speaking, and acting according to a Code that includes all areas of activity. This "Code" is made to function by an individual person who chooses to use one or more parts of the "code," at a time, place, and under those specific conditions that he or she thinks best and correct.

These terms also mean that each person functions as an organization unto him or herself. "Open-Airism" and/or "Universalism" means that each person is his or her own leader, as well as his or her own follower, in the use of what he or she chooses to select from a "code" of behavior that he or she uses as a basic guide. He or she, through the use of that "code," seeks to function as an organized and/or unified body.

> **Notes:** The *United-Independent Compensatory Code/ System/Concept* is a Code to be used as a means of attempting to compensate for the lack of ease and/or ability in organizing and/or maintaining a formal group that is consistently and continuously effective against the activities of the Racists (White Supremacists), and is, at the same time, greatly resistant to those things said or done by Racists to resist the effects of the Code.

Opinion. Use this word with caution. Be wary of the many ways that persons with much power sometimes use the word "opinion." Study the ways that White Supremacists (Racists) sometimes belittle the "reports" or "judgments" of Non-White persons by saying that these "reports" or "judgments" are so-called "mere opinions."

> **Reason:** During the existence of White Supremacy (Racism), the "opinions" of Non-White people are treated as if they are not as important as the "opinions" of White Supremacists (Racists) – particularly if those "opinions" are about the correct ways to replace The System of White Supremacy (Racism) with The System of Justice (balance between people).

Opinion, Official/Opinion, Personal. Avoid using these terms. When others use these terms, ask for a detailed explanation that you can easily understand. Ask questions.

> **Questions:** What, exactly, is the difference between a "personal opinion," and an "official opinion"? What, exactly, is the difference between a decision based on the "opinion" of a person who is "official," and of a person who is said to be "un-official," or "non-official"? Is any "opinion" by a person, a "personal opinion"? Is an "opinion" the same as a "judgment"? If not, what is the difference? Can a "non-official opinion" have the same

effect as a "judgment"? If it does, is that "non-official opinion," in effect, the same as an "official opinion"? What is and is not, "official business"? Can any person who is talking about "official business," offer an "opinion" that is, in effect, an "official opinion"?

Opportunity. Use this word with caution. When others use it, ask for a detailed explanation that you can easily understand.

> **Reason:** That which is sometimes called an "opportunity" is, in truth, a deceptive and non-constructive "enticement." What is sometimes called an "opportunity" is, in truth, an additional burden upon, or an unnecessary obstruction to, the solving of a problem.

> **Example**: During the existence of White Supremacy (Racism), the White Supremacists (Racistman and Racistwoman) sometimes offer a Non-White person a so-called "opportunity" to acquire large sums of money by having him or her do something that is designed to do greater harm to Non-White people.

Opposite Sex. Use this term with caution. Use it to mean either male or female. Use it to mean male and female as different from, and complimentary to, each other. Do not use the terms "opposite sex," or "complimentary sex," to apply to so-called "homo-sex," or "lesbian sex."

> **Reason:** According to Compensatory Logic, the word "sex" applies to male or female, or male interacting with female. The term "opposite sex" does not mean, and should not mean, "opposing sex" or "opposition to sex," or the male and female behaving "in opposition" to each other. According to Compensatory Logic, the term "opposite sex," functionally, means "complimentary sex." The word "sex" itself always means male and/with female, particularly as it relates to sexual intercourse.

According to Compensatory Logic, only males and females can engage in acts of "sexual" intercourse – and only with each other. It is not possible for a male (person) to have "sexual" intercourse with a male (person), or for a female (person) to have "sexual" intercourse with a female (person). According to Compensatory Logic, any attempts to commit such acts can only be correctly regarded as "anti-sex" ("against sex," and/or "behavior that is opposed to sex").

Oral Sex. <u>Use this term</u> to mean any expression of contempt, or of affection, between a male and a female, that involves the deliberate touching of any part of the body of one another, with the lips, tongue and/or mouth, while also thinking about "sexual passion" toward each other.

Ordained. <u>Use this word with caution</u>. When others use it, ask for a detailed explanation that you can easily understand. Ask questions.

> **Questions:** What, exactly, is an "ordained person"? What, exactly, is the "authority" that makes a person "ordained"? Which person is "qualified" to declare himself, herself, or any other person, "ordained"? "Qualifications," based on what? When? Where? By whom? According to what process?

> **Note:** During the existence of White Supremacy (Racism), and according to Compensatory Counter-Racist Logic, every Victim of White Supremacy (Non-White person), by being a Victim of White Supremacy, is automatically "ordained" to think, speak, and act to replace White Supremacy (Racism) with Justice (balance between people).

Ordinary Person. <u>Avoid using this term</u>. When others use it, ask for a detailed explanation that you can easily understand. What, exactly, is an "ordinary person"? What, exactly, <u>makes</u> a person "ordinary"? Is it correct for a person to be "ordinary"? What, exactly, is the "value" of being an "ordinary person"? Is a person "ordinary," <u>all</u> of the time, in <u>all</u> that he or she thinks, says or does?

Organized. <u>Use this word with caution</u>. Study the many ways that others use the word.

> **Questions:** What, exactly, is an "organized" person? What, exactly, are "organized" people? Are all people "organized" to do something, somewhere, at some time? Is there any such thing as an "organization within an organization"? Is an "organization within an organization" not an "organization at all, but truthfully, a "part" of the "organization" that it is "within"?

> **Notes:** An assembly, a crowd, or a group of people, are not necessarily, an "organization" nor are they necessarily, a "nation," etc. During the existence of White Supremacy (Racism), and according to Compensatory Counter-Racist Logic, those White persons of the known

universe who have chosen to practice White Supremacy (Racism) are the most "organized" group of people in the known universe.

During the existence of White Supremacy (Racism), and according to Compensatory Counter-Racist Logic, it is not possible for the Victims of White Supremacy (Non-White persons) to "organize" (as a group) against White Supremacy (Racism). While subject to White Supremacy, and according to a Counter-Racist Code of thought, speech, and action, Non-White people of the known universe can only "organize" as _individual_ persons.

This Counter-Racist "Code" serves to "organize," and "unify" the collective thoughts, speech, and action of each _individual_ Victim of White Supremacy (Non-White person), and do so in a manner that motivates him or her to think, speak, and act effectively to replace The System of White Supremacy (Racism) with The System of Justice (balance between people).

Organized Crime. <u>Use this term</u> to basically, mean the same as "The System of White Supremacy (Racism)".

> **Reason:** As long as The System of White Supremacy (Racism) exists, and according to Compensatory Counter-Racist Logic, there is no group of "criminals" in the known universe who are more "organized," or more powerful, than those White people who believe in, and who practice the crime of White Supremacy (Racism). As long as White Supremacy (Racism) exists, there is no "crime" greater than the "crime" of White Supremacy (Racism). The System of White Supremacy (Racism), by its very existence, makes it the "Universal Crime of Crimes".

Organized Religion. <u>Avoid using this term</u>, except to apply to The System of White Supremacy (The Religion of White Supremacy). Study the many ways that others use the word "religion," and the term "organized religion." Ask questions.

> **Questions:** What, exactly, is a "religion"? What, exactly, is not a "religion"? What, exactly, is an "organized religion"? What, exactly, is a "non-organized religion"?

> **Reason:** During the existence of White Supremacy (Racism), and according to Compensatory Counter-Racist

Logic, no "religion" that exists among the people of the known universe has proven to be more powerful than the "religion" of White Supremacy (Racism), and therefore, in effect, the only truly "organized religion". By comparison, all other "religions" and all other "organized religions," have proven to be too weak, and too ineffective to be called "organized," and/or "powerful."

Original. Use this word with caution. When others use it, ask for a detailed explanation that you can easily understand. Keep in mind that everything has an "origin." What is the "origin" of everything? What is the "origin" of "nothing"?

Our People. Do not use this term. When others use it, ask for a detailed explanation that you can easily understand. Instead of saying "our people," say "people," "the people," "White people," "Non-White people," "Race people," "victimized people," "powerful people," "powerless people," "smart people," "smart-less people," etc.

> **Notes:** The word "our" when applied to the word "people" may cause some to think that it implies "ownership" of people, by people. During the existence of White Supremacy (Racism), and according to Compensatory Counter-Racist Logic, the White Supremacists (Racists) of the known universe claim "functional ownership" of the Non-White people of the known universe. According to the correct concept of Justice (balance between people), it is non-just and incorrect for any people to claim, or attempt to practice, "ownership" of any person.

Outlaw. Avoid using this word. When using it, do not apply it to any specific person. Apply it to the general behavior of all of the people of the known universe. Study the many ways that others use this word. When others use it, ask for a detailed explanation that you can easily understand. Ask questions.

> **Questions:** What, exactly, is an "outlaw"? Are not all persons violating some "law" at some time? At all times? By practicing one "law," are not all persons violating or practicing another "law," at the same time? If so, which "law"? Whose "law"? As applies to what – in order to accomplish what? Is a person an "outlaw" if he or she practices White Supremacy (Racism)? Is a person an "outlaw" if he or she allows themselves to be a Victim of White Supremacy?

Note: According to Compensatory Logic a "law" is, functionally, "anything that is done".

Over-Compensation. <u>Do not use this term</u>. Instead, use the terms "non-compensation," and/or "non-compensatory."

> **Reason:** "Compensation" means "making-up" and/or producing something to place or replace that which is <u>missing</u>. Either something is missing (not there) or it is not. Either something is compensatory or it is not. "Compensation" either exists, or it does not exist.

Owner/Ownership. <u>Use these words with caution</u>. Study the many ways that others use the words "owner" and/or "ownership." Ask yourself, and others, many questions.

> **Questions:** Who, in the universe, "owns" what? Who "owns" water? Who "owns" air? Who "owns" sunshine? Who, or what, makes a person an "owner"? How long can a person "own" something and for what "reason"? Can a person "own" another person? Should a person "own" another person? Who should be an "owner"? Why? In order to do what? Is it correct to regard a person as an "owner" of things if those things were obtained or produced as the result of one person claiming to "own" another person? Is "possession" the same as "ownership"? If so, why? If not, why not? When, exactly, is a person the "owner" of "property"? Why? Based on what? By whom?
>
> During the existence of The System of White Supremacy (Racism), who decides what a Non-White person "owns" or doesn't "own"? If a person can claim "ownership" of land, why not air? Why not sunshine? Is it correct for a person to claim "ownership" of gravity? If so, why? If not, why not? If a person is "owned" by another person, can the person who is "owned" claim to "own" anything? How can a person "own" anything if he or she has a so-called "owner," "controller," "dominator," and/or "master"?
>
> **Notes:** During the existence of White Supremacy (Racism) and according to Compensatory Counter-Racist Logic, justice (balance between people) does not now exist. As long as White Supremacy (Racism) exists, it is not possible for justice to exist. In a situation where justice does not exist, it is confusing to say that a person

"owns" or is qualified to "own" anything. In a situation where justice does not exist, people may or may not "possess" things, and/or they may or may not master other people. Is it correct to think of "ownership" as being something that can come into existence only through the practice of, and only as a result of, "justice"? Justice (balance between people) exists only when no person is being mistreated, and the person who needs help the most, gets the most help. "Owners" only exist in "The System of Justice (balance between people). "Masters" exist in The System of White Supremacy (Racism), and in other forms of Incorrect Government (by people).

P

Pacification. Use this word with caution. When others use the word, ask for a detailed explanation that you can easily understand.

> **Note:** When White Supremacists (Racists) say that they intend to "pacify" an "area," what they often mean is that they intend to do something to "better control" Non-White people for the benefit of White Supremacy (Racism).

Paradise. Use this word only to mean a condition of "peace" between and among all people, all creatures, and all things, everywhere in the known universe. Use it to mean a universal condition in which no person is mistreated, and in which the person who needs help the most, gets the most help. Study the ways that others use this word.

> **Note:** According to the White Supremacists (Racistman and Racistwoman), "paradise" is any situation wherein the Non-White people of the known universe are subject to the direct or indirect domination and control by, of, and for, the White people (White Supremacist White People) of the known universe.

Para-Military. Do not use this term. When others use it, ask for a detailed explanation that you can easily understand. Ask questions.

> **Questions:** What, exactly, is "military"? What, exactly, is "paramilitary"? What, exactly, is "militant"? What, exactly, is "non-militant"? What, exactly, is "non-military"? What, exactly, is the difference between a "militant person," and a "civil" or "non-militant" person? Exactly when is a person a "militant"? Exactly when is a person "civil," "civilized," and/or "non-militant"? Is a

"militant person" civilized? Is a "para-militant person" a person who is "part-civilized"? If so, according to what? If so, according to whom? If so, by which definition and qualification? During the existence of White Supremacy (Racism), and according to Compensatory Counter-Racist Logic, is it correct to think, speak, and act as if all White Supremacists (Racists) are "military," "para-military," "militant," as well as "non-civil" and "non-civilized"?

Parent. Use this word with caution. When others use this word, ask for a detailed explanation that you can easily understand.

Questions: What, exactly, is a "parent"? What, exactly, are the correct qualifications for a person to function as a so-called "parent"? Can a person who is subject to White Supremacy (Racism) be a "parent"? How can people who function as "subjects" to White Supremacy (Racism) also function as "Parents"? If a person is subject to White Supremacy (Racism), is that person a "child"? If so, can a "child" be a "parent"? What, exactly, is a "child"? During the existence of White Supremacy (Racism), are all of the Non-White people who are subject to, or the Victims of White Supremacy (Racism), also the "subject children" of the White Supremacists (Racistman and Racistwoman)? Who are the "parents" of a person who is a "Race-prisoner"? If a "child" can produce "offspring," does that mean that a "child" can also be a "parent"?

Who has so-called "parental authority" over the Victims of White Supremacy (Non-White people) who call themselves "parents"? During the existence of White Supremacy (Racism), is it "The Great White Father" and "The Great White Mother" (White Supremacists, collectively)? What is a "true parent"? What is a "false parent"? Is it correct for children to be "subject" to their "parents"? If so, whom should the "parents" be subject to? If a Non-White person calls him or herself a "parent," how can he or she function as a "parent" when he or she is subject to the dictates of White Supremacists (Racistman and Racistwoman)?

Notes: During the existence of White Supremacy (Racism), and according to Compensatory Counter-Racist Logic, a Non-White person who produces offspring cannot function as a true "parent." The White Supremacists (Racists) only allow him or her to function as a so-called "false-parent," and/or "token-parent."

Part-Black/Part-White. <u>Do not use these terms</u>. Study the ways that others use the terms "part-White," "part-Black," "half-Black," "half-White," "part-Indian," "Eurasian," "part-Non-White," "part-African," "part-brown," "half-yellow," etc.

> **Reason:** All of the aforementioned terms only serve the White Supremacists (Racistman and Racistwoman), who use these and similar terms for the purpose of promoting greater confusion and greater control against the Non-White people of the known universe. Sometimes the White Supremacists (Racists) use such terms with the intention of "flattering" a Non-White person who may not "appear" to be "Non-White." The White Supremacists (Racists) do this with the intention of leading or enticing that Non-White person to speak or act in a manner that best helps to support White Supremacy (Racism).
>
> The White Supremacists (Racists) sometimes use words like "mixed-blood," "mixed-race," etc., in such a manner as to promote hostility, conflict, and confusion between and among the Non-White persons of the known universe, causing the Non-White persons to do great harm to one another.
>
> **Notes:** During the existence of White Supremacy (Racism), and according to Compensatory Counter-Racist Logic, there exist only two major categories of people pertaining to "color" or "non-color," visually speaking, other than the so-called "racial-Racist" category of "White Supremacist," and that is "White people" (non-color people), and "Non-White people". The "Non-White" or "Black" category includes all "shades" of Black" (brown, beige, tan, red, yellow, etc.).
>
> According to Compensatory Counter-Racist Logic and as long as White Supremacy (Racism) exists, the non-color "White," as it pertains to people, has no "shade." There exists no logical and/or constructive reason for a "color/non-color" identification category for a person that can be correctly called a "shade" of "White." There only exists "shades" of "Black."
>
> As long as White Supremacy (Racism) exists, all people who are categorized as "Black," or as a "shade" of "Black," are forced to function as Victims of Racistman and Racistwoman - those "White" persons of the known universe who have chosen to use their "Whiteness" as a

reason for subjugating and mistreating the "Non-White" people of the known universe.

Part-Indian. Do not use this term. Instead, use the term "Indian," and/or "Non-White person," or whatever name or title that a person who says that he or she is "Indian" prefers to be called. If a person tells you that he or she is "Part-Indian," ask that person if he or she is "White" or "Non-White."

> **Reason:** During the existence of (or because of the existence of) The System of White Supremacy (Racism), the terms "Indian," "Part-Indian," "redskins," "redman," "red-people," and/or "half-breed" may or may not be acceptable to people who may prefer to be called by other names and/or titles. Therefore, when in doubt, and in order to minimize conflict, it is best and correct to ask a person if he or she is "White" or "Non-White" and, after receiving an answer, ask that person the name and/or title that he or she would prefer to be called.

Partner. Use this word with caution. Study the ways that others use words like "partner," "mate," "companion," "co-worker," "helper," "comrade," etc.

> **Questions:** How much of a "partner," is a "partner"? Can a person be a "partner" to another person and, at the same time, be subject to that other person? Is a person who is in "partnership" with another person, a "partner" in all things? In most things? In a few things? Can people be "partners" in some things, and enemies or opponents in other things?

Party (for purposes of "constructive" fun) – Use this word in regards to Non-White people to mean one Non-White male person, interacting with one Non-White female person, for the purpose of doing something of constructive value, and including (or not including) acts of sexual intercourse and/or "sexual play." Such activity can be described as a "constructive fun party".

> **Notes:** During the existence of White Supremacy (Racism), participation in a "party" for the basic purpose of "having fun" should never include any more than one Non-White male person ad one Non-White female person. During the existence of White Supremacy (Racism), all other "meetings" of people should be for the basic purpose of making suggestions about ways and means of

ending White Supremacy (Racism), and replacing it with The System of Justice (balance between people).

Patriot/Patriotism. Use these words to apply mostly to yourself and to others at anytime that you (or those others) are speaking and/or acting with the intention of replacing White Supremacy (Racism) with Justice (balance between people.) When others use the words "patriot" and/or "patriotism," ask for a detailed explanation that you can easily understand. When talking with others about "patriots" and/or "patriotism" (while doing what you can to replace White Supremacy with Justice), always make the statement, "I know of no person more patriotic than myself."

> **Notes:** During the existence of White Supremacy (Racism), and according to Compensatory Counter-Racist Logic, there is no greater "patriotism" than the "patriotism" of trying to replace White Supremacy (Racism) with Justice (balance between people.) This is true and logical because there is no way for justice (balance between people) to exist, and White Supremacy (Racism) to exist in the same universe, at the same time. Therefore, the person who is speaking and/or acting to replace White Supremacy with Justice is doing the most "patriotic" thing that a person can do.

What is "patriotic" to a person who is trying to end White Supremacy (Racism) is always "subversive" to a White Supremacist (Racist). It is not possible for a White Supremacist (Racist) to function as a "patriot." A White Supremacist (Racist) is a "Master Subverter" of the production of justice.

A Compensatory Suggestion for Usage:

1. "Patriotism" – speaking and acting to guarantee that no person is mistreated at any time, in any place, in any area of activity, and, speaking and acting to guarantee that the person in need of the most [constructive] help, gets the most [constructive] help.

2. "Patriot" – any person who has guaranteed that no person is being mistreated, and, who has also guaranteed that the person in need of the most [constructive] help, received the most [constructive] help.

Peace. Use this word to mean the result of truth (that which is) being revealed, and used in such a manner as to produce justice (balance between people) and correctness (balance between people, creatures, things, etc.), and maintained in every area of activity, every place in the known universe. Study the ways that others use the word "peace."

> **Note:** According to Compensatory Counter-Racist Logic, there is no way for "peace" to exist and White Supremacy (Racism) to exist in the same universe, at the same time.

Peace-Keeper. Do not use this term.

> **Reason:** "Peace," in order to be "kept," must first be "produced". In a known universe in which many of its people are dominated and mistreated by White Supremacists (Racists), "peace" does not, and cannot exist. "Peace" that does not exist, cannot be "kept."

Peace-Maker. Use this term with caution. Do not use this term to apply to any person in the known universe. When others use the term, ask for a detailed explanation that you can easily understand. Ask questions.

> **Questions:** What person in the known universe has proven to be a "maker of peace"? Where is the "evidence"? What, exactly, are the qualifications for being a "peace-maker"? What, exactly, are the "do's" and "don'ts" that are required for "peace-making"? Which persons are qualified as "peace-makers"? "Qualifications" based on what — and according to whom?

> **Note:** During the existence of White Supremacy (Racism), and according to Compensatory Counter-Racist Logic, there is no way for a person to be a White Supremacist (Racist) and be a "peace-maker" at the same time.

Peer/Peer-Group. Avoid using these terms. When others use these terms, ask for a detailed explanation that you can easily understand.

> **Questions:** What, exactly, is a "peer"? What, exactly, is a "peer-group"? Is every person in the known universe the "peer" of every other person in regards to some thing at some time? If two people breathe air, are those two people each other's "peer(s)"? If five people use the same road, at the same time, are those five people the "peer" of one another? Does being a "peer" mean that there is

something that one person has "in common" with another person? If it does, does that mean that persons who are "peers" to each other are "communists"?

Is a person and a dog each other's "peer" if they both drink from the same river? Are "peers" equal to each other in all things, at all times, in all areas of activity? Are people who grow cucumbers "peers"? Are people who reside in houses "peers"? How many things that people do that are "similar" that makes them "peers"? How much is something "in common" is "in common"? What, exactly, is a so-called "shared value"? Does it mean that a person who "likes" the same thing that another person "likes" is the "peer" of that other person?

Notes: During the existence of White Supremacy (Racism) and according to Compensatory Counter-Racist Logic, it is incorrect to apply the word "peer" to any Non-White person; and the only people in the known universe who are correctly qualified to be identified as "peers," are those White persons who, collectively, practice White Supremacy (Racism). Non-White persons, however, are not "peers," nor are they members of any "peer-group." They are victims of White Supremacy. Victims of White Supremacy are a "group," but they are not a "group" of "peers." They are the "victim group" of the people who are "peers" (The White Supremacists, collectively).

Victims of White Supremacy (the Non-White people of the known universe) are made to appear that they are each other's "peers" by being made "equal" to each other in regards to their being subject to, and the prisoners of, the White Supremacists (Racistman and Racistwoman). According to Compensatory Logic, having some things in "common," does not, necessarily, make two or more persons "members" of a "peer-group."

Since the only "meaningful" thing that a Victim of White Supremacy (Non-White person) has "in common" with another Victim of White Supremacy (Non-White person) is his or her victimization, it is incorrect to regard any Non-White person as being the "peer" of another person (White or Non-White).

People (The). Use this term to apply to all of the people of the known universe, and/or to any of the people of the known universe who do not practice White Supremacy (Racism). When others use the term "the people," or "we the people," seek to learn if they are including any of the people of the known universe who practice White Supremacy (Racism).

> **Note:** During the existence of White Supremacy (Racism), and according to Compensatory Counter-Racist Logic, those White persons of the known universe who practice White Supremacy (Racism), function as "Universal Master Criminals" and, as such, function as "the enemy" of all of the Non-White people of the known universe.

People (We as Black). Do not use this term. Use, instead, the term, "We as people who are intending to end White Supremacy (Racism) and replace it with Justice (balance between people)."

> **Reason:** According to Compensatory Counter-Racist Logic, the only reason for two or more Non-White persons to identify themselves as "a people" is to identify themselves as "people" who are trying to replace White Supremacy with Justice.

People (We the). Use this term to apply to any of the following:

- Any White person who is not a White Supremacist (Racist).

- Any Non-White person who is a Victim of, and/or who is subject to, White Supremacy (Racism), and/or who has functioned as such, either directly or indirectly in regards to any area of activity.

- Any person, White, or Non-White, during the exact time that he or she is speaking or acting in a manner that proves effective in ending Racism (White Supremacy).

- Any person, White, or Non-White, during the exact time that he or she is speaking or acting in a manner that proves effective in producing justice (guaranteeing that no person is mistreated and guaranteeing that the person needing help the most, gets the most help).

People (your/my/our). Do not use these terms. Use the terms "people," "the people," "we people," "we the people," etc. When speaking of anything "racial," use the terms "White people," "Non-White people," or "White Supremacists (Racists)." Avoid using any terms that seem to promote the thinking that it is correct for people to have "ownership" of people. Also, do not use terms that have the effect of causing people to think that you intend to "put" people into "categories" that are not necessary for helping to produce justice (balance between people).

Notes: As long as White Supremacy (Racism) exists, it is necessary in the production of justice (balance between people) to use the terms "White people," "Non-White people," "White Supremacists (Racists)," "Black people," "Race People," "Racist People," "Counter-Race People," "Counter-Racist People," etc. This is for clarity in the process of revealing truth.

Perfect Person. Use this term to apply to any person who has produced and maintained "peace" between and among all people, all creatures, and all things, throughout the known and the unknown universe.

Perfect Storm, The (Racial). Use this term to apply to The System of White Supremacy (Racism) and the way that it works to guarantee that the Non-White people of the known universe are the constant Victims of major conflict, confusion, and non-just death-making.

Performance Evaluation. Use this term with caution. When others use it, study the ways that the words are used in making the so-called "evaluation" of a person's "performance." Study what is, and what is not included and make comparisons. Were differences in circumstances given correct consideration? If there were differences in circumstances, were those different circumstances incorrectly produced? Incorrectly considered? Incorrectly not considered?

> **Notes:** During the existence of White Supremacy and, according to Compensatory Counter-Racist Logic, the White Supremacists (Racists) of the known universe always "evaluate" a person's so-called "performance" according to how "efficient" that person is in speaking and/or acting to support the maintenance, expansion, and/or refinement of The System of White Supremacy (Racism).

Personal/Personal Business. Use these terms with caution. When others use these terms, ask for a detailed explanation that you can easily understand. Ask questions.

> **Questions:** What, exactly, is "personal"? What, exactly, is not "personal"? What, exactly, is "business"? What, exactly, is not "business"? What, exactly, is "personal business"? What, exactly, is "official business"? Is every person a "person"? Is every person an "official"? What, exactly, is a "public person"? What, exactly, is a "private person"? Are all of the people of the known universe directly or indirectly associated with each other as "public

persons" involved in "official business"? To what extent is "personal business" also "public business"?

Note: During the existence of White Supremacy (Racism) and according to Compensatory Counter-Racist Logic, everything that a Victim of Racism (Non-White person) says or does that is intended to help replace White Supremacy (Racism) with Justice (balance between people) is "personal," "personal business," "official business," and "public business."

Personal Problem. Use this term with caution. When others use it, ask for a detailed explanation that you can easily understand.

Questions: What, exactly, is a "personal problem"? What, exactly, is not a "personal problem"? Do all "personal problems" only involve one person? If a "personal problem" involves or affects more than one person, how can it correctly be called a "personal problem"? Are not all of the problems that involve one or more persons in the known universe, both "personal" and "public"?

Note: During the existence of White Supremacy (Racism) and according to Compensatory Counter-Racist Logic, all of the "problems" that a Non-White person has that are directly or indirectly the result of the existence of White Supremacy (Racism), are problems that are both "personal" and "public."

Philosopher. Use this word to mean a person with an "opinion," and/or to mean a person who has a distinct combination of "opinions." When others use the word "philosopher" or "philosophy," ask them to explain, in detail, exactly what they mean, and what they do not mean.

Pictures Don't Lie. Do not use this term.

Reason: When a person looks at a "picture," it is the thinking of that person that determines the so-called "meaning" of the "picture." Not all people think the same thoughts when they look at the same "picture."

Nothing has 'meaning,' unless it has 'meaning'.

Pitiful. Use this word to apply to people who are so extremely lacking in knowledge, understanding, will and/or ability that, for most of what is of constructive value, they are extremely dependent on those who are not lacking in that knowledge, understanding, will, and/or ability. The "Pitiful People" are any and all Non-White people during any period in which White Supremacy exists, and any and all Non-White people who exist in direct or indirect subjugation to White Supremacy, in any area of activity.

> **Example**: The Non-White people of the known universe are "pitiful" when compared (collectively) to the White Supremacists (Racists) of the known universe.

Pitiful Arrangement, The. Use this term to describe the "relationship" between the White people and the Non-White people of the known universe during the existence of The System of White Supremacy (Racism). Use the term "The Tragic Arrangement" to mean the same thing – the tacky, trashy, and/or terroristic manner in which the White people and the Non-White people interact with each other during the existence of White Supremacy (Racism), in all areas of activity, including Economics, Education, Entertainment, Labor, Law, Politics, Religion, Sex, and War/Counter-War.

Pleasant/Pleasing Company (Racial). Use this term mostly to apply to those White people whom you suspect may be White Supremacists (Racists) but are, for the most part, "pleasant," "pleasing," and/or "comforting" to talk with, listen to, look at, and/or be in the "company" of.

Polarized. Use this word with caution. When others use it, ask for a detailed explanation that you can easily understand.

> **Reason:** The word "polarized" is sometimes used in too many different ways for too many different reasons, by too many different people, who have too many different intentions.

Police. Use this word with caution. Use it to apply to any person and/or any force that guarantees that no person is mistreated, and that guarantees that the person who needs help the most, gets the most help. Do not apply the word "police" to any person who is "brutal." Do not apply the word "police" to any person who is a Racist (White Supremacist) or a person who is a Racist Suspect (Suspected White Supremacist). Do not apply the word "police" to any person who enforces any law in such a manner that justice (balance between people) is not the result. Instead, practice applying the term "Law Enforcement Officer" to any person who is said to be directly or indirectly assigned to "enforce law," including any "law" that is, in effect, correct or incorrect.

If a White person says that he or she is a "police officer," but speaks or acts in a manner that indicates that he or she is not a "police officer," but a White Supremacist (Racist), seek to use the term "Suspected Race Soldiering" (a White Supremacist and/or a Suspected White Supremacist) who pretends to be a "police officer".

If a Non-White person says that he or she is a "police officer," but speaks or acts in a manner that indicates that he or she is not a "police officer," but is a person who is using force to help a "Suspected Race Soldier" to enforce the practice of White Supremacy (Racism), it is correct to use the term "Misguided Victim of White Supremacy" to apply to that Non-White person.

> **Notes:** In a known universe dominated by the non-just and incorrect acts of people, it is best and correct not to use the word "police" to apply to any person now in existence. It is best and correct to use the terms "Law Enforcer," "Law Enforcement," "Law Enforcement Officer," "Law Enforcement Official," etc. The terms are best and correct because of what a "law" is. According to Compensatory Logic, a "Law" is anything that is "done". This means that every time any person does anything, he or she is practicing, enacting, enforcing etc., a "law" of whatever it is that is being done. It is important to know and to understand that "law" is not the same as "justice".
>
> Justice is that which is done that results in <u>no</u> person being mistreated, <u>plus</u> that which is done that results in the person needing help the most, getting the most help. "Laws" are a combination of things done that may or may not result in the establishment of justice. So far, in the known universe, justice is yet to be produced. This also means that, so far, in the known universe, so-called "police work" does not exist.

Police Action. <u>Use this term with caution</u>. When others use it, ask for a detailed explanation that you can easily understand. Ask questions.

> **Questions:** Is a so-called "police action" the same as "war"? Is it the same as "Counter-War"? Is it the same as so-called "military action"? Can a "police officer" and a "soldier," be one and the same? Can a "civilian" function as part of a "police action"?
>
> **Notes:** The term "police action" has often been used in a manner that is very confusing. The terms "law and order"

and "police action" have sometimes been used by White Supremacists (Racists) in a manner that helps to "disguise" the action [practice] of White Supremacy (Racism). Therefore, during the existence of White Supremacy (Racism), terms like "police action," "law and order," etc., should be explained in detail, or not used at all.

Police Brutality. Do not use this term. Instead, use terms like "brute-law," "brute-law enforcement" and/or "race/brute-law enforcement."

> **Reason:** "Police" persons do not commit "brutality". Incorrect law-enforcement officers do commit brutality. An incorrect law-enforcement officer is any person who speaks or acts in such a manner that produces or maintains non-justice (non-balance between people.)
>
> "Law" is anything that is done. A "Police" person does not do anything in a manner that helps to produce or maintain non-justice. Therefore, in a known universe in which justice (balance between people) does not exist, there is no evidence that "police" persons exist. What does exist are "law enforcement officers". When a person does something correctly that person has acted as a "correct law enforcement officer". When a person does something incorrectly, that person has acted as an "incorrect law enforcement" officer. It is only incorrect law enforcement officers who enact "brute-law," "brute-law enforcement," or "race/brute-law enforcement."

Police State. Do not use this term. When others use it, ask for a detailed explanation that you can easily understand. Ask questions.

> **Questions:** What, exactly, is a "police," or "the police"? What, exactly, is a "state"? What is the difference between "police" that is not a "state," and "police" that is a "state"? What is the difference between a "police person," a "police state," a "police act," and/or a "police action"?
>
> **Note:** White Supremacists (Racists) sometimes use the term "Police State" in a manner that is intended to confuse and mislead Non-White people.

Policy/Government Policy. Use these terms with caution. When others use the words "policy," "government policy," "rule," "regulation," "guideline," "custom," "practice," etc., ask them if these words have the same meaning as the word "law." When someone says that a "rule" or "regulation" has been "violated," ask if that "violation" is the same as a "violation of law." Ask questions about the differences, if any, between "policies," "rules," "regulations," and "laws." Can a "policy" have the same effect as a "law"? If so, why not call a "policy," a "law"?

Study the ways that White Supremacists (Racists) use the words "policy," "rules," "regulations," "customs," etc., and study how they use the words in a manner that allows White persons to say or do things that Non-White persons cannot say or do without being criticized and/or penalized. Also, when talking about White Supremacy (Racism), never say that White Supremacy (Racism) is the "policy," "law," etc., of any "government" except the "Government of White Supremacy (Racism)".

Political Act/Political Action. Use these terms to apply to anything that is said or done by a person that involves or affects another person. Study the ways that others use these terms, and study the purposes for which these terms are used.

> **Note:** During the existence of White Supremacy (Racism) and according to Compensatory Counter-Racist Logic, it is best and correct to use the word "politics" to mean anything that involves or affects interaction(s) between people. During the existence of White Supremacy (Racism), White Supremacy (Racism) has proven to be the most powerful "political action" and the most powerful "political force" affecting the conduct of the people of the known universe.

Political Asylum. Avoid using this term. When others use this term, ask for a detailed explanation that you can easily understand. During the existence of White Supremacy (Racism), seek to use the term only if you can do so in a manner that will best help to produce justice (balance between people.)

Political Prisoner. Use this term with caution. When others use this term, ask for a detailed explanation that you can easily understand. Study carefully the ways that others use this term. Particularly, study the ways that Suspected White Supremacists (Racist Suspects) use the term. Ask questions.

> **Questions:** What, exactly, is a "political prisoner"? What, exactly, is a "non-political prisoner"? During the existence of White Supremacy (Racism), are all of the

Non-White people "political prisoners" of the White Supremacists (Racistman and Racistwoman, collectively)? What, exactly, is "political"? What, exactly, is a "prisoner"? What, exactly, is "politics"? Are all of the people of the known universe "political"?

Note: During the existence of White Supremacy (Racism) and according to Compensatory Counter-Racist Logic, all of the Non-White people of the known universe are the "political prisoners" of the White Supremacists (Racists) of the known universe.

Political Statement. Use this term to apply to any "statement" that a person makes that involves or affects another person. When others use the terms "political" or "political statement," ask for a detailed explanation that you can easily understand. Ask questions.

Questions: What, exactly, is "politics"? What, exactly, is not "politics"? What, exactly, is a "political statement"? What, exactly, is not a "political statement"?

Notes: According to Compensatory Logic, "politics" is any relationship, or "arrangement" between one person and another. In addition, a "political statement" or a "political remark," is anything said or done by a person that involves or affects another person, in any one or more areas of people activity, including Economics, Education, Entertainment, Labor, Law, Politics, Religion, Sex, and War/Counter-War.

Politics/Politician(s). Use these words to mean any interactions between two or more persons, doing or saying things in such a manner as to have an effect on one another, either directly or indirectly, in any one or more areas of activity. When others use the words "politics," "political," "politician," "political statement," "political correctness," "political prisoner," etc., ask for a detailed explanation that you can easily understand.

Polygamy. Use this word to apply to any act of sexual intercourse and/or "sexual play" by one person with two or more other persons, during the same period of existence. Study the ways that others use the words "polygamy," "monogamy," "marriage," "cohabitation," "multiple marriages," "serial marriages," etc.

Note: During the existence of White Supremacy (Racism), persons classified as "White," who function as "White," and who engage in willful and deliberate sexual intercourse and/or "sexual play" with any Non-White person, are guilty of Direct Racist (White Supremacist) Aggression against all of the Non-White people of the known universe.

Pooling Resources. Use this term with caution. When others use it, ask for a detailed explanation that you can easily understand. Ask questions. Is not everything the result of a "pooling of resources" by someone, at some time, either directly or indirectly? Is not everything that a person receives, the result of the efforts of others – in whole or in part?

> **Note:** During the existence of White Supremacy (Racism), and according to Compensatory Counter-Racist Logic, it is best and correct to use the term "pooling resources" in such a manner as to mean the same as the expression, "Replace White Supremacy (Racism) with Justice (balance between people)."

Poor/Poor People. Use these terms with caution. When others use them, ask for a detailed explanation that you can easily understand.

> **Questions:** What, exactly, is "poor"? "Poor" as compared with what? When? How? What, exactly, is the difference between being "poor" and not being "poor"? How many things of "value" does a person have to have in order not to be "poor"? Can a person be "poor" in one area of activity, and not "poor" in another? Is a person who is "poor" also "powerless"? How much "powerless"? "Powerless," as compared with what? How much "power" does a person need? "Power" to do what? Is there really such a person as a "rich person"? What, exactly, makes a person "rich"? Is it possible for a person not to be "poor" and, at the same time, be subject to the System of White Supremacy (Racism)?

> **Notes:** During the existence of White Supremacy (Racism) and according to Compensatory Counter-Racist Logic, it is best and correct not to apply the terms "rich" or "poor" to any of the people of the known universe. Instead, it is best and correct to use the term "powerful," to apply to those White people of the known universe who participate in the practice of White Supremacy (Racism), and the term "power-less" to apply to those White persons who do not participate in the practice of White Supremacy (Racism), and to those Non-White people who are subject to White people who participate in the practice of White Supremacy (Racism).

Pornography. <u>Avoid using this word</u>. When others use it, as for a detailed explanation that you can easily understand.

Possession(s). <u>Use this word</u> to apply to anything that a person (or creature) has access to, and/or has use of. Study the ways that others use the word "possession(s)." Ask yourself and others questions.

> **Questions:** How much, of what, does a person truly "possess" and when does he or she truly "possess" that which is said to be in his or her "possession"? Does a person "possess" something simply by looking at it at the time that the something is looked at? Does a person "possess" something simply by touching it at the time that the something is touched? Does a person "possess" a sound simply by hearing that sound?
>
> Does a person "possess" the taste of food that is tasted? Does a person "possess" an "experience" during the time that he or she is remembering that "experience"? If a person is not thinking about and/or not touching something that he or she is said to "possess," is that person "in possession" of that something that he or she is not thinking about, and/or not touching? Can a person be "possessed" by his or her "property"?
>
> **Notes:** According to Compensatory Logic, it is incorrect to think, speak, or act as if the word "possession" and the word "property" have the same meaning. A "property" is something acquired by <u>correct</u> thought, speech, and/or action. A "possession" is something acquired by <u>any</u> thought, speech, and/or action - be it correct or incorrect.
>
> **Example:** According to Compensatory Counter-Racist Logic, everything that a White person "possesses" that was acquired as the direct or indirect result of the practice of White Supremacy (Racism), was acquired and/or "possessed" by <u>incorrect</u> thought, speech, and action and, therefore, cannot be correctly called "possession."

Pot Calling the Kettle Black. <u>Do not use this term</u>.

> **Reason:** This is a "slang" term that is often used in a manner that basically expresses White Supremacist (Racist) thinking that anything "black" or "dark" is

dreadful and/or unworthy – especially as it relates to people. All such terms similar to this one do not help to promote the production of justice (balance between people) and, therefore, should not be used. Some other examples of expressions that have no constructive use, are "black day," "black lie," "dark deeds," "dark past," "gloomy mood," "shady character," etc.

Power Father. Use this term to apply to any male person who is classified as "White," and/or who generally functions as and is recognized as "White" in his general interactions with "White" and "Non-White" people, during the existence of The System of White Supremacy (Racism), and who is able to either help or harm a "Non-White" person.

Power Mother. Use this term to apply to any female person who is classified as "White," and/or who generally functions as, and is recognized as "White" in her general interactions with "White" and "Non-White" people, during the existence of The System of White Supremacy (Racism), and who is able to either help or harm a Non-White person.

Power Parent. Use this term to apply to any male or female person (who have offspring) and who are classified as "White," and/or who generally function as, and is recognized as "White" in their general interactions with "White" and "Non-White" people, during the existence of The System of White Supremacy (Racism), and who is able to either help or harm a Non-White person.

Powerless Father/Mother/Parent. Use these terms to apply to any Non-White person(s) who produce offspring, and/or who so-called "adopts" a "child," "infant," etc., while directly or indirectly subject to The System of White Supremacy (Racism), in any one or more areas of activity/existence (Economics, Education, Entertainment, Labor, Law, Politics, Religion, Sex, and War/Counter-War).

> **Notes:** During the existence of White Supremacy (Racism), no Non-White person is allowed to function as a "father," "mother," or "parent." He or she is only allowed to pretend to function as such. Proof of the pretense is shown by the many ways in which the White Supremacists (Racists) practice their power over all that the Non-White people can and cannot do in regard to their offspring.

Prayer. Use this word with caution. Study the ways that others use this word. Ask yourself about "prayer."

Questions: Do you know and understand what a "prayer" is? Do you know and understand what a prayer is not? Is there a way to "pray" without using any special body movements or without using any special body positions? Can a "prayer" be a thought and/or a "perception" in which words are not used? What, exactly, is the correct purpose of "prayer"? When a person "prays," is he or she in "church"? Is "prayer" and "church," one and the same? Is being "in prayer" the same as being "in a church"? "In a temple?" "In a shrine"? Is it correct for a person to be "in prayer" at all times, in all places, in all areas of activity?

Preemptive Attack/Preemptive Strike. <u>Avoid using these terms</u>. When others use these terms, ask for a detailed explanation that you can easily understand. Ask questions.

Questions: What, exactly, is a "pre-emptive attack," and/or a "pre-emptive strike"? Is it correct to use a "pre-emptive attack" to put an end to The System of White Supremacy (Racism)? Is it correct to use a "pre-emptive strike" to help to produce the system of justice (balance between people)?

Pre-Historic. <u>Do not use this word</u>. Instead, use the words "history," "herstory," "theirstory," "ourstory," "mystory," and/or use the terms "known past," "unknown past," "forgotten past," etc. When others use the words "pre-historic," and/or "pre-history," ask for a detailed explanation that you can easily understand. Ask questions.

Questions: What, exactly, is "pre-history"? Is there a "history" that existed before "history"? Is all "history" the "same"? Is the "history" of one moment the absolute same as the "history" of another moment? Is everything in the past interrelated with everything in both the past and the present? What "began" before "the beginning"? How much of what is "past," is everybody's "past"?

Prejudice. <u>Use this word with caution</u>. Use it to mean, "to judge, before knowing and/or understanding the truth," and/or to "judge, without knowing and/or understanding the difference between what is true and what is not true". When others use this word, ask for a detailed explanation that you can easily understand.

Press, The/Media. <u>Avoid using these terms</u>. When others use these terms, ask for a detailed explanation that you can easily understand. What, exactly, is "the press"? What, exactly, is "the media"? Is it a person? A place? A thing? If "the press" or "the media" is a "thing," what is it controlled by? When? Where? How? For what ultimate purpose?

> **Notes:** According to Compensatory Logic, it is best and correct to avoid the use of terms such as "the press" and/or "the media." If something is said, written, and/or printed, it is best and correct to refer to the specific thing that was said, written, and/or printed - and by whom (by what person). It may be true that what is called "the press," is anyone who writes something or "prints" something. It may be true that what is called "the media," is anyone who says something that is "heard" (read, seen, etc.), by another.

Pretty. Use this word to apply to any person, creature, place, thing, feeling, etc., that you think to be "attractively pleasing," "nice-looking," "pleasant," "pleasing in appearance," "sexually-attractive" and/or "pleasant-looking." Also, use the word "pleasing" to mean the same as the word "pretty." Study the ways that others use the word "pretty" – especially the ways that others use the word to apply to the "appearance" of persons. During the existence of White Supremacy (Racism), Racistman and Racistwoman (White Supremacists, collectively) usually promote thought, speech, and action that result in many people thinking, speaking, and acting as if Non-White people, generally, are not as "pretty" as White people.

Preventative Detention. Use this term with caution. When others use it, ask for a detailed explanation that you can easily understand.

> **Questions:** Is all detention "preventative"? What, exactly, is the difference between "detention" and "arrest"? Is there a difference between "detention" and "subjugation"? Is The System of White Supremacy (Racism) a form of "preventative detention" that unjustly subjugates the Non-White people of the known universe? Does the practice of White Supremacy (Racism) "prevent" the production of justice (balance between people)?

Pride Tribes. Use this term to apply to any three or more persons who willfully and deliberately work to accomplish a goal that they made for themselves, mainly for the purpose of "producing pride" in themselves, and doing so with little or no regard for the harmful or non-constructive effects that such "pride production" has on others. This "pride production" may be done in the form of, and/or in the name of, "religion," "patriotism," "fraternalism," "gangsterism," "clubism," "thugism," "sexual show-offism," "anti-sexual (homo-sexual) show-offism," etc.

Primitive.　Use this word to apply to a condition of limited knowledge, and limited understanding, as compared with a greater knowledge, and a greater understanding.　Study the ways in which others use the word "primitive."

> **Notes:** During the existence of White Supremacy (Racism) and according to Compensatory Counter-Racist Logic, the White Supremacists (Racists) of the known universe have a greater knowledge and a greater understanding of what they need to know and what they need to understand in order to subjugate the Non-White people of the known universe. Therefore, the White Supremacists (Racists) are, by comparison, less "primitive" than the Non-White people of the known universe.
>
> The word "primitive" can also be applied to the thought, speech, and action of those persons in the known universe who do not know and understand what should be known and understood, about how to do what needs doing in the most constructive manner.　Use the word "primitive" mostly to apply to all of the Non-White people of the known universe, who are directly or indirectly subject to, and/or dependent upon, the will and/or the skills of the White Supremacists (Racistmen and Racistwomen, collectively) of the known universe.

Prince Charming.　Do not use this term.

> **Reason:**　During the existence of White Supremacy (Racism), the White people of the known universe are generally regarded as "royal" when compared to the Victims of White Supremacy (Non-White people).　For that reason, the term "Prince Charming" has directly or indirectly been used to promote the thinking that a real "prince" is, and should be, not only "charming," but strong, brave, skillful and, more than anything else, "White."　According to the White Supremacists (Racists), the only person in the known universe worthy of the title "Prince" or "Prince Charming," is a White male.

Prison.　Use this word to mean any condition of confinement, restriction, and/or unwanted subjugation that is lacking in spiritual, mental, or physical "comfort," and/or that is the result of incorrect thought, speech, and/or action.

> **Note:** According to Compensatory Counter-Racist Logic, The System of White Supremacy (Racism) is, in function,

a prison system that is specifically designed to unjustly confine, restrict, subjugate, and in other ways mistreat the Non-White people of the known universe for the basic physical, mental, and spiritual comfort, convenience, and pleasure of White people.

Prisoner. Use this word to apply to any person or creature forced into physical, mental, material or spiritual confinement, restriction, and/or subjugation. Use it, particularly, to apply to all of the Non-White persons existing in the known universe during the existence of The System of White Supremacy (Racism).

Prisoners of [Race] War/Race Prisoner(s). Use these terms to apply to the personal and general condition of all of the Non-White people of the known universe during the existence of The System of White Supremacy (Racism).

> **Reason:** During the existence of White Supremacy (Racism) and according to Compensatory Counter-Racist Logic, the Non-White people of the known universe are unjustly confined, restricted, retarded, handicapped, and subjugated by Racistman and Racistwoman (White Supremacists, collectively), at all times, in all areas of activity including, Economics, Education, Entertainment, Labor, Law, Politics, Religion, Sex, and War/Counter-War. This unjust condition that is enforced by the White Supremacists (Racists) is a war against the Non-White people, and they are, in effect, "prisoners of [Race] War," and/or "Race prisoners" (prisoners of Racistman and Racistwoman).

Privilege (Correct). Use this term to apply to the will plus the ability to seek truth, and to use truth in such a manner as to promote the production of justice and correctness.

Private. Use this word with caution. Study the ways that others use the word "private." Ask questions.

> **Questions:** What, exactly, is "private"? What, exactly, is not "private"? How "private" is "private"? How, and in what ways, is "private property" controlled by something (or somebody) called "public" or "the public"? How "private" is the "private business" of a "public person"? How "public" is the "public business" of a "private person"? To what extent is "private" and "public" one and the same? According to what? According to whom? What, exactly, is "private enterprise"? To what extent can

a "private enterprise" and a "public enterprise" be one and the same? If so, according to whom? If so, according to what? Can anything in the known universe be "public" and "private" at the same time? Is it correct to think, speak, and act as if everything that is directly or indirectly associated with The System of White Supremacy (Racism) is the business of the "public"?

Produce/Production. Use these words to apply to causing a result. Practice using the word "produce" in place of the word "develop." Use the word "production" in place of the word "development." Instead of saying, "We must 'develop' the skills to replace Racism with Justice," say, "We must produce the skills to replace Racism with Justice."

> **Reason:** There is reason to believe that some words, sometimes, have a more powerful effect on the thought, speech, and/or action of persons, than other words. The word "produce" seems to be a word that may increase the will of a person to do what needs doing sooner and completely.

Profession. Use this word to apply to anything that is said or done willfully, deliberately, and consistently and/or more than once. When others use this word, ask for a detailed explanation that you can easily understand.

Professional/Professor. Use these words to apply to any person who willfully, deliberately, and/or consistently, says or does something more than once. When others use the words "profession," "professional," and/or "professor," ask for a detailed explanation that you can easily understand. What, exactly, is a "professional"? What, exactly, is a "non-professional"? Who, exactly, is qualified to say that a person is, or is not, a "professor" or a "professional"?

Progress. Avoid using this word. Instead, say what has or has not been done, that needs doing. Study the ways that others use this word. Ask questions.

> **Questions:** What, exactly, is "progress"? Does "progress" truly exist in the absence of justice (balance between people), and in the absence of correctness (balance between people, creatures, things, etc.)? How, exactly, can "progress" be correctly measured during the existence of The System of White Supremacy (Racism)? What, exactly, is "progress" for a Victim of White Supremacy (a Non-White person)?

Progressive. <u>Avoid using this word</u>. When others use this word, seek an exact explanation of what is meant. If necessary, ask questions.

> **Questions:** What, exactly, is "progressive"? Are any people truly "progressive"? Have any people in the known universe become the quality of people that they should be? Are White people (collectively) a "progressive" people? In what ways are Non-White people "progressive"? What is the correct thing to "do with" people who are judged to be "non-progressive"? Should they be dominated by people who are judged as "progressive"? Should so-called "non-progressive people" be displaced and/or replaced by people who are judged "progressive people"? Should people who are not "progressive," be put to death? Is The System of White Supremacy (Racism) a "progressive" way of thinking, speaking, and acting?

Proper/Property. <u>Use these words with caution</u>. Use the word "proper" to mean anything that any person regards as "pleasing," "pleasant," "satisfying," "comforting," etc. Use the word "property" to mean that which is acquired as a result of acts that are just and correct. Do not confuse the word "property" with the word "possession." A "possession" is that which is acquired by any means — whether just and correct, or non-just and non-correct. Study the ways that others use the words "proper" and "property." Particularly, study the ways these words are used by persons who may be White Supremacists (Racists).

Prostitute/Prostitution. <u>Use these words with caution</u>. When others use the words "prostitute" or "prostitution," ask for a detailed explanation that you can easily understand.

> **Questions:** What, exactly, is a "prostitute"? What, exactly, is "prostitution"? What, exactly, is the difference between a "prostitute" and a "whore"? What, exactly, is a "whore"? What does the saying "doing something unworthy for pay" mean?

How many interactions between people are "unworthy"? "Unworthy" to whom? "Unworthy" in what manner? During the existence of White Supremacy (Racism), is a Non-White person a "prostitute," and/or an "unworthy person" if he or she asks a White person for a "job" growing food? Is cooperation with any part of The System of White Supremacy (Racism) a form of "prostitution"? Is participation in any form of non-just activity for "pay," a form of "prostitution"? A form of "whoredom"? Are all of the people who are subject to White Supremacy (Racism) "whores" and "prostitutes"? Are they victims of rape? Are they victims of exploitation? Is The System of White Supremacy (Racism), itself, a form of forced "prostitution" of Non-White people, and, therefore, a form of "mass rape"? Is a retarded person guilty of "prostitution" if he or she does something "unworthy" in return for money? Is a "retarded person" a "whore" if he or she engages in sexual intercourse in return for food, clothing, or shelter?

During the existence of The System of White Supremacy (Racism) are all Non-White persons "retarded"? Does not the activities of Racistman and Racistwoman (White Supremacists, collectively) "retard" and "handicap" all of its victim-subjects (Non-White people) in all areas of activity — Economics, Education, Entertainment, Labor, Law, Politics, Sex, and War/Counter-War? When a White person engages in sexual intercourse with a Non-White person during the existence of White Supremacy (Racism), is the Non-White person a "victim," or a "prostitute"?

In a known universe dominated by people who mistreat people, is there any way for a weak, confused, "misguided," and/or subject-person to avoid being "prostituted"? Are many "marriages" no more than "sophisticated," or acceptable forms of "prostitution"?

Protection/Protected. Use these words with caution. When others use them, ask for a detailed explanation that you can easily understand.

> **Note:** What is sometimes said to be "protection," "protected" and/or "protectionism" may, in truth, be a form of "aggression."

Prove/Proven. Use these words with caution. When others use the words "prove," "proven," and/or "proof," ask for a detailed explanation that you can easily understand.

> **Note:** What seems to be "proof" of something may not be "proof." What is said to be "proven" may not have been "proven."

Prudent. Use this word with caution. When others use it, ask for a detailed explanation that you can easily understand. When you use it, use it to mean to make a judgment based on the revelation of truth and speaking and acting according to that judgment in a manner that best promotes the production of justice (balance between people) and of correctness (balance between people, creatures, things, etc.).

Public, The. Use this word to mean (and to apply to) the existence of and/or activities of, any one or more persons. When others use the word "public," ask for a detailed explanation that you can easily understand.

> **Questions:** If a person is not the same as "the public," then what is "public," a "public," or "the public"? When, exactly, is a person not "public"? What is the exact difference between a person who is "public" and a person who is "private"? Who is correctly qualified to say what is, and what is not, "public" and/or "private"? If a person is "public," is he or she "public" in every area of activity? If so, why, and how? If not, why not? During the existence of White Supremacy (Racism), which part of the activities of a Non-White person is "public," and which part is "private"? Why? For the benefit of who or what?

Public Enemy. Use this term with caution. When others use the term, ask for a detailed explanation that you can easily understand. Ask questions.

> **Questions:** What, or which "public," is the enemy of what, or which "public"? Is it correct to be a "public person" who is the enemy of another "public person"? Is a White person a "public enemy" if he or she is not willing to speak and act to replace The System of White Supremacy (Racism) with The System of Justice (balance between people)? During the existence of White Supremacy (Racism), who are the persons who are correctly qualified to judge who is, and who is not, a "public enemy"?

Public Figure/Public Person. Avoid using these terms. When others use them, ask for a detailed explanation that you can easily understand. Ask questions.

> **Questions:** What, exactly, is a "public figure"? What, exactly, is not a "public figure"? What, exactly, is a "public person"? What, exactly, is not a "public person"? Are all of the people of the known universe "public"? Is a person a "public person" if he or she interacts with or "relates" to another person, in one or more areas of

activity? Who, exactly, is correctly qualified to judge who is, and who is not, a "public figure" and/or a "public person"?

Public Servant. Avoid using this term. When others use it, ask for a detailed explanation that you can easily understand.

> **Questions:** What, exactly, is a "public"? Is a person a "public"? Is a person "the public"? How many of which persons qualify for the title of "public"? What, exactly, is a "public servant"? Who, exactly, is correctly qualified to judge? How many persons must "serve"? How many of which persons are necessary to correctly qualify for the title of "public servant"? "Serve" what? When? Where? How? Are the people who "serve" The System of White Supremacy (Racism), "public servants"? If so, which people do not serve The System of White Supremacy (Racism) during the existence of White Supremacy (Racism)? Who are they, what are they, and what do they "serve"?

> Is it correct to think, speak, and act as if a "public servant" is a person who uses truth (that which is) in such a manner that justice (balance between people) and correctness (balance between people, creatures, things, etc.), is produced and maintained at all times, in all places, in all areas of activity? If so, why? If not, why not? Are all people "public servants"? Are all people "public enemies"? Are all people "serving" themselves and others at the same time that they are speaking and acting as "the enemy" of themselves and others? (See, "Public" and "Public Enemy")

Pull the Wool over their Eyes. Do not use this "slang" term. When others use it, ask for a detailed explanation that you can easily understand.

> **Reason:** During the existence of White Supremacy (Racism), this term may be used mostly to help promote the thought that the hair of Black people is not only like "wool," but should be disdained. The expression "pulling the wool over [the] eyes" may apply to the act of deceiving people by making them "blind" to many worthy things, and/or may apply to making Black people "blind" to their own self-worth by having them believe that their "wool-like" hair is somehow associated with that which is "worthless," or some "wool-like" material that is associated with a hindrance to sight and/or vision.

Note: During the existence of White Supremacy (Racism) Racistman and Racistwoman have often produced and/or promoted the thinking that the hair of Black people, is "wool-like" and, therefore, "ugly," "non-quality," "useless," and not as "socially acceptable" as the hair of White persons.

Pure as the Driven Snow. <u>Do not use this term</u>. Instead, use the term "pure as that, which is pure."

> **Reason:** The term "pure as the driven snow" is, in the thinking of some people, a promotion of "whiteness" in the appearance of people as having the "value" of honesty, "niceness," sincerity, "not being contaminated," "not looking like the color of dirt," etc.

Pure White. <u>Do not use this term</u>. When others use this term, ask for a detailed explanation that you can easily understand. When you use the word "White," do not say "pure White," "part-White," "half-White," "semi-White," etc., simply say "White."

> **Reason:** During the existence of White Supremacy (Racism) and according to Compensatory Counter-Racist Logic, the term "pure White" is sometimes directly or indirectly used to promote thinking in support of "whiteness" in the appearance of people, as being, within itself, "more desirable" and/or "less repulsive," than "darkness," "dark," and/or "Black."

> **Note:** During the existence of White Supremacy (Racism), the term "pure Black" is seldom used as an expression of, or as a description of, something or someone that is "desirable," "pretty," "pleasantly attractive," etc.

Pussy/Dick. <u>Avoid using these terms</u> to describe or apply to sexual organs. Instead, use the terms "vagina," "penis," "birth canal," "reproductive organs," etc. Do not use any "slang" or "pet" expressions when referring to sexual intercourse and/or to sexual organs, except when expected or enticed to do so by a sexual mate in order to increase intimacy and/or to improve communication. Avoid using any terms that are mutually regarded as "profane," "vulgar," insulting, non-caring, and/or non-constructive in effect. To describe the act of sexual intercourse, use the term, "sexual intercourse".

Q

Qualified/Qualification(s). <u>Use these terms with caution</u>. When others use these terms, ask for a detailed explanation that you can easily understand. Study the ways that Racistman and Racistwoman (White Supremacists, collectively) sometime use these terms to confuse their victims (Non-White people). Ask questions.

> **Questions:** During the existence of White Supremacy (Racism) what, exactly, is a White person "correctly qualified" to force a Non-White person to do, or not do, if that White person is a Racist Suspect (Suspected White Supremacist)? If a White person is a Suspected White Supremacist (Racist Suspect), how can he or she be correctly "qualified" to force any Non-White person to do, or not do, <u>anything</u>, in <u>any</u> area of activity, including, Economics, Education, Entertainment, Labor, Law, Politics, Religion, Sex, and War/Counter-War"?

> **Note:** During the existence of White Supremacy (Racism) and according to Compensatory Counter-Racist Logic, all Non-White persons in the known universe are, at all times, correctly "qualified" to think, speak, and/or act in <u>opposition</u> to Racistman and Racistwoman (White Supremacists, collectively).

Quality/Quality Relationship. <u>Use these terms with caution</u>. Use these terms to apply to any and all thought, speech, and/or action that best helps to end White Supremacy (Racism) and/or that best helps to produce justice (balance between people), and correctness (balance between people, creatures, spirits, things, etc.).

Use these terms particularly to apply to the types of interactions that should exist between White people and Non-White people, as well as between Non-White people with each other. Use the term "The Quality Relationship" mostly to apply to the best, correct, and most specific ("codified") way of replacing White Supremacy with Justice. "The Quality Relationship," as applied to the interactions between White people and Non-White people would function according to a list of "do's and "don'ts" in each area of activity.

Practice using the term "The Quality Relationship" as one of the basic results of the process of replacing White Supremacy (Racism) with Justice (balance between people). <u>Do not use</u> any of the following terms: "Black and White together," "color-blind society," "racial diversity," "racial harmony," "racial integration," "racial mixing," etc.

Notes: During the existence of White Supremacy (Racism), and according to Compensatory Counter-Racist Logic, "Quality Relationships" do not now exist any place in the known universe, in any area of activity. What does exist, is "The Tragic Arrangement." (See, "The Tragic Arrangement").

Quota, Racial. Avoid using this word. Instead, use the expression "Replace White Supremacy with Justice." When others use the term "racial quota," ask for a detailed explanation that you can easily understand.

Questions: What, exactly, is a "racial quota"? What, exactly, is a "racial preference"? Do "quotas" exist? If so, where? Do "racial quotas" or "racial preferences" exist? If so, where? When ? How? By whom? For whom? Against whom? Is there any such thing as an "informal racial quota"?

Notes: During the existence of White Supremacy (Racism), and according to Compensatory Counter-Racist Logic, the only purpose for the existence of a "Race" of people is to practice Racism (mistreatment of people based on the factors of "color" and/or "non-color"). During the existence of White Supremacy (Racism), the only form of Racism based on factors associated with the "color" or "non-color" of people, is White Supremacy.

R

Race/Racism/Racist. Use these terms. During the existence of White Supremacy (Racism), use these terms only to apply to those White persons who practice White Supremacy (Racism), either directly or indirectly, in any area of activity (Economics, Education, Entertainment, Labor, Law, Politics, Religion, Sex, and War/Counter-War.) Do not use these terms to apply to any persons in the known universe who are Non-White ("Black," "Brown," "Beige," "Yellow," "Red," "Tan," etc.) – specifically those persons who are "classified" as "Non-White," and who function as "Non-White."

Do not (as long as White Supremacy exists) say that you are a member of a so-called "Race." As long as White Supremacy (Racism) exists, always say that no Non-White person is, or can be, a "Racist." As long as White Supremacy (Racism) exists, always think, speak, and act as if no Non-White person is able to practice "racism." Always think, speak, and act, as if all Non-White persons are "Victims" of Racism. As long as White Supremacy exists, always

309

think, speak, and act, as if "Racism" is White Supremacy, and White Supremacy is Racism.

If a White person says or implies that a Non-White person is a "member" of a so-called "Race" (a Racist) while White Supremacy (Racism) exists, it is correct for all Non-White persons (and all other persons) to regard that White person as a "Racist Suspect," and a "Suspected White Supremacist." Always use the terms "Race," "Racism," and/or "Racist" in direct identification and association with White Supremacy and White Supremacists. Always speak and act as if a member of a "Race" is a White Supremacist (Racist), who is also a member of the only "Race, which is "The White Race".

> **Notes:** As long as White Supremacy (Racism) exists, all Non-White persons are <u>victims</u> of Race/Racism/Racists and/or White Supremacy. A person cannot be a Victim of Racism and, at the same time, be a Racist. "Race" is "Racism." During the existence of White Supremacy, "Racism" is White Supremacy. Counter-Racism, however, is not Racism. Counter-racism is any effective thought, speech, and/or action <u>against</u> the practice of Racism (White Supremacy).

> Use the terms "Race," "Racism" and/or "Racist" to apply to:
>
> (1) A system of thought, speech, and action operated by people who classify themselves as "White," and who use deceit, violence, and/or the threat of violence, to subjugate, use and/or abuse people "classified" as or who function as "Non-White" under conditions that promote the practice of falsehood, non-justice, and non-correctness for the basic purpose of maintaining, expanding, and/or refining the practice of White Supremacy (Racism) in all areas of activity, including Economics, Education, Entertainment, Labor, Law, Politics, Religion, Sex, and War/Counter-War.
>
> (2) <u>Non-just</u> speech, action, (or non-action) based on the "color" or "non-color" of persons, and/or factors associated with the "color" or "non-color," of persons <u>by</u> "White" persons, <u>against</u> "Non-White" persons, during the existence of White Supremacy.
>
> (3) White Supremacy/The System of White Supremacy.

"Race" is "Racism" (the <u>mistreatment of people</u> based on "color"/"non-color"). During the existence of White Supremacy (Racism) the only "Race" of people that exists in the known universe is "The White Race." There is not now, nor can there ever be, a so-called "Human Race." "Humans" do not practice Racism. "Humans" are <u>people</u> who practice "humane-ness." "Humane" people do not practice falsehood, non-justice, or non-correctness. "Humans" practice <u>peace</u> (the use of <u>truth</u>) in such a manner as to <u>result</u> in the practice of <u>justice</u>, and <u>correctness</u>.

It is not possible to be a member of a "Race" and <u>not</u> <u>mistreat people</u>. During the existence of White Supremacy (Racism), it is not possible for any person to <u>be</u>, or to function as, a "human being." The System of White Supremacy (Racism), by its very existence, prevents people from functioning as "Humane-Beings." During the existence of White Supremacy (Racism), <u>all</u> people, both White, and Non-White, function as "Non-Human" and/or "Non-<u>Humane</u>, beings.

The purpose for being a member of a "Race" is to practice Racism. The reason for practicing Racism is to <u>mistreat people</u> for the purpose of "profit," "glory," and/or "fun." Racism is specifically designed to produce "throw-away" <u>Non-White</u> people. Race/Racism should not be supported or defended, at any time, for any reason, regardless of the great "material benefits" that such a System produces. The number of people that are abused and destroyed by The Race/Racism System is proof that such a practice should be replaced with The System of Justice (balance between people).

Justice (balance between people) is, according to Compensatory Logic, <u>better</u> than Race/Racism (The System of White Supremacy). People are a "species." Each "species" is different in many ways. Each "species" is similar in many ways. Each <u>person</u> is different in many ways. Each <u>person</u> is similar in many ways. People are born as a "species." People are born with "color" or with "non-color." No person is born as a "Race Person." No person is born a "Racist." A person, after being born, can "join" a "Race" if he or she chooses to do so, or if he or she is forced to do so. To become a "member" of a "Race," a person must practice <u>Racism</u>. Since the practice of Racism is for purposes of mistreating people because of factors based on the "color"/"non-color" of people, it is therefore correct for all people to <u>oppose</u> the practice of Racism.

People as a "species" (White, Non-White, male, female, tall, small, etc.), should be helped in the production of justice (balance between people). People, as a "Racist Operation" should be persuaded (or if necessary, forced) to stop practicing Racism and help in the production of justice. No entire "species" of people should be forced to, or allowed to, go into non-existence. People who are "White," "Yellow," "Brown," "Black," "Tan," "Red," "tall," "small," "brown-eyed," "white-haired," "broad-nosed," "thin-lipped," "large-eyed," etc., should all be "preserved," and helped to do constructive things. No people should become Racists. The practice of Racism should come to an end.

"Species," however, can be, and should be, protected and constructively supported. By mating substantial numbers of people correctly, every "species" of people in the known universe can and should be "preserved," and helped in doing constructive deeds. All people should, voluntarily, speak and act in a manner that will guarantee that no "species" will disappear from existence in the known universe. When people engage in producing offspring, they should always think and act constructively in regards to the preservation of the "species."

Important: During the existence of The System of White Supremacy (Racism), the only <u>functional</u> form of "Racism" that exists in the known universe, is The System of White Supremacy (Racism). No other form of Racism does, or can, exist.

Race Buffering. <u>Use these terms</u> to apply to the practice by White Supremacists (Racists) of using substantial numbers of Non-White people as "buffers," "blockers," "barriers" etc., between themselves and other Non-White people. The White Supremacists (Racists) do this in order to produce conflict and confusion between Non-White people. This form of Refined Racism is specifically designed to allow the White Supremacists (Racists) to do great harm to some Non-White people, greater harm to most Non-White people, and to blame all Non-White people for all of the harm that was done.

The practice of "Race-buffering" also includes the White Supremacists (Racists) using Non-White people to slander, scandalize, hinder, or kill other Non-White people in order to protect or divert attention away from the non-just harm that the White

Supremacists (Racists) are doing, have done and/or intend to do, against Non-White people. "Race-buffering" is designed to help the White Supremacists (Racistmen and Racistwomen, collectively) to "hide" their Racist activities by claiming that it is not the White Supremacists, but the Non-White people themselves, who are the cause of all of their problems.

It is correct to study the ways that the White Supremacists (Racistmen and Racistwomen, collectively) practice "Race-Buffering" in each area of activity (Economics, Education, Entertainment, Labor, Law, Politics, Religion, Sex, and War/Counter-War.

Race Camp. Use this term to apply to any "place," "residence," "country," "nation," etc., where Non-White people are located during the existence of White Supremacy (Racism).

> **Reason:** During the existence of White Supremacy (Racism), Non-White people do not have or reside in "homes," nor do they have or reside in "countries" or "nations." A "location" is not, necessarily, a "home," a "country" or a "nation." A "location" is a "location." A "location" can also be a "dislocation". During the existence of White Supremacy (Racism), the White Supremacists (Racists) dictate which Non-White people will be "allowed" to "locate" where, when, and how. These "locations" and/or "dislocations," for or against Non-White people cannot be correctly called "homes," "countries," or "nations." They can only, at best, be correctly called "race camps," "tribal camps," "tribal locations," "tribal reservations," etc.

Race Court, Racist Court, Superior Court (Racial), White Court. Use these terms to apply to any White person in the known universe who practices Racism (White Supremacy) and who makes, or has made, any decision that directly or indirectly supports and/or promotes falsehood, non-justice, or incorrectness, among or against Non-White persons.

> **Notes:** The Racist Court, Race Court, etc., is not a building or a geographical location. It is a person. It is any White person in the known universe who practices White Supremacy (Racism) in any place, at any time, in any area of activity. White Supremacy (Racism) is a "Court of Law" itself. Since White Supremacy is a non-just system, it is not possible to produce justice through the will of those who practice White Supremacy.

Racehouse/Raceresidence. Use these terms to apply to any and all "places of residence," "homes," "houses," "states," "locations," etc., where Non-White people may be situated in the known universe, during the existence of White Supremacy (Racism).

> **Reason**: During the existence of White Supremacy (Racism), all of the Non-White people of the known universe are subject to Racistman and Racistwoman (White Supremacists, collectively). According to Compensatory Counter-Racist Logic, all Non-White persons have as their "places of residence" only those places that Racistman and Racistwoman "assign" to them. This means that as long as White Supremacy (Racism) exists, the Non-White people of the known universe do not simply reside in "self-chosen homes," "states," "nations," etc., but in Racist-assigned "Racecamps," "Racehouses," and/or "Raceresidences."

Race-Mate/Racial-Mate. Use these terms to apply to some, any, or all persons who are so-called, "married," "wedded," or "mated" during the existence of The System of White Supremacy (Racism).

> **Reason:** During the existence of White Supremacy (Racism), every person (both White and Non-White) who chooses a so-called "husband," "wife," "spouse," "mate," "help-mate," "care-mate," "marital-partner," etc., does so in a manner that directly or indirectly is a promotion of, and/or is a reaction to, the existence of White Supremacy (Racism).

> **Notes:** During the existence of The System of White Supremacy (Racism), the terms "Race-mate," or "Racial-mate" are two of the simplest and easiest terms that a person can use to apply to any "marriage" between people that are true, correct, and constructive. The terms "Race-mate," and/or "Racial-mate" are specifically designed to focus on the existence of Racism (White Supremacy), and the effects of the existence of Racism (White Supremacy) in regards to male-female relations.

Race-Mixing. Do not use this term. When others use it, ask for a detailed explanation that you can easily understand.

> **Reason:** The term "Race-mixing" is a useless and confusing term. During the existence of White Supremacy (Racism), there exists only one "Race" of people, and that "Race" is the "White Race," "Race Nation," "White Nation,"

and "Racistman and Racistwoman". The term "Race-mixing" is a useless term that actually describes a non-existent condition.

In a socio-material condition dominated by The System of White Supremacy (Racism) "Race" is "Racism." It is not possible to "mix" Racism. Racism (White Supremacy) is a condition that is either maintained, or it is ended. A "Race" [and/or "Racism"] either exists or it does not exist. In a socio-material condition dominated by White Supremacy, Racism is White Supremacy, and White Supremacy is Racism. If a person is "Non-White," he or she cannot be a "part-member" or a "mixed-member" of the "White Race." If a person is "Non-White," he or she can only be subject to, and/or a Victim of, the "White Race" (White Supremacists, collectively).

Racism (White Supremacy) is the social, material, religious, and scientific practice of White people mistreating Non-White people based on factors associated with the "color," and/or "non-color" [White], of people. Because "Race" is the practice of Racism, and Racism is the practice of White Supremacy, there is no such practice as "race-mixing," there are no people who are "mixed-race," and there is no process for "mixing" a "race." During the existence of White Supremacy (Racism), there is only one "Race" – "The White Race" ((Racistman and Racistwoman, collectively), "The Race Nation," "The White Nation," "The White Supremacists," "White Royalists," etc.

"The Race Nation" functions for the purpose of abusing, confusing, and aggressively mistreating the Non-White people of the known universe for the basic "benefit" of people classified as "White." The Race Nation functions for this purpose in all areas of activity – including the use of sexual intercourse and the production of people.

Race Officer/Race Enforcement Officer/Race Soldier. Use these terms only to apply to those White persons who use "law" in such a manner as to aggressively or defensively establish, maintain, expand, and/or refine the practice of White Supremacy (Racism). Do not, however, use any of these terms to apply to specific persons in such a manner as to appear that you are practicing "name-calling." Use the terms only in a manner that causes people to think about some White persons as not functioning as "Police Officers" etc., but as persons who use "law" to enforce and support White Supremacy (Racism).

Do not, under any circumstance, call any person by the title of "Race Officer," "Race Enforcement Officer," "Race Soldier," etc. Instead, when using the terms to apply to specific White persons, use the terms "Race Officer Suspects," "Suspected Race Enforcement Officer(s)," "Suspected Race Soldiers," etc. Also, use these terms to apply to any White person who directly or indirectly helps or forces a Non-White person to use threats, violence, or any other force to harm a Non-White person in a manner that directly or indirectly helps to establish, maintain, expand, refine, glorify, and/or otherwise give strength to The System of White Supremacy (Racism).

Race Tax. Use this term to apply to any and all of the expense, monies, prices, burdens, suffering, sacrifices, "hidden" costs, etc., that a Non-White person is required to experience as a special result of, and as a special condition of, being subject to The System of White Supremacy (Racism).

Race Unit. Use this term to mean the same as the term "White family."

> **Note**: According to Compensatory Counter-Racist Logic, the term "White family" generally applies to two or more White persons who directly or indirectly interact with each other in such a manner as to result in the establishment, maintenance, expansion, and/or refinement of The System of White Supremacy (Racism).

Race Victims' Major Disaster Area. Use this term to mean the general location of any large number of Non-White people who are dying and/or who are being killed as a direct or indirect result of the existence of White Supremacy (Racism).

Racial. Use this word to apply to:

(1) anything said or done that involves White people with Non-White people, in social and/or material activities that are directly or indirectly dominated by White Supremacy (Racism).

(2) anything said or done by any person, in any place, in any area of activity, during any time that White Supremacy (Racism) exists.

(3) any circumstances and/or event that directly or indirectly is caused or affected by the practice of Racism in any one or more areas of activity.

Racial Balance. Do not use this term.

> **Reason:** During the existence of White Supremacy (Racism), and according to Compensatory Counter-Racist Logic, there is only one "Race" of people in the known universe, and that is the "White Race" (White Supremacists, (collectively, Racistman and Racistwoman), "The White Nation," "White Nationalists," "The Race Nation," etc.).

Since the only "Race" in existence is "The White Race", the term "racial balance" cannot be applied to any existing situation, or to any situation that can exist. In order to have so-called "racial balance," at least two "races" must exist. In order for a "race" of people to exist, the members of that "race" must practice Racism. If members of a "race" must practice Racism, it means that they are dominant over and/or more powerful than all of the people who are not "members".

People who are dominated by a "race" cannot, at the same time, be "members" of a "Race." They may pretend to be "members." They are usually told by those persons who are members of a "Race," that they too are members of some [different] "Race." They may pretend to be "members" of a "nation." They may be allowed by the "Race People" to call themselves "members" of a "tribe," "organization," "club," "clique," "gang," "association," etc. In practice, persons who are subject to a "Race" (one or more Racists), do not, and cannot, function as any major category, other than "Race Victim"/"Victim of Racism."

The people of the known universe who are not White Supremacists (Racists) are either "White" persons who do not participate in the practice of Racism (White Supremacy), or they are "Non-White" persons. All of the Non-White people are the Victims and/or the subjects of the "Race People" (White Supremacists, collectively, Racistman and Racistwoman).

Notes: During the existence of White Supremacy (Racism) and according to Compensatory Counter-Racist Logic, the only form of functional Racism is White Supremacy. Therefore, instead of the term "racial balance," it is best and correct to avoid confusion by saying, "Replace White Supremacy (Racism) with Justice (balance between people)".

Racial Desegregation. <u>Do not use this term</u>. When others use it, ask for a detailed explanation that you can easily understand.

> **Reason:** During the existence of White Supremacy (Racism) and according to Compensatory Counter-Racist Logic, there is no such process as "racial desegregation." There is not, nor can there be, any such process as a "desegregation of Racism." During the existence of White Supremacy (Racism), and according to Compensatory Counter-Racist Logic, White Supremacy is Racism, and Racism is White Supremacy. The use of the terms "racial integration" and "racial desegregation," are confusing. Therefore, instead of using the term "racial desegregation," it is best and correct to use, "Replace White Supremacy (Racism) with Justice (balance between people)".

Racial Exhibits. <u>Use this term with caution</u> and only to apply collectively and without insult, to any and all Non-White persons who are selected, and/or greatly publicized (usually by Racists), as examples of the way Non-White persons should or should not speak and/or act while existing in subjugation to White Supremacy (Racism). The term "Racial Exhibitionism" and the term "Racial Showcasing" mean the same thing.

Racial Expert. <u>Use this word</u> to apply to a person who has proven to all that he or she knows everything about Race and/or Racism, including how to practice it, and how to stop it from being practiced.

> **Note:** During the existence of White Supremacy (Racism), and according to Compensatory Counter-Racist Logic, no Non-White person "qualifies" as a "Racial Expert" - only White Supremacists (Racists) do.

Racial Incident. <u>Use this term</u> to apply to any conflict between any White person and any Non-White person, in any situation that is directly or indirectly dominated by White Supremacy (Racism).

Racial Integration. <u>Do not use this term</u>. Use instead, the expression, "Replace White Supremacy (Racism) with Justice (balance between people)." When others use it, ask for a detailed explanation that you can easily understand.

> **Reason:** According to Compensatory Counter-Racist Logic, there is no way to use the term "Racial Integration" in a manner that does not promote confusion. "Race" is "Racism," and "Racism" is White Supremacy. There is no

way to "racially integrate" White Supremacy or "racially desegregate" White Supremacy. Also, there is no way for a White Supremacist (Racist) to be "separated" from" his or her Victim (Non-White people).

According to Compensatory Counter-Racist Logic, the only purpose for the existence of "Race People" or "Racist People," is to mistreat people based on "color" or factors associated with the "color" or "non-color" of people. Since "Race" is "Racism," there is no way to "integrate," "segregate," or "separate from" Racism or Racialism. Racism is a socio-material activity that is either practiced or it is not practiced. Race and/or Racism is a socio-material activity that either exists or it does not exist. The existence of a "Race" of people serves no purpose that is constructive to the production and maintenance of justice (balance between people). The only purpose for being a "member" of a "Race" is to practice Racism.

Suggestion: Instead of using the terms "racial integration," or "racial desegregation," use the terms "ending White Supremacy" and/or "replacing White Supremacy (Racism) with Justice (balance between people)." (See, "Racial Balance," "Racial Desegregation").

Notes: The terms "racial integration," "racial segregation" and/or "racial separation," have often been used by Racistman and Racistwoman (White Supremacists, collectively), to cause confusion in the ways that their Victims (Non-White people) think, speak and act in their efforts to replace White Supremacy (Racism) with Justice (balance between people). According to Compensatory Counter-Racist Logic, there is no way to use the terms "racial integration," "racial segregation" or "racial separation" in any manner that is logical and non-confusing.

Racial Masochism. Use this term to apply to a condition in which a Non-White person has become so "accustomed" to being extremely abused by White Supremacists (Racists), that he or she seeks, expects, and welcomes, the personal "attention" given to him or her through more abuse.

Examples:

- Non-White females in their socio-sexual [subordinate] interactions with White men, and in their social (or "anti-sexual") interactions with White women, during the existence of White Supremacy (Racism).

- Non-White males when interacting directly with White men or White women during the existence of White Supremacy (Racism) find it "easier" and "less offending" to present themselves as "effeminate," or so-called "homo-sexual" ("anti-sexual") and/or as "silly boys," rather than as <u>men</u>.

- Non-White males and females, when in the presence of White people, choosing to interact with White people, and/or with each other, in a manner that can best be described as "pitiful," "primitive," "stupid" and/or "silly."

> **Note:** According to Compensatory Counter-Racist Logic, such behavior is caused and/or promoted by The System of White Supremacy (Racism), either directly or indirectly, in any one or more areas of activity.

Racial Mathematics. <u>Use this term</u> to apply to the sum total of the direct and indirect effects of Racism on what people think, do, and say at any time, in any place, in any one or more areas of activity, including Economics, Education, Entertainment, Labor, Law, Politics, Religion, Sex, and War/Counter-War.

Racial Name. <u>Use this term</u> to apply to a name given to and/or used by a Victim of Racism (Non-White person) that was directly or indirectly given to that Victim by a White Supremacist (Racist) for the purpose of helping to promote White Supremacy (Racism).

Racial Overtone/Racial Undertone. <u>Do not use these terms</u>.

> **Notes:** There is no such thing as a "racial overtone" or a "racial undertone". If an incident or situation is, in any way, directly or indirectly associated with or affected by the practice of Racism (White Supremacy), it is a <u>racial incident</u>.

Racial Plantationalism (Racism). <u>Use this term</u> to apply to the practice of White Supremacy, and the direct and indirect effects of the practice has on any Non-White person, in any one or more areas of activity.

Racial Prejudice. <u>Do not use this term</u>. It is an incorrect term that should not be used to describe any condition.

Notes: To say that a person practices "racial prejudice" is confusing. It is best and correct to say that a person practices "Racism". To exercise prejudice is to judge before knowing and/or understanding the truth about something or someone. A Racist is not, necessarily, a person who is prejudiced against another person. A Racist is not, necessarily, a person who doesn't know and/or understand the truth about their Victims. A Racist is a person who simply intends to subjugate, restrict, and/or mistreat another person, on the basis of color and/or factors associated with color. White Supremacists do not mistreat Non-White people because they lack knowledge and/or understanding of them. White Supremacists mistreat Non-White people because they know and understand that they want to mistreat them - it is their reason for existence.

Racial Segregation. <u>Do not use this term</u>. When others use the terms "racial segregation," or "racial separation," ask for a detailed explanation that you can easily understand.

Reason: According to Compensatory Counter-Racist Logic, "Race" is "Racism" and "Racism" is White Supremacy. A "Racist" is a White Supremacist, and a White Supremacist is a Racist. During the existence of White Supremacy (Racism) the Victims of White Supremacy (Non-White people) are not and cannot be a "Race," nor are they "separate from" the power of the people who dominate them (The White Supremacists/ Racists).

The term "racial segregation" has often been used to imply that, during the existence of White Supremacy (Racism), there is no "contact" between White people and Non-White people. This is not true. During the existence of White Supremacy (Racism), the direct or indirect contact between White Supremacists (Racists) and their victims (Non-White people) is constant, and complete. Without this constant and complete "contact" between the White Supremacists (Racists) and their Victims (Non-White people), White Supremacy (Racism) would not, and could not, exist. Domination means contact. Among the people of the known universe, the White Supremacists (Racists) dominate and maintain contact with, and against, all of the Non-White people of the known universe, at all times, in all places, in all areas of activity.

Racial Show-Offism. Use this term to mean:

1. Non-White people pretending that they are not subject to the will of the White Supremacists (Racists) in any one or more areas of activity.

2. Non-White people bragging about themselves, to each other, while existing in subjugation to the White Supremacists.

3. Non-White people belittling each other, all the while existing in subjugation to the White Supremacists.

Racial Slur/Racist Support Words. Use these terms to apply to any words that are used in a manner that directly or indirectly promotes thought, speech, or action that has the effect of supporting the practice of White Supremacy (Racism) and/or has the effect of giving aid or comfort to a White Supremacist (Racistman and Racistwoman) in any one or more areas of activity.

Racial Subjugation. Use this term during the existence of White Supremacy (Racism) to apply to: (1) White Supremacy (Racism), and (2) treating a person unjustly and/or incorrectly because of factors associated with the color, and/or the shade of color of that person (which is the function of White Supremacy/Racism).

> **Note:** "Racial Subjugation" is sometimes incorrectly called "Racial Segregation".

Racial Subjugationist. Use this term to apply to a White Supremacist and/or a person who practices Racism (White Supremacy).

Racial Zeroism. In "Racist Mathematics," this term means Non-White persons, generally, who are worth nothing (zero) of social or material value, except as subjects of, and servants to, The System of White Supremacy (Racism).

Racism. Use this term to apply to: (1) the scientific practice of unjust subjugation, misuse, mistreatment and/or abuse of persons classified as Non-White, by persons classified as White, on the basis of color or non-color, or on the basis of factors associated with color or non-color; and/or (2) the System of White Supremacy.

> **Notes:** It is incorrect to use the term "White Racism". To use this term is to imply that Racism exists in a form other than White Supremacy. It is important to study the

ways that others use the word "Racism" and to ask many questions about the way it is used.

Racist. <u>Use this word</u> to apply only to a White person who directly or indirectly participates in the practice of White Supremacy (Racism) in any one or more areas of activity. During the existence of White Supremacy, do not use the term "Racist" to apply to any person or the speech or action of any person other than a person "classified" as "White," who functions as "White," and who speaks and/or acts to mistreat any Non-White person, based on factors associated with the person being "Non-White."

During the existence of White Supremacy (Racism), use the word "Racist" to mean the same as a White Supremacist, and use the term "White Supremacist" to mean the same as a "Racist" (as correctly applied to the behavior of a White person in his or her interactions with a Non-White person). Always associate the words "Race," "Racialism," "Racism," "Racist," "Racistman," and "Racistwoman" only with those White persons who directly or indirectly <u>practice</u> White Supremacy.

> **Notes:** During the existence of White Supremacy (Racism) and according to Compensatory Counter-Racist Logic, it is not possible for a Victim of White Supremacy (Non-White person) to practice "Racism," and/or to function as a "Racist." He or she can only function as a "Victim" of White Supremacy (a Victim of the Racists) and/or as a person attempting to end White Supremacy (Racism).

Racist America/Racist Europe, etc. <u>Do not use these terms</u> or words similar to these terms.

> **Reason:** During the existence of White Supremacy (Racism) and according to Compensatory Counter-Racist Logic, a "Racist" is not a "place." A "Racist" is a White Supremacist, and a White Supremacist is a White person who practices White Supremacy (Racism).
>
> There are no "places," "titles of places," directions, locations, "geographical areas," "flags," or "symbols," that can correctly be called "Racist." Only people can correctly be identified as "Racist." A concept of a location, a place and/or the name or title of a concept or a place does not mean that Racism is being practiced. Therefore, it is incorrect to say that Racism is, or can be, practiced by anyone other than a person, and/or by anyone other than a "Racist-coordinated" category of persons. Racists

323

are people. They are people who do not have so-called "allegiance" to any people, any place, any animal, any plant, any "flag," any "God," or any existence, except The System of White Supremacy (Racism).

During the existence of White Supremacy (Racism), and according to Compensatory Counter-Racist Logic, it is not possible for a so-called "America," "American," "Europe," or a "European" to practice White Supremacy (Racism). Only a White Supremacist (Racist) can practice White Supremacy (Racism).

Racist Family/Racist Tribe. Use these terms to apply to White Supremacists, collectively, and/or The System of White Supremacy.

Racist Law. Use this term to apply to: (1) anything said or done by a Racist; and/or (2) anything said or done that results in the establishment, maintenance, expansion, and/or refinement of Racism (White Supremacy) in any one or more areas of activity, including Economics, Education, Entertainment, Labor, Law, Politics, Religion, Sex, and War/Counter-War.

Racist School System. Use this term with caution to mean the sum total of everything that is taught and learned by both White and Non-White people in the known universe, plus the sum total of the result [White Supremacy] of everything that is taught and learned by both White and Non-White people. Use the term "Racist School System" as having the exact same meaning as the term "System of White Supremacy (Racism)."

Racist Suspect/Suspected Racist (White Supremacist). Use these terms to apply to any person who "appears" to be "White," who is "classified" as "White," and/or who functions as an "acceptable member" of "The White Nation" (Race/Racist Nation), and who willfully and deliberately says or does anything that indicates a willingness to participate in any speech, action, or inaction that helps to establish, maintain, expand, and/or refine the practice of White Supremacy (Racism) in any one or more areas of activity.

If a White person is able to be a Racist (White Supremacist), he or she may be one and should be suspect (Racist Suspect).

Examples: A White person is a Racist Suspect (Suspected White Supremacist) if he or she willfully and deliberately does any one or more of the following (during the existence of White Supremacy/Racism):

- Says something to or about a Non-White person that is not true.

- Either withholds or fails to give to a Non-White person, constructive information, and/or give such information in a manner that does not produce the most constructive result.

- Had the opportunity and the ability to give constructive help to a Non-White person who was in need of that constructive help, but did not give that constructive help.

- Engages in so-called "homo-sex," sexual intercourse and/or "sexual play" with (against) a Non-White person, and/or directly or indirectly speaks or acts in support of other White persons who do the same.

- Supports sexual intercourse and/or "sexual play" between White persons, with each other who have not proven that they use most of their time and energy thinking, speaking, and acting to replace The System of White Supremacy (Racism) with the System of Justice (balance between people).

- Produces or supports the use of language, pictures, and/or images in such a manner as to directly or indirectly promote the maintenance, expansion, and/or refinement of The System of White Supremacy (Racism) in any area of activity, including Economics, Education, Entertainment, Labor, Law, Politics, Religion, Sex, and War/Counter-War.

- Refuses to agree with a Non-White person when that person identifies him or herself as a Victim of White Supremacy (Victim of Racism).

- Fails to use most of his or her time and energy to think, speak, and act to replace The System of White Supremacy (Racism) with The System of Justice (balance between people) in all areas of activity.

Racist War Crime. Use this term to apply to any harmful speech or action against a Non-White person by a person classified as "White," that is willful, deliberate, non-just, and incorrect, and that is the direct or indirect result of malice or carelessness associated with the "color," and/or "non-color" of persons, during the establishment or the existence of White Supremacy (Racism). Particularly, use the term "Racist War Crime" to apply to any deceptive and/or deliberate, massive or extreme act by White Supremacists (Racists) that directly or indirectly results in the death or serious injury to one or more Non-White persons.

Notes: White Supremacy (Racism) is "The Crime of Crimes." White Supremacy (Racism) is war against Non-White people. All White Supremacists (Racists) are Master War Criminals. All Master War Criminals (White Supremacists) are opposed to both the concept and the practice of justice (balance between people).

Racket. Use this word to mean any form of deceit, violence and/or threat of violence that is used to mistreat persons, animals, etc. Also, study the ways that others use the words "racket," "racketeer," "racketeering," etc. During the existence of White Supremacy (Racism) and according to Compensatory Counter-Racist Logic, The System of White Supremacy (Racism) is "The Master Racket" and the White people who practice White Supremacy (Racism), are "The Master Racketeers."

Racketeer, Master. Use this term to apply to a White person who directly or indirectly practices White Supremacy (Racism) in any one or more areas of activity/existence including Economics, Education, Entertainment, Labor, Law, Politics, Religion, Sex, and War/Counter-War.

Radical. Use this word with caution. When others use it, ask for a detailed explanation that you can easily understand.

Questions: What, exactly, is "radical" – in each area of activity? What, exactly, is not "radical"? "Radical," according to whom? Who, exactly, is correctly qualified to say what is, and what is not, "radical"? "Radical" when? "Radical" where? "Radical," according to what? As compared with what? Is "slavery" "radical"? Is getting rid of "slavery" "radical"? Is "freedom," a "radical" idea? Is White Supremacy (Racism) a "radical" way for people to interact with each other? Is it "radical" to attempt to eliminate White Supremacy (Racism) and replace it with Justice (balance between people)?

Note: During the existence of White Supremacy (Racism), and according to Compensatory Counter-Racist Logic, the most "radical" political system in the known universe is The System of White Supremacy (Racism).

Raised. Use this word with caution. When others use the words "raise" and/or "raised" to apply to the so-called "maturity," or power of people, ask for a detailed explanation that you can easily understand. Ask questions.

Questions: What, exactly, is a "raised child"? What, exactly, is a person who has been "raised"? Who is correctly qualified to know when a Non-White person has finished being "raised," while he or she is subject to The System of White Supremacy (Racism)? Is it possible for a person to be "raised" and, at the same time, remain subject to The System of White Supremacy (Racism)?

Ransom. Use this word to apply to the forced service that the Non-White people of the known universe render to The System of White Supremacy (Racism) as hostages to Racistman and Racistwoman (White Supremacists, collectively).

> **Note:** During the existence of White Supremacy (Racism) and according to Compensatory Counter-Racist Logic, all Non-White persons who function in subjugation to The System of White Supremacy (Racism) are being held for "ransom" in all areas of activity, including Economics, Education, Entertainment, Labor, Law, Politics, Religion, Sex, and War/Counter-War.

Rap [sound/images]. Use this word to apply to any message that is presented in words and/or words combined with images, pictures, etc. When others use the word, ask for a detailed explanation that you can easily understand.

Rape. Use this word. Use it mostly to apply to everything that is harmful and non-constructive that happens to a Non-White person as a direct or indirect result of the existence of White Supremacy (Racism). Study the ways that others use the word "rape."

> **Note:** During the existence of White Supremacy (Racism), and according to Compensatory Counter-Racist Logic, Racistman and Racistwoman (White Supremacists, collectively) are guilty of the crime of "rape" against all of the Non-White people of the known universe, in all areas of activity.

Rational. Use this word with caution. When others use the word "rational," ask for a detailed explanation that you can easily understand. Ask questions. What, exactly, is the correct "qualification" for deciding what is, and what is not, "rational" during the existence of White Supremacy (Racism), in any area of activity?

Raw Racism. Use this term to mean a "style" of practicing and "presenting" Racism (White Supremacy) in a manner that is direct, open, easily recognized, obvious, and/or not "refined."

Use this term to mean the "style" of practicing and "presenting" White Supremacy (Racism) in a manner that is so crude, and so unsophisticated, that the average Non-White person who has knowledge of the existence of White Supremacy (Racism), recognizes immediately the manner in which it is being practiced.

Ray of Hope. Do not use this term. Instead, use the word, "hope" without saying "ray of hope."

> **Reason:** The use of the word "ray" in association with that which is regarded as constructive, is similar to how some other words are used in direct or indirect support for, and/or the glorification of, White Supremacy (Racism). A "ray" is regarded as associated with "light." The word "light" is often associated with that which is "bright." The word "bright" is often associated with the word "right," and the word "right" is often associated with the word (and the non-color) "white."
>
> During the existence of White Supremacy (Racism), the words "light," "bright," and "right" are directly or indirectly associated with "White" people (people who are "racially-classified" as "White"). The word "right" is also often associated with the word "justice," and the word "justice" is often associated with the images, or the so-called "special values" of "White" people. Thus, during the existence of White Supremacy (Racism), many words that have been made to be associated with things that are regarded as "constructive," have also, either directly or indirectly, been "arranged" to be associated with persons who have been classified as "White."
>
> Many words and word-terms have been indirectly used in such a manner as to promote the thought that a "White" person is a person who is not only "light," "bright," and/or "radiant" in appearance, but also, "right," "righteous," "brilliant," "smart," "good" and/or "just."
>
> **Notes:** During the existence of White Supremacy (Racism), and according to Compensatory Counter-Racist Logic, it is correct to study the use of all words, and all word-terms that are used to directly or indirectly support the concept and practice of White Supremacy (Racism). This includes words and word-terms like "Age Of Enlightenment," "beaming," "brilliant person," "fair," "fair employment," "fair play," "fair and just," "lady fair," "knight (White) in shining armor on a White horse," "light-hearted," "radiant," etc.

Real Estate, White [Racial/Sexual]. <u>Use this term</u> to apply to the vagina and associated "sexual organs" of the body of a White female person during the existence of The System of White Supremacy (Racism).

> **Reason:** During the existence of White Supremacy (Racism) and according to Compensatory Counter-Racist Logic, the vagina and other associated "sexual organs" of the body of a White female person is of Supreme Value to the White Supremacist (Racist) male person and, as such, is absolutely essential to the existence and continuation of The System of White Supremacy (Racism), itself.

Reasonable. <u>Use this word</u> to apply to any and all thought, speech, and/or action that best helps to reveal truth, and use truth in a manner that best helps to produce justice and correctness, in any one or more areas of activity – Economics, Education, Entertainment, Labor, Law, Politics, Religion, Sex, and War/Counter-War. Also, use the words "reasonable," and/or "logical," to apply to any and all thought, speech, and/or action that best helps to result in replacing the System of White Supremacy (Racism) with the System of Justice (guaranteeing that no person is mistreated, and guaranteeing that the person who needs help the most, gets the most help). Study the ways that others use the word "reasonable" – particularly when they say or imply that they are trying to replace White Supremacy (Racism), with Justice.

Rebel/Rebellion. <u>Use these words with caution</u>. When others use them, ask for a detailed explanation that you can easily understand. Ask questions.

> **Questions:** Is Counter-War against the practice of White Supremacy (Racism), a "rebellion," or is it "patriotism"? Is a White Supremacist (Racist) a "rebel" against the production of justice, correctness, and peace? What, exactly, is a "rebellion"? What, exactly, is not a "rebellion"? Who is correctly qualified to decide?

Recession. <u>Avoid using this word</u>. When others use the words "recession," "depression," "poverty," etc., to describe the so-called "economic status" of people, ask for a detailed explanation that you can easily understand.

> **Note:** During the existence of White Supremacy (Racism), and according to Compensatory Counter-Racist Logic, a Victim of White Supremacy (a Non-White person) is, at all times, in a condition of "recession," "depression," and

"poverty" (either mentally, physically, spiritually, materially, or financially).

Recognize/Recognized. Use these words with caution. Study, carefully, the ways that many people use the words "recognize," or "recognized."

> **Reason:** White Supremacists (Racists) sometimes say that they do not "recognize" a person, a law, a "point of view," etc., except when that person, law, "point of view," etc., meets with their approval. White Supremacists (Racists) sometimes declare that they do not "recognize" something that is true by saying or by implying (falsely), that what is true, is not true, because they choose not to "recognize" what is true.

Red/Redskin. Use these words with caution. Do not call a person "Red," or "Redskin," unless that person says to you that he or she wants to be called by that name, title, or description. When others use these words in a manner that applies to people, ask for a detailed explanation that you can easily understand.

Refined Racism (White Supremacy). Use this term to apply to the "ultimate" and most sophisticated form of White Supremacy and to those forms of White Supremacy that usually have many of the following, or similar characteristics and/or results:

- Non-White persons being deceived (fooled) by the White Supremacists (Racists) in a manner that does not "appear" to be deceit.

- Non-White persons denying to themselves and others that White Supremacy (Racism) exists, and/or denying to that White Supremacy (Racism) is a major problem.

- Non-White persons speaking and/or acting as if The System of White Supremacy (Racism) is the best way of conducting the affairs of the people of the known universe.

- Non-White persons speaking, and/or acting as if the destructive things that happen every day as the result of The System of White Supremacy (Racism) are not only so-called "normal" and/or "acceptable," but often desirable.

- Non-White persons preferring to waste time "showing-off," and insulting, fighting, and killing each other, rather than make a serious and sustained effort to rid the known universe of Racism (White Supremacy) and other forms of injustice.

- Non-White persons being serious about matters that are silly, being silly about matters that are serious, and/or being generally confused about the best and correct way to do or say, or not do or say, in regards to Economics, Education, Entertainment, Labor, Law, Politics, Religion, Sex, and War/Counter-War.

Notes: Many White Supremacists (Racists) are greatly skilled in the practice of "Refined Racism" (Refined White Supremacy). This means that they are "The Masters of Deception and Confusion". This means that they know how to cause Non-White people to think, speak, and act in a manner that is mostly, self-destructive. The White Supremacists (Racists) know how to make the destruction appear not to have been caused by White Supremacists (Racistmen and Racistwomen). Therefore, during the existence of White Supremacy (Racism), and according to Compensatory Counter-Racist Logic, it is correct to blame the White Supremacists (Racists) for everything that Non-White people do that <u>should not</u> be done.

<u>Refined Racism</u> is a form of White Supremacy that is designed to make many Non-White people more "comfortable" in mind and body, while, at the same time, helping to make the practice of White Supremacy more sophisticated, stronger, and easier to maintain. Under Refined Racism, Non-White people are helped to learn many things that they were previously not allowed to learn.

Under Refined Racism, Non-White people are allowed to sometimes have better housing, better transportation, and/or more money. Some or many Non-White persons are enticed to have greater and more "open" sexual relations with White people. Some or many are often allowed to do work that is easier. Some or many are allowed to have more food, and of a greater variety. Some or many are allowed to have greater participation in selected social and "business" functions. Better medical care is provided for them.

They are allowed to acquire numerous "toys," and/or so-called "status symbols." They are allowed to have greater participation in so-called "law games" in which they can learn, make and use "law," but not in a manner that produces justice. Praise, compliments, flattery, and awards are sometimes provided in great abundance.

Refined Racism is practiced by Racistman and Racistwoman (White Supremacists, collectively), not for the purpose of starting to end White Supremacy, but to better deceive its Victims [Non-White people] into believing that White Supremacy no longer exists. Refined Racism is designed to promote greater confusion among its Victims. Refined Racism is designed to use "comfort" and "play-acting" as a substitute for justice (balance between people). Much of what is done through Refined Racism is of constructive value, while other things are done that are very destructive, but do not immediately seem to be so. Eventually, the many things that are done that are constructive are "cancelled" by the many things that are done that are destructive. That which is helpful is "mixed in" with that which is harmful. The result is "greater comfort" in some things, and "greater discomfort" in others. With this comes much emotion, but with greater confusion, and less understanding among Non-White people.

During the refinement of White Supremacy (Racism), Non-White people do more things and go more places. They learn more about things, but they are led to understand less about White Supremacy (Racism) – what it is, and how it works. Non-White people remain dependent upon what is decided by Racistmen and Racistwomen (White Supremacists). Many Non-White people are deceived into not knowing or understanding how dependent they are. Under Refined Racism (Refined White Supremacy), many Victims of Racism (Non-White people) seem to be less dependent on Racistman and Racistwoman when, in truth, their dependence is becoming greater.

Under Refined Racism, justice may seem to be in the process of production in spite of the existence of White Supremacy. The Refined Racists (Refined White Supremacists) are very skilled at *pretending* to be working to produce justice while, in truth they work to make their Victims believe that Justice and White Supremacy (Racism) are one and the same.

The Refined White Supremacist is usually greatly skilled in the use of words. He or she is usually very skilled in the science of "taking" the words that a Non-White person says, and "making" those words seem to apply to something other than what the Non-White person intended. A Refined Racistman or Racistwoman can often use words in such a manner as to actually cause a Non-White person to change what he or she intended to say. The Refined Racistman or Racistwoman will then accuse that Non-White person of intending to mean to say what was said in the change.

The Refined White Supremacists usually know how to use words in such a manner as to cause Non-White people to argue and to sometimes fight against each other about problems that could easily be solved by White people. Sometimes, when Non-White persons have a tendency to want to "show-off" how much they know (especially when in the presence of both White and Non-White people), a Refined White Supremacist has proven to be greatly skilled at using words in a manner that results in Non-White persons saying things that only add to confusion and/or animosity between and among Non-White people.

A Refined White Supremacist (Racist) also delights in showing how greatly skilled and "heroic" they, themselves, are when they come to the rescue of Non-White persons who, apparently, are unable to save themselves from a primitive or pitiful circumstance and/or from the results of stupid and/or silly acts.

The first major indication that Refined Racism (Refined White Supremacy) is working "smoothly," is when the greater number of both White people and Non-White people, speak and act as if they have a "silent agreement" to pretend that White Supremacy (Racism) no longer exists, and/or if it does exist, it should not be regarded as if it seriously matters.

Refugee. Use this word mostly to apply to any Non-White person who speaks or acts in such a manner as to show that he or she was trying to keep from being harmed by, and/or trying to put an end to, The System of White Supremacy (Racism). Study the ways that others use the word "refugee." Ask questions. What, exactly, is a "refugee"? What, exactly, is not a "refugee"? When? Where? According to whom?

Regulation(s). Avoid using this word. Practice, instead, using the word "law," or "laws." When others use the words "regulation(s)," "rule(s)," "policy," "guidelines," "general practice(s)," etc., ask for a detailed explanation that you can easily understand. Ask questions.

Questions: Is a so-called "regulation" the same as a so-called "law"? Is a "rule" the same as a "policy"? Is a "policy," a "rule," or a "regulation," the same as a "law"? If so, why? If not, why not? If a "rule" or a "regulation" is required to be "obeyed," does that mean that the "rule" or "regulation" is, in fact, a "law"? If a person is punished for "breaking" a "rule," does that mean, in effect, that the "rule" was in fact, a "law"? If so, why not call that "rule" a "law"? If so, why pretend or imply that the "rule" and the "law" are not one and the same?

Note: According to Compensatory Logic, a "law" is anything that is done (happens, accomplished, etc.).

Rehabilitate. <u>Do not use this word</u> to apply to any process that should be designed to cause a person to be the "quality" of person that a person should be. Instead, use, "correct process," "corrective process," "correct person production" and/or "quality person production". When someone uses the terms "rehabilitated" and/or "habilitated," it is correct to always ask for a detailed explanation that you can easily understand.

> **Reason:** According to Compensatory Logic, no person in the known universe is the "quality" of person that a person should be. Therefore, no situation that now exists with regard to interactions between people is the quality of interactions that should exist between people. No person in the known universe is a so-called "perfect example" of what a person should be. When someone says that a person has been "rehabilitated," it is said to mean that he or she has been changed from what he or she is, to what he or she should be. During the existence of White Supremacy (Racism), there is no reason to believe that a so-called "habilitated" person now exists anyplace in the known universe.

Religion/Religious Person. <u>Use these terms</u>. Use the word "religion" to apply to the sum total of all the things that a person chooses to do or say, or tries to do or say, according to the will that is "given" to him or her, at all times, in all places, in all areas of activity, including Economics, Education, Entertainment, Labor, Law, Politics, Religion, Sex, and War/Counter-War. Use the word "religious person" to apply to any person who does the aforementioned (practices "religion"). When others use the terms "religion," or "religious person," ask for a detailed explanation that you can easily understand. Ask questions.

Questions: Are all people "religious," at some time, in some place, about some thing? What, exactly, is a "non-religious" person? What is the correct way for one person to judge whether another person is "religious" or "non-religious"? Is "religion" and "spiritualism" one and the same? Does all "spiritual guidance" come from the same Creator ("Source," "Master," "God," "Allah," "Maker," "Supreme Power," etc.)?

What, exactly, is the Supreme source of a person's "willpower"? Is a "religious" or "godly" person "good"? What, exactly, is a "good person"? Do such persons exist? If so, where are they? If so, who are they? If so, "good," as compared to what? Which persons are the "experts" in judging who is and who is not "good" and/or "religious"? If a person does not practice all of his or her "religion," is it correct to believe that his or her "religion" is being practiced? Is there such a thing as a "half religion," or a "part religion"? Can a "religion" be practiced "part-time," and be correctly regarded as a "religion" that is practiced "full-time" (all the time)?

Religious Fundamentalism. Avoid using this term. When others use this term, ask for a detailed explanation that you can easily understand. Are all "religions" fundamental? What makes a religion "fundamental"? What makes a religion "non-fundamental"? Does a "non-fundamental" religion have the same "value" as a "religion" that is "fundamental"? If so, why? If not, why not? Who is, and who is not, "qualified" to judge? According to what? Is White Supremacy (Racism), a "fundamentalist religion"? If so, why? If not, why not? According to whom, and based on what "qualifications"?

> **Note:** During the existence of White Supremacy (Racism) and according to Compensatory Counter-Racist Logic, all Victims of White Supremacy (Non-White persons) are correctly qualified to regard (or not regard) The System of White Supremacy (Racism) as a so-called "fundamentalist religion."

Relocate/Relocated. Use these words to apply to the act(s) of going from one place to another place, and doing so willfully. Do not use these words to mean the same as the words "dislocate" or "dislocated." Use the words "dislocate" or "dislocated" to apply to the act(s) of going from one place to another place, and doing so unwillingly, and/or as the result of being forced to do so by others.

Study the ways that others use the words "relocate," "relocated," "dislocate," and "dislocated." Study how, during the existence of

White Supremacy (Racism), the Non-White people of the known universe are often directly or indirectly forced to "dislocate" by the White Supremacists (Racistman and Racistwoman, collectively).

> **Note:** During the existence of White Supremacy (Racism), the White Supremacists (Racists) often cause the "dislocation" of Non-White people under the guise of "relocation" for the purpose of so-called "progress" and/or "improvement".

Remedial Education. Use this term to apply to all acts of learning, all things about all things, and/or learning all things about one thing. When others use the term "remedial education," ask for a detailed explanation that you can easily understand. What, exactly, is "remedial education"? What, exactly, is not "remedial education"? Is all education, "remedial"?

> *The process of learning what one needs to know, when successful, is a 'remedy' for not knowing.*

Report. Use this word to apply, mostly, to statements that best help to reveal truth (that which is) in a manner that best helps to produce justice (balance between people) and correctness (balance between people, creatures, things, etc.). When asked to speak or write of your so-called "gripes," "grievances" or "complaints," say, instead, that you will make a "report." Always say that the "report" that you make is intended to promote the production of justice (balance between people) and/or the production of correctness (balance between people, creatures, things, etc.). Do not say in the report that you are, in any away, intending the report to be "valued" as a "gripe," "grievance" or "complaint." Say that the report should be "valued" as a report – including any and all requests and suggestions that are made.

> **Note:** According to Compensatory Logic, the expression "balance between people" (a meaning for the word "justice") also means in detail, the act(s) of guaranteeing that no person is mistreated, and guaranteeing that the person who needs help the most, gets the most help.

Represent/Representative. Use these words with caution. When others use the words "represent" and/or "representative," ask for a detailed explanation that you can easily understand. Ask questions.

> **Questions:** What, exactly, is a "representative"? Does everything, in some way, "represent" everything else? Can a so-called "symbol" truly "represent" something

336

other than itself?   Can one person truly "represent" another person? Can a word "represent" something that is not a word? Can a sound "represent" something that is not a sound?   Can "something" "represent" "nothing"? Can a Racist (White Supremacist) "represent" a person who is a Victim of Racism (Non-White person)?   Can a "graven image" of a person "represent" that person by serving the exact same purpose of that person to another person?

Republic/Republican. Avoid using these words. When others use these words, ask for a detailed explanation that you can easily understand. What, exactly, is a "Republic"? What, exactly, is not a "Republic"? What, exactly, is a "Republican"? What, exactly, is not a "Republican"? If a "Republican" is "democratic," is he or she also a so-called "Democrat"?   Can a White Supremacist (Racist) be a "Republican"? Can a Victim of White Supremacy (Non-White person) be a member of a "Republic"?

Reservation. Use this word with caution. Study the ways that others use the words "reservation" and "reserved." Ask questions.

> **Questions:** What is the difference between land that is "owned" and land that is so-called "reserved"? If a person has been forced to reside on a "reservation," does that person "own" that "reservation"? Is all land "reserved"? What is the difference between a "reservation" and a "nation"? Is a so-called "territory," a "reservation"? Who is correctly qualified to decide what a "reservation" is, and what a "reservation" is not?   Is a White Supremacist (Racist) qualified to "assign" a "reservation"?

Resettle/Resettlement. Use these words with caution.   When others use these words, ask for a detailed explanation that you can easily understand. Ask for an explanation of the differences, if any, between the meanings of the words "resettle," "relocate," "re-establish," and "dislocate."

> **Note:** According to Compensatory Logic, "dislocation" is always the result of force.

Respect. Use this word with caution. Use it only to apply to "self-respect." When speaking of "self-respect," define it as, "refusing to lie to oneself, and letting all others know of that refusal". Instead of asking others to "respect me," or "show me some respect," ask them, "Will you please be courteous"?

Reason: "Courtesy" is a manner of speaking or acting that is designed to help a person give or receive a "pleasant feeling" while interacting with others.

"Respect" is something that you get only by giving it to yourself. The only [true] respect (involving persons) is the respect that each person produces for <u>himself</u> or <u>herself</u> (self-respect). When a person has "self-respect," it cannot be "taken away" or be "infringed upon" by others.

The word "respect" may mean many different things to many different people. To some, the word "respect" means to speak and act with something called "courtesy." To some, it means not to speak until spoken to. To some, the word "respect" means to speak "with favor" toward and about the person, creature, or thing involved in the interaction with the person who is speaking.

Example: Anytime that you <u>know</u> that you are not telling <u>yourself</u> the truth, you do not have [self] "respect."

Questions: What, exactly, is "respect"? Where does it come from? Do people produce "respect," or is it delivered from some unknown source within, or without, the known universe? Is it correct for a person to depend on another person to "supply" him or her with "respect"? Is it possible to "disrespect" a person if he or she has "self-respect"? If a person has "self-respect," why would he or she try to get "respect" from others? If a person has "self-respect," what "type" of "respect" would he or she need from others that would be <u>better</u> than the "respect" that he or she has "produced" for him or her <u>self</u>? Does "showing respect," mean <u>avoiding contact</u> with those whom you "respect" the most – or does it mean trying to have as much contact as you can with them?

When, exactly, is a person being "disrespected"? Is being "disrespected" the same as being "mistreated"? Is it possible to "disrespect" a person who has "self-respect"? If so, is it better to "get respect" from others, than to supply oneself with "self-respect"? What, exactly, is "self-respect"? How does a person know for certain <u>when</u> he or she <u>has</u> "self-respect"? How does a person know for certain when he or she <u>does not have</u> "self-respect"?

Is "self-respect" the <u>only</u> form of "respect" worth having? If not, what "type" of "respect" is better? What person in the known universe has a "supply" of "respect" that you would like to have for yourself? Do you intend to "beg," "borrow," "buy," "rob" or "steal" the amount of "respect" that you believe others should supply you with? If not, how will you get it? If so, how will you know that you have it, when you have it, and what will be the "true value" of it if, and when, you know that you have it? Is it possible to "have respect" and, at the same time, be subject to, and/or be a Victim of, The System of White Supremacy (Racism)? If so, how? If so, "respect" from what "source"? If so, what is the value of that "respect"? If so, what will the value of that "respect" produce?

Responsible/Responsibility. Use these terms with caution. When others use these terms, ask for a detailed explanation that you can easily understand.

> **Questions:** What, exactly, is "responsibility"? What, exactly, is the "responsibility" that a person has in regards to opposing White Supremacy (Racism), or doing what is necessary to produce justice (balance between people)? What, exactly, is a "responsible person"? What, exactly, is the "responsibility" of a Victim of White Supremacy (Non-White person) to The System of White Supremacy (Racism)? Who is "responsible" for what happens to Non-White people who are subject to White Supremacy (Racism)? Does "responsibility" also include "blame"? If so, who should be "blamed" for all of the mistreatment that happens to Non-White people while they are subject to White Supremacy (Racism)?

> Who should be "responsible" for ending White Supremacy (Racism)? White people? Non-White people? Which White people? Which Non-White people? Should a White person who practices White Supremacy (Racism), be trusted to have the "responsibility" for deciding who should be "in charge" of ending White Supremacy (Racism)? Is anybody "responsible" for not ending White Supremacy (Racism)? Is anybody to blame? What about the White people who are not doing all that they can to end White Supremacy (Racism)? Are they "responsible"? Are they to "blame"? If they aren't, who is?

Restitution. Use this word with caution. Study, in detail, the ways that others use the word "restitution," and the word "restoration." When referring to "making up" for losses by Non-White people as the result of the existence of White Supremacy (Racism), use the word "compensation," along with, or in place of, the words "restitution," "restoration," "reparations," etc. The word "compensation" can and should be used to apply to everything that needs doing, and finally, is done, that is effective in replacing The System of White Supremacy (Racism) with The System of Justice (balance between people).

> **Note:** According to Compensatory Counter-Racist Logic, "compensation," "restitution," etc., for the practice of White Supremacy (Racism) <u>must</u> include the establishment of justice (balance between people) in all areas of activity, including Economics, Education, Entertainment, Labor, Law, Politics, Religion, Sex, and War/Counter-War.

Reverse Discrimination/Reverse Racism. <u>Do not use these terms</u> to apply to any condition that involves "Race," "Racism," or "Counter-Racism." Study the ways that others use the terms "reverse discrimination," "reverse racism," "reverse racial discrimination," etc. Instead of using any of these terms, use the term, "Counter-Racism," and/or the expression, "Replace White Supremacy (Racism) with Justice (balance between people)."

<u>Do not use these terms</u>. They are meaningless and/or confusing terms oftentimes used by White Supremacists (Racists) to pretend that White people are the victims of Black Supremacy. Such pretending is, in turn, used as an excuse to refuse to compensate for the practice of White Supremacy (Racism) in all areas of activity.

> **Reason:** During the existence of White Supremacy (Racism), and according to Compensatory Counter-Racist Logic, the only [functional] form of Racism that can and does exist in the known universe is White Supremacy. This means that as long as White Supremacy (Racism) exists, there is not, nor can there be, any other form of so-called "racial" discrimination in existence, any place in the known universe. There can only be a <u>reaction</u> to the existence of White Supremacy (Racism). That reaction can only take two forms: cooperation with, or resistance to. During the existence of White Supremacy (Racism), and according to Compensatory Counter-Racist Logic, to speak and/or act to resist White Supremacy (Racism) is not "reverse discrimination," or "reverse racism." It is "counter-racism" and/or "anti-racism" (speech or action that is effective in ending White Supremacy/Racism). A Non-White person who is subject to White Supremacy (Racism) cannot, at the same time, practice Racism, nor can he or she be a Racist. He or she can only react to the Racism (White Supremacy) that is being practiced.

Notes: According to Compensatory Counter-Racist Logic, so-called "Reverse Racial Discrimination" does not, and cannot exist, while the System of White Supremacy (Racism) exists. When others use the term "reverse racial discrimination," ask for a detailed explanation that you can easily understand.

Revolution. <u>Avoid using this word</u>. Instead, practice using the words "compensation," and/or "compensatory" (making up for what is missing that is also needed, and should be provided). When others use the word "revolution," ask for a detailed explanation that you can easily understand.

> **Notes:** During the existence of White Supremacy (Racism) and according to Compensatory Counter-Racist Logic, it is best and correct for all of the people of the known universe to produce a so-called "revolution" by first speaking and acting to replace The System of White Supremacy (Racism) with the System of Justice (balance between people) and correctness (balance between people, creatures, things, etc.). The result of this combination of thought, speech, and action should, logically, be a condition of "peace."

Rich. <u>Do not use this word</u> to apply to any person now existing in the known universe. If a person possesses an abundance of money, do not say that he or she is "rich." Instead, say that he or she "possesses an abundance of money." Use the word "rich" to apply to a person only if that person has *produced* justice (balance between people) and correctness (balance between people, creatures, things, etc.), in all areas of activity, including Economics, Education, Entertainment, Labor, Law, Politics, Religion, Sex, and War/Counter-War. Study the ways that others use the word "rich" as applied to people.

> **Notes:** During the existence of White Supremacy (Racism) and according to Compensatory Counter-Racist Logic, there are no people in the known universe who can be correctly described as "rich." It is best and correct to describe those White persons who practice White Supremacy (Racism) as "powerful," and to describe their "Victims" (Non-White persons) as "powerless."

Right. <u>Do not use this word</u> to describe what a person says or does. Instead, use the word "correct." Instead of saying "the person is right," say, "The action of the person was correct." Instead of saying, "They did what was right," say, "They did what was correct." Instead of saying "she has the right attitude," say, "She has the correct intentions."

> **Reason:** The word "right" has been so misused when applied to the actions of people that its meaning is, and has been, confusing. The use of the words "right" and "righteous" by the people of the known universe has often resulted in people speaking and acting to do great harm to themselves, and/or to each other. The use of the word "wrong" should be avoided or not used at all. It is best to use the words "incorrect" or "non-correct," in place of the word "wrong."

> **Notes:** In a world dominated by non-justice among people, it is incorrect to think that any person is correctly qualified to know for sure what is, and what is not "right" or "wrong" as it pertains to any area of activity. The use of the word "right" when compared with the word "left," should be given special consideration. Avoid confusion. Explain in detail.

Right Way/Wrong Way. <u>Do not use these terms</u>. Use, instead, the terms "correct way" or "incorrect way."

> **Reason:** As long as White Supremacy (Racism) exists and, according to Compensatory Counter-Racist Logic, it is best and correct to think that there is no way for a person to know, and/or to understand exactly what is "right" and exactly what is "wrong." The people of the known universe are too "poisoned" by non-justice, and too accustomed to glorifying their flaws to be able to accurately judge what is "right" and what is "wrong." The terms "correct" and/or "incorrect" can be applied to the process of "proving" themselves by measuring cause and effect.

> **Example**: It is correct to believe that fire "burns" by experience with fire. In regards to "right" and "wrong" however, people give opinions usually based on what they intend to do (or not do) regardless of any destructive effects their intentions may have on others.

Right-Wing/Left-Wing (as applied to people relations). <u>Do not use these terms</u> to apply to any so-called "political" interactions between people. Do not use terms like "leftist," "rightist," "right-of-center," or "left-of-center" when making remarks about the "political" acts of people. When others use these terms, ask for a detailed explanation that you can easily understand. Ask questions.

Questions: What, exactly, is a [political] "right-wing"? What, exactly, is the "center"? How does the "center" become the "center"? Is the "center" the same as The System of White Supremacy (Racism)? Is it possible for a Non-White person to be "situated" to the "right" or the "left" of The System of White Supremacy (Racism)? During the existence of White Supremacy (Racism), what "position" does a White Supremacist (Racist) "occupy"? Is it "right-wing"? "Left-wing"? "Center"? "Above center"? "Below center," "Circular,"? "No position"?

Note: During the existence of White Supremacy (Racism), and according to Counter-Racist Logic (the logic used against Racism/White Supremacy), it is correct for Non-White persons to describe their "political position" as "Victim of White Supremacy" – not as "right-wing," "left-wing," etc.

Riot. Use this word with caution. Study the ways that others use the words "riot" and "rioting." What, exactly, is a "riot"? Can a "riot" be a "rebellion"? What is the difference between a "riot" and a "fight"? Can a "riot" be "terroristic"? If a "riot" causes "terrorism," are the people who participate in a "riot," also "terrorists"? Is a "riotous-rebellion" against White Supremacy (Racism) a form of Counter-War against the unjust speech and action caused by Racistman and Racistwoman (White Supremacists, collectively)?

Note: During the existence of White Supremacy (Racism) and according to Compensatory Counter-Racist Logic, a "riot" is any non-constructive activity caused or promoted by people that result in unjust and/or incorrect harm to persons, creatures, and/or things.

Rise Above. Do not use this term to help cause one person to think, speak, or act as if he or she is "better" (more "royal") than other persons. Instead, always describe what any person says or does as being either "correct," or "incorrect." Do not promote the concept that people become the quality of people that they should be by "rising above" other people. Do not describe people as "higher-up" or "low-down," in regards to the quality or non-quality of their interactions with one another. Describe all actions and interactions between all people, creatures, and things as either "correct," or "incorrect."

Rite of Passage [Compensatory Counter-Racist]. Use this term to apply to the combined thought, speech, and action that result in the replacement of The System of White Supremacy (Racism) with The System of Justice (balance between people).

> **Note:** During the existence of White Supremacy (Racism) and according to Compensatory Counter-Racist Logic, it is correct for each Non-White person to think of a "rite-of-passage" as being *nothing less* than the replacement of White Supremacy (Racism) with Justice (balance between people).

Rob/Robbery. Use these words to apply to anything that is done willfully and deliberately by a person that results in another person incorrectly losing, or being prevented from acquiring, something of constructive value. Study the ways that others use the words "rob" and "robbery."

> **Notes:** People can be "robbed" in many different ways. During the existence of White Supremacy (Racism) and according to Compensatory Counter-Racist Logic, the White Supremacists (Racists) of the known universe have "robbed" the Non-White people of the known universe of what is most needed for Non-White people to practice justice (balance between people) and correctness (balance between people, creatures, things, etc.). This robbery continues in every area of activity including, Economics, Education, Entertainment, Labor, Law, Politics, Religion, Sex, and War/Counter-War.

Role Model. Avoid using this term. During the existence of White Supremacy (Racism), do not think, speak, or act as if any person is the "quality" of person ("role model") that a person should be. Instead, produce or use a "code" of correct thought, speech, and action that applies to every area of [people] activity. Use logic. "Follow" logic - don't "follow" people. People make too many mistakes. Study the laws of "cause and effect". Study the *results* of everything that is said and done – and not said and done.

> **Reason:** During the existence of White Supremacy (Racism) and according to Compensatory Counter-Racist Logic, there is reason to believe that no person is correctly qualified to act as a "role model" for any other person. There is reason to believe that all people should think, speak, and act according to a "code" of words with meanings that help to guide people into thinking, speaking, and acting to use the revelation of truth, in such a manner as to result in the production of justice,

correctness and "peace." A "role model" should be a carefully produced "code" of behavior that each person can adopt, for practice, in each area of his or her daily activities. There is reason to believe that if people know and understand exactly what to do, and not do, and exactly what to say, and not say, they will not need a "role model" in the form of a person. A "role model" should always be in the form of correct thought, speech, and action.

Questions: What "role model" came before the first "role model"? What "form" did the first "role model" take? Did the first "role model" have an "instruction list"? If so, where did the "list" come from? Are the correct words, with the correct meanings, the best and correct "role models"?

Romance. Use this word with caution. Do not use it to mean the same as the words "love" or "affection." Use the words "romance" or "romantic" to apply to thought, speech, and/or action that is, in effect, thrilling, exciting, soothing, and/or productive of temporary or artificial "gentle pleasure" to the mind and/or senses. When others use the words "romance" and/or "romantic," ask for a detailed explanation that you can easily understand. Ask questions.

Questions: Is "romance" the same as "love"? Is "romance" the same as "affection"? Does "romance" include justice (balance between people)? Does "romance," necessarily, include "honesty" and "sincerity"? Instead of using the word "romance," is it better to use the word "attraction"? What attracts one person to another? What attracts one person to another, "romantically"? During the existence of White Supremacy (Racism), does "romance" between and among Non-White people have the same meaning as "romance" between and among White people? If so, why? How? If not, why not?

Is it silly or pitiful for a Non-White person to attempt to be "romantic," while subject to The System of White Supremacy (Racism)? Is "romantic activity" among Non-White people no more than a pitiful and theatrical imitation of constructive attraction? Is the concept and practice of "romance" nothing more than "attractive exercises" in the direct or indirect support of the concept and practice of White Supremacy (Racism)?

Royal/Royalist/Royalty. <u>Use these terms with caution</u>. When others use these terms, ask for a detailed explanation that you can easily understand.

> **Questions:** What, exactly, do the terms, "royal," "royalism," "royalist," and/or "royalty" actually mean, <u>in function</u>? What, exactly, <u>should</u> these terms mean? Is being "royal" a way to produce justice (balance between people)? Who is qualified to decide who is "royal," and who is not? How many people in the known universe <u>should be</u> regarded as "royalty," and how many people <u>should not</u> be regarded as such?
>
> Is Racism (White Supremacy) a form of "Royalism"? If Racism (White Supremacy) is a form of "Royalism," should Counter-Racism (<u>ending</u> White Supremacy) be regarded as the form of "royalism" that <u>should be</u> enacted in order to end Racism (White Supremacy)? Is "Royalism" better than Justice? Is "Royalism" the <u>same</u> as justice? Is "Royalism" a means of producing justice? If "Royalism" is not the same as, better than, and/or is not a means of producing justice (balance between people), what, exactly, is its purpose?

Royalism (Racial). <u>Use these terms</u> to apply to the basic general characteristics of The System of White Supremacy (Racism), expressed as a form of "royalism" designed to mistreat people based on "color," with people classified as "White" functioning as a "chosen royal-family," with an unlimited "right" to use and abuse people classified as "Non-White," and to do so in any or all areas of activity, including Economics, Education, Entertainment, Labor, Law, Politics, Religion, Sex, and War/Counter-War.

Some examples of the more "sophisticated" and refined expressions of "Racist (White Supremacist) royalism" are as follows:

- Prominent numbers of "well-known" White persons engaging in so-called "marriages" and/or serious "romances" (sexual intercourse, etc.) with significant numbers of Non-White persons.

- Large numbers of Non-White people deliberately speaking and acting in such a manner as to imitate whatever they believe "sophisticated White people" do and say, without understanding that in the System of White Supremacy (Racism), most of the "most sophisticated" interactions between one White person and another are specifically designed to be supportive of The System of White Supremacy (Racism).

- Prominent numbers of White persons receiving unto themselves the "worshipful trust" and devotion of Non-White persons by speaking and acting as if they have been "chosen by God," and/or by other White persons to show Non-White persons the way to achieve "eternal salvation."

- White persons behaving in such a manner as to indicate that they expect to be "entertained" by whatever Non-White persons are available, whenever those White persons show that they desire to be "entertained."

- White persons indicating to Non-White persons, who is, and who is not, the "best choice" of Non-White persons "qualified" to speak or act for the so-called "betterment" of Non-White people.

- White persons indicating in work situations ("labor," "employment," etc.) that the Non-White persons will not, in any way, act as if they are not subject to the opinions, choices and/or desires of the White persons that they interact with.

- White persons indicating to Non-White persons, that what is called "law" will be interpreted in a manner that indicates that White persons will be, and should be "favored" over Non-White persons, in all things of "best value," in all areas of activity/existence.

- White persons indicating that White persons should directly or indirectly decide what will, or will not, be taught to both White people and Non-White people.

Rules/Regulations/Rules of War, etc. Avoid using these words to apply to anything that is said or done (writings, words, deeds, etc.). Practice, instead, using the words "law" or "laws."

> **Reason:** The words "rules," "rules and regulations," "policies," "guidelines," "general practices" etc., are often used to mean the same as "laws" that must be obeyed only some of the time, by some people, and/or "laws" that must be obeyed all of the time, by all of "some people." When some people use these terms, what they mean, and what they do not mean, is often very confusing.
>
> Racistman and Racistwoman (White Supremacists, collectively) have often used these words in a manner that is intended to frustrate and confuse their Victims (Non-White people). What may be called a "rule," "rule-of-thumb," "regulation," etc., when applied to a White person, may be regarded as a "law," when applied to a Non-White person. White Supremacists (Racistman and Racistwoman, collectively), may sometimes use the terms

"constitutional law" and/or "supreme law" to mean something either exactly alike, or very different from the terms "administrative law," "administrative rules," "administrative policies," etc.

During the existence of White Supremacy (Racism) some words, some times, are expected to have the effect of "laws" without those words actually being called "laws." Instead, they are called "bulletins," "memoranda," "notices," etc.

S

Sacred. Use this word with caution. When others use it, ask for a detailed explanation that you can easily understand.

> **Questions:** What, exactly, is "sacred"? What, exactly, is not "sacred"? Is everything "sacred" to someone, at some time? What, exactly, makes one thing, place, creature, etc., "sacred" and another thing, place, creature, etc., not "sacred"? What person is qualified to judge? Is the entire universe "sacred"? Is speech and action that is designed to replace White Supremacy (Racism) with Justice (balance between people), "sacred"? If so, why? If not, why not? Who is qualified to judge?

Salt-of-the-Earth. Do not use this term to apply to a person being the quality of person that he or she should be.

> **Reason:** The term could have been produced or promoted as a way of saying that salt is special, precious, and supremely useful because of its "whiteness" and, because of its "whiteness," it is akin to being special, precious, and supremely useful, like White people. The term has been often applied as a form of praise for a person. A person has sometimes been described as being the "salt-of-the-earth." During the existence of White Supremacy (Racism), this term, as applied to persons, may easily be used to glorify (directly or indirectly) the existence and practice of White Supremacy (Racism). Therefore, during the existence of White Supremacy (Racism) and, according to Compensatory Counter-Racist Logic, it is best and correct not to use this term to apply to any person.

Sane/Sanity. <u>Use these terms with caution</u>. Study the ways that others use the terms "sane," "sanity," "insane," "insanity," "balanced," "imbalanced," etc. Ask questions.

> **Questions:** What, exactly, is "sanity"? What, exactly, is "insanity"? When, exactly, is a person "sane" in each area of activity (Economics, Education, Entertainment, Labor, Law, Politics, Religion, Sex, and War/Counter-War)? Is a person "sane" if he or she willfully and deliberately kills people? Is a person "sane" if he or she deliberately inhales smoke from materials that are burning [tobacco]? Is a person "sane" if he or she practices White Supremacy (Racism)? Is a person "sane" if he or she submits to, and/or cooperates with, those who practice White Supremacy (Racism)? Are all persons both "sane" and "insane" about some things, at all times? Is it "insane" to "love" everybody? Is "hate" a form of "insanity"?

Santa Claus/Saint Nick. <u>Do not use these terms</u> to "celebrate," "commemorate," or "glorify" any event, circumstance or condition. Unless required by your chosen religion, do not make or "recognize" any person, image, depiction, etc., as being "Santa Claus," and/or "Saint Nick."

> **Reason:** The words "Santa Claus" and/or "Saint Nick" have often been used to describe a "make-believe" White-bearded, White man, who is depicted as a supreme good person, and who is a master-giver of gifts to the "good people" of the place called "planet earth." The concept of "Santa Claus" has most often been used in a manner that has helped to promote, both the concept and the practice, of White Supremacy (Racism). For that reason, and for reasons associated with the revelation of truth (that which is), it is best and correct not to associate "goodness," or "gift-giving" with any thought, speech, action, image, etc., with the name or title of "Santa Claus" and/or "Saint Nick."

Savage(s). <u>Use this term with caution</u>. When others use this term, ask them to explain, in detail, exactly what a "savage" is, and what a "savage" is not. Ask questions.

> **Questions:** Can a person be a "savage" and, at the same time, be a "member" of a so-called "civilization" (civilized society)? If so, how? If so, according to what "standard" – established by whom? Can a person be a "savage" and, at the same time, be very smart and very powerful? Can

a person have great knowledge and great understanding and, at the same time, be a "savage" in the way(s) he or she interacts with others? Can a person be very primitive, very ignorant, and very energetic, and yet not be "savage" in the way(s) that he or she interacts with others? Is a White Supremacist (Racist) a "civilized person," or is he or she a "savage"?

Is it logical that a "savage" could be any person while he or she is speaking or acting to promote falsehood, injustice, and/or incorrectness, in all areas of activity?

Scholar. <u>Use this word</u> to apply to any person who "studies" [attempts to learn]. When others use the word "scholar," ask them to give you a detailed explanation that you can easily understand.

School. <u>Use this term</u> to apply to:

(1) any part of the entire universe (and/or university);

(2) the sum total of all that exists, and/or all that can exist; and

(3) any situation in which something can be learned.

> **Explanation**: Every person, animal, insect, etc., is in school all of the time. Every situation is a learning situation, as long as everything is not known or understood.

Scum-of-the-Earth. <u>Do not use this term</u>. When others use it, ask for a detailed explanation that you can easily understand.

> **Reason:** Much of the earth is dark in color. White Supremacists (Racists) sometimes use the term "scum-of-the-earth" to promote thoughts that are associated with having contempt for "darkness" – particularly in regards to "color" in people. The word "scum" is usually associated with something that is not only "dark," but also filthy and worthless. White Supremacists (Racists) sometimes associate the words "scum," "dirt," and "earthy" with "dark" people. Some other terms that they use are "dirty lie," "dirty joke," "low-down dirty," "mud-people," "mud-race," "soiled," etc. The expression "scum-of-the-earth" is a term sometimes used by White Supremacists (Racists) which is intended to directly or indirectly promote harm to Non-White people. They sometimes use the term "salt-of-the-earth" as a compliment. Salt is "white" in appearance.

Second-Class Citizen. Avoid using this term. Instead, use the term "mistreated person." When others use this term, ask for a detailed explanation that you can easily understand.

> **Questions:** During the existence of White Supremacy (Racism), what, exactly, is a "citizen"? Who, exactly, is a "first-class citizen"? During the existence of White Supremacy (Racism), who is correctly qualified for "citizenship"? According to whom, and what? Can a member of the White Nation (White Supremacists, collectively), at the same time, function as a member of any other "nation," "country," etc.? (See, "Citizen").

Second World/First World/Third World. Do not use these (or similar) terms unless you give them definitions that you, and others, can easily understand. When others use these (or similar) terms, ask for a detailed explanation that you can easily understand.

Secret. Use this term to apply to information known only to one person (yourself).

Secular. Avoid using this word. When others use it, ask for a detailed explanation that you can easily understand. Ask questions.

> **Questions:** What, exactly, is "secular"? What, exactly, is the difference between that which is "secular," and that which is "religious"? When? Where? In which area(s) of activity? What, exactly, makes a "religion" a "religion"? What, exactly, is the specific number of things that a person says or does that is "secular," and not "religious"? Are any "parts" of a "religion" also "secular"? Can an act be both "religious" and "secular" at the same time? Can an act be both "spiritual," and "secular," at the same time?

Secular Religion. Use this term to mean any thought, speech, or action that is willful and deliberate, that is neither "spiritual" nor "religious," and that is neither involved in, nor influenced by, anything that is "material." When others use the terms "religion," "religious," "secular," "secular religion," "spiritual" and/or "spiritualism," ask for a detailed explanation that you can easily understand.

> **Questions:** Are all "religions" also "secular"? Is any "religion" a "secular religion"? Is The System of White Supremacy (Racism), a "secular religion"? Can a "spirit" be involved in that which is "secular"? Can a "religion" be

without "spirit" and/or be without "spiritualism"? Which persons are correctly qualified to judge which "spirits" are "evil" and which "spirits" are "good"? Are all "spirits" neutral, or are they "good"? Are all "spirits" "secular"? Are all people "spiritual"?

Security. Use this word with caution. Study the ways that others use the words "secure" and "security." Ask yourself, and others, what is "secure"? Who is "secure"? "Secure" in regards to what? Can there be "security" without justice (balance between people)? Should there be "security" without justice? If so, "security" for whom? In order to accomplish what?

Security Risk. Use this term to apply to all persons who practice White Supremacy (Racism). It is correct to regard as a "security risk" any person who has the ability to speak and act effectively to replace White Supremacy (Racism) with Justice (balance between people), but fails and/or refuses to do so. Also, regard a "security risk" as any person who refuses to speak and act to support the aforementioned description of "security risk" as being the basic and most important description. Study the ways that others use this term, and look for any contradictions in the ways that the term may be used.

Self-Defense/Self-Preservation. Use these terms with caution. Study and compare all the different ways that people use the terms "self-defense" and/or "self-preservation" in regards to all areas of activity. Ask many questions of self and others. (See, "Selfish").

Selfish. Avoid using this word. Instead use the terms "incorrect," "incorrect speech," "incorrect action," "unjust speech" and/or "unjust action." When others use the word "selfish," ask them to explain, in detail, exactly what they mean – and do not mean.

> **Questions:** Are all people "selfish"? Is not "selfishness" only a matter of degree or comparison? Could it be true that everybody is "selfish"? Could it be said that every person should be "selfish" by being at least half for "self" and at least half for "others"? If a person is half for "self" and half for "others," does that mean that he or she is not only all for "self" but also, all for "others"? If so, all "for" how many others? When? Where? In what ways? What does it mean to be "selfish"? Is it "selfish" to want to produce offspring? Is it "selfish" not to want to produce offspring? Is it "selfish" to help yourself as much as you help others? How can one "prove" to oneself and to others that one is "not selfish"?

Self-Help. Use this term to apply to anything that is done by a person or creature, that is the result of the effort(s) of that person or creature, without any help from any other person or creature, either directly or indirectly, in any one or more areas of activity, including Economics, Education, Entertainment, Labor, Law, Politics, Religion, Sex, and War/Counter-War. When others use this term, ask for a detailed explanation that you can easily understand. Look for the contradictions in the ways that the term may be used.

Self-Made (Man/Woman/Person). Do not use this term. When others use the term "self-made," ask for a detailed explanation that you can easily understand. Ask questions.

> **Questions:** Is any person, creature, place, or thing in the known universe, "self-made"? If so, who, or what, "made" the "self" that was "made"? If asked if "The Creator" of the known universe was "self-made," say, "I do not know" (if you do not know).

Self-Respect. Use this term to mean refusing to lie to oneself and letting all others know of that refusal. (See, Respect).

Semite/Semitic. Avoid using these words except to ask those persons who call themselves "Semites" and/or "Semitic," to explain what a "Semite" is, and what a "Semite" is not. When others use the words "Semite(s)" or "Semitic," ask for a detailed explanation that you can easily understand.   Seek answers mostly from persons who identify themselves as "Semites" or "Semitic."

> **Questions:** What, exactly, is the major goal of a "Semite" that is different from and/or that is opposed to, the major goal of persons who are not "Semites"?   How does a person who is a "Semite" act toward and/or interact with, a person who is not a "Semite," in each area of activity? What should a Victim of White Supremacy (Non-White person) expect a "Semite" to say and do in helping to replace The System of White Supremacy (Racism) with The System of Justice (balance between people) in each area of activity?

Semitism/Anti-Semitism. Avoid using these words until you know and understand exactly what a "Semite" is, what "Semitism" is not, and what "Anti-Semitism" is, and what it is not, in regards to all people, creatures, places, things and spirits, and in regards to all areas of activity.

Senile Person. <u>Use this term</u> to apply to a person who is extremely weak in effective activity and/or any person who has little or no ability to cause or assist in promoting significant help, or deliberate harm to any other person.

Separate. <u>Use this word with caution</u>. Study the ways that others use (or not use) the word "separate". Ask yourself, and others, many questions.

> **Questions:** What, exactly, is "separate"? What, exactly, is not "separate"? Is anything in the known universe completely "separate"? Is anything in the known universe partially "separate"? Does everything in the known universe interact with everything else? Is everything affected by everything else, either directly or indirectly? Are White people and Non-White people "separate" from each other? Is there any interaction between White people and Non-White people in any area of activity?
>
> How "separate" is "separate"? Is "separation" the same as "segregation"? Is segregation the same as "subjugation"? Is "subjugation" the same as "domination"? Is "domination" the same as "mistreatment"? Is a White Supremacist (Racist) "separate" from his or her Victim (Non-White person)?
>
> **Reason:** According to Compensatory Counter-Racist Logic, there is no way for any person, creature, or thing to be "separate" from any other person, creature, or thing and, at the same time, interact with or have an effect that is either "for" or "against" that person, creature, or thing (either directly or indirectly). Therefore, anything that is involved with Racism (White Supremacy) is not, and cannot, be "separate" from the people who are affected by Racism (White Supremacy). This means that the Victims of Racism (Non-White people) are never "separated" from the people who practice Racism [the White Supremacists, collectively] at any time during the existence of Racism (White Supremacy).
>
> **Notes:** It is important to remember that the functional purpose for the existence of Racism (White Supremacy) is for people who are classified as "White," to dominate and mistreat people who are classified as "Non-White," for the enjoyment and basic "benefit" of the people who are classified as "White." As expressed through The System of White Supremacy (Racism), domination, and mistreatment is applied, at all times in every area of

activity. Everything that is said and done in each area of activity is interrelated with each of the other areas of activity. They are not "separate" in effect; they may only appear to be so.

Separate Development. Do not use this term. When others use this term, ask for a detailed explanation that you can easily understand. When others use this term, it is correct to ask for a detailed explanation that you can easily understand. It is correct to ask as many questions as necessary. How "separate" is "separate"? What, exactly, is a "developed" person, creature, or thing, that is also "separate"?

> **Reason:** According to Compensatory Logic, the term "separate development" is meaningless and does not exist among and between the people, creatures, and things of the known universe. According to Compensatory Logic, every person, creature, and thing in the known universe has a direct or indirect effect on every other person, creature or thing, and are interactive with each other, either constructively or destructively.

Separate (but) Equal. Do not use this term. When others use this term, ask for a detailed explanation that you can easily understand. Instead of using the term "separate but equal," use the terms "quality relationship(s)," "correct interaction(s)," and/or "justice."

> **Reason:** According to Compensatory Logic, the terms "quality relationship(s)" and/or "correct interactions," means "balance between people, creatures, things, spirits, etc., in the process of producing 'correct' results." The term "justice" means balance between people and/or the act(s) of guaranteeing that no person is mistreated, and guaranteeing that the person who needs help the most, gets the most help.

Separation, Racial. Do not use this term. When others use it, ask for a detailed explanation that you can easily understand.

> **Reason:** According to Compensatory Counter-Racist Logic, and during the existence of White Supremacy (Racism), the "White Race" is the only "Race," and in order to qualify for the term "Race," the White person must practice Racism (White Supremacy) by being in constant contact with its Victims (Non-White people), directly and/or indirectly, in all areas of activity. Therefore, as long as a person is practicing Racism (White

Supremacy), he or she is not "separate" from the Victims (Non-White persons) of the Racism (White Supremacy) that is being practiced.

According to Compensatory Counter-Racist Logic, there is no way for a Victim of Racism (Non-White person) to be "separate" from the effects of what a Racist (White Supremacist) does. If a way of doing things is "racial," there is no way for the things that are done to be "separate" from the purpose of being "racial." According to Compensatory Counter-Racist Logic, the purpose of any person "being racial" is to either be in favor of the practice of Racism (White Supremacy), or be against it. The only form of functional Racism (according to Compensatory Counter-Racist Logic) now in existence is The System of White Supremacy.

Separation of Church and State. <u>Do not use this term</u>. When others use this term, ask for a detailed explanation that you can easily understand. Ask questions.

> **Questions:** What, exactly, is a "church"? What, exactly, is a "state"? How "separate" is "separate"? Is a "church" involved with people? Is a "state" involved with people? Is a "church" people? Is a "state" people? Is a person a "state"? Can one person be a "church"? Can that one person also be a "state"? What, exactly, is a "statesperson"? What, exactly, is a "churchperson"? Can a person who is a "statesperson" and a "churchperson" be "separate" from him or herself? If so, "separate" how? If so, "separate" in regards to what – or to whom? When? Where? How much? Which persons are correctly qualified to say?

Serious Crime. <u>Use this term with caution</u>. Use it mostly to apply to anything said or done that helps to establish, maintain, expand, and/or refine the practice of White Supremacy (Racism). Study the ways that others use the term "serious crime".

> **Note:** According to Compensatory Counter-Racist Logic and as long as White Supremacy (Racism) exists, it is correct to regard White Supremacy (Racism) as "The Crime of Crimes."

Seriously Flawed Person. <u>Use this term</u> to apply to any person who has not done all that he or she could to replace The System of White Supremacy (Racism) with The System of Justice (balance between people). It is correct to always describe yourself as an example of a "seriously flawed person."

Servant/Service. Use these words with caution. When others use these words, ask for a detailed explanation that you can easily understand. Ask questions.

> **Questions:** What, exactly, is a "servant"? What, exactly, is "service"? Who "serves"? Who is not a "servant"? Does providing a "service" make a person a "servant"? What "kind" of "service"? Does a Racist "serve" The System of White Supremacy (Racism)? Does a Victim of Racism (Non-White person) "serve" The System of White Supremacy (Racism)? Is The System of White Supremacy (Racism) the greatest and most powerful "servant" to the practice of non-justice among the people of the known universe?

> **Note:** According to Compensatory Counter-Racist Logic, White Supremacy (Racism) is the "Crime of Crimes," and all Non-White persons are the direct or indirect "servants-in-crime," to those White Supremacists (Racists).

Sex. Use this word to apply to any interaction that involves a male with a female. This includes interaction that may or may not involve sexual intercourse, or "sexual play." Such interaction may be physical, mental, "spiritual," or verbal. According to Compensatory Logic, having a "sexual experience, can mean any interaction between a male and a female in which "attention" is given, through speech, action, or silence to the "recognition" by a male and a female, that one is male, and one is female. Study the ways that others use the words "sex" or "sexual."

Use the term "Correct Sexual Intercourse" to mean any act of sexual intercourse that directly or indirectly helps to produce thoughts, speech, and/or action against the System of White Supremacy (Racism) and in support of the production of Justice (balance between people).

> **Notes:** According to Compensatory Logic, it is not possible for a male person to have a "sexual relationship" with a male person, nor can a female person have a "sexual relationship" with a female person. "Sex," at all times, means male and female. During the existence of The System of White Supremacy (Racism), it is those White persons who practice White Supremacy (Racism) who deliberately promote sexual confusion among the

Non-White people of the known universe. It is the White Supremacists (Racistman and Racistwoman, collectively), who are the greatest influence in promoting harmful sexual activity among Non-White people.

Important: The White Supremacists (Racists) use and promote so-called "homo-sex" and/or lesbian" ("anti-sex"/"counter-sex") to confuse, weaken, and sometimes destroy many Non-White people. This is one of their standard Racist practices.

Sex (the fair). Use this term to apply to White females only. When others use the terms "fair sex," or "the fair sex," ask for a detailed explanation that you can easily understand.

Reason: According to Compensatory Counter-Racist Logic and as long as White Supremacy (Racism) exists, the word "fair," when applied to a person, always means the non-color "White." During the existence of White Supremacy (Racism), terms like "fairness," "fair play," "fair employment," "fair lady," "fair treatment," etc., are always used in such a manner as to directly or indirectly promote thought, speech, or action in support of White Supremacy (Racism). White females are regarded, not only as "fair" (White) in appearance, but also as so-called "symbolic" of "purity," and of justice (balance between people). "Fair" does not mean "purity," nor does it mean "just." According to Compensatory Counter-Racist Logic, it is incorrect to associate the word "fair" in any manner, with the word "justice."

Sexism/Sex Offense. Use these terms to apply to any harm that is willfully and deliberately done against a male because he is a male, or a female because she is a female.

Sex-Oriented. Use this term to apply to everything that involves interactions between male and female because they are male and female. Study the ways that others use the term "sex-oriented" and/or the term "sexually-oriented." Ask for definitions with explanations that are easily understandable, and logical, to you.

Sex Slaves (Racial). Use this term to apply to all of the Non-White females or Non-White males of the known universe who are directly or indirectly required to, forced to, and/or enticed into, engaging in sexual intercourse and/or "sexual play" in order to obtain food, clothing, shelter, constructive learning and/or any of the things necessary for support, defense, or comfort.

Note: During the existence of White Supremacy (Racism) and according to Compensatory Counter-Racist Logic, the White Supremacists (Racistmen and Racistwomen, collectively) are most to blame for Non-White persons being used as "sex slaves."

Sexual Communication. Use this term to apply to any speech and/or action between male and female based on the needs and/or attraction directly or indirectly motivated by the physical and/or mental qualities or differences between male and female.

Sexual Harassment. Use this term. As long as White Supremacy (Racism) exists, study the ways that the use of the term "sexual harassment" is said to mean anything that White men and White women say that it means. Also, as long as White Supremacy (Racism) exists, use the term "sexual harassment" to mean anything that a White person says or does sexually, or anti-sexually, with or against a Non-White person for the purpose of producing or promoting "pleasure" or entertainment to or for a White person acting in direct or indirect support of White Supremacy (Racism). Study all the details of how others use the term "sexual harassment," "sexism," and/or "sexual offense," etc.

Sexual Intercourse. Use this term to apply to the act of the insertion of the male penis into the female vagina. (See, "Sex").

Sexual Misconduct. Use this term to apply to all sexual activity (sexual intercourse, "sexual play," etc.), that does not directly or indirectly promote thought, speech, and/or action that proves effective in helping to replace White Supremacy (Racism) with Justice (balance between people).

Sexual Perversion. Use this term to apply to:

(1)   Any speech and/or action that causes or promotes non-constructive speech and/or action between male and female.

(2)   Anything willfully and deliberately said or done by a male and female, in their relationship with each other, that does not promote the production of justice and/or correctness.

When others use the term "Sexual Perversion," ask for an explanation that you can easily understand.

Sexual Play. Use this term to apply to:

(1)   Male and female speaking to, acting toward, and/or touching one another, in such a manner as to promote thoughts of sexual intercourse.

(2)   Any contact between male and female that includes deliberate playful and/or sexually stimulating touching of any part of the body of one by the other, particularly the touching of the vagina, penis, buttocks, mouth, breasts, hair, etc.

Sexual Politics. Use this term to apply to any deliberate relationship between male and female persons, based primarily on consideration of sexual differences, and which does or does not include sexual intercourse, and/or "sexual play".

Sexual Remark. Use this term with caution. Use it to apply to anything said to a female person, by a male person, or to a male person by a female person, because of the "differences" between male and female persons. Regard what is said as being either constructive or non-constructive in effect or intent. Study the ways that others use this term. Be wary of the way(s) that Racist Suspects (Suspected White Supremacists) may or may not use the terms "sexual remark," "sexist remark" and/or "sexual harassment."

> **Note:** During the existence of White Supremacy (Racism), a White Supremacist (Racist) will always seek to use all words associated with "sex" in a manner that will directly or indirectly help to maintain, expand, and/or refine the practice of White Supremacy (Racism).

Sexually Trashed/Sexually Sewered (Racial). Use these terms to apply to the socio-political condition or "status" of a Non-White person, while he or she is engaging in any act of sexual intercourse, "sexual play," and/or so-called "homo-sexual" activity, with a White person, under any circumstances directly or indirectly dominated by, or during the existence of, White Supremacy (Racism).

> **Explanation**: According to Compensatory Counter-Racist Logic and as long as White Supremacy (Racism) exists, all acts of sexual intercourse or "sexual play," or all varieties of counter-sexual ("homo-sexual") behavior that involves a White person and a Non-White person, are acts that are non-just and non-correct. All such acts are maximum insults to, and/or maximum acts of aggression against, Non-White persons. All such acts under conditions dominated by The System of White Supremacy (Racism),

are "non-quality" acts between people. All such acts help to promote greater confusion among the Victims of White Supremacy (Non-White people). None of these acts help to produce justice (balance between people) or help to produce the end of Racism (White Supremacy). All of these acts have no "value," except to help produce the direct or indirect "trashing" and "sewering" of all Non-White people. There is no evidence that such activities help to produce "quality relationships" between White people and Non-White people.

Sexy. Use this word to apply to anything said or done that promotes mutual thought, speech, and/or action (between male and female persons) that favors sexual intercourse and/or "sexual play".

Shadow Fighting (Racial). Use this term to apply to Non-White people fighting each other, and/or blaming each other for the existence of White Supremacy (Racism), rather than speaking and/or acting to eliminate it.

Shadow of a Doubt. Do not use this term. Instead, use the word "doubt."

> **Reason:** It is not necessary to associate the word "doubt" with the word "shadow." A "shadow" is "dark." White Supremacists (Racists) often deliberately use any word that is generally associated with "darkness" in a manner that helps to promote thoughts of uncertainty, ugliness, unpleasantness, evil, foreboding, danger, etc. This includes the use of the term "enlightened" - a term that White Supremacists (Racists) indirectly associate with ways and means of thinking against "doubtful shadows" and/or people who are "dark" in appearance. Doubt is doubt, and a shadow is a shadow. Though a shadow is dark, there is no logical reason to associate the word "shadow" with the word "doubt," or the word "doubt" with the word "dark."

> **Example**: According to White Supremacist (Racist) culture, the expression, "I'm in the dark about what happened" means, "I do not know," and/or "I have a doubt."

Shady Background/Character/Shady Deal/Checkered Past. Do not use these terms. When others use them, ask for a detailed explanation that you can easily understand. Ask questions.

Questions: What, exactly, does the word "shady" have to do with the "background" [past] of a person? What, exactly, makes a person's character "shady"? Why say that a deal is "shady"? If a person is saying that a business transaction is incorrect, why not say that it is incorrect? Why call it a "shady deal"?

Why is the word "checkered" used? Does it mean a "past" that is incorrect? If so, why not use the term "incorrect past"? Does "checkered" mean black and white? Does "checkered" mean something derogatory? Does it mean that a person's "past" has not been what it should have been and is, therefore, "checkered"? Does this term mean "white," but with too many black (derogatory) "blocks," "squares" and/or "characteristics"? Why would the word "checkered" be used to describe events in a person's past? Is this term the result of probable Racist (White Supremacist) thinking?

Notes: White Supremacists (Racists) often deliberately use words in combinations that help to directly or indirectly insult or belittle the "dark" (Non-White) people of the known universe. They do this by implying that conditions of uncertainty, ugliness, danger, dishonesty, foreboding, evil, doubt, crookedness, etc., should always, as much as possible, be associated with "darkness," "shady-ness," "shadows," and especially Black, "dark," and/or "Non-White" people.

Shed Some Light on the Subject. <u>Do not use this term</u>. Use, instead, the expression, "reveal the truth about the matter" or "learn what needs to be known," etc.

Reason: During the existence of White Supremacy (Racism), many of the people (White) who have chosen to practice White Supremacy (Racism) sometimes use the word "light" in such a manner as to promote thoughts about the word "light" as being associated mostly with White people, as in, "right," "bright," "wisdom," etc.

Short/Short Time. <u>Use these words with caution</u>. Study the ways that others use the words "short," "short time," "long," "long time," "tall," etc. Ask questions.

Questions: How "short" is "short"? "Short," as compared with what? Has The System of White Supremacy (Racism) existed for only a "short time"? If so, according to whom? If so, as compared to what? What person is correctly qualified to judge? Based on what (as a "correct qualification")?

Show Me/Give Me [some] Respect. <u>Do not use these words</u> when talking to, or about, others in regards to acquiring "respect" for yourself.

> **Reason:** According to Compensatory Logic, it is incorrect to ask a person for an apology, or for "love," or for "respect." An apology and "love" are values that should be produced, and offered voluntarily. "Respect" is a value that a person can only produce and receive for him or herself. The only form of true "respect" is the "respect" that a person "gives" to him or herself. He or she can "give" respect to him or herself, only by refusing to lie to him or herself, and only by letting others know of that refusal. According to Compensatory Logic, it is best and correct not to ask a person for "respect" but, instead, ask all persons to help you to produce justice (balance between people).

Showed Their True Colors. <u>Do not use this term</u>. Instead use the expression, "showed their true intentions."

> **Reason:** During the existence of White Supremacy (Racism), and according to Compensatory Counter-Racist Logic, any mention of the words "color," or "colors" should be avoided except when used in a manner that is favorable to the existence of "color" itself – particularly in regards to the "color" of people.

Showed Yellow. <u>Do not use this term</u> to apply to a person. When talking about a person acting incorrectly, say, "He or she acted incorrectly."

> **Reason:** The term "showed yellow" has often been used by White Supremacists (Racists) to "make fun" of people who act fearful, and/or who act in a so-called "cowardly" manner. White Supremacists (Racists) have often said that a person who shows a lack of courage is "showing yellow." This expression, by association, is sometimes regarded as applicable to a great number of Non-White people who White Supremacists (Racists) have "racially classified" as "yellow" people.

Sick. <u>Use this word with caution</u>. Study the ways that others use it. Ask questions.

> **Questions:** What, exactly, is "sickness"? What, exactly, is "wellness"? How "sick" is "sick"? How "well" is "well"? Is a Racist (White Supremacist) "sick"? Is a Victim of Racism (Non-White person) "sick"? Can the "body" of a person be "well" if that person's "mind" is "sick"?

Silly Question/Stupid Question. <u>Do not use these terms.</u>

> **Reason:** No question is "silly" and/or "stupid." All questions have answers [the answer]. All questions have a correct answer. An "incorrect answer" to a question is no answer to that question.

Sin. <u>Use this term</u> to apply as follows:

(1) Hypocrisy (willfully and deliberately pretending to others that one has a constructive belief and intent that one does not have);

(2) Pretending to believe one thing while, in truth, believing another or pretending to say or do one thing while, in truth, saying or doing something very different and/or contradictory. (<u>See</u>, "Sinner").

Single. <u>Use this word with caution</u>. Try to use this word in ways that will best produce the revelation of truth (that which is). Study the ways that others use this word. Study the ways that people sometimes use the words "apart," "couple(s)," "separate," "triple," "together" and/or "allied." Study how they apply these words to describe interactions between people. Ask questions of yourself and of others.

> **Questions:** Is any person, place, creature, or thing truly "single"? What, exactly, is a "couple"? Can three people holding each other's hands be a "couple"? Can two people who are not touching each other, but who are looking at each other and smiling, be "single"? Are they a "couple"? Are they a "couple" that are "single"? Are all people, creatures, and things in the universe, interrelated? How "single" is "single"? How "double" is "double"? Can a person be "single," and "united," at the same time?

Sinner. Avoid using this word. Do not use the word "sinner" to describe any person, unless that person uses it to describe him or herself. When others use the words "sin" or "sinner," ask for a detailed explanation that you can easily understand.

> **Reason:** The word "sinner" is usually defined in ways that result in confusion among and between the people of the known universe.

> **Questions:** What, exactly, is a "sin"? What, exactly, is not a "sin"? Exactly how many "sins" makes a person a "sinner"? Is a person a "sinner" if he or she "sinned" yesterday, but not today? Is every person a "sinner"? Are some persons who are "sinners" better than other persons who are also "sinners"? If so, why? If not, why not? Are all "sins" equal? Is there such a thing as "degrees" of "sin"?

> **Note:** During the existence of White Supremacy (Racism), and according to Compensatory Counter-Racist Logic, the functional definition of "sin" is *hypocrisy*.

Slant-Eyed. Avoid using this term in a manner that may be thought of as a derogatory remark about a person's appearance.

> **Reason:** White Supremacists (Racists) have sometimes used the terms "slant-eyed" or "shifty-eyed" to describe the eyes of so-called "yellow," "Asian," or "Oriental" people. They have done this for the purposes of being insulting, and producing contempt. According to Compensatory Counter-Racist Logic, it is incorrect to "poke fun" at or make insulting remarks about any part of a person's body.

Slavery. Use this word to apply to any activity and/or condition that results in a person being subject to, and/or being a Victim of, any form of deliberate injustice or incorrectness. Identify The System of White Supremacy (Racism) as the greatest and most powerful form of "slavery" now in existence among the people of the known universe. Study the ways that others use the word "slavery." Ask questions.

> **Questions:** What, exactly, is a "slave"? What, exactly, is not a "slave"? Who is correctly qualified to say what "slavery" is, and what "slavery" is not? Is a person a "slave" to his or her own "ignorance"? Is "ignorance" a form of "slavery"? Is a person who is forced to fight or kill other persons, a "slave" to the person(s) who did the

forcing? Is a person in "slavery" to his or her own destructive or non-constructive habits?

Notes: The word "slavery" has been, and can be, used in many different ways. What one person says is "slavery," another person may say is "business," or a "condition of supply and demand." There should be many questions about what is and what is not a "slave". According to Compensatory Counter-Racist Logic, however, a person who is subject to White Supremacy (Racism), is a "slave" to White Supremacy (Racism).

Slave World. Use this term to apply to any activity and/or any condition in which a person is subject to, or a Victim of, any activity, or condition that is non-correct, or non-just. When others use the term "slave world," ask for a detailed explanation that you can easily understand.

Sleeping With. Do not use this term to apply to sexual intercourse. Use the term "sexual intercourse".

Slope [Racial]. Do not use this word to apply to any person. When others use the word in this manner, ask for a detailed explanation that you can easily understand.

Reason: White Supremacists (Racists) sometimes use this word to be insulting to a so-called "Asian," "Oriental," and/or "yellow" person.

Slut. Do not use this word. When others use this word, ask for a detailed explanation that you can easily understand.

Reason: During the existence of White Supremacy (Racism), the word "slut" has been too easily associated with the words "smut," "smuck," "smudge," "sludge," and "muck." This is done in order to associate "dark" people with places, creatures, and/or things with that which is [regarded as] trashy, useless, unwanted, ugly, immoral, wrong, etc. Through The System of White Supremacy (Racism), Racistman and Racistwoman (White Supremacists, collectively), have produced an entire "language" that is especially designed to make everything associated with "darkness" (specifically in regards to "color" in the appearance of people), to be disgraceful, filthy, unworthy, despicable, etc.

Small Business. Use this term. During the existence of White Supremacy (Racism), use the term "small business" mostly to apply to what the Non-White people do, collectively, as compared with what White Supremacists (Racistman and Racistwoman) do, collectively.

>**Reason:** During the existence of White Supremacy (Racism) and according to Compensatory Counter-Racist Logic, the White people who practice White Supremacy (Racism) are practicing "big business," (the most influential "business" now existing among the people of the known universe). By comparison, all of the things that the Non-White people of the known universe say or do can be correctly regarded as "small business."

Smartest People (the). Use this term to apply only to those White persons of the known universe who practice White Supremacy (Racism). When others use this term, ask for a detailed explanation that you can easily understand. Do not argue. Listen to the reasons others give for saying whatever they say.

>**Reason:** All of the Non-White people in the known universe are, directly or indirectly, subject to the will of those White persons who have chosen to practice White Supremacy (Racism). If the persons who are subject to the practice of White Supremacy (Racism) were as "smart" as the persons who practice White Supremacy (Racism), the persons who are subject to White Supremacy, would not be subject to White Supremacy.
>
>Persons who are subjugated are never as "smart" as the persons who are subjugating them. The White Supremacists (Racists) have proven how "smart" they are. The Victims of White Supremacy [Non-White people] can only "prove" that they are also "smart" when they are no longer Victims.
>
>**Notes:** There is reason to believe that at all times, in all places, among all people, it is the correct duty of the "Smartest People" to guarantee that justice (balance between people) is produced and maintained. There is reason to believe that "smart people" are "allowed" to be "smart" and "allowed" to be in contact with people who are not "smart." There is reason to believe that if people who are "smarter" than other people decide not to produce justice, it is logical for "The Law of Compensation" to cause a condition in which the "not smart" people will become "smart enough" themselves, to "cause" justice to be produced.

During the existence of White Supremacy (Racism) and according to Compensatory Counter-Racist Logic, those White people who have chosen to make the Non-White people of the known universe subject to White Supremacy (Racism), have proven that they are "the smartest people" by making the Non-White people subject to White Supremacy (Racism) in all areas of activity, including Economics, Education, Entertainment, Labor, Law, Politics, Religion, Sex, and War/Counter-War.

Smart-less People. Use this term to apply to:

(1)   Non-White people, generally, and/or collectively;

(2)   All Non-White people who exist in direct or indirect subjugation to Racists (White Supremacists);

(3)   The people of the known universe who are classified as "Non-White" when they are compared, both collectively and functionally, with the people of the known universe who are classified as "White" and who practice White Supremacy (Racism).

(4)   People who are less smart than people who are smart, and/or people who are less smart than people who are the smartest.

Smear. Avoid using this word when applying to the actions between people.

> **Reason:** The word "smear" is sometimes used by White Supremacists (Racists) to apply to an act that is "dark" with oil or grease. Indirectly, the word is made to be associated with something done that is unpleasantly similar to being involved with a "dark" (Non-White) person. Similar words that are used for the same "mental picture" purpose are "tarnish," "smudge," "dirtied," "sludge," "soil," "sully," etc.

Smokescreen. Use this term with caution. Do not use this term to apply to an act of deception that does not refer to the actual use of "smoke". Study the ways that others use this term. If they do not use the term to apply to the presence of actual smoke, ask them why they chose to use that term.

> **Reason:** White Supremacists (Racists) use the word "smokescreen" to sometimes describe something that a person says or does (without actually using smoke), that is intended to deceive other persons, particularly persons who are classified as "Non-White." By using the term

"smokescreen," the White Supremacists (Racists) help to make people think that being deceitful is somehow the same as being "dark," and/or somewhat like being or looking like a dark person ("shady," "shadowy," "smoky," etc.).

Notes: It is the White Supremacists (Racists), more than any other people in the known universe, who have proven to be the masters of malicious deceit. It is also worthy of thought to give attention to the way that the term "whitewash" is used. The term "whitewash" is sometimes used to talk about something said or done that promotes the theory that <u>thinking</u> that has been "washed white," is correct thinking.

Smuck/Smut. <u>Do not use these words</u> to apply to any person, place, thing, etc. When others use these words, ask for a detailed explanation that you can easily understand. Ask questions.

Questions: What, exactly, is a "smuck"? What, exactly, is not a "smuck"? What, exactly, is "smut"? What, exactly, is not "smut"? Do these words mean something derogatory? Why do such words rhyme with or are made to seem associated with other so-called "derogatory descriptions" of persons, places, things, etc.? Why do such words seem to be designed to produce thoughts that are about that which is "unworthy," and associated with "darkness" – particularly darkness in regards to the appearance (color) of people classified as "Non-White"?

Snow White. <u>Use this term with caution</u>. Avoid using the term "Snow White" in any manner that gives "praise" to or produces adulation for a person because of that person's "whiteness" of skin/appearance.

Reason: According to Compensatory Logic, it is incorrect to praise people because of the way that they "appear" in color or non-color. In regards to "whiteness" in skin/appearance, the White people who believe in the practice of White Supremacy (Racism) have used such "whiteness" (in skin appearance) as a so-called "justification" for the mistreatment of the "Non-White" people of the known universe.

Social. <u>Use this word with caution</u>. When others use the words "social," "socialize," "socialist," "anti-social," etc., ask for a detailed explanation that you can easily understand. Ask questions.

Questions: What, exactly, is "social"? What, exactly, is not "social"? What, exactly, does it mean to be "anti-social"? Is a person who is "anti-social," "anti-social" about everything – with everyone? What, exactly, is a "social event"? What, exactly, is a "social gathering" of people? Is a meeting of two White persons who practice White Supremacy (Racism), a "social gathering"? Is a meeting of two Non-White persons who are opposed to the practice of White Supremacy (Racism) a "gathering" that is "anti-social"? What, exactly, is the difference between a "social meeting" and a "business meeting"? During the existence of White Supremacy (Racism), is sexual intercourse between a White person and a Non-White person a "social event," or an "anti-social event"?

Socialism/Socialist. <u>Avoid using these words</u>. When others use these words, ask for a detailed explanation that you can easily understand. Ask questions.

Questions: What, exactly, is "socialism"? What, exactly, is a "socialist"? What, exactly, is not a "socialist"? Is a person who is "socialized," a "socialist"? Does a person who is a "socialist," own anything? If so, what? Can a person be a "capitalist" and a "socialist" at the same time? Is The System of White Supremacy (Racism) a form of "socialism," "capitalism," "fascism," or "royalism"? Is it all of these? Is it none of these? Is The System of White Supremacy (Racism) the most powerful form of "socialism" now in existence among the people of the known universe?

Note: During the existence of White Supremacy (Racism) and according to Compensatory Counter-Racist Logic, there is no form of "government," by people, that is more powerful than the Society of White Supremacy (White Supremacists/Racists, collectively).

Social Legislation. <u>Use this term with caution</u>. Use it mostly to apply to anything that is done by people – be it correct, or incorrect. When others use the terms "social legislation," "social law," or "social action," ask for a detailed explanation that you can easily understand.

Social Obligation. <u>Use this term with caution</u>. Use it mostly to apply to those things that are said or done, that are intended to be of help in ending White Supremacy (Racism), and/or in producing justice (balance between people). When others use this term, ask for a detailed explanation that you can easily understand.

Note: During the existence of White Supremacy (Racism) and according to Compensatory Counter-Racist Logic, the basic "social obligation" of every person in the known universe, is to think, speak, and act with the intention of replacing The System of White Supremacy (Racism) with the System of Justice (balance between people).

Social Security. <u>Use this term with caution</u>. Use it mostly to apply to speech and/or action that result in justice (balance between people). When others use this term, ask for a detailed explanation that you can easily understand. Ask questions.

> **Questions:** What, exactly, is a "socially-secure" person? Is a White Supremacist (Racist) "socially secure"? Is a Victim of White Supremacy (Non-White person) "socially-secure"? How "socially-secure" can a Non-White person be if he or she is subject to White Supremacy (Racism)? How "social" is "social," and in how many areas of activity? How many areas of activity must a person be "secure" in if he or she is to be "socially-secure"? What about "social security" in all The Nine Areas of (People) Activity?

Socially Acceptable. <u>Use this term with caution</u>. Use it mostly to apply to any speech and/or action that is directly or indirectly supportive of, or opposed to, The System of White Supremacy (Racism) in any one or more areas of activity. When others use the term "socially-acceptable," ask for a detailed explanation that you can easily understand. "Socially acceptable" with regard to what? By whom? In order to accomplish what?

> **Note:** As long as White Supremacy (Racism) exists and according to Compensatory Counter-Racist Logic, the term "socially acceptable" can be used in a manner that is, or can appear to be, contradictory.

Society. <u>Avoid using this word</u>. When others use it, ask for a detailed explanation that you can easily understand. Ask questions.

> **Questions:** What, exactly, is a "society"? What, exactly, is not a "society"? How many "parts" of what kind of thought, speech, or action does it take to make a "society"? Can one person be a "society"? How "separate" is a so-called "separate society"? Can Non-White people be a "society" and, at the same time, be subject to The System of White Supremacy (Racism)? What qualifies a "society" to be a "society"? Are all of the people in the

known universe a "society"? What, exactly, is an "independent society"? What, exactly, is a "society within a society"?

Socio-Economic. <u>Use this term</u> to apply to any speech, action, and/or inaction, that affect any part of any person's existence, and/or the use of time and energy, in general.

> **Note:** A better term than "socio-economic" is "socio-material". The word "economics" should be used to express only that speech or action that is just and correct in any one or more areas of activity.

Soil/Soiled. <u>Use these words with caution</u>. Study the ways they are used by others when they talk about a person's so-called "character" or "reputation." Give attention to the ways that the words are sometimes used to talk about people in a harmful way. Study the ways that people sometimes use words associated with "dark," or "darkness," with being not only like the "soil," but with being "trashy," "filthy," despicable, and/or worthless. Study how some other words are used, such as "black," "blackened," "dirty" "sullied," "tarnished," etc.

Soldier. <u>Use this word with caution</u>. Study the ways that others use the word "soldier." Ask questions.

> **Questions:** What, exactly, is a "soldier"? What, exactly, is not a "soldier"? Is a "soldier" a "militant" person? Is a "militant" person the same as a "military" person? Is a White person a "soldier" if he or she participates in the practice of White Supremacy (Racism)? Is a White Supremacist (Racist) the same as a "Race soldier"? Is The System of White Supremacy (Racism) itself, a "military activity" that requires that the White persons who participate in the System think, speak, and act as "Race soldiers" ("militant" White Supremacists)?
>
> Is it true that a "soldier" is any person who participates in a "fight" to accomplish a specific purpose? Is a "soldier" also a "law enforcement officer"? Can a person participate in a "military action" and, at the same time, not be a "soldier"? Are all "soldiers" also "militant"? Are all persons who are "militant" also "soldiers"? If not, what is the difference?
>
> Is the existence of White Supremacy (Racism) a condition of "military aggression"? Is the existence of White

Supremacy (Racism) the greatest and most powerful expression of war? Are the White persons who maintain that war, the most powerful "soldiers" among the people of the known universe?

Somber Colors/Somber Mood/Somber Tones. Do not use these terms. Use instead, the true description of a "color" or a "shade" of color. For example, if a color is "dark blue," say that the color is "dark blue." Do not say that it is a "somber blue," or that blue is a "somber tone." Instead of saying that a person is in a "somber mood," say that he or she is "sad."

> **Reason:** The word "somber" is sometimes associated with the word "sad" or "gloomy," or "foreboding." These words are often used by White Supremacists (Racists) in association with "dark," "Black," "colored," and/or "Non-White" people. For that reason, it is better not to use terms like "somber colors" or "somber tones" because such terms directly or indirectly helps to promote Racist (White Supremacist) thought, speech, and action. The terms "gloomy," "shady" or "shadowy" are sometimes used in a manner that promotes that same kind of thinking.

> **Questions:** Does a "mood" have "color"? What does a "bright mood" actually look like - and why?

Sophisticated. Use this word with caution. When others use it, ask for a detailed explanation that you can easily understand.

> **Notes:** The word "sophisticated" is sometimes used in a manner that is contradictory and/or confusing. During the existence of White Supremacy (Racism) and according to Compensatory Counter-Racist Logic, the White Supremacists (Racistman and Racistwoman, collectively), have proven to be the most "sophisticated" of all the people of the known universe in regards to the most skillful uses of power for the purpose of dominating and mistreating people.

Soul (Racial). Use this term to apply to:

(1) The will plus the ability, to think, speak and act, to use truth in such a manner as to produce justice and correctness; and

(2) The will, plus the ability of a Victim of Racism (Non-White person) to eliminate Racism (White Supremacy).

373

Soul Art. Use this term to apply to any speech, action, thing, etc., that helps to produce the will plus the ability, to find truth, and to use truth in a manner that produces justice and correctness.

Soul Food. Use this term to apply to:

(1)   Anything put into the body that best helps one to think, speak, and act in a manner that produces justice and correctness.

(2)   Any information that best helps one to think, speak, and act in a manner that produces justice and correctness.

(3)   Any food, drink, or information that best helps one to produce the will and the ability to replace Racism (White Supremacy) with Justice (balance between people).

Soul Music. Use this term to apply to:

(1)   Any words and/or sounds that best help one to think, speak, and act in such a manner as to produce justice and correctness.

(2)   Any words and/or sounds that best help one to think, speak, and act to replace Racism (White Supremacy) with Justice (balance between people).

Sound Mind. Do not use this term. When others use this term, ask for a detailed explanation that you can easily understand. Study the ways that others use this term. Ask yourself, and others, many questions.

> **Questions:** What, exactly, is a "mind" that is "sound"? When is a person's mind "sound"? During the existence of White Supremacy (Racism) how can any person "prove" to be of "sound mind"? "Prove" it to whom? What person is correctly qualified to judge? Is a person who practices White Supremacy (Racism) of "sound mind"? Is a person who spends most of his or her time and energy trying to end White Supremacy (Racism), of "sound mind"?
>
> Since The System of White Supremacy (Racism) is maintained by the use of deceit and/or indirect violence, is a person who seeks to end White Supremacy (Racism) by using truth and direct counter-violence, of "sound mind"? Is any person in the known universe truly of "sound mind"? In a world in which all of the people are involved (either directly or indirectly) in unjust and

incorrect thought, speech, and/or action, what person can truthfully say that he or she is of "sound mind"? Whose "mind" is "sound" enough to judge?

Sovereign. Avoid using this word. When others use this word, ask for a detailed explanation that you can easily understand. Ask questions.

> **Questions:** What, exactly, is a "sovereign people"? What, exactly, is not a "sovereign people"? What people in the known universe are truly "sovereign"? Which persons are correctly qualified to judge? During the existence of White Supremacy (Racism), is a person "sovereign" if he or she is Non-White?

Space. Use this word with caution. Study the ways that others use the word. How much "space" exists in what is called "time"? What, exactly, is "inner-space," and why? What, exactly, is "outer-space," and why? What, exactly, is a "space race"? Is space the absence of "time," and the absence of "deed"?

Space Race. Do not use this term. Instead, use the term, "space use." When others use this term, ask for a detailed explanation that you can easily understand. How, exactly, can a person "race" against "space"? Why would a person desire to "conquer" what is known as "space"? Why use the words "conquer space"? Is it not best and correct to say, "use space in a constructive manner," than to say, "race against space" or "conquer space"?

Spot (hit the). Do not use this term. Instead, use the expression "correct speech and/or action."

> **Reason:** The word(s) "spot" and/or "target," are sometimes used by White Supremacists (Racists) as "slang" expressions designed to promote thinking that associates "spots" or "targets" with the [dark] color of Black people. During the existence of White Supremacy (Racism), Racistman and Racistwoman (White Supremacists, collectively), sometimes regard Non-White people as something fit to be hit, "targeted," ("get the tar out"), "erased," and/or so-called "whitened-out."

Spotless. Do not use this word in regard to the interaction between people. Instead, use the word "correct," or the word "corrected."

> **Reason:** The word "spotless" is often used by Racistman and Racistwoman (White Supremacists, collectively), to

apply to White people and/or to apply to the "character" of a person when that person is the person that he or she "should be." The word "spotless," as used by White Supremacists (Racists), is used to imply that something or someone "spotless" is not "like" a Black or dark person. They imply that a "spotless" person is not only "pure," "clean," "good," "pretty," "desirable," etc., but also "White." They imply that a Black Person is like a "spot" or a "blot," something that is "impure," "unclean," "poison," "ugly," and/or "undesirable."

Spy. Use this word with caution. During the existence of White Supremacy (Racism) use the terms "Racist spying" and/or "Racist espionage" to apply to the practices of Racistman and Racistwoman (White Supremacists, collectively), when they seek information about Non-White persons with the intention of using that information to do non-just harm, and/or to directly or indirectly support The System of White Supremacy (Racism). Study the ways that others use the word "spy." Ask questions about what is, and what is not, "spying."

Squatter. Avoid using this word. When others use it, ask for a detailed explanation that you can easily understand. Ask questions.

> **Questions:** What, exactly, is a so-called "squatter"? What, exactly, is not a "squatter"? What, exactly, is a "settler"? Is a "settler" the same as a "squatter"? If not, why not - and according to whom? Who is correctly qualified to judge? Based on what "qualification"? According to whom? Are the White Supremacists (Racists) of the known universe, the "master squatters" of the known universe? If not, who is?

Standard(s). Use this word with caution. Study the ways that others use the word. Ask questions.

> **Questions:** Is The System of White Supremacy (Racism) the major "standard" for power among the people of the known universe? What, exactly, is the "standard procedure" for replacing The System of White Supremacy (Racism), with the System of Justice (balance between people)? Which persons are correctly qualified to produce that "standard procedure"? According to whom?

Stand By Your Work. Use this term to apply mostly to a suggestion that should be repeatedly made to those persons (White or Non-White) who kill, maim, and/or in other ways do harm to others – whether the harm done is correct or incorrect.

Use this term to suggest that every person in the known universe should be willing to voluntarily say to all of the people in the known universe that it was he or she who did whatever harm he or she did to others. The understanding should be that any person who does harm to others, should be willing to "tell the world" that they did the harm, and they did so willingly. To refuse to "stand by [one's] work" is to show contempt for the production of Justice (balance between people).

> **Notes:** Whatever a person does willingly and deliberately, he or she should always also be willing to say, "I stand by my work."

State/Statehood. Use these words with caution. When others use these words, or similar words, ask for a detailed explanation that you can easily understand. Ask questions. According to Compensatory Logic, a "state" is a person, and every person has "status" as a person.

> **Questions:** What, exactly, is a "state"? What, exactly, is not a "state"? What is "statehood"? What is not "statehood"? Can a "state" be one person? Two persons? In The System of White Supremacy (Racism) is a White person one "state," and a Non-White person another "state"? Are the two "state persons" so-called "united"? If so, how? Where? "United states" in regards to what? Can a White Supremacist (Racist) be "united," in "statehood," with a Victim of White Supremacy [Non-White person]? How can one person be "united" with another person if one person is maliciously and destructively dominant over the other? How can one "state," be subject to another "state" and, at the same time, have "status" as a "state"? Does a slave have "united status" with his or her master, or is he or she enslaved by his or her master?

States Rights. Avoid using this term. When others use the term "states rights," ask for a detailed explanation that you can easily understand. Ask questions.

> **Questions:** What, exactly, is a "state"? What is not a "state"? What is the so-called "right" of a "state"? Can one person be a "state"? Is one person a "state of being"? What are the "rights" of one person who functions as a "state of being"? Do White Supremacists (Racists) function as a "state," or do they function as a "state of being"? What are the "states rights" of those White persons who have chosen to practice White Supremacy

(Racism)? Do Victims of White Supremacy (Non-White people) have the "right" to "state" their "right" not to be Victims, and to "state" that "right" in both words and deeds?

> **Note:** White Supremacists (Racists) have sometimes used the term "states rights" as a Racist Code term applying to any speech and/or action that helps to establish, maintain, expand, and/or refine The System of White Supremacy (Racism).

Statesman/Stateswoman. Use these words with caution. When choosing to use these words, use them to apply to any person (male or female) in the known universe who is classified as "White." Use the words "statesperson" to apply to any person(s) in general, White or Non-White, male or female. Study the ways that others use the words "state," "United States," "statehood," "un-United States," "statesman," "stateswoman," "statesperson" etc.

> **Notes:** According to Compensatory Logic and, during the existence of White Supremacy (Racism), each and every person in the known universe functions in the "status" of a "state," and the only functional "United States" is "the United States of White Supremacy (White Supremacists practicing White Supremacy/Racism in unity), in every area of activity including, Economics, Education, Entertainment, Labor, Law, Politics, Religion, Sex, and War/Counter-War.)

Statue of Liberty. Do not use this term. Instead, use the term "image" to apply to anything that is an "image." When others use the term "statue of liberty," ask for a detailed explanation that you can easily understand. Ask questions.

> **Questions:** What, exactly, is a "statue of liberty"? What, exactly, does a "statue of liberty" actually do? What does it actually produce? What does a "statue of liberty" look like? What should a "statue of liberty" look like? Can "liberty" actually be a "picture" or a "graven image" of a person, creature, or thing? What, exactly, is "liberty"? To do what? Should a person have the "liberty" to practice White Supremacy (Racism)? Is it correct for a Victim of White Supremacy (Racism) to have the "liberty" to speak and act to replace White Supremacy (Racism) with Justice (balance between people)?

378

Status Quo (Racial). <u>Use this term</u> to apply to The System of White Supremacy (Racism) and/or injustice in general.

Statute of Limitations. <u>Use this term with caution</u>. When others use this term, ask for a detailed explanation that you can easily understand.

> **Note:** According to Compensatory Logic, there is no correct so-called "limitation(s)" on the production of justice (balance between people.)

Steal/Stolen. <u>Use these terms</u> to apply to anything that is unjustly and/or incorrectly taken from another, particularly by using stealth, deception, and/or confusion. Study the ways that others use these words.

> **Note:** During the existence of White Supremacy (Racism) and according to Compensatory Counter-Racist Logic, it is correct to regard all Victims of White Supremacy (Non-White persons) as having had everything "stolen" from them, by the White Supremacists (Racistman and Racistwoman, collectively), in every area of activity, including Economics, Education, Entertainment, Labor, Law, Politics, Religion, Sex, and War/Counter-War.

Struggle. <u>Avoid using this word</u> – particularly in regards to attempts to end White Supremacy (Racism). According to Compensatory Logic, the use of the word "plan" best helps a person to think about ways to solve a problem. The use of the word "struggle" tends to promote thoughts about the difficulty in solving a problem. Instead of saying things like "the struggle to end White Supremacy (Racism)," say, "I must make a plan to replace White Supremacy (Racism) with Justice (balance between people)."

Student. <u>Use this word</u> to apply to any person who is in the process of learning.

> **Note:** During the existence of White Supremacy (Racism) and according to Compensatory Counter-Racist Logic, the White Supremacists (Racistman and Racistwoman, collectively) of the known universe have, so far, proven to be the greatest, smartest, and most powerful "students" of everything that exists in the universe.

Sub-Culture. <u>Use this term with caution</u>. When others use it, ask for a detailed explanation that you can easily understand. During the existence of White Supremacy (Racism), use the term "sub-culture" to apply mostly to everything that Non-White people say or do while subject to the Racists (White Supremacists) of the known universe.

> **Note:** According to Compensatory Logic, a "culture" is the sum total of everything that a person says and does.

Sub-Human. Use this word to apply to all persons and creatures in the known universe. When others use the terms "sub-human," "non-human," "inhuman," "inhumane," etc., ask for a detailed explanation that you can easily understand.

> **Reason:** According to Compensatory Logic, the people of the known universe are not "human" (not "humane"). They are other than "human," and/or less than "human." They are not "human beings" because they have proven not to be "humane" because they do not interact with each other by using truth in a manner that would result in the production of justice and correctness (balance between people, creatures, things, etc.).

> The White people of the known universe practice White Supremacy (Racism) and/or they allow White Supremacy (Racism) to be practiced. This, alone, disqualifies them from being correctly called "human beings." They are "beings" but not "human beings."

> The Victims of White Supremacy (Racism) (Non-White people) are not "human beings" because those White people who practice White Supremacy (Racism) do not allow their Victims to function as "beings" who are "humane".

Sub-Husband/Sub-Wife. Use these terms to apply to Non-White male and Non-White female persons who are generally regarded as being "married," but whose interactions with each other and with others, is directly or indirectly subject to, the will of White Supremacists (Racists) in one or more areas of activity (Economics, Education, Entertainment, Labor, Law, Politics, Religion, Sex, and War/Counter-War).

Subject(s). Use this term to apply to the Non-White people of the known universe who are directly or indirectly subject to the power of the White Supremacists (Racists) in any one or more areas of activity. Study the ways that others use the terms "subject" and/or "subjects."

Sub-Support Unit. Use this term generally, in place of the terms "Black family," "Non-White family," and/or a "family" that includes a Non-White person who directly or indirectly serves, and/or functions, in subjugation to The System of White Supremacy (Racism).

> **Reason:** According to Compensatory Counter-Racist Logic, a "family" of people, in order to qualify (truthfully) for the title of "family," cannot, at the same time, function as a "family" and be subject to The System of White Supremacy (Racism). Instead of "family," a person or persons [Non-White] who are subject to The System of White Supremacy (Racism) can best be correctly described as a "Sub-Support Unit" [Racial]. Such persons are, directly or indirectly forced by the White Supremacists (Racists) to function in subjugation to The System of White Supremacy (Racism), and are "allowed" to function as "support units" to each other as long as they render "satisfactory service" to The System of White Supremacy (Racism).

Subversive. Use this term mostly to apply to anything said or done that helps to establish, maintain, expand, and/or refine the practice of White Supremacy (Racism) in any area of activity (Economics, Education, Entertainment, Labor, Law, Politics, Religion, Sex, and War/Counter-War). Study the ways that others use the terms "subversive," "subversive activity," etc. Ask questions like, "If The System of White Supremacy (Racism) is not a subversive activity, what is?"

> **Reason:** Of all the people in the known universe, it is the White Supremacists (Racists) who are the most dedicated to subverting the production of justice (balance between people). Therefore, it is correct to regard them as "The Subversives" and/or "The Master Subversives."

> **Note:** During the existence of White Supremacy (Racism) and according to Compensatory Counter-Racist Logic, The System of White Supremacy (Racism), every White person that practices White Supremacy is the "Master Subversive" element opposed to the production of justice (balance between people) among the people of the known universe.

Subversive Activity. Use this term to mean:

(1)   The masterful, willful, and deliberate promotion of falsehood, non-justice, and/or incorrectness.

(2)   The masterful, willful, and deliberate speech, action (or inaction) in support of the establishment of, maintenance, expansion, and/or the refinement of White Supremacy (Racism).

(3)   The System of White Supremacy (Racism).

Success/Successful. Use these words. As long as White Supremacy (Racism) exists, use these words to mean nothing less than the end of White Supremacy (Racism), and the establishment of Justice (balance between people) between the people of the known universe in all areas of activity/existence. Study the ways that others use the words "success," "successful," "successful society," "successful person," "successful operation," etc.

Sully/Sullied/Unsullied. Do not use these words. Instead, use the words "incorrect" or "not correct." Instead of saying that a person's "character" is "sullied," say that it is "incorrect." Instead of saying that a person's "reputation" is "sullied," say that his or her "reputation" appears to be "incorrect" or "not correct".

> **Reason:** During the existence of White Supremacy (Racism), the words "sully," "sullied," "sullen," etc., are usually associated with "darkness," "gloom" "gloomy," "somber," etc., and indirectly have been used to imply that "dark" people are associated with that which is unpleasant, not correct and/or non-constructive.

Super Conquerors/Super Beggars System. Use these terms to mean that during the existence of White Supremacy (Racism), the White people who practice White Supremacy (Racism) are the "Super-Conquerors" among the people of the known universe, and the Non-White people, are the "Super-Beggars."

Super Murder (Racial). Use this term to apply to the death of every Non-White person killed as a direct or indirect result of the existence of The System of White Supremacy (Racism).

Superior. Use this word with caution. During the existence of White Supremacy (Racism) always describe the will and the ability of the White Supremacists (Racistman and Racistwoman, collectively), to practice White Supremacy (Racism) as "superior," and always describe the will and the ability of the Non-White people not to be subject to White Supremacy (Racism), as "inferior."

> **Note:** According to Compensatory Logic, the "captor" is always "superior" (in power) to one who is the "captive." When others use the terms "superior," "inferior,"

"supreme," etc., ask for a detailed explanation that you can easily understand.

Superior Capitalists/Communists. Use these terms to apply to The White Supremacists (Racists) of the known universe, collectively.

Superior Race.   Use this term to apply to White Supremacists, collectively, and the only "Race" of people in the known universe.

Supervisor. Use this word with caution. Use it to apply to a person during that time when he or she is giving advice that is more powerful, in total effect, than the advice that is given by any other person in the known universe. During the existence of White Supremacy (Racism) and according to Compensatory Counter-Racist Logic, it is important to remember that only the White Supremacists (Racists) have proven to be the most powerful "advice givers" and "advice masters" in regards to the effect that they have on, and/or against the Non-White people of the known universe. When others use the word "supervisor" ("superior advice-giver") ask for a detailed explanation that you can easily understand.

> **Notes:**   During   the   existence   of   White   Supremacy
> (Racism) and according to Compensatory Counter-Racist
> Logic, no Non-White person has proven to function as a
> so-called "supervisor" ("superior advice-giver").   Some
> Non-White persons who appear to function as "superior-
> advisors" are, in effect, "non-superior advisors," and/or
> persons who are "assigned" by the White Supremacists
> (Racists) to pretend to be "superior-advisors."

Supporter of the United-Independent Compensatory System. Use this term to apply to:

(1)   Any person, while speaking and/or acting to use truth in such a manner as to effectively promote the production of justice and correctness; and/or

(2)   Any person, while speaking and/or acting to effectively promote the elimination of Racism (White Supremacy).

Supreme.   Use this word with caution.   During the existence of White Supremacy (Racism) and according to Compensatory Counter-Racist Logic, use the term "White Supremacy" to mean that the White people of the known universe who believe in dominating and/or mistreating Non-White people are, in truth, exercising "supreme power" (functionally) over the Non-White people of the known universe.

Notes: The White Supremacist (Racistman and Racistwoman, collectively), exercise this supreme functional power in all areas of activity, including Economics, Education, Entertainment, Labor, Law, Politics, Religion, Sex, and War/Counter-War.

The White Supremacists (Racists) practice "supreme" functional power over/against Non-White people by making all major decisions in regards to the manner in which Non-White people interact with White people, and with each other. A White person, as an individual person is not "automatically" so-called "superior" to a Non-White person, but as a person who functions within The System of White Supremacy (Racism), a person "classified" as "White" is expected to, and/or is directly or indirectly trained to, practice White Supremacy ("supreme" power over and/or against the people of the known universe who White Supremacists regard as "Non-White"). As White Supremacists (Racists), these White persons have proven to be "supremely successful" and "successfully supreme".

Supreme Being. Use this term with caution. When others use this term, ask for a detailed explanation that you can easily understand. Ask questions. Is the "Supreme Being" a "White" person? Is a White Supremacist (Racist) a "Supreme Being"? Is the "Supreme Being" a "spirit"? Is the "Supreme Being" everywhere?

Notes: Do not argue with, fight, or kill people because of disagreements over whether the "Supreme Being" is a person or a "spirit," etc. During the existence of White Supremacy (Racism), speak and act as if Racistman and Racistwoman (White Supremacists, collectively) are the "supreme" promoters of confusion about what is, or is not, a "Supreme Being."

Surplus Population. Do not use this term. When others use it, ask them to explain, in detail, exactly what they mean.

Notes: It has been said that there is no such person as a "surplus person." It has been said that a person takes care of him or herself, or is taken care of by others, or dies, or is killed. It has also been said that, it is the duty of each person to do all that he or she can do to be of constructive help to every other person.

Survival Mate/Caremate/Racialmate. Use these terms when referring to a so-called "marital-partner," or "partner-in-marriage," as applied to Non-White persons (to each other) within The System of White Supremacy (Racism). Do not use these terms to apply to any person other than yourself, unless a person other than yourself approves of your using these terms to apply to him or her. Do all that you can to use words that will best reveal truth (that which is), but do so, at all times, in such a manner as not to call people by the names or titles that they do not approve of. Do your utmost to avoid being involved in "name-calling."

Survival Unit/Basic Support Unit. Use these terms instead of using the term "family," when speaking about or writing about Non-White persons during the existence of White Supremacy (Racism).

> **Reason:** During the existence of White Supremacy (Racism), Non-White people are not permitted to function as a "family." During the existence of White Supremacy (Racism), Non-White people are only permitted to function as "survival units" and/or as person-to-person "support-units" that are directly or indirectly forced to support and defend The System of White Supremacy (Racism) in all areas of activity.

Suspected Race Officer/Suspected Race Enforcer. Use these terms instead of the terms "police" or "police officer" whenever there is reason to believe that a White person who is described as a law enforcement official ("police," etc.), speaks, and/or acts either directly or indirectly as if he or she is practicing Racism (White Supremacy).

> **Notes:** A Non-White person who is serving The System of White Supremacy (Racism) as a so-called "Police Officer" should be referred to simply as a "Law Officer," "Enforcement Officer," and/or "Victim Officer." The use of the term "Police Officer" should be avoided completely as long as The System of White Supremacy (Racism) is in existence. (See, also, "Police").

Suspected Racist. (See, "Racist Suspect").

Suspension/Suspended. Use these words with caution. When others use them, ask for a detailed explanation that you can easily understand. Study the ways that Racist Suspects (Suspected White Supremacists) use the words "suspension," "suspended," "temporary suspension," etc.

Symbol. <u>Use this word with caution</u>. Study the many ways that others use the words "symbol," "symbolic," "sign," "representative," etc.

> **Questions:** What, exactly, is a "symbol"? What, exactly, is not a "symbol"? Is a "word" a "symbol"? Is a person a "symbol"? Is everything a "symbol"? How does a "symbol" become a "symbol"? Which person is correctly qualified to judge what is, and what is not, a "symbol"? Which person is correctly qualified to judge what a "symbol" means and what it does not mean? Do all "symbols" have "meaning"? If so, "meaning" to whom? When? "Meaning" for what purpose? Can the same so-called "symbol" "symbolize" one thing to one person, and something different to another person? If a person can be a "symbol," how many different "symbols" can that person "symbolize"? One? Ten Million? Is it correct to use any creature (person, bird, cow, wolf, etc.), as a "symbol" of anything other than itself? Is it correct to use a bird as a "symbol" of "peace"?

> **Note:** During the existence of White Supremacy (Racism), Racistman and Racistwoman (White Supremacists, collectively) have sometimes used and/or glorified a bird (dove) with white feathers as a so-called "symbol" of "peace" because its feathers are white in appearance.

System, The. <u>Use this term</u> to apply to the sum total of all speech, and all action, by White Supremacists (Racists), that directly or indirectly dominate Non-White people in any one or more areas of activity, including Economics, Education, Entertainment, Labor, Law, Politics, Religion, Sex, and War/Counter-War.

T

Tainted. <u>Avoid using this word</u>. When others use the word to say things like "tainted evidence," "tainted reputation," "tainted background," "tainted character," etc., ask them to explain exactly why the word "tainted" was used. Why not use the term "incorrect evidence" and/or "damaged evidence"? Why not use "reputation for incorrect speech or action," rather than the term "tainted character"? Ask them to be specific about saying what the incorrect speech or action was.

> **Notes:** During the existence of White Supremacy (Racism), the word "tainted" is sometimes used,

indirectly, to promote the thinking that "tainted" is like a "stain," and that "dark" people look like people who have been "stained," and people who have been "stained" have incorrect "reputations," incorrect "character," etc. To use the word "tainted" to apply to food may be correct, but it may be better to use the word "poisoned." During the existence of White Supremacy (Racism), it is best and correct not to use the words "tainted," "dark," "tarnished," "shady" "stained," "blotted," "blackened," etc., in any way to apply to the "reputation" or "character" of a person.

Talent/Talented Person. Use these words with caution. Study the ways that others use these words.

> **Note:** According to Compensatory Logic, there is reason to believe that every person, creature, and thing in the known universe has "talent," for something, at some time.

Tan Your Hide. Do not use this term as a means of telling a person that he or she is to be whipped.

> **Reason:** The expression "tan your hide" is sometimes used by White Supremacists (Racists) as a threat of a whipping of a "light skinned" or "White-skinned" person, until the skin of that person becomes dark or "tan" in color. When the term "tan your hide" is used in this manner, it is often intended to have the effect of a Racist (White Supremacist) insult.

Tarnished Image/Reputation. Do not use these terms.

> **Reason:** The terms "tarnished image," "tarnished reputation," "blackened reputation," etc., have often been used in a manner that is supportive of White Supremacist (Racist) thinking. For example, a person with a "tarnished image" would be thought of as being "dark," as well as being despicable. During the existence of The System of White Supremacy (Racism), the basic intent for the use of such terms is to associate unworthy or destructive behavior with the physical appearance of Non-White people.

Tax Obligation. Use this term with caution. Study the ways that others use the term. Ask questions. What is the true "tax obligation" of a Victim of White Supremacy (Non-White person) to the White Supremacists (Racists)? What is the true "tax obligation" of a White

Supremacist (Racist) to a Victim of White Supremacy (Non-White person)?

Temporary. Use this word with caution. Study the ways that others use the word. Be wary of the many tricky and deceptive ways that White Supremacists (Racistman and Racistwoman) use the word "temporary." Ask questions.

> **Questions:** How "temporary" is "temporary"? "Temporary," as compared to what? What, exactly, is not "temporary"? What, exactly, is "permanent"? What, exactly, is "temporary" as to what, when, to whose advantage, and for what purpose?
>
> **Notes:** As long as White Supremacy (Racism) exists, and as long as any form of injustice exists, it is correct to always be wary of the ways in which terms like "temporary," or "with all deliberate speed," or "for a short time," are used. These terms are often used in a manner that helps to produce confusion or incorrect expectations.

Territorial Possession. Avoid using this term. When others use it, ask for a detailed explanation that you can easily understand. Ask questions.

> **Questions:** What, exactly, is a so-called "territorial possession"? Does a "nation" include "territory"? Does a "territory" include people? Is a person a part of a "territory," or is a "territory" a part of a person? How much "territory" makes a person a "state"? Is each person a "territorial state"? Is each person, correctly "self-possessed"? What, exactly, is the difference between a person and a "state"? Does not every person "occupy" a "territory" at all times? Is a person a "possession"? Can a "possession" be a "state" and, at the same time, be a "territory"? Who are the persons correctly qualified to decide what is, and what is not, a "territory"? Who are the persons correctly qualified to decide against what others have decided?

Territory. Use this word with caution. When others use this word, ask for a detailed explanation that you can easily understand.

> **Questions:** What, exactly, is the true difference between a "territory," a "possession," a "tribe," a "state," a "nation" etc.? Is a person the same as a "state," and is the "state" the same as a "territory"? Can a "territory" be correctly

called a "reservation," a "compound," a "homeland," a "province," and/or a "nation"? How much of the sky is included in a "territory"? How many clouds? How many birds?

Terror/Terrorism. Use these words to apply to any willful and deliberate act committed with the effect of causing or promoting great fear for unjust and/or incorrect purpose(s). Also, use the term "master-terrorism" to apply to anything that is willfully and deliberately said or done by a White Supremacist (Racist) or Suspected White Supremacist (Racist Suspect) that results in great and unjust harmful fear used against a Non-White person (a Victim of White Supremacy). Study carefully the ways that others use the terms "terror," "terrorism," "terrorist," etc. Study the ways that others use the term "counter-terrorism."

Terrorist. Use this word to apply to any person [suspected terrorist] who willfully and deliberately commits an act that has the effect of causing or promoting great fear for reasons and/or purposes that are non-just and/or incorrect. As long as White Supremacy (Racism) exists, use the word-term "Master Terrorist" ["Suspected Master Terrorist"] to apply to a White person who willfully and deliberately commits an act of non-justice that has the effect of causing or promoting great harm to a Non-White person, through the direct and/or indirect non-correct use of fear.

The Longest Holocaust. Use this term to mean all of the destructive things that have happened and are happening to the Non-White people of the known universe as a direct, and/or indirect, result of The System of White Supremacy (Racism).

The People. Use this term to apply to any people who do not practice Racism (White Supremacy), and/or all people, other than Racists (White Supremacists).

The Powers That Be. Use this term to apply to the collective powers of the White Supremacists (Racists).

The Problem. Use this term to apply to The System of Racism (White Supremacy).

The Race. Use this term to mean any one or more of the following: (1) organized Racists (White Supremacists, collectively); (2) Racistman and Racistwoman (White Supremacists, collectively); (3) The System of White Supremacy (Racism); (4) The White Nation (Racist Nation); and/or (5) White Supremacists (Racists, collectively).

Note: "Race," in regards to people, and color/non-color, is Racism. During the existence of White Supremacy (Racism), the only "Race" of people that exist in the known universe is "The White Race" ("The White Nation," "The Race," etc.).

Things Could Be Worse. <u>Do not use this term</u>. Instead, say, "It is the <u>duty</u> of all people, all creatures, and all things, to use truth to produce justice, and to produce correctness, in all areas of existence, at all times."

> **Note:** "Truth" is that, which is. "Justice" means <u>balance between people</u> – which means guaranteeing that no person is mistreated, and guaranteeing that the person who needs help the most, gets the most help. Correctness means <u>balance</u> between people and all other creatures, beings, things, etc.

Thrilling. <u>Use this word</u> to describe many of the things that Racistman and Racistwoman (White Supremacists, collectively), do and/or say. Use this word to also describe many of the things that Racistman and Racistwoman cause other people to think, do, and/or say. Also, study the many ways that Racistman and Racistwoman cause their Victims (Non-White people) to be "thrilled" in <u>all</u> areas of activity, including Economics, Education, Entertainment, Labor, Law, Politics, Religion, Sex, and War/Counter-War.

Study the effects of the "thrills" that Racistman and Racistwoman produce or promote among Non-White people. Study the ways that Racistman and Racistwoman cause <u>destructive</u> speech, and/or action, to have a "thrilling effect" on the ways that Non-White people think, speak, and act.

> **Reason:** The White people of the known universe who have chosen to practice White Supremacy (Racism) have shown that they believe the practice of White Supremacy (Racism) to be the "greatest thrill" in the known universe. Racistman and Racistwoman (White Supremacists, collectively) have proven to be the greatest "thrill-makers" in the known universe. Robbing, killing, terrorizing, deceiving, and promoting sexual conflict and confusion are some of the basic things that Racistman and Racistwoman do, and lead others to do, in order to "thrill," and "be thrilled."

Throwaway People [Racial]. <u>Use this term</u>. Use it to refer to the <u>way</u> that limited numbers of Non-White people are "evaluated" from time to time, and judged to be "fit for extermination" by the White Supremacists (Racists), in order to "better serve" The System of White Supremacy (Racism).

Time. Use this term to mean, "The absence of deed".

Tone Down. Do not use this term. Instead, use the terms "turn down," "quiet," "balance," "compensate [down]," "correct [down]," etc.

> **Reason:** During the existence of White Supremacy (Racism), the word "tone" is often used in association with "color" as it pertains to people. Therefore, to "tone down" is, indirectly, sometimes associated with "darkness," "death," silence, and/or "oblivion." To "tone-up" during the existence of White Supremacy (Racism) could, and sometimes does, apply indirectly to becoming "lighter," "brighter," "correct," "balanced," etc.

Total Disaster [Racial]. Use this term to apply to any situation in which The System of White Supremacy (Racism) has not been replaced with The System of Justice (balance between people) in all areas of activity, including Economics, Education, Entertainment, Labor, Law, Politics, Religion, Sex, and War/Counter-War.

Totalitarian. Do not use this word. When others use the word, ask for a detailed explanation that you can easily understand. Is the System of White Supremacy (Racism), "totalitarian"?

Tragic Arrangement, The. Use this term to apply to all interactions between the White people and the Non-White people of the known universe during the existence of The System of White Supremacy (Racism). Apply this term also to all of the non-constructive effects that The System of White Supremacy (Racism) has on Non-White persons in regards to their interactions with/against each other.

> **Notes:** During the existence of White Supremacy (Racism), the interactions between the White people and the Non-White people of the known universe can best be described as "Tacky," "Trashy," and/or "Terroristic." These interactions can be called "The Three T's," which, when combined, is "The Tragic Arrangement."
>
> According to Compensatory Counter-Racist Logic, this "Tragic Arrangement" should be replaced with "The Quality Relationship." "The Quality Relationship" should be regarded as the combination of all thought, speech, and action (regarding White people and Non-White

people) that actually results in replacing The System of White Supremacy (Racism) with The System of Justice (balance between people).

Tragic Necessity. Use this term to apply to the absolute need to kill and/or eliminate a person, animal, plant, insect, etc., in order to establish and/or maintain justice and/or correctness.

Trash Sex/Toilet Sex/Cesspool Sex. Use these terms as a basic description for any type of sexual intercourse and/or "sexual play" between a White person and a Non-White person during any period in which White Supremacy (Racism) is being practiced in any area of activity, in any place in the known universe.

> **Reason:** As long as White Supremacy (Racism) exists, all sexual intercourse and/or "sexual play" that is enacted between a White person and a Non-White person, has the basic functional effect of helping to make the practice of White Supremacy (Racism) stronger, and more "glorified," in all areas of activity. Such sexual intercourse and/or "sexual play" between White people and Non-White people during the existence of White Supremacy (Racism) has the basic functional effect of making Non-White people sillier and more confused in their attempts to end Racism (White Supremacy).

True Colors. Avoid using this term. When others use the term, ask them to explain, in detail, exactly what they mean.

> **Questions:** What is meant when a person is said to have shown his or her "true colors"? What, exactly, is the "color" of a person that is so-called "true"? What, exactly, is the "color" of a person that is so-called "false"?

Truth. Use this term to mean, "that which is".

Truthful Person. Use this term to apply to a person who has never knowingly, willingly, and/or deliberately said anything that was not true (false).

U

Ugly. Use this word with caution. When others say that a person, creature, or thing is "ugly," ask them to explain, in detail, why they say that the person, creature, or thing, is "ugly." Ask questions.

Questions: Are some persons, creatures, or things "uglier" than other persons, creatures, or things? If so, why? If not, why not? "Ugly," according to what or according to whom? How "ugly" is "ugly"? Compared to what? When? Where? Are White people "ugly"? If so, which White people? Are Non-White people "pretty"? If so, which Non-White people? If so, why? During the existence of White Supremacy (Racism), what makes a Non-White person or a White person "pretty," or "ugly"? Which persons in the known universe are correctly qualified to judge and make the most important decisions about which persons are "pretty," and which persons are "ugly"?

Note: In a known universe in which the people are not in balance with each other, there is reason to believe that any people who do not practice justice, can be correctly regarded as "ugly."

Un-American. <u>Use this term</u>. During the existence of White Supremacy (Racism), use this term to apply to anything said or done (or not said or done) that results in the maintenance, expansion, and/or refinement of White Supremacy (Racism) or any form of non-justice, or non-correctness. When others use the terms "un-American," "un-Asian," or "un-African," ask for a detailed explanation that you can easily understand.

Note: According to Compensatory Logic, the terms "un-American," "un-Asian," and "un-African," all have the same meaning: (1) Mistreatment of people, and (2) failure or refusal to help the person who is most in need of help.

Unauthorized. <u>Avoid using this term</u>. When others use this term, ask for a detailed explanation that you can easily understand. Ask questions of yourself, and/or of others.

Questions: What makes something "un-authored" or "unauthorized"? Who, exactly, authorizes something that exists that is "accepted" like it should exist, though it should not exist? Who "authorizes" the existence of White Supremacy (Racism)? Who, exactly, is correctly qualified to "authorize" a "Code" of thought, speech, and action that is designed to replace White Supremacy (Racism) with Justice (balance between people)? Who, exactly, is "unauthorized" to produce such a "Code"?

Un-churched. <u>Avoid using this term</u>. When others use it, ask for a detailed explanation that you can easily understand. Ask questions.

> **Questions:** What, exactly, is a "churched person"? What, exactly, is an "un-churched person"? What, exactly, is a "church"? What, exactly, does a "churched person" do (or not do) in regards to each area of activity (Economics, Education, Entertainment, Labor, Law, Politics, Religion, Sex, and War/Counter-War)? Can a "churched person" practice White Supremacy (Racism)? Can a "churched person" be subject to the dictates of White Supremacists (Racists) and, at the same time, be a "churched person"? Can a person be "churched" and "un-churched" at the same time?

Uncivil/Uncivilized. <u>Use these terms</u> to apply to any situation in which justice and correctness is not being practiced in every area of activity. When others use the terms "un-civil" and/or "un-civilized," ask for a detailed explanation that you can easily understand. Ask questions.

> **Questions:** What is "civil"? What is "un-civil"? What is "civilized"? What is "un-civilized"? Within The System of White Supremacy (Racism), can any person be correctly regarded as "civilized"? In the absence of justice, can any person truly function as a "civilized" person? Is it true that all people are, in practice, "uncivilized"?

> **Note:** During the existence of White Supremacy (Racism), and according to Compensatory Counter-Racist Logic, all of the people of the known universe function in a manner that is "un-civil" and/or "un-civilized".

Uncle Tom. <u>Do not use this term</u>, except as an explanation that it usually has been applied to any Non-White person who, directly or indirectly cooperates with White Supremacy, and/or with White Supremacists, at any time, in any place, in any area of activity, including Economics, Education, Entertainment, Labor, Law, Politics, Religion, Sex, and War/Counter-War.

> **Note:** It is unjust and incorrect to ever call any person an "Uncle Tom," if it is not a name that that person uses to identify himself. To do so, constitutes name-calling, and serves no constructive purpose.

Undeclared War. <u>Do not use this term</u>.

Reason: According to Compensatory Logic, there is no such war as an "un-declared war." All wars are "declared." A war is "declared" whenever and wherever any person is willfully and deliberately mistreated. A war is also "declared" whenever and wherever a person who is most in need of help, is not allowed to receive that help, by those who are most able to provide the help that is needed.

Notes: During the existence of White Supremacy (Racism) and according to Compensatory Counter-Racist Logic, The System of White Supremacy (Racism) is "The War." All other so-called "wars" are, in truth, "battles" that are a direct or indirect part of "The War." "The War" is, by definition, the sum total of all thought, speech, and action by White Supremacists (Racists) against the Non-White people of the known universe. It is correct to regard any action taken by any White Supremacist (Racistman and/or Racistwoman) that results in non-just or non-correct harm to any Non-White person, as being, in effect, a "Declaration of War."

Underclass. <u>Use this term</u>. During the existence of White Supremacy (Racism), use the terms "underclass" and "power-less class" to apply to all Non-White persons who are classified as, and who function as, "Non-White." When others use this term, ask for a detailed explanation that you can easily understand.

Notes: During the existence of White Supremacy (Racism) and according to Compensatory Counter-Racist Logic, all Non-White persons function in the "category" of the so-called "under-class" or "power-less class." The terms mean, in function, that the Non-White people of the known universe have less power than those White persons who believe in, and who practice, White Supremacy (Racism).

Undeveloped Country. <u>Do not use this term</u>. Instead, use the term "powerless people." When others use this term," ask for a detailed explanation that you can easily understand.

Questions: Is any person so-called "developed"? "Developed," from what, into what, and for what ultimate purpose? Is The System of White Supremacy (Racism) "developed"? Should it be? If so, why? Since no "country" can exist as long as White Supremacy (Racism) exists, how can any "collection of people" be correctly called a "country" ("nation," etc.), other than "The White Country" (Racistmen, and Racistwomen, collectively)?

Undeveloped/Underdeveloped. <u>Do not use these terms</u>. Instead, use the term (when applied to people), "powerless people." Study the ways that others use the terms "undeveloped," "underdeveloped," "under-class," etc.

> **Reason:** During the existence of White Supremacy (Racism), the White people who practice White Supremacy (Racism) often use the terms "undeveloped" or "underdeveloped," to describe the minds and the general activities of the Non-White people of the known universe.
>
> The White Supremacists (Racists) of the known universe use terms like "under-developed" and "undeveloped" as a way of telling themselves and Non-White people that White people are better than Non-White people. The White Supremacists (Racists) also teach themselves and Non-White people that, since White people are "better" than Non-White people, White people are therefore "entitled" to do anything that they choose to do with or against Non-White people. Other terms that can be used in place of the words "underdeveloped" and "undeveloped" are, "immature," "infantile," "lacking," "not equipped," "not mature," "not prepared" and/or "primitive," etc.

Unemployed. <u>Do not use this term</u>. Instead, use the terms "constructive employment," "non-constructive employment," and/or "destructive employment." Study the ways that others use the terms "unemployed," or "employed."

> **Reason:** During the existence of White Supremacy (Racism) and according to Compensatory Logic, all of the people, creatures, and things in the known universe are, at all times, "employed," either constructively, or non-constructively.
>
> **Notes:** During the existence of White Supremacy (Racism), it is the White Supremacists (Racists) who use the words "employment" and "unemployment" mostly for the purpose of saying what people are "worth" and/or "not worth." Therefore, instead of saying that a person is "unemployed," it is best and correct to describe how a person uses time and energy, and/or how he or she produces cause and/or effect.

Unfair. <u>Do not use this word</u>. Instead of using the word "unfair" to mean "incorrect," or "non-just," use the words "incorrect" or "non-just." Do not use the words "fair" or "unfair" to be, in any way, associated with the words "justice" or "injustice."

> **Reason:** During the existence of White Supremacy (Racism), the word "fair" has been deliberately associated with the word "white," and the word "justice" has been deliberately associated with the word "fair." The result has been that the words "fair," "white," and "justice" have been made to appear to have the same associated meaning. Likewise, the word "unfair" has been made to seem to mean "unjust," "not just," and/or "not White." Therefore, it is incorrect and supportive of White Supremacy (Racism) to use the words "fair" or "unfair" in a manner that is associated with the words "justice," "non-justice," "injustice" and/or "un-justice."

Unimportant or Wasted Time (Racial). <u>Use this term</u> to apply to:

(1)   Anything said or done that does not, directly or indirectly, help to eliminate the practice of Racism (White Supremacy); and/or

(2)   Anything said or done that does not directly or indirectly help to produce justice, and/or correctness.

Unisex. <u>Do not use this word</u>. When others use it, ask them to explain, in detail, <u>exactly</u> what they mean. Ask them to explain what a "sexual union" is, and what "sexual union" is not. Instead of the word "unisex," use the words "sex" and/or "sexual union."

> **Reason:** The word "sex" means <u>male</u> or it means <u>female</u>, or it means <u>male with female</u>. To use the word "unisex" is not necessary, and can contribute to confusion.

United/Union. <u>Use these words with caution</u>. When others use the words "united" and/or "union," ask for a detailed explanation that you can easily understand. Ask questions.

> **Questions:** What, exactly, are the qualifications of a so-called "united people"? "United" in regards to what? "United" how? How much? When? "United" for what purpose? What, exactly, is a "union"? What, exactly, is not a "union"? What persons are "united" and/or in "unity" with what persons? When? Where? How? For what purpose? How often? For how long? Every minute?

When people are "united," does it mean that they are, at all times, mutual and harmonious in all that they say and do in all areas of existence, including Economics, Education, Entertainment, Labor, Law, Politics, Religion, Sex, and War/Counter-War? If people disagree, can they disagree, and at the same time, be "united"? Can a person be "subject" to another person and, at the same time, be "united" with the person that he or she is "subject" to?

Can a White Supremacist (Racist) be "united" with his or her Victim (Non-White person)? Is a prisoner "united" with a prison-master? Is a slave "united" with his or her slave master? Is a robber "united" with the person being robbed? Is a victim in "unity" with the victim-maker? What is the true "proof" of the existence of a "union"? If a person is "united" in one thing with another person, but not "united" in another thing with that same person, can it be truthfully said that the two persons are "united"? How much "unity" makes a "union"?

United-Independent Compensatory Code/System/Concept. A term that means, when expressed in practice, the sum total of everything that is thought, said, or done by one individual Non-White person, who is a Victim of Racism [Victim of White Supremacy] that is effective in helping to eliminate Racism (White Supremacy), and/or in helping to "make up" for the lack of justice and correctness, in any one or more areas of activity, including Economics, Education, Entertainment, Labor, Law, Politics, Religion, Sex, and/or War/Counter-War.

United Nations. Do not use this term to apply to any situation that exists in the known universe, at the same time that The System of White Supremacy (Racism) exists. Study the ways that others use the words "nation," "united," and "united nations."

> **Reason:** During the existence of White Supremacy (Racism), and according to Compensatory Counter-Racist Logic, it is correct to regard only those White persons who participate in The System of White Supremacy (Racism) as a so-called "nation" that is worthy of the title of "nation." Therefore, it is correct for all Victims of White Supremacy (Non-White people) to regard themselves as subjects of the only people in the known universe who actually function (collectively) as a "nation." That "nation" is "The White Nation," and/or "The Race/Racist Nation," which consists of all of those White people in the known universe who have functionally agreed with each

other to be "United Racists" (a "United Nation" of White Supremacists).

Suggestion: When talking about people who identify themselves as "The United Nations," use the expression, "People who identify themselves as The United Nations". It is best and correct to avoid "name-calling" by always using the names or titles for people that those people ask you to use.

United States. <u>Use this term with caution</u>. When others use the words "united," "states," and/or "United States," ask for a detailed explanation that you can easily understand. Ask questions.

Questions: What, exactly, is "united"? When is someone, or something, "united"? Does someone who touches someone else become "united" with that person? If one thing "touches" something else, are the two things "united"? If one person looks at another person, are the two persons "united"? If two or more persons talk to each other, are they "united"? Can two or more persons be "united" if they never see each other, touch each other, or talk to each other? Can people be "united" simply by thinking about each other? Are all people "united" in some way at some time? Can two persons be "united" with each other and, at the same time, be "independent" of each other? Can people be "united" in some things, but not in others?

What, exactly, is a "state"? What, exactly, is not a "state"? Is a "state" a person? Can one person be a "state"? Can two persons be two "states"? Can two persons function as "states" that are "united"? If so, how? If so, "united" for what purpose? What is the proof that a person who is a "state," is "united" with another person who is also a "state"? Are all "states" dependent on each other, at some time, for some thing? Is air and water a part of a "state"? If so, what air? If so, what water? What air and what water is the "property" of what "state"? How much air and how much water is a "statesperson" (a person who is a "state") entitled to? When? Where? Why? How much "unity" makes a "union"? What, exactly, is the true "proof" of the existence of a "union"? If a person is "united" in one thing with another person, but not "united" in another thing, can it be truthfully said that the two persons are "united"?

Can a White person who functions as a White Supremacist (Racist) be the same "state" of thought, speech, and action as a Victim of White Supremacy (a Non-White person)? If not, how can one "state of person" be unjustly subject to another "state of person," and the two "stated persons" be "united"?

Is it possible for persons to be "united" in some areas of activity, and not "united," but unjustly subjugated, in other areas of activity? Is it correct to say that a slave is in a "state of unity" with a slave master? Is it correct to say that a prison master is in a "united state" with his or her prisoner? Is a person who rapes another person in a "state of unity" with the person who is being raped?

United States of/for America. Use this term to apply to one or more persons who have guaranteed that no person is mistreated, and who have guaranteed that the person who needs help the most, gets the most help, at all times, in all places, in all areas of activity/existence, including Economics, Education, Entertainment, Labor, Law, Politics, Religion, Sex, and War/Counter-War.

Use this term to apply to those persons who, at all times, in all areas of activity, practice justice (balance between people), who, at no time participate in the practice of White Supremacy (Racism) and who, at no time, give direct or indirect support or comfort to any person who practices White Supremacy (Racism) in any of its forms. Also, use the term to apply to those persons who, at no time, allow themselves to be Victims of White Supremacy (Racism) in any area of activity, or in any area of existence.

Use this term to apply to those persons who have used truth (that which is), and/or who have revealed truth, in such a manner as to have resulted in the establishment and the maintenance of justice (balance between people), and the establishment and maintenance of correctness (balance between people, creatures, things, etc.), in all areas of activity and existence. Also, use the term to apply to those persons who have produced "peace" between and among all people, all creatures, and all things, in all areas of activity and existence. According to Compensatory Counter-Racist Logic, it is correct for all persons to do their best to think, speak, and act to produce "The United States of America".

> **Notes:** During the existence of White Supremacy (Racism), and according to Compensatory Counter-Racist Logic, the so-called "United-States of/for America" does not, and cannot, exist; neither does "Africa," "Asia," or

"Europe". What does exist is The System of White Supremacy (Racism).

Many White people practice White Supremacy (Racism); some White people do not practice White Supremacy (Racism), but all Non-White people are the Victims of White Supremacy. It is important to always say that, according to Compensatory Counter-Racist Logic, it is not possible for The System of White Supremacy (Racism), and any people to exist and function as "Africans," as "Asians," or as "Americans," in the same universe at the same time. (See "America" and "American Dream").

United States/The Union/Sovereign State. Use these terms with caution. Study and ask questions about the ways that others use the terms "United States," "The Union," "Sovereign State," etc. When making reference to those persons who practice White Supremacy (Racism), use one or more of the following terms:

- "The United States of White Supremacy."
- "The United Racists-States."
- "The Union of White Supremacists."
- "The White Supremacist Union."
- "The Union of Racist States."
- "The Race Nation."
- "The Racist Nation."
- "The Race States."
- "The Racist States."
- "The Race."
- "The System of White Supremacy (Racism)."

Notes: During the existence of The System of White Supremacy (Racism), no people in the known universe are more "united" than the White Supremacists (Racists). It is important to know and to understand that "The United States of America" is a concept that should become real, but that is yet to become real. (See, "America").

Universal Compensatory Pledge of Allegiance. Use this term to apply to these words: "I hope to produce the will to pledge allegiance to my Creator, by doing the things my Creator created me to do."

Universal Compensatory Pledge to Flags. Use these words to apply to "flags": "I do, at all times, relate to the flag the exact same way that the flag relates to me."

Universal Compensatory Social Question. Use this term to apply to the questions, "Are you going to help me, or are you going to harm me, and when, where, why, and how"? Ask these questions when you interact with a person in any situation in which it is logical and important that every person involved knows, and understands, that he or she is likely to be either helped, or harmed, by any of the other persons involved.

Universal Counter-Racist Goal. Use this term to always apply to the statement, "Replace White Supremacy (Racism) with Justice (balance between people)," and continue to do so as long as White Supremacy (Racism) exists.

Universal Language. Use this term to apply to any condition of death or suffering, and/or the ability to inflict death and/or suffering.

Universal Man and/or Universal Woman. Use this term to apply to any male and/or any female person, who knows and understands truth, and who has used that knowledge and understanding in a manner that has produced justice and correctness, in all places, in all areas of activity, including Economics, Education, Entertainment, Labor, Law, Politics, Religion, Sex, and War/Counter-War.

> **Notes:** A basic characteristic of a Universal Man is that he is totally "masculine" and not "effeminate" in any of his interactions with others, and only interacts, sexually, with a person of the female gender. A basic characteristic of a Universal Woman is that she is totally "effeminate" in any of her interactions with others, and only interacts, sexually, with a person of the male gender.
>
> Synonyms:
>
> All/Man/All Woman
> Correct Man/Correct Woman
> Good Man/Good Woman
> Holy Man/Holy Woman
> Just Man/Just Woman
> Life Man/Life Woman
> Maximum Man/Maximum Woman
> Peace Man/Peace Woman
> Perfect Man/Perfect Woman
> Total Man/Total Woman
> Ultimate Man/Ultimate Woman
> Whole Man/Whole Woman

Universal Religion. Use this term to apply to:

(1)   The sum total of truth, justice, and correctness;

(2)   Peace;

(3)   The religion of religions;

(4)   Ultimate religion;

(5)   The religion of Universal Woman and Universal Man; and/or

(6)   The unknown and/or non-practiced religion.

Universal Subversive. Use this term to apply to a White Supremacist (Racist).

Universal War (and/or) The War. Use this term to apply to:

(1)   The sum total of all thought, speech, and action by those White persons in the known universe who practice White Supremacy (Racism).

(2)   The practice of Racism (White Supremacy), and the sum total of its effects in helping to promote falsehood, non-justice, and/or incorrectness.

Universal White Community.   Use this term to apply to White Supremacists (Racists) collectively, plus, the sum total of all their speech and action that directly or indirectly helps to maintain, expand, and/or refine their common objective of promoting White Supremacy (Racism).

Unknown, The. Use this term with caution. Use it mostly to apply only to those things that you, personally, do not know – regardless of what it is that others may "know," or not "know."

Unqualified. Use this word with caution. When others use the word "unqualified," ask for a detailed explanation that you can easily understand.

> **Note:** During the existence of White Supremacy (Racism), the words "qualified," "unqualified" and "not qualified," are words that are used by White Supremacists (Racists) to prevent Non-White persons from getting the help that is needed in order to replace White Supremacy (Racism) with Justice (balance between people).

Unreal Realities. Use this term to apply to a condition that seems to exist only in relationship to another condition and, at the same time, seems to not exist at all.

Examples: Death, Deed, Eternal Death, Eternal Life, Existence, Fear, Hate, Life, Love, Motion, Space, Time, and Truth.

Uppity. <u>Avoid using this word</u>. When others use it, ask for a detailed explanation that you can easily understand.

> **Reason:** The word "uppity" is sometimes used by White Supremacists (Racists) to describe the actions of Non-White persons who directly or indirectly try not to be subject to the will of White Supremacists (Racistmen and Racistwomen).

Upwardly Mobile Person. <u>Do not use this term</u>. When others use it, ask for a detailed explanation that you can easily understand. Ask questions. Does "upwardly mobile" include replacing White Supremacy (Racism) with Justice (balance between people)?

Urban Renewal. <u>Avoid using this term</u>. When others use this term, ask for a detailed explanation that you can easily understand.

> **Questions:** What, exactly, makes an urban "renewed"? Are things "renewed"? Are people "renewed"? If people are "renewed," how is the "renewal" measured? Will the "renewal" apply to all areas of (people) activity? Economics? Education? Entertainment? Labor? Law? Politics? Religion? Sex? War/Counter-War? In what ways will the so-called "urban renewal" help to replace The System of White Supremacy (Racism) with the System of Justice (balance between people)?

Us/Them. <u>Use these words with caution</u>. Instead of using the words "us" and "them," it is best and correct to use terms that are more specific. If talking about White persons, say "White persons." If talking about White Supremacists (Racists), say "White Supremacists (Racists)." If talking about Suspected White Supremacists (Racists), say "Suspected White Supremacists." If talking about Victims of Racism [Non-White people], say "Victims of Racism," "Victims of White Supremacy" and/or "Non-White people."

Usual Suspects, The. <u>Use this term</u> to apply to any and all White Supremacists (Racistman and Racistwoman) as being persons who are most to blame for all non-just harm done to any Non-White person, any place in the known universe during the existence of White Supremacy (Racism).

V

Vacation. <u>Use this word with caution</u>. When others use the word "vacation," ask for a detailed explanation that you can easily understand.

> **Questions:** What, exactly, is a "vacation"? What, exactly, is not a "vacation"? Is it possible to take and/or make a "vacation" everyday? Do "vacations" exist in many different forms? If so, how many different forms? Are some forms of "work" also "vacations"? Do White Supremacists (Racists) take a "vacation" from practicing White Supremacy (Racism)? If so, when? Where? How?

Valuable. <u>Use this word with caution</u>. When others use this word, ask for a detailed explanation that you can easily understand. What is "valuable"? What is not "valuable"? What person is correctly qualified to judge what is, and what is not, "valuable" in each area of activity/existence?

> **Notes:** During the existence of White Supremacy (Racism), it is those White persons who practice White Supremacy (Racism), who tell Non-White persons what is, and what is not, "valuable". During the existence of White Supremacy (Racism), it is the White Supremacists (Racistman and Racistwoman) who dictate to Non-White people what is, and who is, "important".

Very Important Person ("V.I.P."). <u>Do not use this term</u>. <u>All persons</u> are <u>very important</u>, and it is correct to regard all persons as "important" <u>and</u> as "very important." A person who needs help, is a "very important person." A person who helps a person who needs help, is also a "very important person." In the known universe, there are <u>no</u> persons who are <u>not</u> "very important persons." It is not necessary to use the term "Very Important Person." When others use this term, ask them to explain, in detail, what a "very important person" <u>is</u>, and what a "very important person" <u>is not</u>, and ask them to explain exactly how these persons become so.

> **Reason:** It is incorrect to promote the concept of one person being "more important" or "less important" than another. To do so, helps to maintain the practice of non-justice (non-balance between people). During the existence of White Supremacy (Racism), the "very important person" concept has been used, and is being used, to promote the mistreatment of Non-White persons by White persons.

During the existence of White Supremacy (Racism), the most powerful form of "Royalism" is White Supremacy (Racism). White Supremacy (Racism) is the supreme expression of, and the only functional form of, "Racist Royalism" now in existence among the people of the known universe. This means that the White people who practice White Supremacy (Racism) are regarded as "very important persons" and/or "the most important persons" when compared to the Non-White people of the known universe.

Veteran and/or Veteran-Victim (Racial). Use these terms mostly to apply to any Non-White person who, either directly or indirectly is, or has been subject to, and/or a Victim of, The System of White Supremacy (Racism) in any one or more areas of activity, including Economics, Education, Entertainment, Labor, Law, Politics, Religion, Sex, and War/Counter-War.

Victim. Use this word mostly to apply to the Non-White people of the known universe during the existence of White Supremacy (Racism). Also use the word "victim" to apply to any person who is directly or indirectly mistreated in regards to any area of activity-existence. Study the ways that others use (and not use) the word "victim." During the existence of White Supremacy (Racism), do not use the term "Victim of Racism" to apply to any White person. If a White person is mistreated by any person (White or Non-White) during the existence of White Supremacy (Racism), say that he or she is the "victim" of mistreatment by the person who did the mistreatment.

>   **Reason:** During the existence of White Supremacy (Racism), "Race" is "Racism," "Racism" is White Supremacy. White Supremacy is "Racism." All Non-White people are Victims of White Supremacy. No White people are victims of White Supremacy. "Black Supremacy" or "Non-White Supremacy" does not exist. Any people can be victims of non-just treatment, by any people, but only Non-White people can be Victims of Racism (White Supremacy), and will continue to be Victims of Racism (White Supremacy) as long as White Supremacy (Racism) exists.

>   **Notes:** The System of White Supremacy (Racism) is specifically designed to cause harm to the Non-White people, either directly or indirectly in all areas of activity. This harm includes much that Non-White people do in regards to Economics, Education, Entertainment, Labor, Law, Politics, Religion, Sex, and War/Counter-War.

Victim Father/Mother/Sister/Brother/Wife. <u>Use these terms</u> to apply to any Non-White persons who interact with each other in a manner of so-called "kin-ship," and/or in some specific manner of association with each other while, at the same time, functioning in subjugation to, or as Victims of, The System of White Supremacy (Racism), in any one or more areas of activity.

> **Notes:** Instead of using the entire word "victim," the letter "V" can be used ("V-Father," "V-Mother," "V-Child," etc.) A "V-marriage" would apply to Non-White persons who are so-called "married" to each other while one or both are subject to The System of White Supremacy (Racism). Such "marriages" are false, or racially-victimized "marriages." They are "non-marriages" because the Non-White persons so involved cannot, functionally, "dedicate" or "devote" themselves to any material partnership with each other that is not subject to the direct or indirect domination of the White Supremacists (Racistman and Racistwoman, collectively).
>
> During the existence of White Supremacy (Racism), those White persons who practice White Supremacy (Racism) are directly or indirectly the functional "Race-Mothers," "Race-Fathers," and "Race-Parents" of all of the Non-White people of the known universe.

Victims Group. <u>Use this term</u> to apply to any so-called "family" of Non-White persons in which any "member" of such "family" is directly or indirectly subject to The System of White Supremacy (Racism) in any one or more areas of activity/existence (Economics, Education, Entertainment, Labor, Law, Politics, Religion, Sex, and War/Counter-War).

Victims Guaranteed Qualification ("V.G.Q."). <u>Use this term</u> to apply to what a Non-White person (Victim of White Supremacy) chooses to <u>say</u> about Race, Racism and/or Counter-Racism during the existence of White Supremacy (Racism), including anything that he or she chooses to say as it pertains to what White Supremacy (Racism) is, how it works, how Non-White persons are victimized by it, and/or what to do (or not do) about it.

> **Notes:** During the existence of The System of White Supremacy (Racism), and according to Compensatory Counter-Racist Logic, every Non-White person who is subject to and/or a Victim of The System of White Supremacy (Racism), is totally "qualified" to <u>say</u> <u>anything</u> that he or she chooses to <u>say</u>, that either directly or indirectly pertains to Race, Racism, and/or Counter-

Racism. Since no <u>White</u> person is subject to and/or is a Victim of White Supremacy (Racism), it is not logical to think, speak, and/or act as if a White person should choose to say anything about Race, Racism, and/or Counter-Racism, unless what is said is in support of the replacement of The System of White Supremacy (Racism) with The System of Justice (balance between people).

Victims of Racism. <u>Use this term</u> to apply to any person who is racially classified as, and/or who is generally considered to be, "Black," "Brown," "Red," "Yellow," and/or Non-White and, who is or has been directly or indirectly dominated by White Supremacists (Racists). (<u>See</u>, "Victim").

Victims Unit/Victims Race-Unit. <u>Use these terms</u> to mean the same as the term "Black family."

> **Notes:** During the existence of White Supremacy (Racism) and according to Compensatory Counter-Racist Logic, all Non-White persons (either individually, or collectively) are, in function, victims of, and subjects to, the power of those White people who participate in The System of White Supremacy (Racism).
>
> The System of White Supremacy (Racism) is a system of government that is designed to guarantee that the White people of the known universe dominate and mistreat the Non-White people of the known universe for the basic "pleasure," "convenience," and/or "benefit" of the White people of the known universe. The System of White Supremacy (Racism) makes "Victim units" out of all Non-White persons in all areas of activity, including Economics, Education, Entertainment, Labor, Law, Politics, Religion, Sex, and War/Counter-War.

Violated. <u>Use this word</u>. As long as White Supremacy (Racism) exists, use the word "violated" to mostly apply to and/or describe what has happened, and what is happening, to the Non-White people of the known universe, because of their interactions with Racistman and Racistwoman (White Supremacists, collectively), in all areas of activity.

> **Note:** During the existence of White Supremacy (Racism), White Supremacy (Racism) has proven to be the most powerful form of violence in existence among the people of the known universe.

Violence/Non-Violence/Counter-Violence. <u>Use these terms with caution</u>. When others use them, ask for a detailed explanation that you can easily understand. Ask questions.

> **Questions:** What, exactly, is "violence"? What, exactly, is "non-violence"? What, exactly, is counter-violence? What forms do they take? Is there only one form of "violence," "non-violence" or "counter-violence"? Are there many forms? What persons are correctly qualified to judge? Is "non-violence" the complete absence of any form of "violence"? If so, how can "violence" and "non-violence" exist at the same time? Is it correct to always "meet" "violence" with "non-violence"? Is it correct to sometimes "meet" "violence" with "counter-violence"? If so, when? where? why? how? by whom? Is it always correct not to use "counter-violence" to force a "violent" person to be "non-violent"? Is White Supremacy (Racism) a form of "violence"? If it is, is it ever correct for a Victim of White Supremacy (Non-White person) to use "counter-violence" against those who practice White Supremacy (Racism)?

> **Notes:** Generally speaking, <u>violence</u> is any unjust and/or incorrect harm to a person, animal, thing, etc., and <u>counter-violence</u> is any speech and/or action used to stop a person, animal, etc. from doing unjust and/or incorrect harm.

> The System of White Supremacy (Racism) has proven to be the most powerful, efficient, and most sophisticated form of "violence" yet produced by the people of the known universe. During the existence of White Supremacy (Racism), "non-violence" does not and cannot exist.

Violent Crime. <u>Avoid using this term</u>. When others use the term, ask them to explain, in detail, exactly what they mean, and what they do not mean. Also, whenever you use the term "violent crime," always explain that The System of White Supremacy (Racism) is the <u>most</u> violent of crimes.

> **Questions:** If a person is "violated," is it a "crime"? What, exactly, is "violence"? What, exactly, is a "crime"? Are all "crimes" "violent" in "effect"? If a "crime" is <u>not</u> "violent" in "effect," is it correct to say that it is a "crime"? How "violent" is "violent"? How "criminal" is "criminal"? How "violently criminal" is a "violent crime"? Is poisoning

409

the land that produces the food that people must eat, a "violent crime"? If so, why? If not, why not?

Visitor. <u>Use this word with caution</u>. When others use the word "visitor," study the ways that the word may or may not be used. Is a "visitor" different from an "owner"? Is an "owner" different from a "resident"? Can a "visitor" and a "resident" be one and the same?

> **Note:** White Supremacists (Racists) always regard the Non-White persons of the known universe as "restricted visitors" who must, at all times, be under the direct or indirect control of White Supremacists (Racistman and Racistwoman, collectively).

Voluntary/Volunteer. <u>Use these words with caution</u>. When others use these words, ask for a detailed explanation that you can easily understand. Study and question the conditions that exist when the words are used, by whom, and for what ultimate purpose. Are the Victims of White Supremacy (Non-White people) "voluntary" victims?

> **Note:** Sometimes what "appears" to be "voluntary," is not "voluntary," but is, in truth, action that was or is the result of coercion, intimidation, and/or deception.

Vulnerable/Vulnerability. <u>Use these words</u> mostly to describe and/or to apply to, the general position or condition of Non-White people during the existence of The System of White Supremacy (Racism).

W

War. <u>Use this word with caution</u>. When others use words like "war," "non-war" and/or "peace," ask for a detailed explanation that you can easily understand. When you use the word "war," use it to apply to any conflict between two or more persons that includes the intent of doing unjust harm to one or more persons. Use it also to apply to any willful and deliberate unjust harm done by any person against another person. When applying the word "war" to The System of White Supremacy (Racism), use the term, "The War."

As long as White Supremacy (Racism) exists, use the term "Counter-War" and/or "Counter-Racist War" to apply to anything said or done that proves effective in replacing White Supremacy (Racism) with Justice (balance between people). The word "war" can and should be used to apply to those things said or done that help to maintain injustice (imbalance between people).

The term "The War" should always be used to describe or apply to those things that directly or indirectly help to maintain, expand, and/or refine the practice of White Supremacy (Racism) in any one or more areas of activity. All other conflicts between people should be called "battles," "fights," "violent acts," "major disagreements," etc.

> **Note:** During the existence of White Supremacy (Racism), it is best and correct to regard all conflicts between White persons as being disputes about how The System of White Supremacy (Racism) should or should not be maintained, expanded, and/or refined.

War Crime(s)/War Criminals. <u>Use these terms</u> mostly to apply to The System of White Supremacy (Racism), and/or to apply to those White persons who practice White Supremacy (Racism) in any one or more areas of activity – Economics, Education, Entertainment, Labor, Law, Politics, Religion, Sex, and War/Counter-War. When others use the terms "war," "war crime(s)," "war criminal(s), and/or "anti-war," ask for a detailed explanation that you can easily understand. Study the many different ways that others may or may not use these terms.

> **Notes:** The System of White Supremacy (Racism) is the most powerful form of war making among the people of the known universe. It is also the most sophisticated form of war making, and the greatest of crimes by people, against people, ever produced by people, among the people of the known universe. The people (White) who established, maintained, expanded, and refined The System of White Supremacy (Racism) have proven themselves as the greatest, most powerful, and most intelligent warriors, criminals, and "war criminals," ever to function among the people of the known universe. By producing a system of mistreatment based on deceit and direct violence against people whom they "classify" as "Black," "Brown," "Red," "Yellow," and/or "Non-White," the Racemen and Racewomen (White Supremacists) of the known universe have manufactured a condition of "war" that can be correctly called "The Crime of Crimes." It is correct to regard the people (White) who practice White Supremacy (Racism) as being "the Master War-Criminals" of the known universe.

Warfare. <u>Do not use this word</u>. Instead, use the word "war."

> **Reason:** The word "war" does not need the word "fare" added to it. "War" is "war." By adding the word "fare" to the word "war," a person may be lead to believe that "war" is "fair" - that "fair" is "white" and that "fair," "white," "just," "justice"

and "war," are all one and the same when used in association with a White person.

During the existence of White Supremacy (Racism) the word "fare" may be confused with the word "fair," which usually is associated with the word "white." The word "fair" may also be associated with the words "just" and "justice." Therefore, the term "warfare" may be confused with the words that could produce thoughts that a "war" fought by White people is a "war" that is "fair" and, therefore, must be a "just" war and/or a "war for justice."

War Games. Avoid using this term. When others use the term "war games," ask for a detailed explanation that you can easily understand. Ask questions.

Questions: Is "war" a "game"? Should "war" be thought of as being a "game"? Is a "game" the same as "sport" or "entertainment"? If so, is it correct to regard killing, maiming, and/or abuse, as a form of "sport" or "entertainment"?

War, Rules of. Use this term with caution. When others use this term, ask for a detailed explanation that you can easily understand. What, exactly, is "war"? What, exactly, are the "rules of war"? Who makes these "rules"? Who is correctly qualified to make and to enforce these "rules of war"? Is it correct to produce "rules of Counter-War" as a compensatory counter-action against "war-making" and the "rules of war-making"?

War of Wars. Use this term to apply to everything that is or has been said or done that has helped to establish, maintain, expand, and/or refine The System of White Supremacy (Racism).

Note: During the existence of White Supremacy (Racism), and according to Compensatory Counter-Racist Logic, the term "Counter-Racist Counter-War" applies to any speech or action that proves effective in replacing The System of White Supremacy (Racism) with The System of Justice (balance between people).

Wedlock. Use this word with caution. When others use it, ask them to explain, in detail, exactly what they mean. Ask questions. Is being in a condition of "wedlock" the exact same as being "married"? If so, why? If not, why not?

Wedlock (outside of). Use this term with caution. When others use it, ask for a detailed explanation that you can easily understand.

> **Questions:** Can a person be "in wedlock" and, at the same time, not be "married"? Can a person be "outside of wedlock," and at the same time, be "married"?

Welfare. Use this word with caution. When others use the words "welfare," "welfare recipient," "welfare system," etc., ask for a detailed explanation that you can easily understand. Ask questions about acts or situations that may appear to be what is said to be "welfare," but may not be described as "welfare."

> **Questions:** What, exactly, is "welfare"? What, exactly, is not "welfare"? What, exactly, is a "welfare recipient"? Are all Non-White people who are subject to The System of White Supremacy (Racism) "welfare recipients"? Is The System of White Supremacy (Racism) a system designed for the "welfare" of White people? Do the White people of the known universe "fare well" and/or "fare better" than Non-White people because of The System of White Supremacy (Racism)? Are all people, at all times, receiving "welfare," of some kind, in some form? Are many "Kings" and "Queens," "welfare recipients"?

> **Suggestion:** When there is controversy or confusion about what "welfare" is, or is not, use the term "welfare" to apply to the speech and/or action that results in a person, or persons, receiving help from others.

West/Western Civilization/Western Culture/Western World. Avoid using these terms. Do not use them to describe any known so-called "political condition." When others use any of these terms, ask them to give you a detailed explanation that you can easily understand. Ask questions.

> **Questions:** What, exactly, is the "West"? What persons are best and correctly qualified to say what the "West" is, as compared with what the "East" is – when, where, and why? How far "west" is "west"? How far "east" is "east"? Is "west" a way of thinking? If so, thinking how? Thinking about what, in order to do what? What does it mean to be "Eastern," or "Northern," or "Southern"? What should it mean? Does the term "Western Culture" mean White Supremacist (Racist) Culture?

Wetback (Racial). <u>Do not use this term</u> to apply to any person because he or she swims through or crosses water for the purposes of seeking a better socio-material condition.

> **Reason:** The term "Wetback" has often been used by White Supremacists (Racists) to be insulting to some Non-White persons who are forced to cross water to get help from White people.

White. <u>Use this word with caution.</u> During the existence of White Supremacy (Racism) use the word "White" to apply to persons who are "classified" as, and who "function" as "White" in regards to their actions, interactions and/or reactions to persons who are "classified" as, and/or who function as, "Non-White."

Study the many ways that this word is used, as compared to words such as "black," "blackened," "brown," "yellow," "red," "dark," "darkened," "dull," "enlightened," etc. Study the many ways that the word "white" is used to support and refine the practice of White Supremacy (Racism). Study how the White Supremacists (Racistman and Racistwoman, collectively), use words in a manner that they believe will do the most to result in most people thinking, speaking, and acting in support of The System of White Supremacy (Racism).

White Blood. <u>Avoid using this term</u> for purposes of identifying a person as being a "White" person. When others say that a person has "White blood," ask for a detailed explanation that you can easily understand. If a "White" person has "White blood," does that mean that Non-White people have "black," "brown," "red," "tan," "beige," or "yellow" blood?

White Christian/Black Christian. <u>Avoid using these terms.</u> When others use the terms "White Christian," "Black Christian," "Asian Christian," "Conservative Christian," "Fundamentalists," etc., ask for a detailed explanation that you can easily understand. Ask if it is necessary to use these terms and why. Why not simply say, "Christian"? Is it necessary to say, "short Christian," or "tall Christian"? Is it necessary to say "fat Christian," or "thin Christian"?

White Christmas. <u>Do not use this term.</u>

> **Reason:** There is reason to believe that it is not necessary for what is called "Christmas" to be "White," and/or to be associated with any specific "color" or "non-color" of any person(s), creature(s), or thing(s). During the existence of White Supremacy (Racism), the use of the term "White

Christmas" is too easily associated with speech and action that is supportive of White Supremacy (Racism).

White-Collar Crime. <u>Do not use this term</u>. When others use it, ask for a detailed explanation that you can easily understand. If an act is a "crime," call it a "crime." Do not call it a "White-collar crime," or a "Blue-collar crime," or a "Black coat crime."

> **Reason:** During the existence of The System of White Supremacy (Racism) a so-called "White-collar crime" means, indirectly, that because the word "White" is involved, the "crime" is less harmful.

White-Collar Worker. <u>Avoid using this term</u>.

> **Reason:** The term "White-collar worker" has often been used to mean, indirectly, "smart worker," "sophisticated" and "refined worker," and/or a worker who is more worthy of special praise, honor and rewards. This term has also been used to indirectly apply to those White persons who are "in command," and/or who are in so-called "decision-making positions" that require greater "brain" usage than so-called "menial-muscle."

White Community, The. <u>Use this term</u> to mean the same as "The System of White Supremacy (Racism)". When others use the terms "The White Community," "White Society," "The White World," "The White Power Structure," "The White Church," "White Culture," etc., ask for a detailed explanation that you can easily understand.

> **Note:** According to Compensatory Counter-Racist Logic, the only reason for White people to function as a so-called "White Community" etc., is to practice White Supremacy (Racism).

White Culture. <u>Use this term</u> to mean the same as the term "White Supremacy (Racism)." When others use the term "White Culture," ask for a detailed explanation that you can easily understand.

> **Note:** "Culture" is whatever is being done. "Culture" is the combination of whatever people think, say, and do, at the time and place that they are thinking, saying and doing.

> **Example**: If some White people function in such a manner as to produce a way of thinking, speaking, and acting that can be correctly called a "White Culture," then

it is reasonable to believe that the basic purpose for that so-called "White Culture" is to practice The System of White Supremacy (Racism). There is no other logical reason for any activity among or between people being called or recognized as a "White Culture."

White Dove of Peace. Do not use this term. When others use it, ask for a detailed explanation that you can easily understand.

> **Reason:** White Supremacists (Racists) sometimes use the term "White dove of peace" to associate "whiteness" in both creatures and people, with "harmlessness," "tenderness," correct intent, and "peace."

> **Notes:** In the White (Supremacists) Culture, birds that are black, are usually associated with thoughts and/or deeds that are "evil" and/or connected with "death and destruction". According to White Supremacist (Racist) thinking, the darker the creature, the more that creature is likely to be a robber, a thief, or a malicious and "unfeeling" killer of the "innocent".

White Family, The. Use this term to apply to two or more White people who practice White Supremacy (Racism) and who directly or indirectly speak and/or act in a manner that helps to maintain, expand, and/or refine, the existence of White Supremacy (Racism)

> **Explanation**: As long as White Supremacy exists, it will, by the definition of its existence, be the dominant motivating force among the people of the known universe. This means that no other "family" of people can exist at the same time that "The White Family" exists. The existence of The White Family cancels, and/or nullifies, the existence and/or function of all other so-called families, tribes, political groups, etc. The term "White Family" always refers to a racial purpose.

> As long as White Supremacy (Racism) exists, the use of the term "family" can, truthfully, refer only to persons who practice White Supremacy (Racism). Any other so-called "families" of people do not exist, and are functionally, simply two or more persons who associate with each other on the basis of limited social and/or material interests.

> Those White persons who do not practice White Supremacy are not members of The White Family, nor do

they function as a family of any kind. They function as infantile persons who, because of physical or mental limitations, are generally incapable of doing deliberate harm to others, on a significant scale.

White people can choose to be members of The White Family. An effective number of them have chosen to do so. All other White persons have either chosen to function against The White Family (White Supremacists, collectively), or they have been so infantile or senile that they were not physically or mentally able to make a choice. As long as White Supremacy exists, <u>all</u> Non-White people are subject to White Supremacy. Since all Non-White people are subject to the White Supremacists (White Family), no Non-White person can function as a member of any "family".

The existence of the superior power and purpose of "The White Family" automatically prohibits any Non-White people from functioning as a family. Two or more Non-White people may appear to function as a family, but they cannot function as such as long as they are directly or indirectly subject to The White Family (White Supremacists, collectively). No people can correctly call themselves "family" and, at the same time, be subject to a family. Such persons are "subjects," not "family". (See, Family).

White Folks. <u>Do not use this term</u>. Instead, say "White people," or "White person(s)."

> **Reason:** The term "White folks," when used by a Non-White person during the existence of White Supremacy (Racism), may sometimes be regarded as offensive or sarcastic.

White Hat(s)/Black Hat(s). <u>Do not use these terms</u> in such a manner as to associate the "color" (or non-color) of hats with acts of "good," "evil," "justice," "injustice," etc.

> **Reason:** During the existence of White Supremacy (Racism) nearly everything "black," or "dark," has been deliberately associated with that which is "evil," non-just and/or incorrect. Nearly everything "white," or "light," has been deliberately associated with that which is "good," "just," "correct," "righteous," "desirable," etc.

White Hope. <u>Do not use this term</u>. When others use it, ask for a detailed explanation that you can easily understand.

White Jew. <u>Do not use this term</u>. When others use the terms "White Jew(s)," "Black Jew(s)," "Yellow Jew(s)," etc., ask for a detailed explanation that you can easily understand. Seek to know and understand the functional difference(s) if any, between a Jew who is "White," and a Jew who is "Non-White." Seek to know and understand how each functions, and/or is expected to function, in each area of activity – Economics, Education, Entertainment, Labor, Law, Politics, Religion (including interaction with persons of other religions), Sex, and War/Counter-War.

> **Note:** According to Compensatory Logic, if you are <u>not</u> a "Jew," and you seek information about "Jews," it is best and correct to have all of your questions about "Jews" answered by persons who say they are "Jews".

White Lie. <u>Do not use this term</u>. When others use terms like "white lie," "black lie," "shading the truth," "dark deception," etc., ask for a detailed explanation that you can easily understand.

> **Notes:** During the existence of White Supremacy (Racism) the term "White lie" has often been used to apply to a falsehood that has been told that was said to be "harmless," and/or that was told in a manner not intended to do harm. During the existence of White Supremacy (Racism) a so-called "Black lie" is taught to apply to a lie (deliberate falsehood) that is regarded as the "worst," most "evil," and most "destructive" kind.

White List/Black List. <u>Do not use these terms</u>. Instead of using these terms, use expressions like "list of correct deeds," "list of incorrect deeds," etc. When others use terms like "White list," "Black list," etc., ask for a detailed explanation of why "color" and/or "non-color" is included in the making of lists that, apparently, have no functional connection with "color" or "non-color."

White Man/White Women. <u>Use these terms with extreme caution</u>. Study carefully the ways that others use these terms.

> **Notes:** It is best and less confusing to use the terms "Racistman," "Racistwoman," and/or "White Supremacist (Racist)," only when applying to White persons who practice Racism (White Supremacy). Racistman and/or Racistwoman are more descriptive than the broader terms White Man, and/or White Woman. The terms

Racistman, Racistwoman, and White Supremacists refer exclusively to those White people who practice Racism; the terms White Man or White Woman may or may not. To avoid confusion, it is best not to use the terms White Man or White Woman to describe people who practice Racism. A person is not necessarily a Racist because he or she is White.

White Man's Burden. Do not use this term. Instead, use the term, "White people's duties" (to replace The System of White Supremacy with The System of Justice).

> **Reason:** It has been said that Non-White people are an "aimless collection" of people in the known universe who are generally primitive, weak-minded, child-like, and, when compared to the White people of the known universe, greatly in need of help from White people. Because of these sayings, some White people have described Non-White people as being the "White Man's Burden."
>
> Considering that The System of White Supremacy (Racism) has not resulted in the establishment of Justice (balance between people) it is best and correct for all people to think, speak, and act as if the "duty" of all people is to replace White Supremacy (Racism) with Justice (balance between people). This process should not be regarded as a "burden" to anybody – White or Non-White. The process of producing justice should be regarded as a "pleasant duty" by all, to all, and for all.

White Muslim/Black Muslim. Do not use these terms to describe any persons unless those persons ask you to use these terms to describe or identify them. At all times, it is best and correct to call people by any name or title that those people ask you to call them by. To produce understanding, and to minimize conflict or end confusion, is it best and correct to ask people what they believe, what they do, and what they intend to do. It is best and correct to get the answers to all questions, about any people, from the people you are asking about. Then study the answers, in detail.

White Nation. Use this term to apply to:

(1)   Any one or more White persons who practice White Supremacy (Racism);

(2)   The sum total of all speech and action by those White persons who practice White Supremacy, in any one or more areas of activity; and/or

(3)   White Supremacists, collectively.

White/Black Neighborhood. Avoid using these terms. Instead, use the terms "White location(s)," to mean places where White people are, and "Black location(s)," to mean places where Black people are.

> **Reason:** During the existence of White Supremacy (Racism), and according to Compensatory Counter-Racist Logic, all of the people of the known universe are located near each other. They may or may not be "neighbors".

> **Questions:** What, exactly, is a "neighborhood"? What, exactly, is not a "neighborhood"? What, exactly, is a "neighbor"? What, exactly, is not a "neighbor"? Is a person a "neighbor" if he or she is not "neighborly"? Exactly how "close" to each other must two or more persons be in order to be correctly called "neighbor(s)"? What is the exact distance? Is a "neighborhood" the same as a "community"? Can people be "neighbors" and not be a "community"? What, exactly, is the difference between a "neighborhood," and a "community"? Are the White Supremacists (Racists) of the known universe, "members" of the "same neighborhood," regardless of how "distant" they may be from each other?

White of you (that's). Do not use this term. When others say, "That's White of you," or when they say something similar, ask for a detailed explanation that you can easily understand.

> **Note:** During the existence of White Supremacy (Racism), this "slang" expression has sometimes been used to indicate that a person's speech or action is "good," "proper," "correct," "desirable," etc., because such speech or action is "characteristic" of that of a White person.

White Paper Report. Avoid using this term. When others use it, ask for a detailed explanation that you can easily understand. What, exactly, is the purpose of a so-called "White paper report"? What, exactly, would be the purpose of a "Non-White paper report"?

White Perfection(ism). Use these terms to apply to speech and action specifically designed to produce the replacement of White Supremacy (Racism) with Justice (balance between people) while, at the same time, guaranteeing that the "whiteness" of the "White" people of the known universe will be "preserved," "conserved," and "protected." As long as White Supremacy (Racism) exists, it is correct for all people to speak and act in support of "White perfection" and "White perfectionism."

> **Notes:** According to Compensatory Counter-Racist Logic, the best and correct way to maintain the "whiteness" of "White" people is to guarantee that White people engage in sexual intercourse and/or "sexual play" only with White people, as long as White Supremacy (Racism) exists. In addition, it is logical that after the end of The System of White Supremacy (Racism), a just and correct plan for the preservation of "White" people as a "White species," should be mutually established as a part of the Universal Man/ Universal Woman fulfillment, according to the System of Justice (balance between people).

White Person. Use this term to apply to:

(1) Any person who considers him or herself "White" and who is considered "White" by a substantial number of other persons who consider themselves as "White," who function as "White" and are accepted as "White" in all areas of activity.

(2) Any person classified as "White," and/or Caucasian who function as a "White" person in his or her relationships with other White persons, and/or in his or her relationships with Non-White persons.

(3) Any person not classified as Non-White, who does not consider him or herself as Non-White, and who does not function as a person who is considered to be or has been classified as Non-White.

White Power. Use this term. During the existence of White Supremacy (Racism), use it to mean the same as White Supremacy (Racism). When others use the term "White power," ask for a detailed explanation that you can easily understand.

White Power Structure (the). Do not use this term. Instead, use the term, "The System of White Supremacy (Racism)."

> **Reason:** During the existence of White Supremacy (Racism) and according to Compensatory Counter-Racist Logic, it is best and correct not to use the term "White Power Structure." In racial matters, there is no "Racial

421

Power Structure" other than The System of White Supremacy (Racism). No Non-White person has proven that he or she has greater or dominant power than the power expressed by the White Supremacists (Racistmen and Racistwomen, collectively). White Supremacy (Racism) is the total, supreme, and exclusive power to practice Racism. It is confusing to say, "The White Power Structure." It is best and correct to say "The System of White Supremacy (Racism)." A so-called racial "power structure," other than The System of White Supremacy (Racism), does not exist.

White Racism. Do not use this term.

> **Explanation**: White Supremacists (Racists) are the only people in the known universe who actually practice effective Racism. As long as White Supremacy exists, no other "Racism" can exist. The term "White Racism" should not be used as long as White Supremacy is the dominant socio-material force among the people of the known universe. The term "White Racism" implies that there exists some other form of "Racism". For that reason, the term should not be used. Racism, functionally, is White Supremacy, and White Supremacy is Racism. A Racist is a White Supremacist, and a White Supremacist is a Racist.
>
> As long as White Supremacy exists, all Racists are White people, but all White people may or may not be Racists. As long as White Supremacy exists, no Non-White person can function as, or be a Racist while existing in subjugation to White Supremacy. It is not possible for a person to be a Victim of Racism, and be a Racist at the same time. One who is a prisoner, is not the same as one who is a Prison Master. "Non-White Supremacy" does not exist; White Supremacy does exist.

White Russia [Belarus]. Use this term with caution. Before deciding on how best to use the term, study the ways that others use the term. Ask for detailed explanations that you can easily understand.

White Sacrifice. Use this term to apply to a person classified as "White," who, during the existence of White Supremacy (Racism) is killed, maimed, neglected and/or in other ways harmed, as a result of his or her inefficiency, and/or as a result of his or her dedication to, or lack of dedication to, the maintenance, expansion, and refinement of, The System of White Supremacy (Racism).

Notes: During the existence of White Supremacy (Racism), and according to Compensatory Counter-Racist Logic, no White person is, or can be, a Victim of White Supremacy (Racism). He or she can only be a victim of other forms of harm that may or may not be in the form of a "White Sacrifice." Only a Non-White person is, or can be, a Victim of White Supremacy (Racism).

White Slavery. Do not use this term. When others use it, ask for a detailed explanation that you can easily understand. Ask why the term is used and/or was used.

White Supremacist (Racist)/Racistman/Racistwoman. Use these terms to apply to any person who knows and understands that he or she is "classified" as White, who functions as White, who is generally accepted by White people as White, and who benefits from being "White" by participating in the practice of White Supremacy (Racism).

A White Supremacist (Racist) is a White person who directly or indirectly helps to establish, maintain, expand and/or refine the subjugation of Non-White people on the basis of "color" and/or factors associated with "color" for the basic purpose of "pleasing" and/or serving all White persons at all times in all areas of activity: (Economics, Education, Entertainment, Labor, Law, Politics, Religion, Sex, and War/Counter-War.

> **Notes:** During the existence of White Supremacy (Racism) and according to Compensatory Counter-Racist Logic, a White person can be a Racist (White Supremacist) only if he or she is able to function as a Racist (White Supremacist). Therefore, if a White person is able to function as a Racist (White Supremacist), it is correct to suspect that he or she probably is one (Suspected White Supremacist).

White Supremacy. Use this term to apply to:

(1) The direct or indirect subjugation of all Non-White people by White people, for the basic purpose of pleasing and/or serving all White persons, at all times, in all places, in all areas of activity.

(2) The only functional Racism in existence among the people of the known universe that is based on color and/or non-color in the physical make-up or physical appearance of persons.

(3) Racism for the sake of Racism.

White Wedding. <u>Do not use this term</u>. When others use the term "White wedding," ask for a detailed explanation that you can easily understand.

> **Notes:** The term "White wedding" has often been used to apply to the white garments that a female wears during a sacred "marriage" ceremony. The "whiteness" of the garments has sometimes been said to represent "honesty," "purity," "faithfulness," "innocence," etc. During the existence of White Supremacy (Racism), the "whiteness" of garments worn at a wedding ceremony has often been associated (directly or indirectly) with the glorification of White Supremacy (Racism). The use of the term "white wedding" is often intended to cause people to think that deeds that are "serious," "wholesome," "pure," "honest," and/or "sacred," should be, or must be, associated with "whiteness," with White people, and/or with the practice of, and the glorification of, White Supremacy (Racism).

Whore. <u>Use this word with caution</u>. During the existence of White Supremacy (Racism), and according to Compensatory Counter-Racist Logic, use the words "whore," "whoring" and/or "whoredom," to apply to any one or more of the following (but only for the purpose of an agreed-upon constructive exchange of views):

- Any act of sexual intercourse and/or "sexual play" by any person that directly or indirectly helps to establish, maintain, expand and/or refine The System of White Supremacy (Racism).

- Any act of sexual intercourse and/or "sexual play" by any person that is not intended to produce thought, speech, and/or action that helps to result in replacing The System of White Supremacy (Racism) with The System of Justice (balance between people).

- Any act of sexual intercourse and/or "sexual play," by any person that does not <u>result</u> in replacing The System of White Supremacy (Racism) with The System of Justice (balance between people).

- Any act of so-called "homo-sex," or "lesbian sex," (anti-sex) that involves a Non-White person.

> **Note:** During the existence of White Supremacy (Racism), and according to Compensatory Counter-Racist Logic, any speech, or action by any Non-White person that

directly or indirectly results in support for The System of White Supremacy (Racism), can be correctly described as "whoring," etc.

Whoremonger. <u>Use this word</u> to mean the following:

(1)   A male person, who, when choosing to have sexual intercourse with a female person, <u>does not</u> on each occasion, <u>tell</u> that person about the previous [last] occasion that he had sexual intercourse with another person, and the reason for doing so.

(2)   A male person, who, during the existence of White Supremacy (Racism) engages in an act of sexual intercourse, and/or an act of "sexual play" for reasons that do not include helping to produce or promote thought, speech, and action that is intended to end White Supremacy (Racism).

> **Notes:** It is incorrect to call a person a "whoremonger." This word should only be used to define what the word means. Also, according to Compensatory Logic, it is, at all times, best and correct to avoid "name-calling" by calling a person only the names and/or titles that the person chooses for him or herself. (<u>See</u> "Whore," "Whoring").

Whoring/Whoresome. <u>Use these terms with caution</u>. Do not apply any of these terms to persons in a manner that is likely to be regarded as "name-calling." When others use any of these terms, ask for a detailed explanation that you can easily understand.

> **Questions:** What, exactly, is a "whore"? Is a "whore" the same as a "prostitute"? Is a "whore" the same as a "harlot"? Can a "married" person be a "whore" to his or her "wife" or "husband"? Can a person be a "whore" in his or her interaction with another person, without making any body contact with that person? Are the Non-White people who are subject to, and who cooperate with, The System of White Supremacy (Racism), "whores"? During the existence of White Supremacy (Racism), which Non-White persons are not "whores" to The System of White Supremacy (Racism)? Is a person "whoring" if he or she submits to and/or cooperates with, a person who practices injustice (imbalance between and/or mistreatment of people)? (<u>See</u> "Whore").

Wife/Husband. Use these words with caution. When others use the word "wife" or "husband," ask for a detailed explanation that you can easily understand. Ask what a "wife" or "husband" does, and does not do, in each area of activity, including Economics, Education, Entertainment, Labor, Law, Politics, Religion, Sex, and War/Counter-War.

> **Reason:** According to Compensatory Counter-Racist Logic, no [Non-White] person can be a "husband" or a "wife" if he or she is, at the same time, subject to The System of White Supremacy (Racism). During the existence of White Supremacy (Racism), Non-White persons can only function as "mates" or "partners" to each other while serving The System of White Supremacy (Racism). According to Compensatory Counter-Racist Logic, and as long as White Supremacy (Racism) exists, only White persons can function as "wives" or as "husbands," and only to each other. Non-White persons are all subject to the dictatorship of Racistman and Racistwoman (White Supremacists, collectively), and, therefore, have no major control over the factors that determine what they (Non-White people) do, or do not do in regards to what they call "marriage."

> **Questions:** How can a Non-White person truly function as a "husband," or a "wife," and, at the same time, be forced to function according to what the White Supremacists (Racistman and Racistwoman, collectively), want or do not want? Is it correct for some persons to decide what does, and what does not make a "marriage" for two or more other persons? Is any person "qualified" to truthfully say when other persons are "married" or "not married"? If so, what qualifies that person to do so?

> Is it correct for any Racist (White Supremacist) or Suspected Racist (Suspected White Supremacist) to say, or imply, that he or she is qualified to judge which Non-White persons are "wives" and "husbands"? During the existence of White Supremacy (Racism) how can a Non-White female have the same so-called "powers," "duties," "benefits," "obligations," etc., as a White female, in regards to being a "wife" when, within The System of White Supremacy (Racism), a White female is not subject to White Supremacy (Racism) and a Non-White female is?

> **Suggestion:** During the existence of White Supremacy (Racism), it is best and correct for Non-White persons to

426

avoid saying that they are "married," and, instead, say something similar to one or more of the following:

- "I am attempting marriage."
- "We are attempting marriage."
- "I have attempted marriage four times."
- "This is my first attempted marriage."
- "I am an attempted husband."
- "She is my second attempted wife, and I am her first attempted husband."
- "We have attempted marriage for more than five thousand days."

Notes: Be cautious, particularly when applying these terms to Non-White males and females during the existence of White Supremacy (Racism). When others use the terms "wife" or "husband" to apply to Non-White persons while they are subject to White Supremacy (Racism), ask them (the others) to explain exactly how a Non-White person can function as a "husband," or as a "wife," and at the same time, be subject to The System of White Supremacy (Racism). Also, make a major effort to explain to others that during the existence of White Supremacy (Racism), no Non-White person can function as a "husband," or as a "wife."

Instead of using the terms "wife," or "husband," to apply to Non-White persons during the existence of White Supremacy (Racism), it is correct (according to Compensatory Counter-Racist Logic) to practice using terms such as "mate," "legal mate," "victim-mate," "race-mate," "caremate," "choicemate," "helpmate," etc.

During the existence of White Supremacy (Racism), all persons who are classified as "Non-White" and/or who function as "Non-White" persons, are subject to The System of White Supremacy (Racism). Therefore, during the existence of The System of White Supremacy (Racism), no person who is subject to The System of White Supremacy (Racism) is qualified to function as a so-called "husband," or as a so-called "wife."

Wild. Avoid using this word. When others use it, ask for a detailed explanation that you can easily understand. Ask questions.

Questions: What, or who is "wild"? What, or who is not "wild"? Who is correctly qualified to truthfully say who, or what, is "wild" or "not wild"? Who, or what, is "tame," or "not tame"? Is a White Supremacist "wild" or "tame"? Is a Victim of White Supremacy (Non-White person) "wild" or "tame"? Is a "savage" "wild" or "tame"? Is a White Supremacist (Racist), a "savage"?

Reason: White Supremacists (Racists) often use the terms "wild," "wilderness," "jungle," or "hostile territory," in a manner that applies to <u>Non-White</u> people, and/or in a manner that applies mostly to the places where Non-White people inhabit.

Wild and Wooly. <u>Do not use this term</u>. When others use it, ask for a detailed explanation that you can easily understand.

Reason: During the existence of White Supremacy (Racism) Non-White people are often described as "wild." The hair of Non-White people is often described as "wooly," and/or like the "wool" of a "wild" creature or a "wild" animal. During the existence of White Supremacy (Racism) many White people are trained to believe that Non-White people, basically, are "wild" people and, since the hair of many Non-White people is often regarded as like "wool," the expression "wild and wooly" is often directly or indirectly meant to be a derogatory way of describing a Non-White person. "Wooly hair" is what it is because it is what it should be. It exists neither for purposes of "bragging," nor for shame, pride, or the subject of derogatory remarks.

Wise. <u>Use this term</u> to mean knowing and understanding truth, and using truth, at all times, in a manner that produces justice and correctness in all areas of activity, including Economics, Education, Entertainment, Labor, Law, Politics, Religion, Sex, and War/Counter-War.

Wise Person. <u>Use this term</u> to apply to:

(1)   A person who knows and understands all that needs to be known and understood, and who has produced justice and correctness in all places, at all times and in all areas of activity;

(2)   A person who has used truth in a manner that has produced justice and correctness in all places, at all times, in all areas of activity; and/or

(3)   A Non-Existence person (in the known universe).

With. Use this word with caution. Study carefully the many ways that others use the word. Ask yourself, and others, these (and similar) questions.

> **Questions:**   When, exactly, is one person truly "with" another person? When, exactly, is one person truly not "with" another person? Is a person "with" another person because he or she is in the "presence" of that other person? Is it possible for one person to be "with" another person, and, at the same time, not "touch" that person, look at that person, and/or think about that person? Is it possible to look at a person, but not be "with" that person because you are not thinking about that person? Is it possible to "touch" a person, and, at the same time, not be "with" that person, or that person "with" you? Can two or more people be "with" each other, while doing "completely different" things because while doing those things, they are thinking about each other?
>
> Is it possible for two or more persons to be "with" each other, and, at the same time, "against" each other? When people argue, are they "with" each other, or "against" each other? Are all people, at all times, both "with" each other, and not "with" each other? If so, how, how much, why, and according to whom? Can a person "own" or "possess" something, and, at the same time, not be "with" the something that is "owned" or "possessed"? Does "with" mean the same as "being together"? Is thinking about a person a form of being "with" that person?
>
> During the existence of White Supremacy (Racism) are most White people "with" or "against" Non-White people? If so, or if not, when, where, how, and why, and in regards to which areas of activity (Economics, Education, Entertainment, Labor, Law, Politics, Religion, Sex, War/Counter-War)?

Within the Context/Out of Context. Use these terms with caution. When others use these terms, ask them to explain, in detail, exactly what they mean.

> **Questions:**   When, exactly, is a statement made that is "within context"?   Where, exactly, are the "limits" or "boundaries" of a so-called "context"? What person is best qualified to say? What person is not qualified to

say? When, exactly, is a remark, or an event, "out of context" with other remarks or events? What person is best qualified to say? Where would such a person get such "qualification"?

Is a Racist (White Supremacist) qualified to say what is, or what is not, "within context" in matters that pertain to Race, Racism, and/or Counter-Racism? During the existence of White Supremacy (Racism), is it "within context" to say that it is correct to blame the White Supremacists (Racists) for everything that Non-White people do that should not be done? Is everything that Non-White people do, done "within the context" of The System of White Supremacy (Racism)? Do all White people, interact with all Non-White people, "within the context" of White Supremacy (Racism)? When a White person has sexual intercourse with a Non-White person, is the sexual intercourse "within the context" of White Supremacy (Racism), or "out of the context" of White Supremacy (Racism)?

Woman. Use this word with caution. During the existence of White Supremacy (Racism), avoid using the word "woman" to describe or to identify any Non-White female. Instead, use the words "female" or "lady" to describe, identify, or apply to any Non-White female. Use these words as long as White Supremacy (Racism) exists.

> **Reason:** During the existence of White Supremacy (Racism) Non-White females are not permitted to function as "women." During the existence of White Supremacy (Racism), Non-White females are only permitted to function as "female-girls," "infants," "children," "ladies," "whores," etc. During the existence of White Supremacy (Racism), only those persons who function as "White females," are permitted to be treated as "women."

> **Notes:** According to Compensatory Counter-Racist Logic, no Non-White female can be subject to, and/or be a Victim of The System of White Supremacy (Racism), and, at the same time, function as a "woman."

> During the existence of White Supremacy (Racism), all Non-White females are subject to, and are the Victims of, The System of White Supremacy (Racism). Therefore, during the existence of White Supremacy (Racism), the only persons in the known universe who function as "women" are those persons who are "classified" and who function as "White" females.

430

As compared with "Non-White" females, "White" females are regarded as the only people in the known universe who are so-called "correctly qualified" to function as "women" in all areas of activity (Economics, Education, Entertainment, Labor, Law, Politics, Religion, Sex, War/Counter-War).

Womanizer/Manizer. <u>Do not use these terms</u>. When others use them, ask them to explain, in detail, exactly what they mean.

> **Questions:** What, exactly, is a "womanizer," or a "manizer"? Is a male person who has had sexual intercourse with more than one female person during his existence, a "womanizer"? Is a female person who has had sexual intercourse with more than one male person during her existence, a "manizer"?

Work. <u>Use this word</u> to apply to all use of time, energy, and/or materials, to directly or indirectly produce a result – either intentional, or unintentional. When others use the word "work," study how the word is used. All persons, creatures, and things do something that can be called "work" - they either "work" constructively, or they "work" destructively.

Worker. <u>Use this word</u> to apply to any person, creature, thing, etc., that uses time, energy, and/or materials, to directly or indirectly produce a result that is either intentional or unintentional.

> **Note:** All persons, creatures, etc., either directly or indirectly are "workers" - they are either constructive "workers" or they are destructive "workers".

Working Class. <u>Do not use this term</u>. Use the term "worker(s)."

> **Reason:** In the known universe, all people, all creatures, and all things, do something called "work" – they either "work" constructively or destructively – either correctly, or incorrectly. Therefore, there is no such "class" as a "working class" of people, creatures, or things.

Working With. <u>Use this term with caution</u>. Study, know, and understand the difference(s) between "working with" someone, "working for" someone, "working for" yourself, "working against" yourself, and/or "working against" someone else.

> **Questions:** While subject to White Supremacy (Racism), is it possible for a Non-White person to "work with" the

White Supremacists (Racists), "work for" the White Supremacists (Racists), and, at the same time, "work for" him, or herself? If so, when? Where? Doing what?

Notes: The interactions between the people of the known universe take many forms – both known and unknown. It is not always easy to know and understand the difference(s) between what is, and what seems to be. Sometimes it may seem that one person is "working with" another person, when, in truth, he or she may be "working for" him or herself.

Worthless People, The. Use this term with caution to apply to the Non-White people of the known universe during the existence of The System of White Supremacy (Racism).

Explanation: All Non-White people in the known universe exist in subjugation to the White Supremacists of the known universe. It is the White Supremacists who determine the worth of Non-White people in comparison with the worth of White people.

Under White Supremacy, it is not possible for any Non-White person to be equal to and/or to be worth more than any White person, at the same time that that Non-White person is subject to White Supremacy. Therefore, if a Non-White person cannot be equal to, and/or worth more, than a White person in a socio-material system dominated by White Supremacy (Racism), then it is impossible for that Non-White person to be "worth" anything other than "less".

The fact that Non-White people do exist in subjugation to White Supremacy, makes them worth less to themselves than they are worth to the White Supremacists (Racists). Their worthlessness is evident in all areas of activity, including Economics, Education, Entertainment, Labor, Law, Politics, Religion, Sex, and War/Counter-War.

Wrong Attitude. Do not use this term. When others use it, ask for a detailed explanation that you can easily understand. Ask questions.

Questions: What, exactly, is a so-called "attitude"? Can an "attitude" be "measured"? If so, how? What, exactly, is the "standard" for measuring "attitude"? Who is qualified to set that "standard"? What, if anything, is the "standard" for measuring "attitude" based on?

Suggestion: Rather than speak of the "attitude" of persons, speak of what it is that persons say or do, or not say or do. Instead of mentioning "right attitude" or "wrong attitude," ask a person what it is that he or she is trying to do or not trying to do – for what purpose, and in order to accomplish what.

Y

Yellow. <u>Use this word with caution</u>. Do not describe or identify people as "yellow" unless those people, as individual persons, say that they prefer to, and/or have no objection to, being described or identified as "yellow."

Questions: What, exactly, is "yellow"? Who, exactly, is "yellow"? Do "yellow" people truly exist? Who is correctly qualified to say which persons are "yellow," and which persons are not "yellow"? Are people who are "yellow" really "light brown"? Is "yellow," in truth, a "shade" of, and/or a "variation" of "Black"? Is it true that during the existence of White Supremacy (Racism) all people "classified" as "Non-White" ("Brown," "Beige," "Tan," "Red," "Yellow," etc.) are all "shades" of "Black"?

Your Attitude. <u>Do not use this term</u>. Rather than speak of a person's so-called "attitude," ask, "What is your intention in regards to this matter and why"?

Questions: What, exactly, is an "attitude"? How is it "measured"? By whom? Based on what? What, exactly, is a "bad attitude"? What, exactly, is a "good attitude"? What, exactly, is a "perfect attitude"? During the existence of White Supremacy (Racism) what persons have proven that they have the "correct attitude" about White Supremacy (Racism)?

Notes: There is reason to believe that it is best and correct not to talk about a person's "attitude." This word is used too easily by too many people, to mean too many different things. The expression, "not having the right attitude" has been used by many persons to say things about other persons in a way that has helped to promote conflict and confusion.

Your Place (Racial). Use this term with caution.

> **Reason:** During the existence of White Supremacy (Racism) The White Supremacists (Racistman and Racistwoman, collectively), have often directed the terms "your place," and/or "stay in your place" to Non-White people. According to the White Supremacists (Racists) the so-called "place" for Non-White people is whatever and wherever the White Supremacists (Racists) say it is. According to the White Supremacists (Racists) the so-called "place" for the White people of the known universe is wherever White people choose to be.
>
> According to the White Supremacists (Racists) every "place" in the known universe is, and should be, "owned" by the White Supremacists (Racistman and Racistwoman, collectively).

You're The Cream in My Coffee. Do not use this term.

> **Reason:** This term is a "slang" term that has sometimes been used by White Supremacists (Racists) to help promote the concept that "dark" ("coffee-colored") people are "improved" by "intimate interactions" with White ("non-color") people. The expression is directly or indirectly sometimes used to imply that "dark" people are lacking in "refinement" unless they are "closely-associated" with White people in one or more areas of activity (usually sexual).

Z

Zeroism/Zeroistic Behavior (Racial). Use these terms to apply to things said or done, or not said or done, that directly or indirectly have the effect of not helping to promote the replacement of The System of White Supremacy (Racism) with The System of Justice and Correctness (balance between all people, all creatures, all things, etc., in all areas of activity-existence and non-existence).

APPENDIX
Index of Word-Terms and Notes Section

A

A Basic Product of the System of
White Supremacy (Racism)
Able-bodied
Acceptable White Losses/White
Sacrifices
Acting White/Acting Black
Acting with the Approval of those
in Power
Acutely Ghetto-Impaired or "AGI"
Administrative/Administrator
Adult
Adultery
Advisor/Advocate
Affectionkin/Aff[e]sexkin/Soul-
Mate
Affirmative Action
Affirmative Action (Racial)
African-American
African Diseases
African Dream/American
Dream/Asian Dream
Africanized Killer Bees
Afrikaner
Afrocentric/Americentric/
Asiacentric
Age of Consent
Aggression/Aggressor
Albino
Alien/Alienated
All
All-American
All Deliberate Speed
All the Facts
Allies
Alone
America
American Culture/American Flag/
Americanism
American Dream (the)
Anti-American
Anti-Black and/or Pro-Niggerized
Entertainment
Anti-Capitalist
Anti-Communist
Anti-Racist Expert
Anti-Semite/Anti-Semitic
Anti-Sexual Behavior, Anti-Sexual
Intercourse/Anti-Sexual Play
Anti-Social
Anti-Terrorist

Apartheid
Apparent
Appropriate
Arab/Arabic
Aristocrat/Aristocratic
Aristocratic-Refined Racism
Army
Arrest
Art
Aryan/Aryan Blood
Asia/Asian/Asiatic
Asian Flu
Assassin/Assassination
Assignment (An)
Assignment (The)
Attack
Attitude
Attraction Enhancer(s)/Repulsion
Enhancer(s)
Authority/Authorized
Average American

B

Baby Boy/Baby Girl (Racial)
Background/Personal History)
Bad
Bad Hair
Balance Between People
Barbarian
Basic Compensatory Constructive
(Sexual) Arrangement
Basic Compensatory Support Unit
Basic Ten "Stops" for Victims of
Racism
Beauty/Beautiful Person
Beauty Contest
Beg/Begging
Being
Benign Neglect
Best and the Brightest (the)
Better
Bias
Big Business
Big Government (Racial)
Bi-Sexual and/or Transsexual
Black
Black Achievement/Black
Progress
Black Arts (the)

Black Bag Jobs/Black Balled
Black Book
Black Capitalism
Black Child
Black Christian
Black Church/White Church
Black Comedy
Black Community (the)
Black Confine/Black Corral
Black Credentials
Black Crime
Black Culture/White Culture
Black Day
Black Death (the)
Black English
Black Family
Black Fascism
Black Flag/White Flag
Black Future
Black Ghetto Thug
Black (Happens to Be)
Black Hats/White Hats
Black Heart/Black-Hearted
Black (and) Hispanic
Black History
Black Institution
Black Jew
Black Leader(s)
Black Lie
Black Lifestyle
Blacklisted
Black Magic
Blackmail
Black Man/Black Woman
Black Mark
Black Middle-Class
Black Monday (Tuesday, etc.)
Black Mood
Black Muslim/Black
Christian/Black Pluralist
Black Nationalism
Black People's Contributions
Black Person
Black Power
Black Pride
Black and Proud (I am)
Black Race
Black School(s)
Black Sheep of the Family
Black Supremacy/Black
Supremacist
Black Underclass
Blacken (His/Her Name)
Black(ened) Reputation
Blacks
Blacks and Browns
Blacks and Jews

Blacks and Puerto
Ricans/Cubans/Pacific Islanders
Blame/Blameworthy
Blemish (on his or her record)
Blue-Collar Worker
Born-Again Christian
Boss
Boundary
Boys
Brave
Bright
Brighter Day (a)
Brown
Buck-Naked
Business Clothes/Business Suit

C

Capital
Capitalist/Communist
Caucasian/Caucasoid
Center (right of/left of)
Character
Character (blot on his/or her) or
reputation
Character (good)
Character (having)
Character (shady)
Character (stained)
Character (swarthy)
Child/Children
Children Having Children
Chinks (Racial)
Chosen People (the)
Church
Churchism
Church and State (separation of)
Church Work
Citizen
Citizen's Council
Civic Duty
Civil/Civilized
Civil Law
Civil Rights
Civil Servant/Civil Service
Civil War
Classical Music
Classified Information
Closest Person/Closest Mate
Code White
Code Work
Codify
Colonialism/Colony
Color/Colored (Racial)
Color Blind/Color-Blind Society
(Racial)

Colored Blood/Black Blood/Indian
Blood/White Blood, etc
Colorful Language
Colorism
Colorless (Racial)
Combatants/Non-Combatants
Combat Zone
Common
Common Basic Objective
Common Sense
Commonwealth
Commune
Communicate
Communist/Communism
Community
Community Standards
Community Ties
Comparable/Non-Comparable
Worth
Compensate/Compensation
Compensatory Communications
Associate
Compensatory Concept/
Compensatory Logic
Compensatory Counter-Racist
Contact
Compensatory Counter-Racist
Copulation
Compensatory Counter-Racist
Family
Compensatory Counter-Racist
Networking
Compensatory Counter-Racist
Suggestion
Compensatory Functional
Definition
Compensatory Functional
Identification
Compensatory Functional
Supreme Value
Compensatory Investment Request
Compensatory Law
Compensatory Marriage/Counter-
Racist Marriage
Compensatory Nuance-Niche
Compensatory Self-Support
Requests
Compensatory Universal Prayer
Compensatory Variables
Complain/Complaint
Comrade
Concentration Camp
Conditions (could be worse)
Confidential
Confiscation
Conflict of Interest
Conquest

Conservative (General)
Conservative (Racial)
Constitution, The
Constructive
Constructive Engagement
Contact
Containment
Contra(s)
Contract
Cooperation
Correct Intentions
Correctness
Correct Speech
Counter-Attack
Counter-Racism
Counter-Racist
Counter-Racist Intellisex
Counter-Racist Labor Union
Counter-Racist Logic/Counter-
Racist Science
Counter-Racist and Production of
Justice Studies
Counter-Racist System
Counter-Terrorism
Counter-Violence
Counter-War
Country
Country (my/our/this)
Coward/Cowardice
Cream (of the crop)
Create
Creation versus Evolution
Creator, The
Credit to your (his, her, our) Race
Creed
Crime/Criminal
Crime (does not pay)
Crime of Crimes
Crime Victim
Criminal Law
Crusade
Cult
Culturally-Deprived
Culture
Culture (Correct)
Culture (The White)
Cultured
Custom
Customer
Cycle Racism (Closed-Circle
Racism)

D

Dance
Dangerous
Dark

Dark Ages
Dark Chapter
Dark Cloud(s)
Dark Deeds
Dark Horse
Dark Journey
Dark (keep in the)
Dark Mood
Dark Realities
Dark Side
Darkest Hour
Darkest Moment(s)
Darkness (forces of)
Darkness (heart of)
Darky
Death
Decent
Deed
Deliberate Speed
Democracy
Democrat
De-Niggerization
Depression
Destructive
Detention
Devastated People (the)
Develop/Development
Diaspora
Dictate/Dictator
Dingy
Direct Order
Dirt/Dirty
Dirt-Cheap
Disaster, The
Discriminate/Discrimination
Disease
Dislocate/Dislocated/Dislocation
Disorder/Disorderly Conduct
Disrespect/Disrespectful
Divorce
Doctor
Domestic/Domesticated
Domestic Enemies
Domestic Violence
Domino Theory (the)
Doom and Gloom
Dress for Success
Drug Abuse
Duty

E

East/Eastern
Eat Crow
Eclectic Pluralism
Eclectic Plurist
Eclipse/Eclipsed

Economical
Economics
Education/Educated Person
Educational Excellence
Effective Majority (The)
Eggshell White
Eight Ball
Eight-Balling (Racial)
Embarrass/Embarrassment
Emergency
Eminent Domain
Employed/Employee/Employment
Enemy
Enemies (Foreign and Domestic)
Enlightened
Entertainment
Entitled
Environmental Error Factor(s)
E. Pluribus Unum
Equal
Equal Opportunity
Equality (Racial)
Espionage/Counter-Espionage
Ethical
Ethnic/Ethnic Group
European Continent
Evidence
Evil Empire/Evil Religion
Evil Shadow/Shadow of Evil/Evil
Darkness
Existence
Exotic
Expert
Explorer(s)
Extremist

F

Fact
Faded Into Obscurity
Failure
Fair
Fair (be)
Fair Trial
Fairy Godmother
Faith-Based Initiative
Falsehood
Familiar Mystery (the Most)
Family
Family Reunion
Family Values
Fanatic
Fascism/Fascist
Father
Fatherless/Motherless
Fear
Fired

First Americans/Native Americans
First World/Second World/Third World
Flag, Compensatory
Follow
Follow the Logic
Force
Forces of Darkness/Forces of Light
Foreign/Foreign-looking/Foreign-sounding
Foreigner and/or Alien (Racial)
Fornication
Founding Fathers (the)
Fraud
Free/Freedom Fighter/Free Enterprise
Friend
Functional
Fuzzy Idea/Fuzzy Plan/Fuzzy Thinking

G

Gal
Gamble
Game
Gang/Gangster
Gay
Genocide
Gentleman
Gentlemate
Getting Ahead
Getting the Kinks Out
Ghetto (Racial)
Ghetto Glorification
Ghettoized
Ghetto Smart
Gifted
Gifted Student
Girl
Gloomy
God
God and Country
God-Fearing
Good
Good Black People/Good White People
Good Education
Good Faith
Good Hair
Good Looking
Good Speaker
Good Time(s)
Gook
Gossip
Government

Government (Correct)
Government (Incorrect)
Government Official
Government (Racist)
Government (Subversive)
Government (The)
Government (The Master)
Grandparent
Gray Area
Great
Great Spectator
Great White Father/Mother
Greater Confinement
Greatest Insult (the)
Greatest War in History (the)
Grotesque
Grown/Grown-Up
Guidelines
Guilt/Guilty
Guttersex

H

Habitat
Half-White
Handicapped/Retarded
Handsome
Happy/Happiness
Harass/Harassment
Harmony
Hate
Have/Having
Haven't Got a Chinaman's Chance
Head of Household
Health/Healthy
Health Hazard
Heathen
He likes Black Females/She likes Black Males/He likes White Females/She likes White Males
Heritage
Hero/Heroine
High/Low
High-Class Person
High-Crime Area
High Yellow
Higher Education
Higher-Ups/Upper Class
Historian
Holiday
Holy
Holy Land
Holy Matrimony
Holy War
Home/Homeland
Home-less
Home-Maker

Home-Rule
Honorary White Person
Hostage
House
House Arrest
House-Keeper
House-Wife
Human/Humane
Humanitarian
Human Nature
Human Race
Human Rights

I

Ignorant
Illegal
Illegal Alien
Illegitimate
I love America/I love Africa
Imitation of Life
Immaculate
Immediate Power
Immoral
Important
Impossible
Incentive
In Common
Incorrect
Incorrect Sexual Intercourse
Indecent
Independent/Independence
Indian
Indian Blood
Indian-Giver
Indian Sub-Continent
Indivisible
Ineffective Minority
Infant/Infantile Person (Racial)
Inferior
Infinite-Comparative
Compensationalism
Information
In God We Trust
Initiative
Inner-City/Inner-City Crime
Innocent White Person
Insane/Insanity
Insane Person(s)
Insensitive Remark(s)
Insubordinate/Insubordination
Insurgent
Insurrection
Intelligence/Counter-Intelligence
Intelligence Quotient or "IQ"
Intelligent Black Person
Intelligent Fear (Racial)

International
International Thug(s)
Interracial
Interracial Marriage
Intimidate/Intimidation
Invade

J

Jap(s)
Jesus
Jew
Jewish
Jewish Blood
Jewish-looking
Job
Join
Judge/Judgment
Jungle
Jurisdiction
Jury
Just Doing my Job/Just Doing my
Duty
Justice
Justice Department/Department
of Justice
Justice for All
Justice is Blind
Justifiable Homicide
Justified

K

Kin
Kinky/Kinky Hair/Kinky Sex

L

Labor/Laborer
Labor (Skilled/Unskilled)
Labor Union
Lackluster
Lady
Ladymate
Land-Owner/Land Ownership
Land Reform
Law
Law Abiding/Law Abiding Citizen
Law, against the
Law and Order
Law (Compensatory Counter-
Racist)
Law of Counter-Racist White
Credibility
Law (Court of)
Law (of the Jungle)

Law (taking the law into your own Hands)
Law (under color of)
Law Maker/Law Making
Law Man/Law Woman
Lawyer
Lazy
Leader (Racial)
Learning Date
Left/Leftist/Left-Wing
Legal
Legal Assistance/Legal Assistant
Legal-Mate
Legal-Mated/Legally-Mated
Liable/Liability
Liberal (Racial)
Liberal/Liberty/Libertarian
Lie
Life
Life, Liberty and the Pursuit of Happiness
Lighten Up
Lighter Shades of Black (Racial)
Light-Hearted
Like
Lily White (Racial)
Little White Lies
Living
Living in Sin
Living Together
Logic
Long/Long Time/Long While
Longest Journey, The
Look on the Sunny Side
Lord/Lords
Love
Love (making)
Low/Low as Dirt/Low Class/Low Down
Lynch/Lynching (Racial)

M

Majority
Majority (Racial)
Malicious
Man
Man Friday (my)
Manager/Management
Man's Shadow/Shadow of a Man
Marriage/Married
Marriage (Compensatory Counter-Racist)
Massacre
Mass Murder
Masses, The

Master Capitalist/Communist
Master Child Abuser
Master Crime Families
Master Criminal (Racial)
Master Organization, The
Master Race
Master-Racket/Master Racketeer(s)
Master Security Risk
Master Terrorist
Master-Universal Subversive Elements
Maximum-Emergency Compensatory Action
Maximum Racist Aggression
Maximum Racist Insult
Media (the)
Medical Care
Meeting (constructive)
Meeting (non-constructive)
Mental Patient
Mentor
Mercy
Merit
Middle-America/Middle-American
Middle-Class/Middle-Class Values
Middle-East/Middle-West
Migrant/Immigrant
Militant
Military/Military Law/Military Target/Militia
Mind Rape
Minor/Minority
Miscegenation
Misconduct
Misfitted Person (Racial)
Misfitted/Zeroistic Speech or Action
Misfitted/Zeroistic Thinking
Mismarriage
Miss America/ Mr. America
Mistake
Mistreat/Mistreatment
Mistreatment (Comforting)
Mixed-Blood/Mixed Race
Mmmmmm
Mob/Mobster
Modern
Money
Money Masters
Monkey on His Back
Monster and/or Monstrosity Behavior
Moral/Morality
Moral Majority (the)
Moslem/Muslim
Mother/Motherland/Fatherland

Motivational Speaker
Mud
Mud (down in the)
Mud (your name is)
Mud-People (the)
Mud-Races (the)
Mud-Slinging
Muddle Along/Muddled Thinking/
Muddle-the-Water
Mulatto
Multi-Race/Multi-Racial
Music (Classical)
Music (Rap)
Music (Soul)
Mutant
Mutual Mates/Mutually Mated
My Rights

N

Nation
National Defense/National
Security
Nationalism
Native(s)
Native American(s)
Natural/Unnatural
Natural War and/or Counter-War
Negative/Negative
Attitude/Negative Thinking
Negress/Negro/Negroid/Nigger
Negro Fun and/or Niggerized Fun
Negroism and/or Niggerism
Neighbor/Neighborhood
Neo-Colonialism
Neo-Fascism/Neo-Nazism/Neo-
Racism
Neutral/Neutrality
New World/Old World/Third
World
Nice (facial) Features
Nice/Nice Person
Nigger
Nigger-Lover
Nightmare
Nine Major Areas of Activity
No Man's Land
Non-African/Non-American/Non-
Asian
Non-Black Person
Non-Person/Nothing Person
Non-Existence
Non-Human Being/Non-Humane
Being
Non-Justice
Non-Just People
Non-Justice, The Masters of

Non-Organized Unification
Non-Person/Nothing Person
Non-Profit
Non-Race
Non-Racial
Non-Racists
Non-Truth
Non-Violence
Non-White Person
Normal
Normal Person
Number One (Racial)

O

Oath (under)
Obscene/Obscenity
Occident/Occidental
Off-Color
Official/Official
Business/Unofficial Business
Official and/or Master Lynch
Force
Off-White/Half-White/Part-White
Old Person
On "Automatic"
On the Bright Side/Lighter Side
On Top
One Zero (1/0)
Open-Airism and/or Universalism
Opinion
Opinion, Official/Personal
Opportunity
Opposite Sex
Oral Sex
Ordained
Ordinary Person
Organized
Organized Crime
Organized Religion
Original
Our People
Outlaw
Over-Compensation
Owner/Ownership

P

Pacification
Paradise
Para-Military
Parent
Part-Black/Part-White
Part-Indian
Partner
Party (for purposes of
"constructive" fun)

Patriot/Patriotism
Peace
Peace-Keeper
Peace-Maker
Peer/Peer Group
People (the)
People (we as Black)
People (we the)
People (Your/My/Our)
Perfect Person
Perfect Storm, The (Racial)
Performance Evaluation
Personal Business
Personal Problem
Philosopher
Pictures Don't Lie
Pitiful
Pitiful Arrangement, The
Pleasant/Pleasing Company
(Racial)
Polarized
Police
Police Action
Police Brutality
Police State
Policy/Government Policy
Political Act/Political Action
Political Asylum
Political Prisoner
Political Statement
Politics/Politician(s)
Polygamy
Pooling Resources
Poor/Poor People
Pornography
Possession(s)
Pot Calling the Kettle Black
Power Father
Power Mother
Power Parent
Powerless Father/Mother/Parent
Prayer
Preemptive Attack/Preemptive
Strike
Pre-Historic
Prejudice
Press, The/Media
Pretty
Preventive Detention
Pride Tribes
Primitive
Prince Charming
Prison
Prisoner
Prisoners of (Race) War/Race
Prisoner(s)
Privilege (Correct)

Private
Produce/Production
Profession
Professional/Professor
Progress
Progressive
Proper/Property
Prostitute/Prostitution
Protection/Protected
Prove/Proven
Prudent
Public, The
Public Enemy
Public Figure/Public Person
Public Servant
Pull the Wool over their Eyes
Pure as the Driven Snow
Pure White
Pussy/Dick

Q

Qualified/Qualifications
Quality/Quality Relationship
Quota (Racial)

R

Race/Racism/Racist
Race Buffering
Race-Camp
Race Court, Racist Court, Superior
Court
Racehouse/Raceresidence
Race-Mate/Racial-Mate
Race-Mixing
Race Officer/Race Enforcement
Officer/Race Soldier
Race Tax
Race Unit
Race-Victims Major Disaster Area
Racial
Racial Balance
Racial Desegregation
Racial Exhibits
Racial Expert
Racial Incident
Racial Integration
Racial Masochism
Racial Mathematics
Racial Name
Racial Overtone/Undertone
Racial Plantationalism (Racism)
Racial Prejudice
Racial Segregation
Racial Show-offism
Racial Slur/Racist Support Words

Racial Subjugation
Racial Subjugationist
Racial Zeroism
Racism
Racist
Racist America/Racist Europe
Racist Family and/or Racist Tribe
Racist Law
Racist School System
Racist Suspect/Suspected Racist
(White Supremacist)
Racist War Crime
Racket
Racketeer, Master
Radical
Raised
Ransom
Rap (sound/images)
Rape
Rational
Raw Racism
Ray of Hope
Real Estate, White (Racial/Sexual)
Reasonable
Rebel/Rebellion
Recession
Recognize/Recognized
Red/Redskin
Refined Racism (White
Supremacy)
Refugee
Regulation(s)
Rehabilitate
Religion/Religious Person
Religious Fundamentalism
Relocate/Relocated
Remedial Education
Report
Represent/Representative
Republic/Republican
Reservation
Resettle/Resettlement
Respect
Responsible/Responsibility
Restitution
Reverse Discrimination/Reverse
Racism
Revolution
Rich
Right
Right Way/Wrong Way
Right-Wing/Left Wing
Riot
Rise Above
Rite of Passage (Compensatory
Counter-Racist)
Rob/Robbery

Role Model
Romance
Royal//Royalist/Royalty
Royalism (Racial)
Rules/Regulations/Rules of War

S

Sacred
Salt-of-the-Earth
Sane/Sanity
Santa Clause/Saint Nick
Savage(s)
Scholar
School
Scum-of-the-Earth
Second-Class Citizen
Second World/First World/Third
World
Secret
Secular
Secular Religion
Security
Security Risk
Self-Defense and/or Self
Preservation
Selfish
Self-Help
Self-Made (Man/Woman/Person)
Self-Respect
Semite/Semitic
Semitism/Anti-Semitism
Senile Person
Separate
Separate Development
Separate (but) Equal
Separation, Racial
Separation of Church and State
Serious Crime
Seriously Flawed Person
Servant/Service
Sex
Sex (the fair)
Sexism/Sex Offense
Sex-Oriented
Sex Slaves (Racial)
Sexual Communication
Sexual Harassment
Sexual Intercourse
Sexual Misconduct
Sexual Perversion
Sexual Play
Sexual Politics
Sexual Remark
Sexually Trashed/Sexually
Sewered (Racial)
Sexy

Shadow Fighting (Racial)
Shadow of a Doubt
Shady
Background/Character/Shady
Deal/Checkered Past
Shed Some Light on the Subject
Short/Short Time
Show Me/Give me (some) Respect
Showed Their True Colors
Showed Yellow
Sick
Silly Question/Stupid Question
Sin
Single
Sinner
Slant-Eyed
Slavery
Slave World
Sleeping With
Slope (Racial)
Slut
Small Business
Smartest People (the)
Smart-less People
Smear
Smokescreen
Smuck/Smut
Snow White
Social
Socialism/Socialist
Social Legislation
Social Obligation
Social Security
Socially Acceptable
Society
Socio-Economic
Soil/Soiled
Soldier
Somber Color/Mood/Tones
Sophisticated
Soul (Racial)
Soul Art
Soul Food
Soul Music
Sound Mind
Sovereign
Space
Space Race
Spot (hit the)
Spotless
Spy
Squatter
Standard(s)
Stand By Your Work
State/Statehood
States Rights
Statesman/Stateswoman

Statue of Liberty
Status Quo (Racial)
Statute of Limitations
Steal/Stolen
Struggle
Student
Sub-Culture
Sub-Human
Sub-Husband/Sub-Wife
Subject(s)
Sub-Support Unit
Subversive
Subversive Activity
Success/Successful
Sully/Sullied/Unsullied
Super Conquerors/Super Beggars
System
Super Murder
Superior
Superior Capitalist/Communists
Superior Race
Supervisor
Supporter of the United-
Independent Compensatory
System
Supreme
Supreme Being
Surplus Population
Survival
Mate/Caremate/Racialmate
Survival Unit/Basic Support Unit
Suspected Race Officer/Suspected
Race Enforcer
Suspected Racist
Suspension/Suspended
Symbol
System (The)

T

Tainted
Talent/Talented Person
Tan Your Hide
Tarnished Image/Reputation
Tax Obligation
Temporary
Territorial Possession
Territory
Terror/Terrorism
Terrorist
The Longest Holocaust
The People
The Powers that Be
The Problem
The Race
Things Could Be Worse
Thrilling

Throwaway People (Racial)
Time
Tone Down
Total Disaster (Racial)
Totalitarian
Tragic Arrangement, The
Tragic Necessity
Trash Sex/Toilet Sex/Cesspool
Sex
True Colors
Truth
Truthful Person

U

Ugly
Un-American
Unauthorized
Un-churched
Uncivil/Uncivilized
Uncle Tom
Undeclared War
Underclass
Undeveloped Country
Undeveloped/Underdeveloped
Unemployed
Unfair
Unimportant and/or Wasted Time
Unisex
United/Union
United Independent Compensatory
Code/ System/Concept
United Nations
United States
United States of/for America
United States/The
Union/Sovereign State
Universal Compensatory Pledge of
Allegiance
Universal Compensatory Pledge to
Flags
Universal Compensatory Social
Question
Universal Counter-Racist Goal
Universal Language
Universal Man and/or Universal
Woman
Universal Religion
Universal Subversive
Universal War and/or The War
Universal White Community
Unknown, The
Unqualified
Unreal Realities
Uppity
Upwardly-Mobile Person
Urban Renewal

Us/Them
Usual Suspects (the)

V

Vacation
Valuable
Very Important Person ("VIP")
Veteran and/or Veteran-Victim
Victim
Victim Father/Mother/
Sister/Brother/Wife
Victims Group
Victims Guaranteed Qualification
("V.G.Q.")
Victims of Racism
Victims Unit/Victims Race Unit
Violated
Violence
Violence/Non-Violence/Counter-
Violence
Violent Crime
Visitor
Voluntary/Volunteer
Vulnerable/Vulnerability

W

War
War Crime(s)/War Criminals
Warfare
War Games
War (Rules of)
War of Wars
Wedlock
Wedlock (outside of)
Welfare
West/Western
Civilization/Western
Culture/Western World
Wetback (Racial)
White
White Blood
White Christian/Black Christian
White Christmas
White Collar Crime
White Collar Worker
White Community (the)
White Culture
White Dove of Peace
White Family, The
White Folks
White Hat(s)/Black Hat(s)
White Hope
White Jew
White Lie
White List/Black List

White Man/White Woman
White Man's Burden
White Muslim/Black Muslim
White Nation
White /Black Neighborhood
White of you (that's)
White Paper Report
White Perfection(ism)
White Person
White Power
White Power Structure (the)
White Racism
White Russia (Belarus)
White Sacrifice
White Slavery
White Supremacist (Racist)/
Racistman and/or Racistwoman
White Supremacy
White Wedding
Whore
Whoremonger
Whoring/Whoresome
Wife/Husband
Wild

Wild and Wooly
Wise
Wise Persons
With
Within the Context/Out of Context
Woman
Womanizer/Manizer
Work
Worker
Working Class
Working With
Worthless People, The
Wrong Attitude

Y

Yellow
Your Attitude
Your Place
You're the Cream in my Coffee

Z

Zeroism/Zeroistic Behavior (racial)

NOTES

NOTES

NOTES

NOTES

NOTES

NOTES

NOTES

NOTES

NOTES

NOTES

NOTES

NOTES

NOTES

NOTES

NOTES

NOTES

NOTES

NOTES

NOTES